KU-325-526

Environmental Policy in the European Union

DISPOSED OF
BY LIBRARY
HOUSE OF LORDS

Environmental Policy in the European Union
Actors, Institutions and Processes

Edited by

Andrew Jordan

EARTHSCAN

Earthscan Publications Limited, London • Sterling, VA

First published in the UK and USA in 2002 by
Earthscan Publications Ltd

Copyright © Andrew Jordan, 2002

All rights reserved

ISBN: 1 85383 795 4 paperback
         1 85383 755 5 hardback

Typesetting by Composition and Design Services (www.cdsca.com)
Printed and bound by Creative Print and Design (Wales), Ebbw Vale
Cover design by Declan Buckley

For a full list of publications please contact:

Earthscan Publications Ltd
120 Pentonville Road
London, N1 9JN, UK
Tel: +44 (0)20 7278 0433
Fax: +44 (0)20 7278 1142
Email: earthinfo@earthscan.co.uk
http://www.earthscan.co.uk

22883 Quicksilver Drive, Sterling, VA 20166–2012, USA

A catalogue record for this book is available from the British Library

Library of Congress Cataloging-in-Publication Data

Environmental policy in the European Union : actors, institutions and processes / edited
by Andrew Jordan.
         p. cm.
    Includes bibliographical references and index.
    ISBN 1-85383-755-5 (cloth) — ISBN 1-85383-795-4 (pbk.)
    1. Environmental policy-European Union countries. I. Jordan, Andrew, 1968-

    GE190.E85 G85 2001
    363.7'0094–dc21

                                                                    2001023292

Earthscan is an editorially independent subsidiary of Kogan Page Ltd and publishes in association with WWF-UK and the International Institute for Environment and Development

This book is printed on elemental chlorine-free paper

Contents

Part 3   Policy Dynamics

Part 4   Making Environmental Policy

Part 5   Future Challenges

List of Illustrations

Figures

Tables

List of Contributors

Henning Arp is a Cabinet member to the European Environment Commissioner, Margot Wallström, at the European Commission, Brussels, Belgium. Email: Henning.Arp@ece.eu.int

Jonathan Golub is Lecturer in politics in the Department of Politics, University of Reading, Reading, UK. Email: J.S.Golub@reading.ac.uk

Adrienne Héritier is Director of the Max Planck-Project group 'Common Goods: Law, Politics and Economics' in the Max-Planck Institute, Bonn, Germany. Email: heritier@mpp-rdg.mpg.de

Philipp M Hildebrand is at the World Economic Forum, Geneva, Switzerland.

Andrew Jordan is Lecturer and Programme Manager of the ESRC Centre for Social and Economic Research on the Global Environment (CSERGE) in the School of Environmental Sciences, University of East Anglia, UK. Email: a.jordan@uea.ac.uk

David Judge is Professor of Politics at the University of Strathclyde, Glasgow, UK. Email: d.judge@strath.ac.uk

Ida Koppen teaches at the University of Siena and the Johns Hopkins University Bologna Centre. She is also Director of the Sustainability Challenge Foundation. Email: koppen@unisi.it

Duncan Liefferink is Lecturer in European environmental politics in the Department of Environmental Policy Sciences, University of Nijmegen, The Netherlands. Email: D.Liefferink@bw.kun.nl

Sonia Mazey is a Fellow of Hertford College, University of Oxford, Oxford, UK. Email: sonia.mazey@hertford.ox.ac.uk

Geoffrey Pridham is Professor of European Politics at the University of Bristol, Bristol, UK. Email: g.pridham@bristol.ac.uk

Jeremy Richardson is Director of the Centre for European Politics, University of Oxford, Oxford, UK. Email: jeremy.richardson@nuffield.ox.ac.uk

Alberta Sbragia is Director of the Centre for West European Studies, University of Pittsburgh, PA, USA. Email: sbragia+@pitt.edu

Mikael Skou Andersen works in the Department of Policy Analysis at the Danish National Environmental Research Institute, Rosskilde, Denmark. Email: msa@dmu.dk

Albert Weale is Professor of Government in the Department of Government, University of Essex, Colchester, UK. Email: weala@essex.ac.uk

David Wilkinson is Senior Research Fellow at the Institute for European Environmental Policy (IEEP) in London, UK. Email: dw@ieeplondon.org.uk

Anthony Zito lectures in the Department of Politics, University of Newcastle, Newcastle, UK. Email: A.R.Zito@newcastle.ac.uk

List of Sources

Earthscan and the editor would like to thank the authors and copyright holders for permission to reprint the contributions appearing in this volume.

Chapter 2: 'The European Community's Environmental Policy, 1957–1992', from the *Journal of Environmental Politics*, 1993, Vol.1, No.4, pp13–44, Frank Cass Publishers.

Chapter 3: 'Maastricht and the Environment', from the *Journal of Environmental Law*, 1992, Vol.4, No.2, pp221–239, Oxford University Press.

Chapter 4: 'Step Change or Stasis? EC Environmental Policy After the Amsterdam Treaty', from the *Journal of Environmental Politics*, 1998, Vol.7, No.1, pp227–236, Frank Cass Publishers.

Chapter 5: 'Strategies of the "Green" Member States in EU Environmental Policy-making', from the *Journal of European Public Policy*, 1998, Vol.5, No.2, pp254–270, Routledge/Taylor & Francis Ltd, www.tandf.co.uk/journals.

Chapter 6: 'National Environmental Policy-making in the European Framework: Spain, Greece and Italy in Comparison', from *Regional Politics and Policy*, 1994, Vol.4, No.1, pp80–101, Frank Cass Publishers.

Chapter 7: 'The Role of the European Court of Justice' from J. D. Liefferink, P. D. Lowe and A. P. J. Mol, *European Integration and Environmental Policy*, 1993, pp126–149, John Wiley & Sons.

Chapter 8: 'Predestined to Save the Earth: The Environment Committee of the European Parliament', from the *Journal of Environmental Politics*, 1992, Vol.1, No.4, pp186–212, Frank Cass Publishers.

Chapter 9: 'Environmental Groups and the EC: Challenges and Opportunities', from the *Journal of Environmental Politics*, 1992, Vol.1, No.4, pp109–128, Frank Cass Publishers.

Chapter 10: 'Task Expansion: A Theoretical Overview', from *Environment and Planning C*, 1999, Vol.17, No.1, pp19–35, Pion Ltd.

Chapter 11: 'The Accommodation of Diversity in European Policy-making and its Outcomes', from the *Journal of European Public Policy*, 1996, Vol.3, No.2, pp149–167, Routledge/Taylor & Francis Ltd.

Chapter 12: 'Environmental Rules and Rule-making in the European Union', from the *Journal of European Public Policy*, 1996, Vol.3, No.4, pp594–611, Routledge/Taylor & Francis Ltd.

Chapter 13: 'State Power and Institutional Influence in European Integration: Lessons from the Packaging Waste Directive', from the *Journal of Common Market Studies*, 1996, Vol.34, No.3, pp313–339, Blackwell.

Chapter 14: 'Integrating the Environment into the European Union: The History of the Controversial Carbon Tax', from *The State of the European Union, Volume 3: Building a European Policy?*, pp431–448, Carolyn Rhodes and Sonia Mazey (eds). Copyright © 1995 by Lynne Rienner Publishers, Inc. Used with the permissions of the publisher.

Chapter 15: 'Technical Regulation and Politics: The Interplay Between Economic Interests and Environmental Policy Goals in EC Car Emission Legislation', from J. D. Liefferink, P. D. Lowe and A. P. J. Mol, *European Integration and Environmental Policy*, 1993, pp150–171, John Wiley & Sons.

Chapter 16: 'Institution-building from Below and Above: The European Community in Global Environmental Politics' from A. Stone Sweet and W. Sandholtz (eds), *European Integration and Supranational Governance*, 1998, pp283–303, Oxford University Press.

Chapter 17: 'The Implementation of EU Environmental Policy: A Policy Problem without a Political Solution?' from *Environment and Planning C*, 1999, Vol.17, No.1, pp69–90, Pion Ltd.

Chapter 18: 'European Environmental Policy by Stealth: The Dysfunctionality of Functionalism?' from *Environment and Planning C*, 1999, Vol.17, No.1, pp37–51, Pion Ltd.

List of Acronyms and Abbreviations

BAT	Best Available Technology/Techniques
CAP	Common Agricultural Policy
CEFIC	European Chemical Industry Council
CFC	Chlorofluorocarbon
CFSP	Common Foreign and Security Policy (EU)
CITES	Convention on International Trade in Endangered Species (UN)
CO_2	Carbon Dioxide
CoM	Council of Ministers (EU)
CSD	Commission on Sustainable Development (UN)
DDT	Dichlorodiphenyltrichloroethane
DETR	Department of the Environment, Transport and the Regions (UK)
DG XI	Directorate General for the Environment (EU)
DoE	Department of the Environment (UK)
EAP	Environmental Action Programme (EU)
EC	European Community (now part of the EU)
ECJ	European Court of Justice (EU)
ECOFIN	Council of Finance Ministers (EU)
ECSC	European Coal and Steel Community (now part of the EU)
EEA	European Environment Agency (EU)
EEC	European Economic Community (now part of the EU)
ELR	European Law Report (EU)
EMAS	Environmental Management System
EMU	European Monetary Union (EU)
ENDS	Environmental Data Services
EP	European Parliament (EU)
EU	European Union
FRG	Federal Republic of Germany
GATT	General Agreement on Tariffs and Trade
GMO	Genetically Modified Organism
GNP	Gross National Product
HL	House of Lords (UK)
HOLSCEC	House of Lords Select Committee on the European Communities
IGC	Intergovernmental Conference (EU)
IMPEL	Implementation Network (EU)
IPC	Integrated Pollution Control
IPPC	Integrated Pollution Prevention and Control
MEP	Member of the European Parliament (EU)
NGO	Non-governmental Organization
NO_x	Nitrous Oxide
OECD	Organization for Economic Co-operation and Development
OJ	Official Journal (EU)

QMV	Qualified Majority Voting (EU)
PCP	Phencyclidine
SEA	Single European Act (EU)
SO_2	Sulphur Dioxide
TEU	(Maastricht) Treaty on European Union (EU)
UK	United Kingdom
UN	United Nations
UNCED	UN Conference on Environment and Development
UNCTAD	United Nations Conference on Trade and Development
UNECE	United Nations Economic Commission for Europe
UNEP	United Nations Environment Programme
US	United States
USSR	Union of Soviet Socialist Republics
VAT	Value Added Tax
VOC	Volatile Organic Compound
WWF	World Wide Fund for Nature
WTO	World Trade Organization

1

Introduction: European Union Environmental Policy – Actors, Institutions and Policy Processes

Andrew Jordan

Analytical Puzzles

At its founding in 1957, the European Union (EU) had no environmental policy, no environmental bureaucracy, and no environmental laws. The European Economic Community (EEC), as it then was, was primarily an *intergovernmental* agreement between six like-minded states to boost economic prosperity and repair political relations in war-torn Europe. When Britain joined in 1973, the EEC had adopted a very limited number of environmental policies but they were primarily directed at safeguarding human health and removing internal barriers to trade.

Today, the EU has some of the most progressive environmental policies of any state in the world although, curiously, it does not possess many of the formal attributes of a sovereign state such as an army or a formal constitution. In fact, over the course of the last 40 years, EU environmental policy has gradually expanded to an extent that is unique among international organizations, although of course the EU is not a conventional international organization dominated by states. The purpose of this book is to act as a guide to the history and institutions of EU environmental policy, to explain how policy is made and implemented, and to introduce some of the main debates within the study of EU public policy and politics.

One of the more puzzling characteristics of EU environmental policy is its remarkable capacity for steady growth. For the most part, it has been (and remains) largely unaffected by the political and economic vicissitudes, periodic budgetary crises and recurrent waves of Euro-pessimism that have continually frustrated European integration in related policy sectors such as social and energy policy. Another puzzling feature is that EU environmental policy now adds up to considerably *more* than the sum of national environmental policies. In fact, as far as environmental policy is concerned, the EU currently enjoys powers, such as the ability to negotiate externally with other states in international meetings and to levy financial sanctions on those actors (ie states) that do not uphold its laws and policies, that are normally the sole preserve of states. The third analytical puzzle is that the pre-existing environmental policies of the Member States are no longer politically or legally separate from EU environmental policy. In fact they have undergone a progressive change through their involvement in EU policy-making. In other words, the Member States have created an institutional entity to perform certain tasks, which has, in turn, deeply affected the way they perceive and act against environmental problems. The relationship between the two main levels – international and national – of this unique system of *multi-level* environmental governance, has been and remains genuinely *two-way*, creating new opportunities and constraints for the various actors involved.

An Overview

Against the odds, environmental policy has come a very long way since the EEC adopted a Programme of Action in 1973. This guide charts and tries to explain the startling transformation of EU environmental policy from a series of what Philipp Hildebrand in Chapter 2 describes as a series of 'incidental measures' to a sophisticated, multilevel governance system in which policy-making powers are shared between supranational, national and subnational actors (Marks et al, 1996; Sandholtz and Stone Sweet, 1998). Throughout the 1970s and early 1980s, items of EU environmental policy were agreed by the Council of Environment Ministers on the basis of proposals submitted by the Commission. In the 1980s, this bilateral arrangement gradually gave way to a more diffuse web of activities centred on a set of trilateral links between the Council, the Commission, and the European Parliament's Environment Committee. Matters which had been contained in discrete intergovernmental committees of national bureaucrats and state-sponsored scientists entered the political mainstream, energizing national and international pressure groups, disrupting national practices and exciting public interest. In turn, these groups have had to be accommodated in the EU policy-making process through extensive systems of consultation, negotiation and lobbying (see Chapter 9). Consequently:

> *Just as policy-making in the Member States can no longer be explained exclusively in national terms, so it is impossible to understand the development of [EU] regulatory policy-making as if the only important political actors were the national governments* (Majone, 1991, p98).

This guide draws together in one volume a number of influential accounts of the making of EU environmental policy, written from different disciplinary and theoretical perspectives. The chapters are grouped into five parts. Part 1 ('The Historical and Institutional Context') describes the history and institutions of

EU environmental policy, and explains the formal rules for making policy. Different actors (some state, some non-state) work within these rules to attain their policy objectives, as shown in Part 2 ('Actors'). A number of commentators have sought to identify general patterns and processes using theories of national and international politics, which is the subject of Part 3 ('Policy Dynamics'). However, the best (and perhaps only) way to fully appreciate how the EU environmental policy process really works is to undertake detailed empirical and theoretical studies of actual policies. Part 4 ('Making Environmental Policy') contains four in depth case studies of how particular environmental policies were made in the EU. Finally, Part 5 ('Future Challenges') explores some of the remaining problems and looks forward to the next phase in the development of EU environmental policy. This collection assumes no prior knowledge of the EU. Readers requiring a more detailed review of the history, law and institutions of the EU should consult some of the books listed in the Further Reading section.

Before moving on, it is important to clarify the meaning of some of the confusingly similar terms used to describe the EU. Until the ratification of the Single European Act (SEA) in 1987, the European Union was officially known as the EEC. The SEA officially re-christened this entity the European Community (EC), a term which remained in popular use until 1993 when the Maastricht Treaty created the European Union with a three 'pillar' structure. Strictly speaking, environmental policy is still made within the first 'pillar' of the EU (ie the EC). Although it is still correct to use either EC or EU, most people now use the acronym 'EU' to cover all its policy responsibilities. Just to confuse matters still further, many of the legal articles of the Treaty referred to in the text below were re-numbered by the 1999 Amsterdam Treaty. So, for example, the environmental Article 130r, s and t (SEA) is now Articles 174–6 of the Amsterdam Treaty, and so on (see Chapter 4).

Part 1: The Historical and Institutional Context

It seems almost remarkable today, but the word 'environment' was not even mentioned in the 1957 Treaty of Rome. As Philipp Hildebrand explains in Chapter 2, there was no formal recognition that there might be environmental limits to economic growth, or that environmental factors should be a vital component of every policy area. It was only after the surge of environmental awareness in the late 1960s and early 1970s, which culminated in the 1972 United Nations environment conference in Stockholm, that the Member States of the EEC started to deal purposively and intensively with the environmental repercussions of European integration.

As is so often the case in Europe, it was the Commission that first seized the initiative, submitting a proposal to the Council of Ministers (CoM) on the need for a formal programme of action. Acting on the political direction of the European Council of Member State leaders, the Commission subsequently drew up a short but detailed Programme of Action on the Environment in 1973. Although a few legal measures had been adopted on chemicals as long ago as 1967, and other actions were taken to combat noise and vehicle emissions in 1970, the programme is now widely regarded as marking the beginning of a co-ordinated and purposeful European environmental policy. Throughout the 1970s policy continued to develop but in a very ad hoc and incremental manner, according to the whims of different states. In many crucial respects, the EEC functioned just like any other international organization. States held a 'double veto' over all affairs: one during the process of policy adoption in the CoM, the other during the subsequent process of implementation (Puchala, 1975, p510). In theory this two-pronged constraint on the development of the *acquis communautaire* – the corpus of principles, policies, laws, treaties and practices adopted by the EU – should have allowed states to cherry-pick their preferred policies. After all, proposals had to secure the support of every state in the CoM before they could be adopted.

Having formally established an environmental role for the EEC in 1972, state leaders moved on to address other, more pressing economic and political issues of which there were many. In 1973 the Yom Kippur war broke and the first oil shock followed. In Europe, the ensuing economic recession coincided with declining levels of political support for integration in the wake of the 1965 'empty-chair' crisis when the French President, General De Gaulle, brought Community business to a virtual standstill. Politically speaking, the decade from the mid-1970s to the launch of the Single Market Programme in the mid-1980s was a lost or 'stagnant epoch' in the history of the EU (Weiler, 1991, p2431). But in less overtly political policy areas, such as the environment, European integration (that is the shifting upwards of decision-making powers to supranational bodies) continued slowly to inch forward. In the 1980s, the trickle of legislation turned into a stream as EU environmental policy underwent a relatively rapid and profound transformation, spurred on by rising levels of public concern for environmental matters.

Philipp Hildebrand shows how the SEA helped to entrench and formalize the EU's involvement by placing environmental policy on a firm legal footing. Crucially, the SEA provided the institutional means to achieve still higher standards by altering the decision rule in the CoM to qualified majority voting for proposals linked to the single market (Article 100a). It also called for greater inter-sectoral integration and for new standards to be based on a high level of protection. These changes, which are described by David Wilkinson in Chapter 3, were subject to further amendment when states negotiated and ratified the 1993 Maastricht Treaty. Andrew Jordan (Chapter 4) brings the story right up to date with an analysis of the amendments introduced by the 1999 Amsterdam Treaty.

Part 2: Actors

The system of rules described in Part 1 comprises the legal 'hardware' of EU environmental policy. However, the development of the environmental *acquis* has often run ahead of the formal (ie state directed) process of amending the founding treaties, inviting us to speculate about whether and to what extent the expansion of the environmental *acquis* was or remains under state control. In order to explain this puzzle, analysts must first examine the motives and activities of the different actors that populate the institutional venues of EU policy-making.

In the 1970s, the cast list of actors involved in making environmental policy was relatively short. Political leaders paid little sustained attention to environmental issues and European environmental pressure groups were conspicuous by their absence. Nigel Haigh (1996) has described the early 1970s as the 'dark ages' of EU environmental policy, when unanimous voting meant standards developed at the pace of the most reluctant state. Supranational institutional structures were weakly developed and in several key respects EEC environmental policy functioned like a normal international organization, with lowest common denominator decision-making in the CoM. By the early 1980s there were around 60 legislative texts dealing with the environment.

However, beneath the surface a series of powerful 'subterranean mutations' were gradually shifting the delicate balance of political power between states and supranational bodies (Weiler, 1991, p2408). Weiler argues that gradual extension of Community competence in areas of 'low politics', produced a powerful political undertow:

> *The momentum [of political integration] was directed at a range of ancillary issues, such as environmental policy, consumer protection, energy and research, all important of course, but a side game all the same. Yet, although these were not taken very seriously in substance (and maybe because of that) each ... represented part of the brick-by-brick demolition of the wall circumscribing Community competences (ibid, p2449).*

These processes did not emerge by chance. The founding fathers of the EEC, notably Jean Monnet and Robert Schuman, firmly believed that the cause of political integration would be best served if the Commission focused its energies on building transnational cooperation in areas of 'low politics' in the hope that enthusiasm for European solutions would eventually 'spill over' into more sensitive areas such as the economy and foreign and defence policy. In these most technical of policy areas the Commission found it could work up proposals for new European legislation relatively unsupervised by pressure groups and national bureaucracies. With some notable exceptions, democratic oversight by the European Parliament (see Chapter 8) and national parliaments remained weak and inconsistent. Every now and again a particular proposal would provoke conflict between states, but for the most part the EEC remained a very weakly developed polity. National pressure groups concentrated on domestic affairs because that was where the locus of environmental policy was thought to lie (Chapter 9).

Although the environmental *acquis* expanded in the political space thereby provided, legal constraints meant that the aims of very early environmental measures such as the common classification, labelling and packaging of dangerous substances, remained relatively modest in the sense that they did not depart significantly from the EEC's core mission, which was to achieve a common market. But in the 1980s, the number of policies began to expand much more rapidly, rising to over 200 by 1987. Moreover, many of the new policies, which related inter alia, to seals, natural habitats, sewage treatment, genetically modified organisms and climate change, went well 'beyond any conceivable standards that would be strictly necessitated by a concern to ensure a single functioning market' (see Weale, Chapter 12). Nowadays, the environmental *acquis* comprises well over 500 legislative items and until recently was one of the fastest growing areas of EU activity. Between 1989 and 1991, the EU adopted more environmental statutes than in the previous 20 years combined.

What explains the sudden step change in the scope and stringency of EU environmental policy that occurred in the period after the mid-1980s? Many chapters of this book contain examples of the greener (or 'leader') states such as Germany, The Netherlands and Denmark, pushing the EU to adopt standards that are as high if not higher than their own, national standards. Having unilaterally adopted high standards in their own territories, these states had an obvious incentive to share the political and economic pain (as well as reap 'first mover' advantages) by 'exporting' them to other, less environmentally progressive EU states. In their chapter (Chapter 5), Duncan Liefferink and Mikael Skou Andersen describe the various mechanisms used by 'leader' states to achieve this. In the southern Member States, the pressure to conform to increasingly stringent environmental standards pursued by the Northern states has often felt like a 'cold but bracing wind from the North' (Pridham, Chapter 6). While the Mediterranean states are not, as Geoffrey Pridham describes, nearly as environmentally 'backward' or 'raggardly' as is sometimes claimed, deficiencies in their domestic environmental management systems mean they have often been the back markers in the regulatory 'competition' to set environmental standards in Europe.

The European Court of Justice (ECJ) has also played an important but greatly overlooked role in raising and also maintaining high environmental standards in the EU. In Chapter 7, Ida Koppen usefully describes how important rulings in the 1960s and 1970 helped to legitimize the Commission's activities and tighten the legal framework of compliance with EU rules. Although it was originally very weakly represented, the European Parliament's role has also grown substantially since the late 1970s, to the extent where it shares responsibility for setting new standards with the CoM under a complicated institutional procedure known as co-decision-making (Chapter 3). As David Judge explains in Chapter 8, the Parliament has also been a persistently powerful advocate of higher environmental standards. Finally, national environmental pressure groups have, as Mazey and Richardson explain (Chapter 9), learnt to exploit the political opportunities presented by European integration to achieve considerably higher environmental standards than might otherwise have emerged through national action.

Part 3: Policy Dynamics

Putting these different actors together with the rules and the institutions described in Part 1 produces an extremely complicated and dynamic picture ('a strange animal' – see Chapter 15), which does not appear to correspond to any commonly accepted model of how policy is normally made in states (see Chapters 9 and 12). In order to identify enduring patterns and possible explanations, political scientists have therefore turned to different explanatory theories. At first, the main question which preoccupied EU scholars then was whether and to what extent states or non-state actors controlled the expansion of the environmental *acquis*. In an early contribution, Rehbinder and Steward (1985, p400) argued that it was not states (who remained fairly passive), but the very supranational agents that they had established to perform relatively routine tasks, that engineered the shift in governance described above:

> *Using a pragmatic, incrementalist approach and concentrating on problems where the benefits of common action were evident, [the Community institutions] have, step by step, established a network of ... legislative texts for the protection of the environment, thereby creating a mosaic of precedents ... which will be hard to overrule. The deficiencies in the legal basis ... were compensated by the political will of the Member States.*

Other commentators have fundamentally disagreed with this interpretation, believing that the *acquis* represents the lowest common denominator of state preferences (Huelshoff and Pfeiffer, 1991). In Chapter 10, Anthony Zito weighs the evidence in support of both sides. Not surprisingly, he finds no clear 'winner'. Instead, some theories appear to work better at certain levels and stages of the policy process than at others. Specifically, macro-level theories such as intergovernmentalism appear to offer a more credible account of the creation of a new policy area such as the environment, whereas meso-level theories such as policy networks, are better employed if the aim is to understand the genesis and administrative implementation of specific directives or regulations.

Adrienne Héritier (Chapter 11) believes the 'patchwork' pattern of EU environmental policy derives from the inter-actor competition discussed above. Her chapter, which draws heavily on evidence from the air pollution sector, suggests that leaders can shape the political agenda by moving first in Europe, but once an issue 'escapes' into the open and other actors become involved, the eventual outcome becomes more difficult to predict, and less coherent. Consequently, we find that 'distinctive regulatory elements are not systematically linked in a comprehensive European policy scheme, but simply added to one another'. Albert Weale (Chapter 12) tries to gauge the extent to which states are formally in control of this process. Having considered the evidence he concludes that the process is too densely populated with veto players (ie actors whose views have to be taken into account) for any actor or group of actors (including states) consistently to dictate the direction of integration. More often than not, environmental standards 'are the aggregated and transformed standards of their original champions modified under the need to secure political accommodation from powerful veto players' – or what Héritier terms a 'policy patchwork'.

Part 4: Making Environmental Policy

In an effort to better understand the process through which policy is made, EU scholars have narrowed their frame of analysis still further by looking at how key pieces of legislation emerge on to the political agenda, are bargained over then implemented. All the chapters in Part 4 employ a 'process tracing' approach to understanding EU environmental policy (see also Chapters 8, 9 and 11). Although the authors realize the dangers of relying too heavily on a single case or cases, their accounts do shed important new light on the actual political mechanics of policy-making. Jonathan Golub (Chapter 13) meticulously analyses the 1994 directive on packaging waste and finds compelling evidence of both state control and supranational entrepreneurship, which he uses to re-interpret the theoretical predictions set out in Chapter 10. Anthony Zito's chapter on the Commission's unsuccessful attempt to establish an EU carbon energy tax (Chapter 14) powerfully underlines the limits to non-state control of policy-making. In his chosen case, the Commission made progress but was unable to overcome deeply rooted state opposition, so the proposal failed. Henning Arp's analysis of the regulation of car emissions (Chapter 15) reaches similar conclusions, though it places particular emphasis on the power of industry lobbying across all stages and levels of the policy process.

The only chapter to find strong evidence of supranational entrepreneurship is Alberta Sbragia's (Chapter 16) on the EU as an emerging international environmental actor. As well as dealing with environmental problems within its own borders, she explains that the EU has also steadily enhanced its role in global environmental policy-making ('parallelism'). Picking up on points made in Chapters 7 and 10, she identifies the ECJ as a prime mover in granting the Commission a stronger external presence. In developing the doctrine of implied (or 'parallel') powers, the Court effectively rejected a state-sanctioned approach to integration. Thereafter, the Community's powers could expand automatically, even without the express approval of the Member States (Nollkaemper, 1987). Although the Commission's environmental Directorate does not (at least yet) enjoy quite the same level of responsibility (or competence) as the trade Directorate (which represents, rather than sits alongside, the Member States in international trade negotiations), the emergence of the EU as a creative force in international environmental diplomacy must rank as one of its greatest achievements.

Part 5: Future Challenges

Irrespective of their theoretical position, most analysts agree that EU environmental policy has come a long way since the 1970s. But, important challenges remain. The first is how to ensure that all the EU's activities take account of and support fully the achievements of its environmental policy. The first 30 years of EU policy were arguably spent crafting an identifiable environmental policy. That task is close to being completed. However, since the 1970s environmentalism has gradually mutated into the more diffuse and politically complicated concept of 'sustainability'. Sustainable development challenges the advocates of strong environmental rules to be less isolated and introspective in their outlook by building alliances with actors in cognate policy domains. More specifically, sustainability means finding ways to integrate the environmental *acquis* into the wider and long-term political, social and economic priorities of the EU. The 1992 Fifth Action Programme marked a turning point in the EU's attempt to achieve environmental policy integration, but there are many significant obstacles to further progress. As the legal and political pressure for greater environmental policy integration continues to grow, the axis of future political conflict in Europe will become much more inter-sectoral (eg *Environment Council* vs *Agriculture Council* etc). This should create interesting new political alliances, possibly spanning the traditional state-supranational (eg the CoM vs the Commission or the Parliament) divide. If the 1980s and 1990s were dominated by conflicts between different *levels* of governance, then the 2000s look set to be characterized by more and more conflicts between different *parts* of the Commission and different sectoral formations of the Councils of Ministers.

The second problem is improving the implementation of EU environmental policy at the national level. Andrew Jordan (Chapter 17) argues that because EU policy is 'European' – ie born of ideas and practices plucked from many states – and not purely 'national', it is more likely to be refracted and mutated when it is implemented in the diverse political and legal circumstances of the 15 Member States. He explains why EU policy is particularly prone to implementation 'deficits' or 'gaps', and appraises the Commission's recent efforts to address them.

This leads to the third and final challenge: enlargement. The imminent enlargement of the EU to encompass states from the former Eastern bloc means that implementation problems are likely to get a lot worse before they start getting better. This is primarily because an enlarged Europe is likely to have a somewhat looser and more devolved structure than the current EU of 15 states. Enlargement will almost certainly necessitate a significant overhaul of the structural funds and the common agricultural policy. So one way or another, EU environmental policy faces a period of significant political turbulence.

So how well prepared is the EU to overcome these challenges? On the face of it, the EU is in remarkably good shape: the environmental *acquis* is much more deeply rooted in the law and institutions of the EU, and the national societies of the Member States, than it ever was in the early 1970s. But important – some would say fundamental – weaknesses remain. In Chapter 18, Albert Weale argues that until now, the environmental *acquis* has tended to develop 'by stealth' rather than via a series of strategic decisions, explicitly taken by political leaders. Commission officials have, as described in Parts 1 and 2, become adept at working behind the scenes in technical committees, employing the 'Monnet method' to coax states into accepting deeper integration; a process which involves disaggregating problems into their functional and technical elements, rather than debating them openly and in the round. Weale argues that the 'Monnet method' may have produced an impressively large corpus of environmental policies, but it is 'pervaded by pathologies'. Thus for Weale, the EU is very good at doing some things, but weak at doing others. The problem is that it is being prevented (mainly by states) from doing more of the things it is good at, while continuing to do the things it is weaker at. So what EU environmental policy really needs at the dawn of a new millennium is a thoroughgoing debate about its structure and purpose to prepare itself for the transition to sustainability. The unfortunate paradox is that until now, EU environmental policy has expanded by avoiding, delaying or working around such questions. It became too good at 'muddling through' problems in its youth, to easily embrace the more strategic and comprehensive approach to future problem-solving currently being demanded by the sustainability agenda. Time will tell whether the EU has the capability to unlearn the habits of the past in order to adjust to the progressive politics of sustainable development in a rapidly enlarging Europe.

References

Haigh, N. (1996) '*A Green Agenda for the IGC: The Future of EU Environmental Policy*', paper presented at a conference at Kings College, London, March, copy available from Institute of European Environmental Policy, 52 Horseferry Road, London SWIP 2AG.

Huelshoff, M. and Pfeiffer, T. (1991) 'Environmental Policy in the EC: Neo-functionalist Sovereignty Transfer or Neo-realist Gatekeeping?', *International Journal*, Vol.47, pp136–158.

Majone, G. (1991) 'Cross-national Sources of Regulatory Policy-making in Europe and the US', *Journal of Public Policy*, Vol.11, Part 1, pp79–106.

Marks, G., Scharpf, F., Schmitter, P. and Streek W. (1996) *Governance in the EU*, London: Sage.

Nollkaemper, A. (1987) 'The European Community and International Environmental Co-operation: Legal Issues of External Community Business', *Legal Issues of European Integration*, Vol.2, pp55–91.

Puchala, D. (1975) 'Domestic Politics and Regional Harmonisation in the European Communities', *World Politics*, Vol.27, pp496–520.

Rehbinder, E. and Steward, R. (1985) 'Legal Integration in Federal Systems: European Community Environmental Law', *The American Journal of Comparative Law*, Vol.33, pp37–447.

Sandholtz, W. and Stone Sweet, A. (1998) *Supranational Governance: the Institutionalisation of the European Union*, MIT Press, Cambridge, MA.

Weiler, J. (1991) 'The Transformation of Europe', *The Yale Law Journal*, Vol.100, pp2403–2483.

Part 1
THE HISTORICAL AND INSTITUTIONAL CONTEXT

2

The European Community's Environmental Policy, 1957 to '1992': From Incidental Measures to an International Regime?

Philipp M Hildebrand

This chapter describes and analyses the evolution of the European Community's (EC) environmental policy. The chosen time frame covers the period from January 1958, when the Treaty of Rome came into effect, to '1992', the target-date for the completion of the Single European Act (SEA) which entered into force on 1 July 1987.[1]

It is often stated that, prior to 1973, there was no EC environmental policy. In principle this assessment is correct. Nevertheless, a number of pieces of environmental legislation had been adopted during that period. For that reason and in order to present an historically and analytically complete picture, the entire period will be assessed here.

At the outset it is necessary to ask two questions. First, how did the EC environmental policy evolve? Second, what were the determining factors of this evolution? At a time when the EC's environmental policies are increasingly being followed by the public, private corporations as well as various interest groups (Sands, 1990, p2), it is important to gain a thorough understanding of the historic evolution of European environmental policies as a whole.[2] The introduction of the SEA has brought about significant changes. Yet, relatively little has been written on the subject and, although '1992' has become every European's catchword, few seem to be aware of the potential environmental consequences of these recent developments.

Before laying out the structure of this chapter, it is necessary to discuss briefly the legal instruments that the relevant Community institutions are equipped with, in 'order to carry out their task'.[3] They are applicable to all issue-areas within the competence of the EC and have not been changed by the amendments introduced by the SEA or the Maastricht Treaty creating the European Union (EU). Article 189 of the EEC Treaty sets out five different types of legal instruments. The first paragraph states: 'In order to carry out their task the Council and the Commission shall, in accordance with the provisions of this Treaty, make regulations, issue directives, take decisions, make recommendations or deliver opinions.' The last two have no binding force and should therefore not 'properly be regarded as legislative instruments' (Haigh, 1990, p2).

A regulation has general application and is 'binding in its entirety and directly applicable in all Member States' (Article 189/2). It has generally been used for precise purposes such as financial matters or the daily management of the Common Agricultural Policy (CAP). Only rarely has it been used for environmental matters (Haigh, 1990, p2).

A directive is 'binding, as to the result to be achieved', while it leaves it to the national authorities as to the 'choice of form and method' (Article 189/3). According to Nigel Haigh, 'it is therefore the most appropriate instrument for more general purposes particularly where some flexibility is required to accommodate existing national procedures and, for this reason, is the instrument most commonly used for environmental matters' (Haigh, 1990, p2).[4]

Finally a decision is 'binding in its entirety upon those to whom it is addressed' (Article 189/4). With respect to environmental protection, decisions have been used in connection with international conventions and with certain procedural matters.

For analytical purposes I have divided the period to be covered here into three different phases. The first one begins with the entry into force of the Treaty of Rome and the establishment of the European Economic Community (EEC) in 1957 and ends in 1972 with the Stockholm Conference on the Human Environment. With the approval of the first Community Action Programme on the Environment by the Council of Ministers in November 1973, the second phase begins which, according to this chronology, lasts until the adoption of the SEA in Luxembourg in December 1985. On 17 and 28 February the SEA was signed in Luxembourg and The Hague and, after ratification by the 12 national parliaments (and referenda in Denmark and Ireland), it came into force on 1 July 1987. The ratification of the SEA represents the onset of the third phase, in the midst of which the EC's environmental policy is presently unfolding.[5]

I have attempted to describe and label each of the three phases in a distinct manner. According to this typology, the first one, from 1956 to 1972 is best understood as a time of pragmatic measures as opposed to proper policy. The overriding objective of the EC during that time was to harmonize laws in order to abolish trade impediments between the Member States. The pieces of environmental legislation that were adopted throughout those years were, as one observer has described them, 'incidental' to the overriding economic objectives (McGrory, 1990, p304).

After 1972, one begins to witness the emergence of an EC environmental policy. Specific actions and measures were initiated in a response to a number of circumstances and events. First, mounting public protest against environmental destruction exerted a considerable degree of pressure upon elected government officials. This pressure, in turn, seems to have had a positive effect on the dynamics and innovation of official EC policy. Second, during the 1970s and the early 1980s the world was witness to a number of environmental disasters which provided a dramatic backdrop to the emerging environmental sensitivity. Last, but by no means least, Member States became concerned about uncoordinated local environmental protection measures causing intra-community trade distortions.

With the third phase, which essentially coincides with the SEA, EC environmental policy becomes more substantive. The Title VII amendment to the original Treaty of Rome introduced important new ideas and methods of environmental policy. Within this context, it is important to keep a proper perspective and avoid a sense of 'europhoria'. The new provisions of the SEA are, although potentially far-reaching, rather abstract. Dirk Vandermeersch (1987, p407) describes them as giving a 'constitutional' base to the Community's environmental policy, and as defining its objectives. Nigel Haigh and David Baldock (1989, p20) take this line of thought one step further arguing that, depending on how one views the relevant articles of Title VII, they may 'do no more than legitimize what was happening anyway'. Yet, at the end, their final judgement is a positive one. They conclude that the new provisions contain interesting elements and result in subtle consequences.

This brings me to the concept of an international regime, to which I referred in the title of this chapter. Throughout the past decade, a significant amount of international relations and political science literature has been concerned with the concept of international regimes. As a result, a whole range of different definitions and approaches has emerged. Arguably, the most promising path is the one that perceives an international regime as a form of international institution or 'persistent and connected sets of rules (formal and informal) that prescribe behavioural roles, constrain activity, and shape expectations' (Keohane, 1989, p3). Within this tradition, Robert Keohane defines international regimes as institutions with explicit rules, agreed upon by governments, that pertain to particular sets of issues in international relations. Similarly, Oran Young (1992, p165) defines international regimes as 'institutional arrangements that deal with specific issue-areas'.

Another recent and related definition stems from Otto Keck (1991, p637) who views an international regime as an institutional arrangement for the collective management of problematic interdependencies of action, meaning problems that simultaneously touch upon the interests of several states and that cannot, or only inadequately, be resolved by individual states without resorting to coordination or co-operation with other states.[6] Applying this kind of concept of an international regime to the EC's environmental policy allows us to embark upon a dynamic analysis. Regimes do not just come into existence; they develop over time. The same applies to the EC's environmental policy. This development takes place via a process of increasing institutionalization, which is the gradual recognition by participants that their behaviour reflects, to a considerable extent, the established rules, norms and conventions and that its meaning is interpreted in light of this recognition (Keohane, 1989, p1).

Throughout the following discussion of the evolution of the environmental policy of the EC I shall pause at the end of each of the three phases mentioned above in order to assess to what extent this process of institutionalisation can be said to have taken place. In the conclusion I shall briefly address the question of the benefits of using a regime or institutional framework in an analysis of the EC's environmental policy.

1957–1972: 'Incidental' Measures

When the Treaty of Rome, establishing the European Economic Communities (EEC), was signed on 25 March 1957, it did not include any explicit reference to the idea of environmental policy or environmental protection. The primary aim of the six founding Member States was to establish a 'common market' in which goods, people, services and capital could move without obstacles (Article 3). There are two articles in the original Treaty that can be regarded as a direct indicator that, as Rolf Wägenbaur (1990, p16) has pointed out, 'the ambitions of the founding fathers went far beyond' the objective of the common market. First, Article 2 of the Treaty of Rome calls for the promotion throughout the Community of 'a harmonious development of economic activities, a continuous and balanced expansion, an increase in stability, an accelerated raising of the standard of living and closer relations between the states belonging to it'. The Community institutions tend to interpret this mandate to include not only an improved standard of living but also an improved quality of life (Rehbinder and Steward, 1985, p21). Although this interpretation, which suggests that environmental protection might be among the Community's objectives, is not uncontroversial, the general view of the literature seems to be that it is 'reasonable to interpret the Preamble and Article 2 of the EEC Treaty as including economic concepts of environmental pollution, such as those of external cost and of the environment as a common good' (Rehbinder and Steward, 1985, p21).

Second, Article 36 refers, at least implicitly, to the protection of the environment. It states that it is justifiable to restrict imports, exports or goods in transit on grounds of 'public morality, public policy or public security; the protection of health and life of humans, animals or plants; the protection of national treasures possessing artistic, historic or archaeological value'. In both cases therefore there exists a certain obligation to safeguard the environment. However, given the very general phrasing of Article 2 and the negative provision of Article 36, allowing for trade restrictions for reasons of public health and the protection of humans, animals and plants only as a derogation from the supreme principle of freedom of exchange, it is obvious that it was the 'common market' and the four 'freedoms' that constituted the core of the Treaty's objectives (Wägenbaur, 1990, p16). Within this context it is worth noting that the European Court of Justice made an attempt to define the substance of the common market, stating that it involves 'the elimination of all obstacles to intra-Community trade in order to merge the national markets into a single market bringing about conditions as close as possible to those of a genuine internal market'.[7] Again, there is some room to perceive environmental protection as being related to the objective of such a common market but only insofar as it touches upon intra-Community trade obstacles, particularly non-tariff barriers.

During those early years, EC environmental legislation was therefore subject to a twofold restriction. First, there were no explicit, formal legal provisions to support any Community-wide action and, second, whatever action could be taken under the available general provisions had to be directly related to the objective of economic and community harmonization (McGrory, 1990, p304). This meant that the pace of environmental protection was essentially set by strongly environmentally-oriented Member States as opposed to anyone on the Community level.

As a result of the uncertainty about the jurisdictional basis for Community environmental protection measures, the Community institutions have, at least until the SEA, based their environmental policy primarily on Article 100 and, to a lesser extent, on Article 235 of the Treaty of Rome. Article 100 authorizes the Council, provided it acts unanimously, to 'issue directives for the approximation of such provisions laid down by law, regulation or administrative action in Member States as directly affect the establishment or functioning of the Common Market'. Article 235 is also based on unanimous decision. It accords the Council the authority to take 'appropriate measures' to 'attain, in the course of the operation of the Common Market, one of the objectives of the Community' where the 'Treaty has not provided the necessary powers' to do so. Obviously the 'justification for using these two articles as the foundation of a common environmental policy depends ultimately on basic Community goals' (Rehbinder and Steward, 1985, p20). According to Article 3 of the EEC Treaty, 'approximation of the laws of the Member States' is to 'promote the proper functioning of the Common Market and the Community's objectives set out in Article 2' (Rehbinder and Steward, 1985, p20). As a result, the use of Article 100 and Article 235 was essentially dependent on a generous reading of Article 2.[8] To sum up, while politically it was possible to use Article 100 and Article 235 for environmental objectives, these provisions as Rehbinder has pointed out, were originally:

> *designed to give Community institutions powers to ensure the establishment and functioning of the Common Market as an economic institution and were not aimed at environmental protection as such* (Rehbinder and Steward, 1985, p16).

Despite the absence of a coherent framework, the Council passed several concrete pieces of environmental legislation prior to the First Action Programme on the Environment. Between 1964 and 1975 a number of initiatives were adopted under Articles 30, 92, 93 and 95 of the EC Treaty to prevent excessive subsidization of the regeneration or incineration of used oil (Rehbinder and Steward, 1985, p16). In 1967 a directive was used for the first time to deal with environmental matters, establishing a uniform system of classification, labelling and packaging of dangerous substances.[9] The jurisdictional basis for Directive 67/548 was Article 100 of the Treaty of Rome. In March 1969 this directive was modified, again on the basis of Article 100.[10] In 1970, Directives 70/157, regulating permissible sound level and exhaust systems of motor vehicles, and 70/220, limiting vehicle emissions, were again passed with reference to Article 100 of the EEC Treaty, while Regulation 729/70 with respect to countryside protection in agriculturally less favoured areas was based on Articles 43 and 209. In 1971, the only 'environmental' directive that was passed extended the deadline for the implementation of the 1967 directive on dangerous substances. In the last year of the first phase, the Council passed three directives that can be considered to have an environmental impact, two of which were related to agricultural issues and therefore took their jurisdictional basis from Articles 42 and 43 of the EEC Treaty. Directive 72/306, regulating vehicle emissions caused by diesel engines, once again referred to Article 100.

While environmental measures were not altogether absent during the first 15 years of the EC's history, they cannot be regarded as adding up to any sort of proper and coherent policy. Only nine directives and one regulation were adopted during that time and, on the whole, these measures were incidental to the overriding economic objective (McGrory, 1990, p304). This is reaffirmed by the fact that all 'environmental' directives, with the exception of the ones pertaining to agriculture, were adopted on the basis of Article 100 and thus perceived as approximation measures with respect to the 'establishment or functioning of the common market'.

During this first phase, it is inappropriate to speak of an institutionalization process in terms of environmental protection. A limited number of pieces of legislation were passed but these were not based on an established set of rules pertaining to the protection of the environment. In fact, the issue-area of the environment did not yet exist per se. It was therefore impossible for the participants to perceive their behaviour as a reflection of a set of rules within this issue area.

1972–1986: The 'Responsive' Period

The Paris Summit Conference on 19 and 20 October 1972 marks the onset of the second phase in the evolution of Community environmental policy. In Versailles, the heads of state or government of the six founding Member States and of the new members (United Kingdom, Denmark and Ireland) called upon the institutions of the Community to provide them with a blueprint for an official EC environmental policy by 31 July 1973. Accordingly, the Commission forwarded a 'Programme of environmental action of the European Communities' to the Council on 17 April 1973. Pursuant to this Commission initiative, the First Community Action Programme on the Environment was formally approved by the Council and the representatives of the Member State on 22 November 1973.[11] The programme must be regarded as a landmark in the evolution of Community environmental efforts. It marked the beginning of an actual policy in that it set the objectives, stated the principles, selected the priorities and described the measures to be taken in different sectors of the environment for the next two years. As Eckhard Rehbinder (Rehbinder and Steward, 1985, pp17–18) states, it 'opened up a field for Community action not originally provided for in the treaties' and, according to the Commission, 'added a new dimension to the construction of Europe'.[12]

The objective of Community environmental policy, as expressed in the First Action Programme, was 'to improve the setting and quality of life, and the surroundings and living conditions of the Community population'.[13] In order to achieve this objective, the Council adopted 11 principles, determining the main features of the policy. Three of these principles deserve particular mention here. First, the emphasis was laid on preventive action. Second, it was asserted that 'the expense of preventing and eliminating pollution should, in principle be borne by the polluter'.[14] Finally, the programme stipulated that 'for each different type of pollution, it is necessary to establish the level of action' befitting the type of pollution and the geographical zone to be protected.[15] With respect to the Commission this meant that it had the authority to act 'whenever lack of action would thwart the efforts of more localized authorities and whenever real effectiveness is attainable by action at Community level'.[16] Overall, the First Action Programme called for measures in three different categories: the reduction of pollution and nuisances as such; the improvement of the environment and the setting of life as well as the joint action in international organizations dealing with the environment. The second category of measures essentially fell under common policies, such as the common agricultural policies (CAP), social policy, regional policy and the information programme.[17]

The first Action Programme was followed in 1976 by a second, more encompassing programme covering the period from 1977 to 1981. It was approved by the Council on 9 December 1976 and formally adopted on 17 May 1977.[18] The transition from the First to the Second Action Programme coincided with the publication of the first report, by the Commission, on the state of the environment in the Community, as provided for in the 1973 programme, reviewing all the environmental measures taken up to the end of 1976.[19] The aim of the Second Action Programme was to continue and expand the actions taken within the framework of the previous one. Special emphasis was placed on reinforcing the preventive nature of Community policy. Furthermore, the programme paid special attention to the non-damaging use and rational management of space, the environment and natural resources. With respect to the actual reduction of pollution, the programme accorded special priority to measures against water pollution. Prior to the adoption of the third environmental programme in 1983, the second programme was extended by one and a half years. Due to the problems of institutional transition caused by the accession of Greece and the upgrading of the Environment and Consumer Protection Service to a Directorate-General for Environment, Consumer Protection and Nuclear Safety, the extra time was needed to make the necessary adjustments (Rehbinder and Steward, 1985, p18).

The continuity of Community environmental policy was assured on 7 February 1983 when the Council adopted a resolution on a Third Community Action Programme covering the years 1982 to 1986.[20] While the third programme certainly remained within the general framework of the policy as outlined in the previous two, it introduced a number of new elements. Most importantly, it stated that, while originally 'the central concern was that, as a result of very divergent national policies, disparities would arise capable of affecting the proper functioning of the common market',[21] the common environmental policy is now motivated equally by the observation that the resources of the environment are the basis of – but also constitute the limit to – further economic and social development and the improvement of living conditions. It therefore advocated 'the implementation of an overall strategy which would permit the incorporation of environmental considerations in certain other Community policies such as those for agriculture, energy, industry and transport'.[22] According to the resolution, the EC environmental policy could, in fact, no longer be dissociated from measures designed to achieve the fundamental objectives of the Community.

This acceptance of environmental policy as a component of the Community's economic objectives was fundamental in that it was the first attempt to do away with the clear subordination of environmental concerns vis-à-vis the overriding economic goal of the common market. Admittedly, the wording of the resolution was carefully chosen. Yet, with the Third Action Programme, environmental policy had clearly gained in terms of its political status. Besides the integration of an environmental dimension into other policies (see Chapter 1), the programme again reinforced the preventive character of Community policy, specifically referring to the environmental impact assessment procedure. It also established a list of actual priorities, ranging from atmosphere pollution (Directive 89/779/EEC), fresh-water and marine pollution (Directive 76/464/EEC; Directive 78/176/EEC), dangerous chemical substances (Directive 79/831/EEC; Directive 67/548/EEC), waste management (Directive 78/319/EEC) to the protection of sensitive areas within the Community and the co-operation with developing countries on environmental matters. Finally, the programme also included a commitment by the Commission to use certain considerations as a basis for drawing up their proposals such as, for instance, the obligation to evaluate, as much as possible, the costs and benefits of the action envisaged.[23]

Not surprisingly, these novelties resulted in a significant increase in terms of environmental legislation. Between February 1983 and the adoption of the SEA in December 1985, over 40 directives, eight decisions and ten regulations that all had at least some regard to the environment were adopted by the Council.

The designated final year of the Third Action Programme was 1986. The negotiations about a follow-up fourth programme were well under way by 1985, at which time it had become clear that the EEC Treaty would be supplemented by the SEA by way of which a separate chapter on the environment would be introduced in the Treaty. Although the Fourth Action Programme was not formally adopted until October 1987,[24] a new phase in the evolution of Community environmental policy was about to begin by the end of 1985, the legal basis of which would be provided by the SEA.

The preceding paragraphs have outlined how the Community's environmental policy evolved quite significantly during the second phase; both in terms of the underlying political attitude towards environmental protection as well as the actual number of adopted pieces of legislation. It must be remembered, however, that the actual legal basis for the policy remained relatively weak. In other words, even by the mid-1980s the Community lacked the formal competences to deal with many environmental problems. Two writers have evoked the image of a 'grey zone' of Community competences in this respect (Teitgen and Mégret, 1981, p69). Rehbinder and Steward (1985, p19) have gone even further by stating that the 'Community's expansion into this policy area is a considerable extension of Community law and policy at the expense of Member States without any express authorization'. To put it differently, until the SEA, the evolution of Community environmental policy took place in the absence of an evolution of its formal legal basis (see Chapter 7).

All said, the second epoch of the EC environmental policy portrays a peculiar image. On the one hand, the jurisdictional basis, being limited from the outset, did not evolve until the adoption of the SEA. On the other hand, the development towards a common environmental policy framework was, though arguably far from satisfactory, remarkable. Within the context of this dichotomy, I shall, in the following paragraphs, make an attempt to shed some light upon the driving forces behind Community environmental policy during these years.

With the unequivocal establishment of economic growth as the goal for post-war Europe, there was simply no room for environmental concerns at the time of the foundation of the EEC. This situation was accentuated by the fact that, at the time, the majority of the public and certainly most politicians probably did not perceive the need for particular efforts in the domain of the environment. The general degree of environmental degradation had not yet reached today's dimensions and even where that was not necessarily true, relatively little reliable scientific information was available. Within this context, it is interesting to note that even progressive politicians, such as, for example, Lester Pearson, had little doubt as to the political supremacy of economic growth.[25]

By the early 1970s, this premise was no longer uncontested. In many parts of the developed world, environmental concerns started to surface on political agendas. In the United States, the Environmental Protection Agency was founded in 1970, accompanied by the Clean Air Act and the subsequent Clean Water Act of 1972. American public opinion was mobilized through organizations such as Friends of the Earth and the Conservation Foundation which later merged with the WWF USA. During the late 1960s Europe witnessed the emergence to prominence of environmentalists such as Bernhard Grzimek in Germany and Jacques Cousteau in France. They made effective use of the mass media to sensitize the public to their causes. Greenpeace International also started to make an important impact with its much publicized and often spectacular missions on behalf of the environment. In the Federal Republic of Germany, Willy Brandt put environmental protection on his 1969 election platform. As Chancellor, he then set a precedent by granting environmental protection a high political priority. In fact, in October 1971, his government launched an official environmental programme (Hartkopf and Bohme, 1983, pp84–118, Bechmann, 1984, pp55–65, Müller, 1986, pp57–96). At least formally, France went even further, becoming the first European country to establish its own environmental ministry. Finally, in the summer of 1972, the United Nations convened the Stockholm Conference on the Human Environment with the extensive acid rain damage to a large number of Swedish lakes as a dramatic backdrop. Under the leadership of Maurice Strong the conference succeeded, despite diplomatic isolation of the West, in establishing a United Nations Environmental Programme (UNEP).

Within the context of this newly emerging international sensitivity towards environmental protection, France seized the opportunity of her EC presidency to bring about the decision to establish the first Environmental Action Programme on the Environment at the 1972 Paris Summit in Versailles. Juliet Lodge has pointed out that the Member States' interest in an EC environmental policy was:

> *spurred not so much by upsurge of post-industrial values and the Nine's*[26] *endeavours to create a 'Human Union' or to give the EC a 'human face' as by the realization that widely differing national rules on industrial pollution could distort competition: 'dirty states' could profit economically by being slack* (Lodge, 1989, p320).

The Federal Republic of Germany and The Netherlands were among the strongest supporters of a concerted Community environmental policy. Their actual and foreseen national environmental standards were relatively strict, causing some concern about the resulting economic burdens. The German and Dutch industrial lobbies therefore argued for equal economic cost of environmental protection throughout the EC via the adoption of their standards on a Community-wide basis.

To sum up, the impetus for the First Action Programme was essentially threefold. First and, as we have seen, most importantly, there prevailed an increasing concern among the Member States about the relationship of environmental protection and trade distortions. Second, governments felt the need to initiate a coherent response to the increasing political pressure from environmentalists both on the national as well as on the international level. Finally, considering the inherently transnational characteristics of much of Europe's pollution, it was recognized that, in order to be effective, concerted supranational efforts were needed which could be based on the existing political structures of the EC (McCarthy, 1989, p3).

In the years following 1972, there is another factor that affected the further course of Community environmental policy. Environmental disasters demonstrated the urgent need for further strengthening of the existing principles of environmental protection. Flixborough in 1974 and Seveso in 1976 were perhaps the most dramatic representations of the 'daily environmental abuse by petro-chemical and other industries, urban programmes and "high-tech" agricultural methods' that grew exponentially during the 1970s and 1980s (Lodge, 1989, p319). The oil shocks of the 1970s resulted in a temporary deceleration of environmental policy.[27] At the latest, by the late 1970s, however, environmental protection had once again become an important item on Europe's political agenda. Several European countries experienced fierce debates about the expansion of civil nuclear capacities and by 1982, with the disclosure of the widespread forest destruction in Germany, environmental policy had become a matter of first priority, a status that even surpassed the one it enjoyed in the early 1970s (Weizsäcker, 1989, p27).[28]

Not surprisingly, the 1983 Stuttgart European Council reacted to these developments. Reviewing the state of Community environmental policy, it concluded that there is an 'urgent need to speed up and reinforce action', drawing special attention to the destruction of the forests (Johnson and Corcelle, 1989, p3).

With the 1985 Brussels session of the European Council, the status of environmental protection policy was once again upgraded in so far as it was now perceived as a fundamental part of economic, industrial, agricultural and social policies within the Community (Johnson and Corcelle, 1989, p3). What this meant is that, by the mid-1980s, the view had emerged that environmental protection was an 'economic and not simply a moral imperative' (Lodge, 1989, p321). This final step in the evolution of Community policy during the second phase must be understood as a result of the increasing realization of the link between economic growth stimulated by further integration and the resulting costs in terms of adverse environmental encumbrances (Haigh and Baldock, 1989, p45). The ensuing integrated approach towards environmental protection leads directly to the last of the three phases that were outlined at the outset.

The second phase of Community environmental policy can be summarized as an active one that undoubtedly furthered environmental protection in the EC. At the same time, however, it was characterized by a considerable degree of uncertainty. It lacked the truly integrated approach based on a sound legal basis that emerged in the third phase with the Fourth Action Programme and the SEA. The policy until 1985 was a 'responsive' one in that it evolved according to the momentary economic, political and social circumstances. Its initial and probably most important impetus was, as described above, the general concern of environmental protection as a potential cause for trade distortions. Public pressure and the direct effects of environmental accidents later accelerated the process. Finally, there was the realization that economic progress and the protection of the environment are so closely interlinked that one cannot be considered without the other. The nature of the policy evolved at each stage depending on the given set of circumstances. Generally speaking, the circumstances as they presented themselves during the second phase favoured a progressive evolution of the policy although, in the case of the 1973 oil shock, they temporarily worked in the opposite direction.

This type of policy had certain advantages. As a whole it remained flexible, not having to rely on rigid principles that quickly become outdated. In other words, it was possible to readjust quickly the policy to a newly arisen situation or set of circumstances. The disadvantage rested in the fact that under these conditions, environmental protection would always be relegated to a subordinate position in relation to Community economic aims. Whether this disadvantage has been eliminated successfully without undermining some of the positive aspects of the second phase will be discussed in the following section. Before that, however, I shall briefly review the most important pieces of legislation of the second phase. Given the significant number of environmental directives, regulations and decisions between the First Action Programme and the SEA, it would, of course, exceed the limits of this study to review them all. I have therefore chosen a small representative selection.

Ernest von Weizsäcker (1989, p42) has identified just over 20 directives as being the most important pieces of Community environmental legislation between 1973 and 1985. For the sake of simplicity I shall base my review on this selection.[29] The relevant directives can conveniently be grouped together in six different categories according to the environmental problem they are addressing:

1. Water
2. Air
3. Noise
4. Waste
5. Emissions
6. Lead in petrol

In addition there are a number of other directives that do not readily fit into any of these categories: the 'Seveso' directive, a directive on chemicals, one on birds and their habitat and one on sewage sludge. Weizsacker's selection of directives is useful in that it more or less represents the full spectrum of EC environmental activities.

In the fight against water pollution, there are four directives, all of which are based both on Article 100 and Article 235 of the EEC Treaty. Directives 75/440 and 80/778 are concerned with drinking water while directive 76/160 regulates bathing water.[30] Directive 76/464 deals with dangerous substances in water.[31] The air quality efforts are represented by three directives: 80/779 on smoke and sulphur dioxide, 82/884 on lead and 85/203 on nitrogen dioxide.[32] Again the legal basis for all three directives rests in Article 100 and Article 235 of the Treaty of Rome. The same applies to the three directives on waste: 75/442 outlines a general waste framework while 78/319 and 84/631 deal with toxic waste and transfrontier shipment of waste respectively.[33] In terms of emission standards. Directive 83/351 on vehicle emission only refers to Article 100, whereas Directive 84/360 on emission from industrial plants is again based on Article 100 and Article 235.[34] The two directives on the approximation of laws of Member States concerning lead content in petrol (85/210 and 78/611) are solely based on Article 100 of the Treaty of Rome.[35] The same is true of Directive 79/831, amending for the sixth time Directive 67/548 on the approximation of the laws, regulations and administrative provisions relating to the classification, packaging and labelling of dangerous substances, as well as Directive 79/117 on use restrictions and labelling of pesticides.[36]

Directive 79/409 on birds and their habitat, on the other hand is exclusively based on Article 235. This is, of course, to be expected, since animal protection has hardly any direct effect on the 'establishment or functioning of the common market' as expressed in Article 100 of the Treaty of Rome.[37] Finally, there are two more directives that need to be mentioned here, both of which were adopted under Article 100 and 235. Directive 82/501 on the major accident hazards of certain industrial activities was a Community response to the dioxine disaster in Seveso, and Directive 85/337 on the assessment of the effects of certain public and private projects on the environment set out an important new priority of Community environmental policy.[38]

This selective review of EC environmental 'legislation' between 1973 and 1985 re-emphasizes a point made earlier. Although the Community institutions were engaged in a considerable amount of environmental activity, the available legal foundations remained limited. There was no explicit jurisdictional mandate for the protection of the environment; the Community therefore proceeded with its environmental efforts on the basis of what Ernst Weizsäcker has called a '*Kunstgriff*', or knack, using Articles 100 and 235 of the original EEC Treaty (see Chapter 18). This is, of course, the most fundamental difference with respect to the present phase of Community environmental policy as it has been unfolding since the adoption of the SEA.

During this second phase, the institutionalization process mentioned at the outset is becoming discernible. Member states begin to understand that certain collective actions are necessary in order to address a more or less specific set of problems in the newly defined issue-area of the environment. As I have pointed out, however, the environment does not stand on its own feet yet. It is still at least partly subordinated to the paramount objective of economic growth. Furthermore, although explicit rules exist in the form of the various directives passed, their ability to prescribe behavioural roles, constrain activity and shape expectations is limited because of the absence of an unambiguous legal foundation. Despite an ongoing gradual process of institutionalization, no proper EC environmental regime can therefore be in place. Though explicit and agreed upon by the Member States' governments, the rules in fact remain weak and exert little independent compliance pull.

1985–'1992': The 'Initiative' Phase

An analysis of EC environmental policy after 1985 is rendered more complicated by the fact that, although there exists an element of continuity, it would be too simplistic to regard it as a mere continuation of previous policy developments. In terms of its general approach, the Fourth Action Programme is certainly related to the previous one, despite the fact that it was differently structured and that it initiated a number of new policy directions such as environmental educational efforts and a focus on gene-technology. It essentially completed and formalized the notions of earlier Community policy. In fact, EC policy, as laid down in the programme, is virtually all-encompassing. It demands integration of social, industrial, agricultural and economic policies, an objective that, as mentioned earlier, began to emerge with the Third Action Programme in 1983. Besides this factor of continuity, however, post-1985 EC environmental policy is shaped by a second strand of influence which manifests itself in the SEA amendment to the Treaty of Rome. Interestingly enough, the forces behind the emergence of the SEA have little to do with the environment. As Rolf Wägenbaur (1990, p17) has stated, the impetus stemming from the original EEC Treaty gradually weakened in the 1980s and 'it was felt that a new initiative was necessary. The so-called Single European Act came to the rescue.' The initiative was also related to the enlargement of the Community from the original six Member States to the present 12 (UK, Ireland, Denmark: 1973; Greece: 1981; Spain and Portugal: 1986). In light of the extended membership, the original Treaty was clearly in need of revision. There were intensive discussions as to what sort of reform the Treaty should undergo: a social charter, an environmental chapter, research and development programmes, a regional policy, the strengthening of the European Parliament, majority voting in the Council: all these issues were brought onto the agenda. The most important outcome of these negotiations, however, was the decision to go ahead with the completion of the internal market.

The commitment to achieve this goal within a specific time limit was laid down in Article 8a of the Treaty. This states that the Community 'shall adopt measures with the aim of progressively establishing the internal market over a period expiring on 31 December 1992'. The internal market is defined as 'an area without internal frontiers in which the free movement of goods, persons, services and capital is ensured'. With Lord Cockfield's White Paper, the Commission presented a plan as to what it perceived to be the specific measures that needed to be adopted in order to complete the internal market (COM 85/310).[39] This relatively sudden acceleration in the process of European integration put an end to perceptions of 'eurosclerosis' and caused great optimism as to the economic effects of the Single European Market.[40] The Cecchini Report on 'the economics of 1992' estimated that the internal market would result in an economic gain of 4.5–7 per cent of the Community's GNP. Such an increase in economic activities would affect the state of the environment. In the absence of any changes in policies or technologies, the environment could clearly be expected to deteriorate. It is within this context that, in 1989, a Commission Task Force published a report on 'The Environment and the Internal Market' in which it stated that the creation of a single market, as well as the need to decouple economic growth from environmental degradation requires a fundamental review of existing environmental policy at EC level and in the Member States (Wägenbaur, 1990, p18). By including Title VII on 'Environment' in the new EEC Treaty, the authors of the SEA provided the formal legal foundation on the basis of which such a fundamental review could take place.

Figure 2.1 shows the two strands that defined the post-1985 EC environmental policy. As mentioned earlier, it is the formal legal foundation as expressed in the SEA that distinguishes Community policy after 1985 from the earlier one. The chart indicates that the dynamics of the first and second phase are still operating (b). However, it is strand (a) that is the primary determinant of the third phase of Community environmental policy.

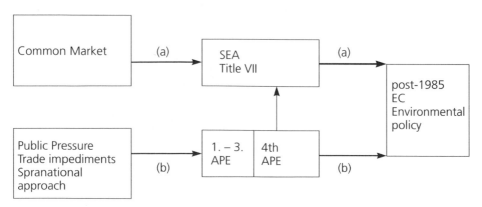

Figure 2.1 *Factors that Shaped EC Environmental Policy Post-1985*

Obviously the distinction between the two strands is somewhat schematic and therefore not entirely correct. The connecting line between the two strands suggests that the SEA amendment is also a result of Community environmental policy as it had been developing since 1972, culminating in the Fourth Action Programme in 1987. Nigel Haigh and David Baldock (1989, p20) make this point, arguing that the lack of a clear legal base for the EC's environmental policy had been much criticized. Within this context they see the 'Environment' title as a 'response to this criticism'. Nevertheless, the distinction is analytically useful if one works with the hypothesis that the adoption of the SEA had a significant effect on the nature of EC environmental policy. The following pages attempt to shed some light upon the question of whether or not this hypothesis is valid.

The SEA affected Community environmental policy in three different ways: First, through the general institutional changes – majority voting and the co-operation procedure; second, through the objective of completing the internal market; and third through the new legal provisions that actually define Community environmental policy (Haigh and Baldock, 1989, p12).

Institutional Changes

The first of the two institutional changes instigated by the SEA is the 'co-operation procedure' with its second reading by Parliament as expressed in Article 149 of the EEC Treaty. In response to criticism of lack of openness of the EC legislation process and charges of a 'democratic deficit', the 'co-operation procedure is designed to allow the European Parliament to play an effective but qualified role in the legislative process' (Lodge, 1989, p69).[41] In terms of environmental protection, there is some significance to Article 149 in that it effectively allows public opinion, represented by the Parliament, to have more of an impact on the process of environmental policy formation. Considering that environmental consciousness has undoubtedly been heightened throughout the Community in the past few years, this source of public influence could prove to become quite relevant.[42]

The co-operation procedure is limited in that it only applies when a vote is taken in Council by qualified majority. Qualified majority voting, as laid down in Article 148 of the EEC Treaty, is not a new phenomenon; it was already contained in the original Treaty. What is new, however, is that under Article 100a, it is now possible to use it for environmental purposes (Haigh and Baldock, 1989, p14). This stands in contrast to Article 100 and Article 235 on which most pre-1985 pieces of environmental legislation were based, as well as to the new Article 130s which I will discuss below. In all three cases, unanimity is a requirement for any action. As Nigel Haigh and David Baldock (1989, p15) point out, one of the problems with majority voting in the context of the environment is the uncertainty that prevails about how 'a choice is made for environmental measures between Article 130s (unanimity) and Article 100a (majority voting)'. Although Article 100a is, in principal, reserved for traded products, it is difficult to categorize all cases along these lines. Not surprisingly, the Commission and the Council do not see eye to eye on this question. The Commission's view is that Article 100a is the proper legal base whenever the specified conditions are fulfilled. According to this view. Article 130s 'only comes into consideration when the conditions of Article 100a are not fulfilled or when, for instance, the impact of the product on competition is very small as compared with the impact on the environment as such' (Wägenbaur, 1990, p21).

The European Court of Justice had been expected for some time to clarify the legal confusion arising out of the tension between these two articles (see Chapter 1). With the June 1991 ruling in the titanium dioxide case 300/89, it has finally done so.[43] The Court clearly gives preference to Article 100a, thus supporting majority voting. This could well set the path for future EC environmental legislation. In anticipation of the actual effect of the Court's position, Nigel Haigh's conclusion can be accepted that, while majority voting may not have revolutionized environmental policy, it has made it more difficult for one or two countries to block certain proposals, as Denmark discovered when it failed to prevent the adoption of Directive 88/76 on emission from large cars (Haigh and Baldock, 1989, p15).

Completion of the 'Internal Market'

In order to achieve the objective of completing the internal market by 31 December 1992 (Article 8a), the SEA introduced Articles 100a and 100b concerning the harmonization of national laws, including environmental laws. Article 100a(3) states that the Commission essentially takes as a base a 'high level of protection' in its harmonization efforts. Article 100a(4) allows Member States to apply more stringent national environmental standards provided they are 'not a means of arbitrary discrimination or a disguised restriction on trade between Member States'. There is also a safeguard clause (Article 100a(5)) that allows Member States to opt out of harmonization efforts in appropriate cases as provided for in Article 36. Article 100b requires the Community to draw up an inventory of national measures 'which fall under 100a and which have not been harmonized pursuant to that Article'. By majority voting, the Council then is to decide which of these can 'be recognized as being equivalent'. All others presumably have to be harmonized at that point (Haigh and Baldock, 1989, p18). These harmonization measures designed to complete the internal market have an impact on environmental policy to the extent that most environmental protection standards that affect the functioning of the internal market will be set at EC level. Whether or not the EC will seek to harmonize standards for emission (to air or water) or for environmental procedures (eg safety requirements at factories, disposal standards at vast sites), which 'have the potential to affect the "functioning of the common market" (Article 100) or the "establishment of the internal market" (Article 8a) remains uncertain' (Haigh and Baldock, 1989, p19).

Environmental Title

The SEA inserted Title VII entitled 'Environment' in part III of the EEC Treaty which is concerned with the 'policies' of the EC. This is worth noting since it suggests that with the SEA it is no longer just de facto but de jure correct to speak of an environmental policy. The relevant Treaty provisions are numbered

130r to 130s. Article 130r specifies the objectives of Community environmental policy and lays down the principles and guidelines that such a policy must follow. It also deals with Member State versus Community competences in terms of environmental protection and finally calls for co-operation with third countries and international organization in matters involving the environment. Article 130s, as discussed earlier, stipulates the legislative process for the formulation of environmental laws and Article 130t allows states to introduce more stringent protective measures as long as they are compatible with the rest of the Treaty.

There are a number of ways in which these new provisions have affected Community environmental policy. First, Title VII has given symbolic importance to environmental protection policy, reinforced by the preamble to the SEA in which the Community commits itself to 'promote democracy on the basis of the fundamental rights recognized in the constitutions and laws of the Member States'. As Haigh and Baldock (1989, p21) have pointed out, 'more than a third of the Member States have accorded constitutional status to the protection of the environment or recognize environmental rights'. Second, the Community environmental policy objectives outlined in Article 130r(1) are sufficiently broad – to preserve, protect and improve the quality of the environment; to contribute towards protecting human health; to ensure a prudent and rational utilization of national resources – to bring almost any environmental issue within the competence of Community legislation. Third, Article 130r(2) gives legal force to the principle which, as discussed earlier, gradually evolved in the 'Action Programmes on the Environment': principle of prevention, rectification at source and polluter pays. In addition. Article 130r(2) formalizes the new principle that environmental 'protection requirements shall be a component of the Community's other policies'. Fourth, Article 130r(3) states four basic factors that the Community needs to consider in its policy adoption: (a) available scientific data, (b) environmental coordination in the various regions of the Community, (c) the potential benefits and cost of action or lack of action and (d) the economic and social development of the Community as a whole and the balanced development of its region. Fifth, Article 130r(4) lays down the principle of subsidiarity which determines whether appropriate action is to be taken at the Community or at the Member States level. The article states:

The Community shall take action relating to the environment to the extent to which the objectives referred to in paragraph I can be attained better at Community level than at the level of the individual Member States, thus expressly reserving residual jurisdiction to the Member States (Vandermeersch, 1987, p422).

Before addressing the question of whether or not these effects are negative or positive in terms of actual environmental protection, I shall, once again, turn to a brief review of environmental legislative measures of the third phase. As was the case for the second phase, this review is highly selective. I have, however, tried to make the selection as representative as possible of the totality of measures adopted. The survey begins with the entry into force of the SEA on 1 July 1987 and ends in August 1990.

Of the nine directives and two regulations that I have selected to review, there is not a single one that is based on Article 100 and/or Article 235. Regulation 3143/87, amending Regulation 3626/82 on the implementation in the Community of the convention on international trade in endangered species of wild fauna and flora, and Directive 88/302, amending for the ninth time Directive 67/548 relating to the classification, packaging and labelling of dangerous substances, make no reference to any specific legal foundations at all. They simply have 're-gard to the Treaty of the EEC'.[44] There are four directives and one regulation that take Article 130s as their legal basis: Directive 87/416 amending Directive 85/210 on approximation of the laws of the Member States concerning lead content of petrol;[45] Directive 88/347, an amendment of Directive 86/280 on DDT, carbon tetrachloride and pentachlorophenol;[46] Regulation 3322/88 on certain chlorofluorocarbons and halons which deplete the ozone layer;[47] Directive 90/219 on the contained use of genetically modified micro-organisms[48] and Directive 90/415 on dangerous substances in water.[49] The remaining four direc-tives – 88/76 and 88/77, both on emissions from vehicles; 88/436, amending an earlier directive on vehicle emission (70/220); and 90/220 on the deliberate release into the environment of genetically modified organisms[50] – were adopted on the basis of Article 100a of the EEC Treaty which, of course, implies that they were essentially harmonization measures agreed on by qualified majority voting and subject to the co-operation procedure.

This limited survey reveals a number of interesting points. First, it is clear that the legal basis used during the first and second phase – mainly Article 100 and Article 235 – have been replaced by the new provisions provided by the SEA amendments to the Treaty of Rome. Second, it reaffirms the fact that, prior to the titanium dioxide case, there reigned uncertainty about which article – 100a or 130s – was to serve as the legal foundation for a given piece of environmental legislation (see Chapters 3 and 7). The range of problems that qualify as having an effect on the 'establishment of the internal market' does not seem to have been rigorously established. Finally, the evidence from our review indicates that Article 100a, implying majority voting and the co-operation procedure, was not used as frequently as one might have expected. Thus, at least until late 1991, much of the Community's environmental policy continued to be contingent on a unanimous decision by the Council.

While it is difficult to assess unfolding events, there are, however, a number of observations about EC environmental policy since the SEA that can already be made. For this purpose it is useful to recall that I set out to examine the hy-pothesis that the SEA is likely to result in a dramatic change of EC environ-mental policy. There are a number of indications that would validate such a hypothesis. Community environmental policy has undoubtedly gained momen-tum since the SEA. Title VII of the EEC Treaty has important symbolic conse-quences. The protection of the environment is now formally of equal or even superior status to all other Community objectives. The possibility of majority voting provides a framework for adopting a much greater amount of environ-mental legislation. The principle of subsidiarity, as expressed in Article 130r(4), may well have significant psychological effects on Member States. Using the example of the UK, Nigel Haigh and David Baldock (1989, p24) have demonstrated how, in terms of the environment, Europe, including its subnational units, is likely to increasingly perceive itself as a whole, thus moving ever closer to the 'union among the peoples of Europe' called for in the preamble to the Treaty of Rome. From such a point of view, the SEA has indeed had dramatic effects; not only in terms of a much broader and more effective environmental policy but also in terms of accelerating the process of integration among the European people in general.

As so often in international politics, there is, however, a perspective that points in the opposite direction. It is conceivable that the new provisions on majority voting could have negative effects in that they allow some Member States to overrule others which will then, in the absence of an effective European enforcement agent, be tempted to simply ignore their implementation obligations. Anxiety has also been expressed with respect to the subsidiarity principle, arguing that, from a Community perspective, it is clearly a step backwards (Vandermeersch, 1987, p422). Prior to the SEA:

> the issue was whether or not the EC had competence to act or not, now measures can be challenged in terms of whether or not the EC or the Member States could better deal with the issue (Lodge, 1989, p323).

In that sense, the SEA has widened the possibilities for challenging EC environmental action which could result in an overall weakened and less effective Community environmental policy.

These examples should suffice to demonstrate that there is indeed significant potential in the Community environmental policy as laid down in the SEA amendments to the EEC Treaty. At the same time, many of the provisions are abstract and leave much room for manoeuvring the thrust of the policy in either direction. Much will therefore depend on the political interpretation of the policy and the nature of future amendments to its jurisdictional basis.

Conclusions

Is it possible to argue that the institutionalization process as described at the start of this study has progressed to the point where it is useful to describe the present state of the European Community's environmental policy in terms of an international regime? Let us once again look at Robert Keohane's definition of an international institution as 'persistent and connected sets of rules (formal and informal) that prescribe behavioural roles, constrain activity, and shape expectations'. The rules are clearly established. There is a large and growing body of legislation in the various areas of European environmental protection. This legislation is based on a relatively unambiguous jurisdictional basis. Formally, there is no doubt that it prescribes behavioural roles, constrains activities and shapes expectations. In fact, its tendency to shape expectations has even reached beyond the present Community Member States. The central and eastern European countries which are aspiring to an eventual accession to the EC are already involved in adjusting or, in some cases, establishing their domestic environmental legislative bodies in such a way as to make sure that they will eventually be compatible with the expectations as expressed in the Community rules. Within this context the conclusion imposes itself that the institutionalization process of the EC's environmental policy, notwithstanding the above-mentioned weaknesses, has progressed far enough to warrant the description of an international environmental regime.

The conclusion that the EC's environmental policy has reached the state of an international regime is therefore no cause for complacency. In many ways the task has only just begun. We are, after all, not dealing with an obscure intellectual puzzle. The issue at hand is the increasing threat to our environment. It is in our immediate interest to start examining the effectiveness of the EC's environmental regime as one of the available institutional arrangements to address this situation. The first set of conceptual guideposts has been provided by the advocates of international institutional approaches. It certainly seems worthwhile and, for the time being, promising to try to build on them.

Acknowledgements

The author wishes to thank Andrew Hurrell, Andrew Walter, David Wartenweiler and David Judge for their helpful comments on earlier versions of this study.

Notes

1. The first time '1992' was officially mentioned was in the Commission president's statement to the European Parliament on 14 January 1985. Referring to the next European Council, he said: 'Now that some Heads of State and Government have decided to set an example ... it may not be over-optimistic to announce a decision to eliminate all frontiers within Europe by 1992 and to implement it' (Commission, of the European Communities (1985b) 'The Thrust of Commission Policy', *Bulletin of the European Communities*, Supplement 1/85, 14 and 15 January). The idea was formally approved by the Brussels European Council on 29–30 March 1985 and adopted in December 1985 in Luxembourg. See Lodge, 1989, p9.
2. The terms 'European' and 'European Community' are used interchangeably throughout this chapter. When referring to other parts of Europe, the proper specification will be made; ie 'Eastern European', 'Southern Europe', and so on.
3. Article 189, Treaty Establishing the European Economic Community as Amended by Subsequent Treaties, Rome, 25 March, 1957; subsequently referred to as Treaty of Rome.
4. See also House of Lords' Select Committee on the European Communities Transfrontier Shipment of Hazardous Wastes, 9th Report Session 1983–1984, HMSO.

5. It remains to be seen whether the changes incorporated in the Maastricht Treaty, creating a European Union will, in itself, represent a new phase of Community environmental policy or follow in the footsteps of this third phase. I will briefly comment on this question in the final section on Maastricht.
6. Citation translated by author.
7. Gaston Schul Judgement of 1982, Case 15/18, 1982 ECR 1409, p1431.
8. For a thorough discussion of the legal details of Article 100 and Article 235 see Rehbinder and Steward (1985, pp21–8).
9. Directive 67/548 EEC of 27 June 1967 on classification, packaging and labelling of dangerous substances, JO No.196, 16.8.1967, p1 (French ed).
10. Directive 69/81 EEC of 13 March 1969 modifying the directive of 16.8.1976 on classification, packaging and labelling of dangerous substances, JO No.L68,19.3.1969, p1 (French ed).
11. OJ No.C112.20.12.1973, p3. See also Seventh General Report of the EC (Brussels, 1973), point 258; Bulletin of the EC, 11–1974, point 1203, pp11–12.
12. 7th Report EC, 1973, point 258, p235.
13. See OJ No.C112, 20.12.73, p5.
14. 7th Report EC, 1973, point 262.
15. OJ No.C112, p7.
16. 7th Report EC, 1973, point 263.
17. ibid, point 264.
18. OJ No.C139, 13.6.1977; Bulletin EC 5-1977, point 2.1.40.
19. See, 'State of the Environment: First Report', 1977.
20. Action Programme of the European Communities on the Environment (1982 to 1986) in OJ No.C46, 17.2.1983, p1.
21. OJ No.C46, 17.2.1983, p3.
22. 17th General Report on the Activities of the European Communities, 1983, point 372. p158.
23. See OJ No.C46. p2.
24. In December 1986, the Council adopted a resolution on the strengthening of Community action in favour of the environment in which it welcomed 'the submission by the Commission of detailed proposals for a Fourth Environmental Action Programme and considers that such a programme provides an opportunity to strengthen decisively Community action in this area, building on the achievements of the past, and to determine a coherent framework within which specific Community actions can be formulated, coordinated and implemented over the period of 1987–1992'. It also refers to the SEA which 'will constitute a new legal basis for the Community environmental policy'. OJ No.C3, 7.1.1987, p3.
25. See, Pearson Report, Bericht der Kommission fur Internationale Entwicklung, Wien, München, Zurich, 1969, pp48–51.
26. By the time of the Paris Summit, the adherence to the Community of the UK, Ireland and Denmark was already decided. Weizsäcker argues that one of the objectives of the 1972 Action Programme was to get it through and then present it to the new Member States as a 'fait accompli'.
27. For a discussion of the German example see Müller (1986, pp97–102).

28. It is worth noting that 1982 was also the year when the Greens were first elected to the German 'Bundestag'.
29. The total number of environmental legislative pieces for the entire second phase amounts to 120 directives, 27 decisions and 14 regulations.
30. Directive 75/440, OJ No.L194, p26; Directive 80/778. OJ No.L229, 30.08.1980, p11; Directive 76/160, OJ No.L31, 05.02.1976, p1.
31. Directive 76/464, OJ No.L129, 18.05.1976, p23.
32. Directive 80/779, OJ No.L229, 30.08.1980; Directive 82/884. OJ No.L378, 31.12.1982; Directive 85/203. OJ No.L87, 27.03.1985, p1.
33. Directive 75/442. OJ No.L194, 25.07.1975, p39; Directive 78/319, OJ No.L84, 31.03.1978, p43; Directive 84/631, OJ No.L326, 13.12.1984, p31.
34. Directive 83/351, OJ No.L197, 20.07.1983, p1; Directive 84/360, OJ No.L188, 16.07.1984, p20.
35. Directive 85/210, OJ No.L96, 03.04.1985, p25; Directive 78/611, OJ No.L197, 22.07.1978, p19.
36. Directive 79/831, OJ No.L259, 15.10.1979, p10; Directive 67/548, OJ No.L196, 16.08.1967; Directive 79/117, OJ No.L33, 08.02.1979, p36.
37. Directive 79/409, OJ No.L103, 25.04.1979, p1.
38. Directive 82/501, OJ No.L230, 05.08.1982, p1; Directive 85/337, OJ No.L175, 05.07.1985, p40.
39. Commission of the EC, Completing the Internal Market: White Paper from the Commission of the European Council (the Cockfield White Paper), Luxembourg, 1985.
40. Although the phrase 'Single European Market' has come into widespread use, it is not used in the SEA. It simply combines the SEA and the internal market, at the expense of conferring the original meaning of the word 'Single' in the SEA 'which was so-called because it combined in a single legal instrument two texts that had different origins, one amending the Treaty of Rome (Title II) and one dealing with cooperation in the sphere of foreign policy'. See Haigh and Baldock (1989, p10).
41. For a detailed discussion of the 'cooperation procedure' see Lodge (1989, pp68–79).
42. This is illustrated by the case of Directive 88/76 on emissions from small cars. See Haigh and Baldock, (1989, pp51–54).
43. Titanium dioxide is a white pigment, generally thought to be harmless. It is used in paints, plastic and other products in order to reduce reliance on toxic substances such as lead and zinc. The problem is that its manufacture results in the discharge of acid waste contaminated by metals. EC legislation on titanium dioxide dates back as far as the early 1970s.
44. Regulation 3143/87 QJ-No.L299, 22.10.1978, p33; Regulation 3626/82 OJ No.L3K4. 31.12.1982, p1; Directive 88/302 OJ No.L133, 30.05.1988, p1.
45. Directive 87/416 OJ No.L225, 13.08.1987, p33; Directive 85/210 OJ No.L96, 03.04.1985. p25.
46. Directive 88/347 OJ No.L158, 25.06.1988, p35; Directive 86/280 OJ No.L181, 04.07.1986. p16.

47. Regulation 3322/88 OJ No.L297, 31.10.1988. p1.
48. Directive 90/219 OJ No.L117, 08.05.1990, p1.
49. Directive 90/415 OJ No.L219, 14.08.1990, p49.
50. Directive 88/76; Directive 88/77; Directive 88/436; Directive 70/220; Directive 90/220.

References

Bechmann, A. (1984) *Leben wollen,* Koln.
Haigh, N. (1990) *EEC Environmental Policy and Britain,* 2nd revised edition, Essex: Longman.
Haigh, N. and Baldock, D. (1989) *Environmental Policy and* 1992, London: Department of the Environment.
Hartkopf, G. and Bohme, E. (1983) *Umweltpolitik, Band 1: Grundlagen, Analysen und Perspektiven,* Opladen.
Johnson, S. P. and Corcelle, G. (1989) *The Environmental Policy of the European Communities* (International Environmental Law and Policy Series), London: Graham & Trotman.
Keck, O. (1991) 'Der neue Institutionalismus in der Theorie der Internationalen Politik', *Politische Viertelsjahresschrift,* 32, Jahrgang, Heft 4, pp635–53.
Keohane, R. O. (1989) *International Institutions and State Power: Essays in International Relations Theory,* Boulder, Co: Westview Press.
Lodge, J. (1989) 'Environment: Towards a Clean Blue-Green EC', in Lodge, J. (ed) *The European Community and the Challenge of the Future,* London: Pinter.
McCarthy, E. (1989) *The EC and the Environment,* European Dossier Service II.
McGrory, D. P. (1990) 'Air Pollution Legislation in the United States and the European Community', *European Law Review,* Vol.15, No.4, August.
Müller, E. (1986) *Innenwelt der Umweltpolitik,* Opiaden.
Rehbinder, E. and Steward, R. (eds) (1985) *Environmental Protection Policy, Volume 2: Integration Through Law – Europe and the American Federal Experience,* Firenze: European University Institute.
Sands, P. (1990) 'European Community Environmental Law: Legislation, the ECJ and Common Interest Groups', *Modern Law Review,* Vol.53, No.5, September, p685.
Teitgen, P.-H. and Mégret, C. (1981) 'La fumée de la cigarette dans la "zone grise" des competences de la C.E.E.', *Revue Trimestrielle de Droit Européen,* 68.
Vandermeersch, D. (1987) 'The Single European Act and the Environmental Policy of the European Economic Community', *European Law Review,* Vol.12, No.6.
Wägenbaur, R. (1990) 'The Single Market Programme and the Protection of the Environment', in *Environmental Protection and the Impact of European Community Law,* papers from the Joint Conference with the Incorporated Law Society of Ireland, Dublin: Irish Centre for European Law.

Weizsäcker, E. U. von (1989) *Erdpolitik: Oekologische Realpolik an der Schwelle zum Jahrliundert der Umwelt,* Darmstadt: Wissenschaftliche Buchgesellschaft.

Young, O. R. (1992) 'The Effectiveness of International Institutions: Hard Cases and Critical Variables', in Rosenau, J. N. and Czempiel, E.-O. (eds) (1992) *Governance without Government: Order and Change in World Politics,* Cambridge: Cambridge University Press.

3

Maastricht and the Environment: The Implications for the EC's Environment Policy of the Treaty on European Union*

David Wilkinson

Introduction

'Two steps forward, one step back' might be the most appropriate way of describing the impact on the EC's environmental policy of the Treaty on European Union signed at Maastricht on 7 February 1992.

On the one hand, the Treaty has strengthened the EC's commitment to environmental protection. Now included as one of the EC's basic tasks is the promotion of 'sustainable and non-inflationary growth respecting the environment'. Environmental policy is to be based on the 'precautionary principle', and the existing Treaty requirement that environmental protection should be integrated into other EC policies has been reinforced.

In addition, EC environmental policy can be expected to continue to develop into new areas. The principle of 'subsidiarity' – which seeks to confine EC intervention to those areas where it will be more effective than national action, and then only to the minimum extent necessary – is stated in so general a way that Member States seeking to limit EC activity through European Court rulings upholding the principle could well face disappointment.

On the other hand, complicated changes introduced to the EC's legislative process are set to cause confusion and delay. Where before there were two procedures for adopting EC environmental legislation, there will now be four – and it

---

* This is a revised version of a paper published in April 1992 by the Institute for European Environmental Policy (IEEP), London.

is unclear from the text of the new Treaty when each will apply. Lengthy legal disputes could now hold up agreement to new environmental measures.

Qualified majority voting (QMV) in the Council of Ministers now becomes the norm for environmental measures. By removing the ability of an individual Member State on its own to veto proposals, QMV in principle can be expected to speed up agreement to new legislation. At the same time, the legislative powers of the European Parliament have been extended. While this goes some way to redressing the 'democratic deficit' in the Community, the complicated new 'co-decision' procedure involving the Parliament can be expected to produce new delays of its own.

Tightening up the implementation and enforcement of EC environmental legislation in the Member States should also become easier with significant new powers for the European Court of Justice to fine Member States which persist in flouting Court judgements. A new Cohesion Fund should also help poorer Member States pay the often substantial costs of introducing the higher environmental standards required by EC legislation.

The new Treaty builds on the significant changes introduced five years ago by the Single European Act (SEA). This provided, for the first time, an explicit legal basis for the Community's environment policy and introduced the important principle that the environment was to be a component of the EC's other policies. But the SEA was drafted quickly and with little discussion, leaving much scope for further Treaty reform.[1]

The Maastricht Treaty, however, suffers from many of the limitations of its predecessor (see Chapter 2). It certainly introduces important changes to the principles underlying EC policy, and to the way in which environmental legislation is decided and implemented. But the text of what was agreed is often unclear and its practical effects will take some time to emerge.

General Principles

Sustainability

The Treaties establishing the EC were written in a period before concerns about pollution and the depletion of resources had come to prominence. This was reflected in Article 2 of the 1957 Treaty of Rome, which included among the tasks of the Community 'a continuous and balanced expansion', and 'an accelerated raising of the standard of living' of the Member States. No concern was expressed for the quality of that expansion, nor the conservation of resources, nor the needs of future generations (see Chapter 2).

Just over 30 years later, EC heads of State and Government reflected how far perceptions had changed when in December 1988 they issued a Declaration on the Environment that 'sustainable development must be one of the overriding objectives of all Community policies'. A number of EC Member States, and the European Parliament, subsequently sought to use the opportunity presented by the two inter-governmental conferences to ensure that environmentally-sustainable development should be enshrined in the Treaty as one of the EC's governing principles.

In the event, the Maastricht Treaty amended Article 2 to include as one of the Community's tasks the promotion of 'sustainable and non-inflationary growth respecting the environment'. Article B of the Common Provisions of the Treaty similarly refers to 'economic and social progress which is balanced and sustainable'.

Many environmentalists have expressed disappointment that the widely supported formulation in the 1987 Report of the Brundtland Commission – 'sustainable development' – failed to find a place in the Treaty. Certainly, on its own and unqualified, the term 'sustainable growth' is easily confused with 'sustained growth', which amounts to much the same as 'continuous expansion'. Nevertheless, Article 2 now places environmental protection on an equal footing with economic concerns as one of the Community's objectives. This is an important symbolic change and represents at least some progress towards the 'greening' of the EC Treaty.

A High Level of Protection

Article 130r(2) of the Maastricht Treaty declares that Community policy, on the environment 'shall aim at a high level of protection'. This extends to *all* aspects of environmental policy a provision first included by Article 100a(3) of the SEA (which is retained in the new Treaty). This required the Commission to take as a base a high level of environmental protection in making proposals for the approximation of measures affecting the functioning of the internal market, such as those relating to product or pollution control standards. The requirement is now extended to environmental measures proposed under Treaty articles other than 100a (see below). Its force, however, is limited by the qualification in Article 130r(2) that the high level of protection should take into account 'the diversity of situations in the various regions of the Community'. Existing standards of environmental protection vary markedly between, say, Germany and Portugal, and the let-out clause could be used by the Commission as a justification for proposing measures which are pitched below the highest standards in the Community, or, more likely, by the Council as a reason for adopting them.

The Precautionary Principle

Now included for the first time in the Treaty is the requirement that the Community's environmental policy 'shall be based on the precautionary principle'. This is in addition to the principles that 'preventive action should be taken, that environmental damage should as a priority be rectified at source, and that the polluter should pay', which were already included by the SEA in Article 130r(2). The precautionary principle is most well developed in Germany where the *Vorsorgeprinzip* was first enunciated by the Federal Government in 1976.[2] How the principle should be applied in practice is by no means clear, but it might, for example, include the requirement that protective measures should be developed before specific environmental hazards are evident, and that the onus of proof that environmental damage will not occur should be placed on the polluter.

However, developing policies to counter an environmental threat before its cause has been established beyond doubt can be both technically and politically problematic. Nevertheless, with the precautionary principle now informing the EC's environmental policy, pressure can legitimately be applied for the application of tighter pollution control standards.

Integration

The SEA provided a major boost to the Community's environmental policy when it included in Article 130r(2) the provision that 'environmental protection requirements shall be a component of the Community's other policies' (see Chapter 2). The Maastricht Treaty clarifies and extends this requirement. Article 130r(2) now states:

> *Environmental protection requirements must be integrated into the definition and implementation of other Community policies.*

Annexed to the Treaty is a 'Declaration by the Member States on Assessment of the Environmental Impact of Community Measures' which reinforces this commitment. It states that:

> *The Conference notes that the Commission undertakes in its proposals, and that the Member States undertake in implementing those proposals, to take full account of their environmental impact and of the principle of sustainable growth.*

Since the SEA, the Commission has not made great progress in reforming its internal administrative procedures so as to put the principle of integration into practice. It has, however, published a number of 'integrative' documents relating to agriculture, tropical rainforests, energy, the urban environment, carbon dioxide emissions, and transport. Moreover, limited procedures have been introduced to screen programmes and projects supported by the Structural Funds – but environmental damage still continues.[3] The Fifth Environmental Action Programme[4] places great emphasis on the need to integrate environmental protection into policies at every level of government and among all social and economic actors, but it remains silent on how this might be done in practice.

Article 162 of the Treaty – which Maastricht leaves unchanged – requires the Commission to 'adopt its rules of procedure so as to ensure that both it and its departments operate in accordance with the provisions of this Treaty. It shall ensure that these rules. are published.' The Commission is therefore under a legal obligation to publish how it intends to fulfill the commitment in Article 130r(2) to 'green' the policies of other Commission directorates.

Subsidiarity

The *potential* for the EC to intervene in the entire area of environmental protection was established in 1987 by the SEA in the broad-brush Article 130r. This described the objectives of EC environmental policy in very wide terms:

- to preserve, protect and improve the quality of the environment;
- to contributre towards protecting human health;
- to ensure a prudent and rational utilization of natural resources.

However, while the EC's potential legal competence in the Community's internal environmental policy is defined in comprehensive (but not exclusive) terms, *in practice* the extent to which it seeks to intervene should be limited by the 'principle of subsidiarity'. This attempts to draw a boundary between the respective activities of the Community, the Member States, and, possibly, local and regional authorities so that action is taken at the Community level only where that is more effective than national action – and then only to the minimum extent necessary. In the SEA, the principle appeared only with reference to environmental policy, in Article 130r(4).

In the early stages of the Intergovernmental Conference on European Union, some Member States and members of the European Parliament argued that the principle of subsidiarity should be extended to all Community activities and be given a detailed form that could be enforced in the European Court. They called for a clear allocation of policy areas between the EC on the one hand and the Member States on the other that would prevent the Community from intervening, as UK Foreign Secretary Douglas Hurd put it, in 'every nook and cranny' of national affairs.

In the event, the treatment of subsidiarity at Maastricht was less ambitious. Article 3b states:

> *In areas which do not fall within its exclusive competence, the Community shall take action, in accordance with the principle of subsidiarity, only if and in so far as the objectives of the proposed action cannot be sufficiently achieved by the Member States and can therefore, by reason of the scale or effects of the proposed action, be better achieved by the Community.*

This general statement supersedes the specific reference to environmental policy in Article 130r(4), which has now been dropped.

The new formulation of the subsidiarity principle is worded more restrictively than in the SEA ('only if, and insofar as ...'). In future, some Member States – possibly outvoted in the Council on an issue they consider to be essentially a domestic affair – may well seek to challenge the legality of legislation on the grounds that it contravenes the subsidiarity principle as set out in Article 3b. The Commission will also now need to think rather more carefully than in the past about the justification for new policy initiatives.

Nevertheless, the new formulation is very imprecise, and such actions in the Court of Justice on balance seem unlikely to succeed. Environmental protection is *par excellence* one area where action often needs to be international to be effective. The need to harmonize product standards, eliminate pollution havens, protect migrating wildlife, and contribute to the solution of regional and global environmental problems all argue for some form of Community involvement. The question then becomes: to what level of detail should EC intervention extend? (See Chapter 18.)

In one particularly sensitive area – town and country planning, which some commentators had argued should be exclusively reserved for the Member States as having few international effects – the Maastricht Treaty in fact establishes a clearer legal basis for Community intervention. Article 130s for the first time introduces into the Treaty specific references to planning. Ironically, these were included as part of a predominantly Spanish-led attempt to establish some safeguards for Member States by requiring the continued use of unanimous voting in certain areas.

The Maastricht Treaty therefore does not place clear limits on the further development of EC policy into areas such as urban policy, the protection of coastal areas, or the establishment of controls on neighbourhood noise.

The Legislative Process

Introduction

The 1987 SEA introduced two separate methods for agreeing EC environmental legislation. Article 130s in the SEA's new chapter on environmental policy required measures to be adopted in the Council of Ministers on the basis of unanimity, with the European Parliament's role restricted to non-binding consultation. Where, however, a proposal related to the harmonization of environmental standards, with effects on the operation of the internal market, then decisions were to be made on the basis of Article 100a. In this case, the Council was to proceed on the basis of QMV where votes are weighted roughly in accordance with each Member State's population. At the same time, the influence of the European Parliament on legislation proposed under 100a was increased through a 'co-operation procedure' which gives MEPs a second reading of legislative proposals. The Parliament has normally sought to tighten up the environmental standards incorporated in Commission proposals and the 'common positions' of the Council.

QMV removes the ability of a Member State on its own to veto a proposal for legislation – indeed, two large Member States jointly opposing action can be overruled by the other Member States. Other things being equal, QMV can therefore speed up Council decisions, and, arguably, makes higher environmental standards easier to agree.

In practice, there has been great uncertainty in some specific cases whether Article 100a or 130s should apply – notably where proposals relate to discharges from an industrial plant which affect its competitive position. An important ruling by the European Court of Justice in June 1991 on the legal basis for a directive regulating pollution from the titanium dioxide industry (see below) has been interpreted as widening the areas where Article 100a should apply, but the situation still remains far from clear (see Chapter 7).

The Treaty on European Union has *not* clarified the legislative process for environmental policy, nor has QMV been introduced for all environmental matters as many Member States and non-governmental organizations (NGOs) had hoped. But the area where it does apply has been considerably extended, and QMV can now be regarded as the 'norm'.

At the same time, the European Parliament's influence has been increased, in two principal ways. Since QMV is required more often, the use of the co-operation procedure involving the Parliament has been extended in parallel. In addition, for some issues a new procedure of 'co-decision' has been introduced. (The term 'co-decision' appears nowhere in the Treaty but the term has been coined to describe the process set out in Article 189b). This gives MEPs an equal say with the Council and includes a conciliation, procedure aimed at re-solving differences between the two institutions. Under co-decision – which is described more fully below and in Appendix I – the Parliament ultimately has a veto (by an absolute majority of its members) over legislative proposals to which it remains opposed. The co-decision procedure is complicated and can in some cases run to 11 separate stages stretching over many months.

While these changes go some way to redressing the 'democratic deficit', it is ironic that they could well have the effect of slowing down agreement to pro-posals which otherwise will have had a speedier passage through the Council be-cause of QMV.

Far from clarifying the legislative process for environmental matters, the Maastricht Treaty has further complicated it. Where, under the SEA, there were two possible procedures, there will now be no less than *four*:

Under Article 130s:

1. QMV in the Council and the co-operation procedure with Parliament. This is now the norm for environmental legislation.
2. QMV in Council and co-decision with Parliament. This applies in the case of 'general action programmes'.
3. Unanimous voting in Council, and consultation with the Parliament (for some exceptional cases specified in Article 130s) – the 'consultation proce-dure'. The Maastricht Treaty retains the existing Treaty provision allowing the Council to decide unanimously to proceed on the basis of QMV in these areas. Under Article 100a.
4. QMV and co-decision for those matters relating to the establishment of the single market.

Voting in the Council of Ministers

In what Circumstances does QMV Apply?

Article 130s(1) indicates that environmental matters will normally be adopted by the Council of Ministers on the basis of QMV, in co-operation with the Euro-pean Parliament (the co-operation procedure). This is essentially the same proce-dure that has applied under Article 100a of the SEA.

However, Article 130s(2) lists several areas where *unanimity* in the Council will continue to be required. In these cases, the European Parliament is con-sulted, but its Opinions have no binding force. The areas are:

- provisions primarily of a fiscal nature;
- town and country planning, land-use (with the exception of waste management and 'measures of a general nature', where QMV will apply) and the management of water resources;
- measures significantly affecting a Member State's choice between different energy sources and the general structure of its energy supply.

These categories are very imprecise. For example, does the term 'land use' encompass nature conservation measures to protect wildlife habitats? In the same context, the meaning of 'measures of a general nature' is obscure. It could, perhaps, refer to proposed amendments to Directive 85/337 on Environmental Impact Assessment, which in that case would be agreed by QMV. Also unclear is whether 'the management of water resources' applies to proposals relating both to the quantity and quality of water. The Dutch text of the Treaty refers specifically to 'quantitative water management', which would suggest that water quality measures are to be adopted by QMV.

The reference to fiscal measures seems to refer to proposals which are fiscal *in essence* – including, presumably, proposals for an EC carbon/energy tax to reduce carbon dioxide emissions. Measures with only minor fiscal implications would be decided by QMV under Article 130s(1). The significance of the reference to energy sources and supply is similarly unclear. One interpretation is that it would apply in the case of issues such as imposing limits on nuclear powered electricity generation, or the use of 'dirty' fuels like lignite. It could well encompass proposals to tighten up Directive 88/609, which allocates reduction targets for SO_2 and NO_x emissions between Member States from existing large combustion plants. (Proposals for amending the national reduction targets and/or the dates for achieving them are due from the Commission in 1994). By the same token it might also include future Commission proposals for allocating national reductions of CO_2 emissions to help reduce global warming.

When Does Article 100a Apply?

The requirement for unanimity in the exceptional areas described above no longer stands if Article 100a applies. The scope of application of Article 100a seems to have been significantly extended by a June 1991 ruling of the European Court (Case C-300/89) regarding the legal base of Directive 89/428 on pollution reduction measures in the titanium dioxide industry. The Commission proposed the Directive under Article 100a on the grounds that the measure was primarily aimed at harmonizing pollution control standards, which affected the operation of the free market. By contrast, the Council argued that this was incidental, that the main aim of the measure was to eliminate pollution, and that Article 130s (requiring unanimity) therefore applied. It proceeded to adopt the directive unanimously on this basis, and the Commission, supported by the European Parliament, took the Council to the European Court.

The Court ruled that in this case the goals of environmental protection and the removal of market distortions were indivisible. It pointed out that in the SEA,

Article 100a expressly made reference to the Commission's obligation when proposing measures for approximating the laws of Member States to take as their basis a high level of environmental protection; and that Article 130r stated that environmental protection should be a component of the Community's other policies. Therefore a measure did not automatically fall within Article 130s simply because it was aimed equally at environmental protection (see Chapter 7).

As a result of this benchmark ruling, the Commission might be expected to make a generous interpretation of the applicability of Article 100a. Some land-use issues – for example, the classification and treatment of contaminated land – are likely to be proposed with 100a as their basis. It should be borne in mind that the Maastricht Treaty amended Article 100a to give the European Parliament powers of *co-decision* with the Council. The number of environmental measures being decided on the basis of QMV and co-decision could therefore be greater than a simple reading of the new Article 130s might suggest (see below).

However, an important political consequence of the reform of the EC's legislative process is that the triangular relationship between the Commission, the Council and the European Parliament that has prevailed since the SEA is likely to change. Under the SEA, both the Commission and the Parliament often joined forces against the Council and pressed for legislation to be based on Article 100a rather than Article 130r-t. The Commission did so because it wanted QMV; Parliament because it wanted the co-operation procedure. Under the Maastricht Treaty, QMV and the cooperation procedure becomes the norm under 130s, so now all three parties might be content with 130s. It is, however, possible that Parliament will push for 100a, since this gives them co-decision, but the Commission and Council might find this time-consuming and try to avoid 100a.

Co-decision with the European Parliament

The *co-operation procedure,* which in conjunction with QMV in the Council now becomes the standard legislative procedure for environmental matters, gives the Parliament two opportunities to propose amendments to proposals for legislation. But it is the Council which has the final say. By contrast, the system of *co-decision* allows the Parliament to veto proposals which MEPs consider inadequate, even if the Council is unanimously in favour of them. Before this stage is reached, however, the system of co-decision provides for negotiations to be held between the Council and the Parliament in a Conciliation Committee, giving MEPs an opportunity to try to ensure that their amendments form part of legislation that is finally agreed. Co-decision therefore represents a significant advance in the powers exercised by the Parliament (see Appendix I).

In addition to those matters decided under Article 100a, co-decision will now apply, according to the new Article 130s(3), to 'general action programmes setting out priority objectives to be attained'. The Maastricht Treaty contains no comparable reference in relation to other policy areas, and exactly what these programmes are is very unclear.

'General action programmes' would most obviously seem to include the Action Programmes on the Environment, setting out general objectives, which the Commission publishes every few years. (The Fifth Action Programme is expected to be approved by a Resolution of the Council before the Maastricht Treaty is ratified, and therefore not under Article 130s(3).) The European Parliament's Environment Committee, however, has argued that the Parliament should interpret 'general action programmes' in the widest possible sense, to include, for example, pollution reduction targets in specific sectors over set timescales (as in Directive 88/609 on reducing emissions from large combustion plants).[5] It remains doubtful whether this interpretation can be sustained, since a reference to such programmes 'in specific policy areas' was removed during the IGC negotiations, underlining that they need to be of a general character to fall within Article 130s(3).

Differing National Standards

EC Heads of State and Government took a significant step at Maastricht towards a 'variable speed Europe' when they agreed to allow the UK to opt out of further moves towards implementing the 1989 Social Charter on workers' rights. New provisions in the Environment Title could also be interpreted as moving towards a more explicit acceptance of different national standards of environmental protection.

Derogations

Voting in the Council by qualified majority implies that individual Member States will be obliged to accept and implement EC environmental measures to which they are opposed. Some of these measures – particularly relating to water quality – can entail very large capital expenditure programmes which may seem prohibitive, particularly in the poorer Member States.

For the first time in the Treaty, where a Member State considers the costs of a particular measure to be prohibitive, formal provision is made in Article 130s(5) for temporary derogations, and/or financial assistance from a new Cohesion Fund, to be incorporated into that particular item of legislation. Although such derogations are to be 'temporary', what this means in practical terms is not defined. Spain and Portugal, for example, secured a ten-year delay in implementing some of the provisions of Directive 88/609 on large combustion plants.

Any Member State (not just the poorer ones) can seek a temporary derogation in the following circumstances:

- The measure from which the Member State seeks to derogate must be one that is adopted under Article 130s(1) – by QMV in co-operation with the European Parliament. Strangely, where the measure is adopted under Article 100a, there is no provision for derogation, even though the impact on a Member State could be the same.
- The costs which are deemed disproportionate have to be incurred by the Member State's *public* authorities. Costs arising for private industry – or newly-privatized utilities – cannot therefore be taken into account.

It is not clear who is to decide whether such costs are, in fact, disproportionate, nor how the terms of the derogation are to be established. Article
130s(5) states that the Council must include appropriate provisions in the
particular measure, but this could well include a requirement for approval
by, or at least notification of, the Commission.

The Cohesion Fund

In addition, or as an alternative, to derogation, eligible Member States may seek
financial support from the Cohesion Fund. Only those member States with a
per capita GNP of less than 90 per cent of the EC average – currently, Greece,
Ireland, Portugal and Spain – will be entitled to such support. Article 130d and
a Protocol on Economic and Social Cohesion attached to the Maastricht Treaty
limit the scope of its activities to projects in the environmental field, and 'trans-
European networks in the field of transport'. A Regulation establishing the Cohesion Fund is currently being developed within the Commission, and a number of environmental NGOs are seeking to ensure that environmental conditions are attached to its use. The Protocol referred to above restricts eligibility for
assistance from the Fund to those Member States which have adopted programmes
'leading to the fulfilment of the conditions of economic convergence'. There is
some force in the argument that a further similar condition should be included
relating to compliance with EC environmental directives.

While in some respects, therefore, the Fund could be a useful instrument
for improving the implementation of environmental legislation, there could also
be a danger that Member States which unsuccessfully bid for Cohesion Fund
money might subsequently be disinclined to fulfil their legal obligations, thus
eroding the 'polluter pays' principle.

Higher National Standards

While the possibility of derogating from particular items of EC legislation holds
out the prospect of a 'slow lane' in the movement towards higher EC environmental standards, the Maastricht Treaty at the same time re-affirms in Article
130t an existing right for Member States to maintain or introduce more *stringent* protective measures, providing they are compatible with the Treaty and are
notified to the Commission. This general right seems to over-ride the more limited provision in Article 130r(2) for Member States to take provisional 'safeguard' measures when harmonization measures are agreed.

The flexibility to apply higher national standards is also retained from the
SEA in Article 100a(4) of the new Treaty. A benchmark ruling in 1988 by the
Court of Justice upholding a Danish law requiring the use of returnable bottles
(Case 302/86) established that a conflict between the internal market and environmental protection need not always be decided in favour of the market. The
Court's judgement suggested that Member States can go considerably beyond the
requirements of EC environmental legislation, even though the effect may be to
distort trade. However, a widely-accepted view is that the right to maintain
higher standards under Article 100a is restricted to those Member States already

applying such standards in existing legislation.[6] There may therefore be an important distinction between what is permissible under Article 130t, and the possibly more restrictive Article 100a.

In short, Articles 100a and 130t, in conjunction with opportunities for temporary derogations under Article 130s, may have the effect of allowing considerable variations across the Community in national standards of environmental protection.

Implementation

One of the consequences of extending qualified majority voting in the Council of Ministers is that individual Member States will from time to time be obliged to adopt and implement policies to which they are opposed. This makes it likely that the non-implementation of EC environmental legislation will become a problem even more serious than it already is (see Chapter 17). Support from the new Cohesion Fund may help to sugar the pill; but not all Member States are eligible for its support, and not all instances of failure to comply are for financial reasons.

The EC's heads of State and Government annexed a Declaration to the Maastricht Treaty which stressed how important it was that 'each Member State should fully and accurately transpose into national law the Community Directives addressed to it within the deadlines laid down therein', and that 'measures taken by the different Member States should result in Community law being applied with the same effectiveness and rigour as in the application of their national law'.

Member States have now been given a greater incentive to implement EC environmental legislation properly by an amendment to Article 171 relating to the enforcement of judgements of the European Court. The changes agreed at Maastricht mean that if the Commission considers that a Member State has not complied with a judgement of the Court, it may in the final analysis refer the matter back to the Court with a recommendation that the Member State should pay a specified lump sum or 'penalty payment'. The final decision on whether to impose a fine, and how much, will rest with the Court.

Although the Maastricht Treaty does not address the matter further, subsequent failure by a Member State to pay a fine imposed in this way could presumably result in the freezing of sizeable payments from the EC's Structural Funds, or of transfers from other sources, such as the Guarantee Section of the Agriculture Fund.

A further change introduced by the Maastricht Treaty to improve implementation involves the European Parliament. MEPs are given the formal right in Article 138c to establish temporary committees of inquiry to investigate 'alleged contraventions or maladministration in the implementation of Community law'. This amendment does no more than give legal backing to an already existing practice – although under the Parliament's current rules of procedure only one such committee may be set up at any one time. Jointly with the Council and the Commission, the Parliament is to define more precisely how its new right of inquiry is to be exercised.

Appendix I

The EC's Legislative Procedures

The Consultation Procedure

The bulk of existing EC environmental legislation was adopted by a procedure requiring unanimous agreement in the Council, and consultation with the European Parliament. This procedure now applies only to the limited number of areas of environmental policy listed in Article 130s. In these areas, the Parliament's role is restricted to giving an Opinion, which is advisory only. The procedure is as follows:

1. Commission proposes legislation (Directive, Regulation, or Decision).
2. Parliament gives opinion (and may suggest amendments).
3. Council adopts legislation (possibly in amended form).

The Council cannot adopt legislation until Parliament's Opinion is received.

The Co-operation Procedure (Article 189c)

The Single European Act introduced qualified majority voting (QMV) for some environmental legislation and in those cases the Council has to act 'in co-operation with the Parliament'. The Maastricht Treaty will make the procedure the normal way of adopting environmental legislation. Article 130s sets out when it is used. Its principal stages, set out in Article 189c, are as follows:

1. Commission proposes legislation.
2. Parliament adopts an opinion by a simple majority (the 'first reading').
3. Council adopts a 'common position' by qualified majority (QMV).
4. Parliament, within three months, approves, amends or rejects the Council's 'common position'. This is known as the Parliament's 'second reading'. Amendment or rejection can only be by absolute majority of those entitled to vote, ie by 260 votes – half the number of seats (518) plus one.
5. Commission may, within one month, revise its proposal 'taking into account' the amendments proposed by the Parliament.
6. Where the Parliament has proposed an amendment the Council, within three months, may do one of four things:
   - adopt, by qualified majority, the revised Commission's proposal;
   - adopt, by unanimity, Parliament's amendments not approved by Commission;
   - amend and adopt, by unanimity, Commission's proposal;
   - fail to act.
7. If the Parliament rejects the proposal the Council can then only agree it by unanimity.
8. The Commission may, at any time before the Council has adopted the proposal, amend or withdraw its proposal. Although a final decision still always rests with the Council, and the Commission still has the power to amend or withdraw its proposal, the Parliament has the ability to send a powerful

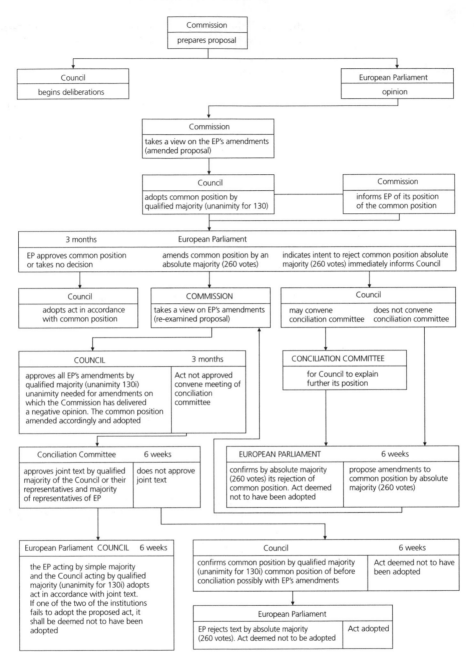

Figure 3.1 *The Co-decision Procedure*

message to the Commission and Council telling them to think again. If the Commission accepts the Parliament's amendment then together they can put considerable pressure on the Council since it can only change the revised proposal by unanimity.

The Co-decision Procedure (Article 198b)

Under the Maastricht Treaty the co-decision procedure will be required for any legislation adopted under Article 100a for measures aimed at establishing the internal market, including the harmonization of environmental standards. Co-decision is also required under Article 130s for 'general action programmes'. The co-decision procedure – which is even more complicated than the co-operation procedure – is shown in Figure 3.1. (The diagram was produced for the European Parliament's Environment Committee by David Earnshaw.)

The Council proceeds on the basis of QMV (with some limited exceptions), and if there are differences with the European Parliament, a Conciliation Committee is established in order to seek to resolve them. In the final analysis, the European Parliament may block the adoption of proposals which it considers inadequate, even though the Council may be in favour of them.

Acknowledgements

The paper owes much to the insights and observations of a number of people: my colleagues Nigel Haigh and Jonathan Hewett at IEEP London, together with Graham Bennett and Barbara Verhoeve at IEEP Arnhem (The Netherlands); Professor Richard Macrory at Imperial College Centre for Environmental Technology; and a number of officials at the UK Department of the Environment. It has also been influenced by unpublished papers written by Ken Collins MEP, David Earnshaw, and Richard Corbett from the staff of the European Parliament, some financial support for producing the original paper was received from the UK Department of the Environment and the Dutch Ministry of Housing, Physical Planning and Environment.

Notes

1. The implications for the EC's environmental policy of the Single European Act are discussed in N. Haigh and D. Baldock, *Environmental Policy and 1992*, IEEP, 1989. An analysis of relevant Treaty amendments put forward for discussion in the Intergovernmental Conference on Political Union is contained in D. Wilkinson, *Greening the Treaty: Strengthening Environmental Policy in the Treaty of Rome*, IEEP, 1990.
2. Konrad Von Moltke, *The Vorsorgeprinzip in West German Environmental Policy*, IEEP, 1987.
3. D. Baldock and M. Wenning, *The EC Structural Funds – Environmental Briefing 2*, World Wide Fund for Nature – UK and IEEP London, 1990.

4. Commission of the European Communities, *Towards Sustainability: A European Community Programme of Policy and Action in relation to the Environment and Sustainable Development,* 1992.
5. European Parliament Committee on the Environment, Public Health and Consumer Protection: Opinion for the Committee on Institutional Affairs on the Results of the Intergovernmental Conferences, 26 February 1992, Doc EN/RR/205692.
6. See, for example, Ludwig Kramer, *EEC Treaty and Environmental Protection,* London, 1990.

4

Step Change or Stasis? EC Environmental Policy after the Amsterdam Treaty

Andrew Jordan

Forty years after the historic signing of the Rome Treaty that gave birth to the European Economic Community in 1957, the European Community (EC) – politically speaking, now the first 'pillar' of the European Union (EU) – stands on the cusp of great changes, facing monumental challenges. This chapter describes the provenance of the June 1997 European Council meeting held in Amsterdam to revise the founding Treaties of the EU, outlines the 'history making' changes that were agreed there by political leaders and considers the future prospects for EC environmental policy.

The 1996 Intergovernmental Conference Agenda

The European Council meeting of EU leaders, held in Amsterdam on 16–17 June 1996, was the culmination of an intergovernmental conference (IGC) process stretching back over a year. IGCs are the means by which states change the founding Treaties of the Union. Two were held in 1991 prior to Maastricht, one on political the other on monetary union. IGCs are long and complicated affairs (all Treaty amendment decisions require unanimity), and operate at many different levels, involving several European Councils and occasional meetings of Foreign Ministers to take stock of progress and give the whole process a firm steer. The 1996 IGC, the fourth major constitutional change to the EC, was formally requested in the Treaty on European Union (TEU) (the 'Maastricht Treaty') (Article N) (House of Lords Select Committee on the European Communities, 1995). The intention was to prepare the EU for the internal pressures thrown up by the introduction of a single currency and the accession of new Member States. The European Monetary Union (EMU) has it own separate institutional track and timetable, while CAP (Common Agricultural Policy) reform, BSE and a host of other problems currently bedevilling the EU were not on the agenda of the Amsterdam IGC.

Almost as soon as the IGC commenced in Turin in March 1996, the EU found itself thrown headlong into a divisive battle over BSE. Impending elections in France and Britain more or less put the whole process on hold, then employment burst onto the political agenda threatening to eclipse everything else. When negotiations actually commenced, it soon became apparent that states had very different expectations about the final outcome. For some, not least the UK, it was a 'conference too soon': the EU, in the words of UK Ministers, needed a '3000 mile service' not another disruptive period of institutional reform. Their aim therefore was to make the IGC a 'non-IGC' (George, 1996, p52). The date of the IGC was fixed when everyone assumed the ratification of the TEU would be completed in 1992. As it was, the Danish 'nej' and the French 'petit oui' put the process back by many months. This meant that the new institutional innovations introduced at Maastricht, such as co-decision-making involving the European Parliament and the 'pillar two' and 'pillar three' powers in the areas of foreign and security policy (CFSP) and justice and home affairs (JHA) respectively, were still properly to find their stride when the IGC opened.

For others, it presented an important opportunity to improve the transparency and accountability of the EU, reconsider the operation of the second and third pillars, and address matters like enlargement and reform of the Commission which had been deferred at Maastricht. All states recognize the need for changes in voting and decision-making arrangements, especially a re-balancing of voting power in the Council of Ministers (CoM) and changes to the size and composition of the Commission, to underpin the rapid expansion of the Union. The expansion process could culminate in a membership of 30 or so states by 2010. Because of considerable uncertainties as to how the political and legal complexion of this new Europe might work, there is much to disagree about over these institutional arrangements. Contrary to popular opinion, the small states are currently politically and legally over-represented and the Union needs to find a better balance between voting power and population. These are vitally important questions because they affect the delicate balance of power between small and big states, and environmental 'leaders' and 'laggards' in an enlarged Union (see Chapter 5). Arguably, the resulting dynamic is vital for all policy areas, the environment included, although it was barely addressed in the Fifth Action Programme.

So consumed were states with these 'macro' issues that environmental issues nearly did not feature at all in the deliberations despite intense lobbying by European environmental groups (Climate Network Europe, EEB, 1995) and DG XI, and careful preparations by national environmental departments (eg IEEP, 1995). The Commission, understandably, was preoccupied with other matters and none of the 'big three' states, namely France, Germany and the UK, listed the environment as a priority in their opening submissions. The environment might have vanished altogether had it not received a strong push from the new, post-1995, Member States (ENDS Report, 1996). But even after it had been added to the formal agenda, the then Conservative British Government remained opposed to any extension of qualified majority voting (QMV) and reform of the Parliament's co-decision powers, which allow it to veto new proposals in certain circumstances (see Chapters 3 and 7). Other, equally minimalist demands included the withdrawal of Commission proposals after a specified period of time, the inclusion of 'sunset clauses' into new statutes triggering automatic reviews after a specified period of time, and more systematic consultation with business interests before proposals are published.

The Formal Outcomes of the Summit

In many important respects, the Amsterdam European Council unsurprisingly delivered a draft that will satisfy neither maximalists nor minimalists. Key issues like flexibility and institutional reform were again deferred and there will need to be a further IGC before the first wave of entrants join in about 2002. Maximalists will be disappointed that leaders failed to reach a decision on the thorny question of re-weighting votes in the CoM and on the future structure of the Commission. Similarly, that are to be no fundamental changes to the CFSP and no big increases in EU powers. On the other hand: the new UK Government led by Tony Blair agreed to reverse its Social Protocol opt out; QMV will be introduced or extended in several new areas including public health (Article 129), equal opportunities (Article 119), fraud (Article 209) and customs; and the complicated arrangements governing the activities of the Parliament are to be simplified and co-decision-making extended to many new and existing Treaty areas including employment, social, environmental, transport and public health policy. Parts of the third pillar will be communitized, although the UK and Eire secured an opt out.

EC Environmental Policy after Amsterdam

What of the environment? The Maastricht Treaty introduced a number of far reaching reforms to EC environmental policy (see Chapter 3), and the new draft builds upon them in a number of important respects. The most significant are as follows:

Sustainable Development

The achievement of sustainable development becomes a fundamental objective of the EU enshrined in Article 2 and is also mentioned in the preamble of the draft Treaty – a goal which environmentalists have fought for since the dawn of EC environmental policy (House of Lords Select Committee on the European Communities, 1980). The inclusion of a new 'chapeau' completes the job only half completed under the TEU, when the original Treaty of Rome, whose goal was a 'harmonious development of economic activities, a continuous and balanced expansion ...', was amended to 'sustainable and non-inflationary growth respecting the environment'. The 1991 version is said to have reflected an unsatisfactory compromise between the two IGCs that delivered the TEU. Supporters of this particular amendment claim that it will underline the importance of protecting the environment and lend weight to the principle of integrating environmental considerations into other policy areas (IEEP, 1995, p2), although significantly there is no new institutional machinery in place to ensure it.

Integration

A new Article 3d requires that 'environmental protection requirements must be integrated into the definition and implementation of Community policies and activities ... , in particular with a view to promoting sustainable development'. Like Article 3b (subsidiarity), the intention is that this amendment will function horizontally across the many strands of EC activity. Previously, integration had been tucked away in the environmental section of the Treaty (Article 130r) and was somewhat ambiguous with respect to its scope. In a Declaration attached to the final draft, the Commission also promised to prepare environmental impact assessment studies when making proposals which have significant environmental impacts. The Danes along with prominent environmental groups had battled for the insertion of an environmental reference into each and every Title of the Treaty. This would have been extremely complicated and negotiators instead opted for a more cautious amendment of Articles 2 and 3. Arguably, though, controversy is just what the environment needs to emphasize the difficult choices required to implement sustainable development.

However modest, the change is likely to be welcomed by DG XI which in the past has had to rely upon softer, 'bottom up' approaches to greening other Directorates-General (Wilkinson, 1997). Finally, Article 100a(3) is also amended to extend the obligation placed on the Commission to take as the basis of its proposals a high level of protection to the Parliament and the Council.

The European Parliament

Changes to Article 189, which extend co-decision-making (Chapter 3) to the main environmental article. Article 130s(1), replacing co-operation (which is abolished except for EMU), may strengthen the possibility of more wide-ranging environmental legislation. Under the procedure, which is extremely complicated, where the Parliament and the Council cannot agreed on a proposal, a Conciliation Committee involving the two has to be convened (see Chapter 3). It considerably enhances the power of the Parliament and goes some way to addressing the 'democratic deficit'. To date, the conciliation procedure, which has been available since late 1993, has worked well in areas like packaging waste, failing on only one occasion to deliver a joint text (HOLSCEC, 1995, p35).

The 'Environmental Guarantee'

One of the most complex and controversial amendments was that made to the all important Article 100a (approximation of laws), allowing states to introduce national rules to protect health and the environment that are sricter than Community norms under carefully specified circumstances. Under the current Article 130t, greener states have only been able to 'maintain' higher standards (ie those implemented prior to membership), not introduce new ones, although this interpretation is disputed. The basic idea of the amendment, which was pushed with particular enthusiasm by the Scandinavian Member States, is that states will make a case for any new and stricter rules to the Commission, which will then investigate whether they breach free trade rules. Environmentalists wanted the burden of proof to lie in favour of the applicant (that is, in favour of the environment), but this was rejected (Climate Network Europe et al, 1995, p19).

The changes were heralded as a major breakthrough when they appeared in the Dutch Presidency's first draft of May 1997 since they appeared to support the notion of different national environmental standards, but the received view is that with so many restrictions the amendment is likely to remain a dead letter. In many ways, the controversy and legal case work that is likely to be generated by this single amendment cuts to the heart of the complicated debate about free trade rules and environmental protection measures that has troubled the EC since the 1970s and which was only partially resolved by the landmark 'Danish bottles' case. Any restrictions are likely to be fiercely resisted by Austria, Finland and Sweden who fear that their existing standards will have to be compromised to facilitate free trade. One or all is likely to bring a landmark case before the European Court of Justice (ECJ) to establish the scope for introducing higher national environmental standards, with interesting implications for the meaning and legal status of the precautionary principle in EC policy. For the time being though, the general presumption remains that trade liberalization will take precedence over the desire of any Member State to attain higher environmental standards. However, it could be that the Commission's use of Article 100a as the legal basis of action decreases with the extension of co-decision-making to Article 130s(1).

Access to Information

A new Article 191a confers a right of access to any citizen to documents held by the CoM, the Commission and the European Parliament, subject to several exemptions. Each organization will now elaborate specific rules for disclosure. Of all the changes, this could be the most far reaching. It could, for example, portend the end of secret votes in the CoM and the custom of attaching unpublished 'interpretative minutes' to directives.

Subsidiarity and Proportionality

A new Protocol is attached which lays down clear markers for the Commission. It states that the Community 'shall not go beyond what is necessary to achieve the objectives of the Treaty'. In future, DG XI will have to state more carefully the justification for its proposals using 'qualitative or, wherever possible, quantitative indicators'.

The Committee of the Regions

The environment is added to the list of areas where the Committee has to be consulted.

There were also a number of disappointments for environmentalists:

QMV

The Dutch Presidency failed in its bid to extend QMV to all aspects of environmental policy via an amendment to Article 130s(2). The current exceptions, namely land use planning, fiscal measures, energy and water resources, were put in place by the TEU. The Danes, environmental groups and the Commission were particularly keen to remove the second of these to facilitate environmental tax reforms, but an extension to all four was theoretically possible. However, the Dutch Presidency tried to do this in one fell swoop and ran into fierce resistance, reportedly from the Germans.

The ECJ

Currently, the Court may only levy an Article 171 fine on a state for non-implementation when a previous ruling has been ignored. By then, however, the environmental resource in question may have been irretrievably damaged.

Citizens' Rights

The Swedes and the Commission were keen to provide a legally expressed right to all citizens to a healthy environment. This would throw up all sorts of conceptual and practical problems (Macrory, 1996) and was rejected. However, an amended Article F strengthens the EU's commitment to human rights and allows for a partial suspension of any state found to be in breach of them.

Public Access to Justice

EC law is rooted in a series of grand intergovernmental bargains. Currently there are restrictions placed upon individuals and environmental groups which prevent them bringing public interest cases against states before the ECJ. No changes were made, but the Commission is known to be actively considering the idea of improving access to environmental justice at the national level.

Nuclear Power

Environmental groups would like to amend the Treaty Establishing the European Atomic Energy Community (EURATOM) phased out and replaced with a set of arrangements that reflect the undesirability of nuclear power as a long-term energy source. EURATOM, Article 1 of which calls for the 'speedy establishment and growth of nuclear industries', was not reviewed in 1991 either, but sits uneasily with the avowedly anti-nuclear energy policies of some of the newer Member States.

Conclusion

The draft Treaty agreed at Amsterdam looks set to consolidate the solid achievements made by EC environmental policy since the 1970s rather than introduce a step change in the level of protection offered. Significantly, the changes made to

Articles 2 and 3 entrench environmental requirements to an extent unprecedented in the history of the EC. Last minute fears that the status quo would prevail proved to be groundless following a strong, late push by greener Member States.

The obvious questions is just how important are big 'history-making' summits like Amsterdam to the evolution of the EU? (See Chapters 10 and 12.) Do they mark important changes of direction or do they merely endorse the products of a slower, evolutionary process of change? On a very practical level, all that leaders agreed to in Amsterdam was a draft of a new Treaty which still requires further work. At the time of writing, the agreement has been signed by states but awaits ratification by national parliaments. If, and this is the big question, ratification proceedings run smoothly at the national level, the new Treaty should come into force early in 1999, although its practical effects will take time to emerge. Following the massive public backlash against Maastricht, smooth entry into force can no longer be assumed and there may have to be complicated 'opt outs' for individual states that run counter to the idea of an *acquis communitaire*.

Acknowledgements

The author is indebeted to Tim O'Riordan and Martin Hession for their helpful comments and suggestions. All remaining errors and omissions are his alone. The research underpinning this paper was funded by the ESRC's Global Environmental Change Programme.

References

Climate Network Europe, European Environmental Bureau, European Federation for Transport and Environment, FoE Europe, Greenpeace International Europe, WWF (1995) *Greening the Treaty II*, Utrecht: Stichting Natuur en Milieu.

European Environmental Bureau (EEB) (1995) *Greening The Treaty: A Manifesto for the IGC From UK Members of the EEB,* London: Campaign for the Protection of Rural England.

ENDS (1996) 'IGC Set to Alter Framework for EC Environmental Policy', *ENDS Report,* Vol.255, pp40–2, April.

George, S. (1996) 'The Approach of the British Government to the 1996 IGC', *Journal of European Public Policy,* Vol.3, No.1, pp45–62.

House of Lords Select Committee on the European Communities (1980) *Environmental Problems and the Treaty of Rome,* HL Paper 68, Fifth Report, Session 1980–81, HMSO: London.

House of Lords Select Committee on the European Communities (1995) *Intergovernmental Conference: Report,* HL Paper 105, 21st Report, Session 1994–1995, London: HMSO.

Institute of European Environmental Policy (IIEP) (1995) *The 1996 IGC: Integrating The Environment into Other EU Policies,* A Report for the UK DoE, London: IEEP.

Macrory, R. (1996) 'Environmental Citizenship and the Law', *Journal of Environmental Law,* Vol.8, No.2, pp219–35.
Wilkinson, D. (1997) 'Towards Sustainability in the EU?', *Environmental Politics,* Vol.6, No.1 (Special Issue), pp153–73.

Part 2
ACTORS

5

Strategies of the 'Green' Member States in EU Environmental Policy-making

Duncan Liefferink and Mikael Skou Andersen

Introduction

Environmentally progressive 'pioneers' are important forces behind the development of international and European Union (EU) environmental policy. On the basis of their own domestic regulations they promote the adoption of stringent environmental policies at the international level. This serves a dual goal. On the one hand, strict international measures lead to the reduction of transboundary flows of pollution and thus contribute to achieving national environmental policy goals. On the other hand, competitive disadvantages for industry in the 'pioneer' countries will diminish if others have to take similarly costly measures. The 'leader–laggard' dynamic in international environmental policy currently enjoys considerable academic interest (see Chapters 11 and 12) (eg Haas, 1993; Héritier, 1994; Héritier et al, 1994; Sbragia, 1996; Holzinger, 1997; Andersen and Liefferink, 1997a).

In the specific case of the EU, the increasing attention paid to the role of 'leaders' versus 'laggards' can be linked to shifts in the political context of environmental policy-making. Until recently, Germany, Denmark and The Netherlands were generally regarded as the most environmentally minded Member States, acting as the 'motors' of EU environmental policy-making. This view was held not only by political scientists (cf for instance the references above) but also by authors more directly involved in the policy-making process in Brussels (eg Krämer 1992, pp52–3; Johnson and Corcelle, 1995, p8). On 1 January 1995 Sweden, Finland and Austria entered the Union. Domestic environmental standards in those countries are at a level comparable with or even higher than those of the former 'green troika'. They were therefore broadly expected to strengthen the group of 'pushers' in EU environmental policy-making (cf Sbragia, 1996; Axelrod, 1997; Aguilar Fernández, 1997). The future enlargement of the Union by a number of

Central and Eastern European countries may further increase the importance of the 'leader-laggard' dynamic by making the EU (even) more diverse than it is now. Although the precise mechanisms are as yet uncertain, this will almost inevitably lead to greater flexibility with regard to the differentiation of standards in the EU and thus to more freedom for environmentally progressive Member States to develop their own policies.

In most studies of 'leaders' and 'laggards', however, there is a tendency to treat the categories in a rather undifferentiated way.[1] The main point of interest being the dynamic of the policy process in Brussels, differences within the groups are hardly taken into account. In this chapter we will argue that such differences do exist and that they are indeed relevant for understanding the two-level game being played in the EU. In doing so, we will focus on the group of environmental 'leaders'.

In the following, we will first propose a typology of 'green' strategies in the EU, distinguishing between different kinds of pushers and forerunners. Based on that, we will consider in detail the positions and strategies of the 'green' Member States in the first year after the accession of Sweden, Finland and Austria. The exploration will address policy-making in the Council and its subordinate bodies as well as relations with the Commission and the European Parliament (EP). Apart from policy documents and secondary literature, empirical data derive from a series of interviews with key policy-makers in the six countries under consideration.[2]

Strategies of Influencing EU Environmental Policy

Domestic policies have often been designed on a predominantly domestic background, with limited attention paid to the impact that such policies may have abroad. More than any other form of international policy-making, however, regulatory policy-making in the EU has a reciprocal, two-level character (Putnam, 1988; Andersen and Liefferink, 1997b). On the one hand, negotiations in Brussels are to a large extent determined by the 'input' from the Member States (eg Weale 1996, p607). On the other hand, processes and outcomes at the EU level often have an impact on domestic policies. This leads to a continuous inter-relation and exchange between policy-making processes at both levels. Considering the growing importance and impact of EU environmental policy, this also implies that domestic policies in this field are increasingly designed with a deliberate view to the possible impact on EU policy-making. In the national context, far-reaching domestic measures have sometimes even been justified by their expected impact at the EU or international level.

It is possible to range the various types of 'green' positions on a spectrum, ranging from defensive forerunner to active pusher strategies, as we have done elsewhere (Andersen and Liefferink, 1997b; Liefferink and Andersen, forthcoming). However, this simple distinction does not leave room for the observation that progressive forerunner positions may be taken either with or without an explicit view to the impact in Brussels. In the former case, a forerunner position can (but does not necessarily have to) be combined with active pusher efforts at the EU level. Moreover, even if stringent national policies are implemented for purely domestic reasons, they may still trigger activity in Brussels. In this context it is useful to distinguish between pusher effects that are channelled directly into *environmental* policy-making, and effects that occur via *internal market* policies. In order to accommodate this kind of gradation in the possible strategies applied by 'green' Member States for influencing EU environmental policy-making, we propose a more systematic classification.

Table 5.1 presents a scheme according to which a Member State can act as a 'pioneer' in principally four different ways, with varying emphasis on the aspects of being a forerunner and a pusher. A 'forerunner' is defined as a Member State which is 'ahead' of EU environmental policy in the sense of having developed more advanced policies with a higher level of protection. The table distinguishes between forerunner policies developed in a more incremental, historical process, and those which have been adapted more purposefully with an eye to the EU policy-making process. 'Pushing' can take place directly with regard to environmental policy-making or, more indirectly, usually by interfering with internal market policies. Our approach thus provides a refinement of the 'first mover' strategy as recently described by Héritier (1996), particularly by raising the possibility of less intentional pusher and forerunner roles. The first field (a), where a Member State acts as a purposeful forerunner and pushes directly, is the situation where unilateral action is taken in order to influence EU environmental policy-making. This can be referred to as a *pusher-by-example*. A good example is Denmark's unilateral introduction of a CO_2 tax, introduced not least to promote an EU-wide CO_2 tax (Andersen and Liefferink, 1996, pp114–15).

In the second field (b), the forerunner position of a Member State has been achieved incrementally, without a view to the EU process and usually primarily for domestic reasons. The Member State may nevertheless seek to push EU environmental policy-making directly by building alliances with the Commission's experts or with other Member States. This type of impact is often referred to as the *constructive pusher* strategy, because it is basically oriented towards finding a compromise, possibly at the expense of slightly lower EU standards than domestic ones. An example is the influence exerted by Germany, The Netherlands and Denmark regarding the rather ambitious level of waste water treatment agreed upon in the urban waste water directive, which followed, to a great extent, the standard in water treatment achieved in these countries over many years.

In the third field (c), the forerunner position of a Member State has been adopted deliberately, but the pushing of EU policy-making is done more indirectly, at least from the point of view of the Member State. It does not explicitly

Table 5.1 *Strategies of influencing EU environmental policy*

Forerunner:	*Purposeful*	*Incremental*
Pusher:		
Direct	(a) Pusher-by-example	(b) Constructive pusher
Indirect	(c) Defensive forerunner	(d) Opt-outer

present its unilateral action as a model for environmental policy in the EU. Instead, the pushing effect is a result of interference with EU policies in other fields, mostly internal market policy. This type of impact can be referred to as the *defensive forerunner,* because the Member State is more concerned with protecting its own environment, rather than that of the EU as a whole. The implications for the EU may nevertheless be considerable. The classical example is the Danish bottle system and the matching ban on cans, which was introduced in 1982 (cf Koppen, 1993). The ban was perceived by the Commission as being in conflict with the single market. Denmark never proposed introducing the system at the level of the EU, but after the European Court of Justice had basically acquitted Denmark, the issue formed a significant part of the background for the drafting of the present packaging waste directive.

In the fourth field (d), the pushing of EU environmental policy is indirect too, but the forerunner position has been developed more incrementally. As in the previous category, the impact on EU policy-making is caused by conflicts between domestic environmental standards and the functioning of the internal market. The difference is that national measures in these cases somewhat unexpectedly turn out to be out of step with EU measures, something which may lead the Member State to *opt out.* As an example of this category, we refer to the German and Dutch bans on the wood-preservative pentachlorophenol (PCP). As the EU established a more lax standard for PCP, it led both countries (and later also Denmark) to invoke Article 100a(4) of the Treaty in order to uphold the forerunner position achieved. France successfully challenged the use of Article 100a(4) at the Court of Justice. The impact of the PCP issue on EU policy-making was not really oriented towards a specific directive, but it helped to revitalize an ongoing discussion among the Member States about the freedom to act nationally in the context of EU environmental policy (see Chapter 4).

With regard to a concrete issue, the above strategies may in fact be combined. It is also conceivable that strategies shift in time. In the case of the introduction of catalytic converters in cars in the 1980s, for instance, Germany successfully combined the role of pusher-by-example with the threat of becoming a defensive forerunner by making advanced preparations for the unilateral introduction of catalytic converters (Holzinger, 1994). The scheme provides us with a tool to distinguish the different strategies analytically.

Strategies of the 'Green' Member States

In this section, we will discuss the strategies of the six allegedly 'green' Member States in the first year after the accession of Sweden, Finland and Austria, ie in 1995. We will start by focusing on forms of indirect pushing (fields (c) and (d)). As we will see, some countries seek to combine these with more direct pushing-by-example (field (a)). Finally, we will examine to what extent various ways of constructive pushing (field (b)) are practised by the environmental 'leaders'. This may involve working through the Council and its subordinate bodies and building alliances with like-minded Member States, but also, for instance, influencing the Commission or lobbying the EP.

Indirect Pushing

Under EU law, the room for introducing or maintaining strict national legislation is limited by the effects of such measures on the functioning of the internal market. Article 36 of the Treaty states this principle in general terms for situations where no specific EU legislation exists or where measures have been taken under the Treaty's environmental section (Article 130r-t). The exact balance between environmental and market interests, however, has to be struck in each individual case. The Danish bottle case, referred to above, was one such case that went all the way to the Court of Justice. It showed that some trade barriers may be allowed for pressing environmental reasons (see further, eg Krämer, 1992; Koppen, 1993). If harmonization measures already exist at the EU level. Article 100a(4) of the Treaty further specifies the conditions under which Member States may be permitted to apply stricter national provisions.[3] Particularly in Denmark and Sweden, Article 100a(4) has gained considerable political importance and has become known as the 'environmental guarantee'.

In Denmark, Article 100a(4) became a major issue in the period of the referendum about the Single European Act in 1986. It was a concession from the other Member States to Denmark and used by the Danish government as an argument against the widespread fear of a loss of national control and autonomy owing to the introduction of qualified majority voting in the environmental field. If Denmark were outvoted in the Council, it was argued, the 'environmental guarantee' would release Denmark from the obligation to accept a relaxation of domestic standards. The implication of this argument was entirely defensive. And in fact, also one year earlier when it blocked the so-called Luxembourg compromise on car exhaust standards for small cars (cf Holzinger, 1994, pp258–61; Liefferink, 1996, Chapter 6), Denmark had shown a readiness to jeopardize a compromise at the European level in order not to belie national policy objectives. Against this background, there can be little doubt that the Court's ruling in the PCP case in 1994 (see above) came as a disappointment to the Danish government. In this judgement, the Court of Justice nullified the Commission's authorization of a German ban on the use of PCP on the grounds of insufficient motivation of environmental necessity. Although the Court had chosen a very careful wording and left open the possibility of the application of Article 100a(4) under other circumstances,[4] the judgement made clear that Article 100a(4) can indeed not be taken as a 'guarantee'. As Koppen (1993, p141) points out, its interpretation is a political rather than a juridical matter. This insight does not necessarily reduce the importance of Article 100a(4), however. Recently, a shift has been observed in Denmark in the direction of a somewhat less defensive and more 'activist' approach to EU environmental policy-making owing, among other things, to the key role of environmental issues in the domestic EU debate and the growing ambition to act as the leader of at least the Nordic core of a new 'green' group in the EU. While the minimization of the EU's impact on the domestic policy space will no doubt continue to be a strong focus, the dynamic potential of going-it-alone in the European policy process, either with or without invoking Article 100a(4), may come somewhat more to the fore.

Pushing-by-Example

Among the new Member States, concern about the possible consequences of membership for national environmental policy is probably greatest in Sweden. In the accession debate therefore the 'environmental guarantee' played a role quite similar to the one it played in Denmark, but beyond defending domestic arrangements for their own sake, Sweden appeared to want more. Both the Swedish government and the environmental movement linked the room for national policies to the ambition of showing a 'good example' to other countries (Naturvårdsverket, 1993; Nielsen, 1994). The government emphasized the need to combine the example strategy with more constructive pushing within the Union. As potential 'good examples' in the EU context, they particularly referred to the system of producer liability for car exhaust cleaning equipment (EU, EES och miljön 1994, pp140–1) and to ozone-depleting substances (Det svenska miljöarbetet i EU, 1994–5, pp43–4). In both areas, however, the accession agreement had already explicitly permitted Sweden to be a forerunner (EU, EES och miljön, 1994, Chapter 10). More interesting in this respect is the field of chemicals. Here Sweden was granted a four-year transition period, whereas the EU committed itself to reviewing its own legislation in this field during this period. It is quite obvious that Sweden's strict policies, for instance with regard to pesticides, can serve as an example for the EU (Det svenska miljöarbetet i EU, 1994–5, pp21–3). It is unclear, however, what will happen if a gap between Swedish and EU requirements remains after the transition period. For the time being, the Swedish government appears to be quite reluctant about the option of going-it-alone and to prefer a strategy based on discussion and co-operation (EU, EES och miljön, 1994, pp141–5; Det svenska miljöarbetet i EU, 1994–5, pp21–3), but a conflict is likely to evolve on this point in the years to come.

Also, Austria and Finland, as well as the 'old' members Germany and The Netherlands, acknowledge the relevance of national experiences as examples of practicable, feasible policy alternatives during negotiations about specific measures in Brussels. Contrary to Sweden, however, they hardly regard them as vehicles to instigate new policies at the EU level. Considering this, it may be questioned how relevant the more provocative variants of a forerunner strategy, ie the unilateral introduction of stricter national measures, still are at this moment. Germany used to be the champion of this strategy in the 1980s (eg the 'clean' car case, cf Holzinger, 1994), but is not likely to resume this role soon. With its 'good example' ambitions, Sweden may be regarded as Germany's most obvious successor, but so far has not stressed this type of approach. As noted above, Denmark has recently turned to a more 'activist' attitude in EU environmental policy-making. In view also of its highly committed Environment Minister, Svend Auken, this country now seems to be the Member State most inclined to embark upon confrontational pusher-by-example or defensive forerunner strategies.

Constructive Pushing 'Inside' Brussels

After having discussed strategies based on the direct or indirect impact of domestic policies in the EU context, we will now turn to strategies applied by the six when they take part in the policy process in Brussels, ie the more constructive approach distinguished above. We will subsequently do so by examining the Member States' dealings in the Council and its subordinate bodies, the opportunities for building alliances in the Council and their various ways of influencing the Commission and the EP.

The Council

Agendas for meetings of the Council of Ministers are set by the Member State holding the Presidency of the Council. In the EU-15, however, Member States are in this position only once in seven and a half years. Moreover, the Presidency is restricted by the fact that a large portion of the agendas are predetermined by proposals already under way in the EU machinery and by external influences, such as major international negotiations in which the EU has to take a common position. During the six months' term of a Presidency, in other words, a Member State is mainly able to affect the order rather than the content of the work of the Council (cf Wurzel, 1996, pp277, 280). In addition, all Member States have the right to submit items to the Council agenda on an ad hoc basis. In the environmental field, Denmark in particular often makes use of this option in order to demand attention for topical issues. Often, however, such interventions are primarily aimed at the domestic audience, as the environment plays a relatively important role in Danish politics (Andersen, 1997). Our study confirms the finding by Pellegrom (1997), however, that other Member States are prepared to go along with this only to a limited extent. A Member State repeatedly overloading the Council agenda with 'other business' runs the risk of losing the goodwill of its partners.

The most conspicuous element of the workings of the Council is their voting procedure. In the Single Act, qualified majority voting (QMV) was introduced for environmental decisions directly related to internal market harmonization (Article 100a). The Maastricht Treaty on European Union extended this, with a number of exceptions, to the entire environmental policy field (Article 130s) (see Chapter 3).

Unlike the former 'troika', the present six 'green' Member States hold sufficient votes to block QMV decisions. Although no doubt important in specific cases, for instance where a lowering of standards is at stake, the impact of this should not be overstated. In the first place, actual voting seldom takes place. Even under the QMV rule, negotiations in the Council are usually carried on until the moment consensus is reached, or is at least very close, so that voting is no longer relevant. Second, it must be realized that a 'green' blocking minority is not, so to speak, very 'shock-proof'. If either Germany or two of the other countries defect, for instance, the coalition loses all formal impact. And even if an alliance holds together, in the third place, the power of the six under QMV is only negative. They can in principle block legislation that does not satisfy them, but they cannot force the adoption of environmentally progressive proposals without the support of a considerable number of other members. Finally, as discussed in further detail below, Member States may have reasons of a more general strategic kind to be reluctant about constructing something like a 'green block'.

Nevertheless, the opinion was widely shared among policy-makers in the six Member States that the last enlargement had caused a certain strengthening of the 'green' input in the Council. Allegedly, 'green' standpoints are being taken more seriously and some noted a refining of consensus-seeking processes under QMV. This phenomenon has been described as the 'shadow of the vote'. According to Weiler (1991), the mere possibility of voting in case of a deadlock enhances the pressure to make concessions for the sake of reaching a compromise. Besides, parties that have *the potential* to form a blocking minority, as the six indeed do, may take advantage of this effect. The circumstance that it seldom comes to an actual vote may in fact even heighten this effect, as Member States do not have to lay all their cards on the table (for an illuminating game-theoretical analysis of decision-making under QMV underpinning several of these points, see Holzinger, 1997).

The Council's Subordinate Bodies

Apart from the work in the Council of Ministers itself, the lower levels of the Council apparatus are highly relevant for pushing issues and preferences. These levels include the Committee of Permanent Representatives (COREPER) and the Environment Group, consisting of the environmental attaches of the Member States' Permanent Representations in Brussels, usually assisted by experts from the capitals. In addition, in some cases permanent or ad hoc working groups at the expert level exist. It goes without saying that the vote casts a shadow in these bodies too, but at the same time discussions are far more detailed and substantive than in the Council meetings. In particular, the Environment Group, which meets more than once a week, operates at the crossroads of politics and technical expertise (Pellegrom, 1997).

Currently, the new Member States seem to focus on the technical aspect of the work in the Group. Especially in Sweden and Austria, good substantive argumentation and a coherent, well-prepared input into the daily policy process are seen as a major way to exert influence in Brussels. Domestically, efforts are made to ensure the high quality of this input. The Swedish Environment Ministry and the Environmental Protection Agency *(Naturvårdsverket)*, for instance, take their task in preparing for EU negotiations particularly seriously, and the environment was the first policy sector in Sweden boasting an official strategic memorandum about EU co-operation (Det svenska miljöarbetet i EU, 1994–5, published in March 1995). In the eyes of other countries, the input notably of Sweden is sometimes regarded as overly driven by arguments that do indeed have a firm basis but leave little room for political wheeling and dealing.

While Denmark can be characterized as putting more emphasis on the political side of the work in the Environment Group, Germany, The Netherlands and to some extent Finland generally show a more pragmatic approach. They acknowledge that expertise can be a major resource in the Environment Group, but in the end it is seen as part of the larger political game. Eventually, one might say, achieving a common solution is considered more important than to be fully in the right. Technical details thus become subject to a process of give-and-take in an earlier stage than they do for countries that strongly stress the technical and scientific basis of their positions. This 'conflation' of political and technical aspects already at the Group level makes it possible to respond more flexibly to political opportunities, but it also reduces domestic control of the behaviour of negotiators in Brussels. As long as there is agreement on the broad lines of the national position, this need not be a problem. If there are serious differences be-tween the domestic parties involved, however, it may give rise to continuous conflicts. According to Pehle (1997), the latter situation exists to some extent in Germany, mainly owing to a protracted struggle about international competen-cies between the Ministry of the Environment and other sectoral ministries.

Co-ordination and Alliances Between Member States

Particularly for the formation of blocking minorities, but also in order to exert more positive pressure on the political process in Brussels, alliance-building be-tween countries is important. Alliances between the 'green' Member States, how-ever, are by no means given. They have to be formed on an issue-by-issue basis and remain liable to defection. Long-term inter-issue reciprocity does not play an important role, neither within nor outside the circle of 'green' Member States. The assessment of the merits of each individual case, rather than general loyalties, determines the process of seeking allies in Brussels, at least in the environmental field. With this in mind it is obvious that potential allies are not restricted to a small group but in principle include all Member States. France, for instance, was drawn into a group supporting a special declaration regarding the application of the 'best available technology' in the framework of the directive on integrated pollution prevention and control (IPPC), a group which was not joined by Ger-many and Austria (cf *Europe Environment* No.457, pp1–13). Belgium and Lux-embourg participated in an informal meeting of eight Member States advocating more effective climate policies, held at the instigation of the Dutch government in The Hague in January 1996 (Europe Environment No.471, p1–11), in which Germany again appeared as the most reluctant partner. The need to have a broad basis in order to produce positive results under the QMV rule, and in the 'con-current majority' system of the EU in general (cf Weale, 1996), of course rein-forces the tendency to recruit partners from as broad a range as possible.

Alliance-building in the Council or Council working groups is to a large ex-tent an implicit process. Like-minded countries tend to 'find' each other in the course of negotiating in Brussels. And if they do decide actively to co-ordinate their strategies, this largely happens at the dally work level, ie between envi-ronmental attaches at the Permanent Representations in Brussels. In addition, regarding issues of major importance, bilateral contacts between capitals may occur, particularly in order to win doubters for one side or the other. Sub-EU meetings, like the one on climate policy in The Hague in January 1996, are in fact an exception, but in this case it may be explained by the wish to give an un-orthodox impulse to the exceptionally slow and cumbersome process in this field. There can, of course, be no doubt that governments are aware that some Mem-ber States are more likely to join them than others. It is also probable that they anticipate this and, either implicitly or explicitly, adjust their strategies in the Council to take advantage of perceived opportunities in specific cases. Closer and regular co-ordination between a 'green core' of Member States, however, appears to be in contradiction with the open and case-by-case character of alliance-building in the Council. If the 'green' Member States wish or need the support of as many others as possible, every suggestion of 'cliquism' has to be avoided.

Seen in this light, it is not surprising that actual attempts made to establish more regular forms of co-ordination between a limited group of Member States were received with little enthusiasm by most countries, including those that were supposed to be part of the group. After the accession of Sweden and Finland, Denmark in particular made an effort to arrange informal meetings between the ministers of the Nordic Member States immediately before Council sessions. Although the meetings were neither secret nor closed, it was felt that they might be associated with the formation of a Nordic 'bloc'. Finland, which generally gives lower priority to environmental issues in the EU than Denmark and Sweden and has a particularly strong geo-political interest in not becoming isolated, was especially eager not to create this impression.

A case in point is the Nordic campaign concerning the review of the Basle Convention on hazardous waste shipment in September 1995 (cf *Europe Environment*, Nos 451–7). Earlier that year, Denmark had proposed that in this review the EU should go for a total ban on the export of hazardous waste destined for disposal and for recycling or recovery. After the Danish proposal had been turned down by the Commission, Denmark, together with Sweden, Finland and Norway, submitted an amendment of similar purport directly to the Secretariat of the Convention. In March 1995, however, the Council agreed on a considerably more modest common standpoint. Formally, and under the threat of a Court case, the Nordic Member States should now have withdrawn their own amendment to the Convention, leaving it to the Norwegians to keep up the position unilaterally. Denmark refused to do so and managed to get Sweden and Finland on its side. A political and juridical fight evolved about the affair. Helped by some pressure from the EP and after a stiff internal debate, in late April the Commission changed its mind and adopted the Nordic amendment, which was endorsed in June by the Council. The Commission even succeeded in pushing through the export ban during the Convention meeting with many exemptions *(Europe Environment* No.462, p1–5). The eventual effectiveness of the action cannot be denied, in sum, but the Danish self-will was looked upon critically, not only by the Commission and the other Member States but also within the Nordic 'coalition'.

Episodes like the confrontation on the Basle Convention are therefore bound to remain the exception. Generally speaking, it must be concluded that the Nordic countries have insufficient critical mass to play a role in the environmental field comparable with that of the French–German co-operation on the integration process at large. Owing to its limited political weight, the risk of a Nordic 'green core' being isolated appears to be greater than its opportunity to function as a 'nucleus' for wider coalitions. When thinking of possibilities to broaden the basis of a 'green core group', the crucial role of Germany is evident. Being by far the largest of the environmentally progressive countries in the EU, Germany's participation in such a group would give substance to the threat of a blocking minority and thus make it a power to be reckoned with by all Member States.

The construction of a standing environmental coalition led or at least joined by Germany seems very unlikely, however, not only in view of the many factors that would actually divide the members of such a coalition, but also because of the basically pragmatic and ad hoc character of alliance-building in the Council, for the reasons pointed out above.

The Commission

If new policies are to be initiated at the EU level, the Commission cannot be circumvented. The Commission has the exclusive right to submit proposals for new legislation to the Council. For that reason, good relations with the Commission are of crucial importance, particularly for Member States attempting to push forward a policy field. For the new Member States, the building up of such relations is among the highest priorities.

The part of the Commission most obvious in this regard is the Directorate-General for Environment, Nuclear Safety and Civil Protection (DG XI), which is in charge of the majority of environmental policies in the EU. DG XI is generally quite receptive to new developments in the policy field and is regarded by the 'green' Member States primarily as an ally against 'unwilling' DGs and Member States. In this context it is an illustrative detail that some of our interviewees talked about 'supporting' rather than 'influencing' DG XI. Contacts at the expert level, (participation in) the formulation of various kinds of preliminary policy proposals and position papers, and what may be called the strategic employment of nationals in Brussels are the most common ways for Member States to exert influence on the Commission's policies, and we will now consider these ways in some detail.

Experts from the Member States meet in Brussels basically for two purposes. In the first place, meetings of civil servants specializing in the issue at stake, usually from the relevant ministries or related government agencies, are convened by the Commission in the preparatory phase of a proposal for new legislation. The experts comment on the technical aspects of the proposal but are also supposed to give a first idea of the political support to be expected later in the Council. Second, there are several kinds of committee composed of national civil servants controlling the implementation of EU legislation, a system often referred to as 'comitology'. Both the committees in the preparatory phase and the implementation committees obviously give room for influencing the Commission's policy choices. Apart from that, they also function as a breeding-ground for new steps. An expert committee may identify the need for follow-up policies or it may be a suitable place for a Member State to first test a new idea. Because of its large proportions and its opaque character, Pellegrom (1997) qualifies 'comitology' as 'a limitation on the coordinated input from the capitals, after all'. This may be correct from the point of view of central co-ordination by the Permanent Representations and, behind them, the Ministries of Foreign Affairs. From the perspective of policy-makers at the ministries and agencies directly involved, however, the evaluation may turn out somewhat differently. In most cases, the expert taking part in the consultations for new legislation is from the same specialized unit in the ministry as the one delegated afterwards to the implementation committee regarding the directive in question, if it is not the same person. In addition to this, the same people are usually involved in preparing positions for the Council negotiations that take place in the mean time. This offers excellent opportunities for governmental actors at the professional level consistently to propagate certain views or priorities throughout the policy process. These opportunities are recognized by all 'green' Member States. The Environment Ministries, particularly in the new Member States, attach great value to a well-prepared and competent input into the various EU expert committees.

A second way to influence Commission policy is through various types of written statement. These can range from suggestions or designs for specific policy measures to general strategic memoranda. Apart from informal discussions with the Commission and, if relevant, other Member States, such papers may be presented to the Environmental Policy Review Group (EPRG). This group was set up in the early 1990s in order to improve communication between the Member States and the Commission, and it brings together the Directors-General of the Environment from all Member States and the EU. A document that is well received by this forum can hardly be neglected by the Commission. A Dutch position paper on a new structure for environmental framework directives was launched this way in May 1995. Regarding proposals for a framework directive on ecological water quality, a route via the Council was followed. Dissatisfied with the first draft directive submitted by the Commission in late 1994, The Netherlands and a number of other Member States decided to prepare quite detailed position papers containing alternative proposals. These papers were first discussed in the Council's Environment Group. Via the EP and the Council itself, the issue was eventually referred back to the Commission, which came up with an encompassing communication on 'European Community water policy' in February 1996 (COM(96)59; cf *Europe Environment*, Nos 457, 465; also Van As, 1995).

The third and probably the most effective method for a Member State seeking to have an impact at an early stage is to penetrate into the Commission directly, that is, to place personnel at strategic places in the Commission. For this purpose the system of so-called national experts is very helpful. In many DGs, including DG XI, personnel temporarily 'on loan' from the Member States play an important role. All Member States make use of this by sending specialists in prioritized fields to the Commission. In this way, for example, the preparation of the Fifth Environmental Action Plan was led by a Dutch national expert (cf Kronsell, 1997). Shortly after its accession, Sweden seconded an expert to Brussels to help revitalize the area of acidification. Influencing the employment of regular EU personnel is more complicated, as this depends more on vacancies and other factors beyond the control of Member State governments. Particularly for the lower ranks, one of the main things a Member State can do is to try to ensure that it has a proportional share of the total number of employees. Stimulating sufficiently high-quality people to apply for jobs in the Commission appears to be a problem especially in Sweden, the most Eurosceptic of the three new Member States. Appointments at the level of Directors and Directors-General, and of course of Commissioners themselves, are strongly determined by political factors, thus leaving more room for strategic manoeuvres by Member States.

Conspicuous examples are the stable presence of the French at the highest level of DG VI (Agriculture) and the succession of two Dutch Directors-General in DG XI, Laurens-Jan Brinkhorst (1986–1994) and Marius Enthoven (1994–1997). National networks in the Commission consisting of both permanent and temporary staff can be very important. In the first place, they can function as a basis for 'lobbying' for concrete issues inside the Commission. Depending on the issue at stake, like-minded Commission officials from other Member States can be relevant here as well. Second, such networks can help in diffusing a certain way of thinking about environmental problems and policies. New Member States obviously have to make up arrears in this field but, as they are all well aware of the potential impact of such networks, this is mainly a matter of time.

The European Parliament

As the EP has often in the past delivered relatively progressive amendments and resolutions with regard to the environment (cf for instance Judge, 1992; Arp, 1992) (see Chapter 8), it may be seen as a partner, especially by the 'green' Member States. Some of our interviewees, however, pointed to a certain unpredictability in the EP's stances. This may have to do with the EP's permanent involvement in an inter-institutional struggle for more power, which sometimes tends to prevail over substantive considerations. In the case of a further increase of the Parliament's formal powers, moreover, influence on its positions will be sought by a growing range of interested actors and it is doubtful whether the 'green' image will be maintained to the same extent as it has been so far.

Member States maintain contacts to the EP mainly through 'their own' contingent of parliament members (MEPs). The best and most well-structured relations were reported to exist between the British MEPs and London, among other things in the form of briefings and regular meetings. Most 'green' Member States see the UK as an example in this respect and are in different stages of improving their relations with national MEPs. A number of countries, including Germany, already inform 'their' MEPs of their positions in Council negotiations on a routine basis. Among the new Member States, only Finland appears to be more or less regularly sending briefing notes on environmental matters to its MEPs. Austria as well as Denmark are currently working on this. In all six countries, direct meetings still take place largely ad hoc, with an obvious focus on major and controversial issues. Furthermore, contacts are not always initiated by the Member States themselves. MEPs often seek information or assistance from their respective capitals or Permanent Representations. So this is one more way for Member States to propagate their viewpoints, to be sure, but it indicates that cultivating contacts with the EP is hardly regarded as a top priority.

It should be added that, in this context, the EP is a considerably more important partner for the Commission. In the co-operation and co-decision procedures, amendments by the EP supported by the Commission are difficult to resist by the Council. A certain amount of co-ordination between the EP and the Commission in this sense is no exception.

Conclusion and Outlook

It must be stressed that this discussion on the strategies of the six 'green' Member States in EU environmental policy was based on only one year, 1995. For the three new members, moreover, this was the first year of full membership. An evaluation of their role in particular should take into account that they were still in the process of defining their positions on the rolling train of the EU. Even with this limitation, however, there can be little doubt that Denmark is currently the most articulated 'green' Member State in the EU. It is important to realize, however, that the Danish activism has a strong defensive tendency. In the 1980s, the predominant Danish strategy was that of a defensive forerunner. A focus on developing and maintaining strict national policies was combined with an uncompromising approach in Brussels. Furthermore, the central role of the 'environmental guarantee' in the domestic debate showed that the idea of opting out was always present. Denmark is currently placing more emphasis on the pusher potential of its forerunner position, or in the terminology of our scheme: its potential as a pusher-by-example. This may be associated, among other things, with the fact that the environment is one of the few fields where the Danish government may be able to convince the Euro-sceptical population of the assets of EU membership (see Andersen, 1997; Liefferink and Andersen, forthcoming). Some major disappointments in the environmental field or a further decrease of Danish confidence in the EU, for instance, in relation to the most recent Treaty revision, may change this situation. In that case, a retreat to more defensive strategies seems likely.

Considering its rhetoric in the accession debate, as noted above, Sweden could have been expected to assume a role close to that of Denmark. In the first year of membership, and perhaps partly owing to relative inexperience in EU work, Sweden did not immediately choose a confrontational strategy. Rather, it adopted a more constructive approach based on good arguments and expertise. The end of the four-year transition period, especially with regard to the important issue of chemicals and pesticides, however, may force Sweden to make a more explicit choice between meagre results at the negotiating table in Brussels and the preferences of the domestic constituency. Although ambitions in the accession debate had not been set as high as in Sweden, Austria appears to be in a somewhat similar situation. In daily policy-making, the country so far mainly acted in a constructive manner, but the explosive issue of road transport through the Alps may lead to a direct conflict between domestic and EU policies and trigger a greater emphasis on Austria's forerunner position. In both countries, moreover, increasing Euro-scepticism among the population may enhance these trends.

While in Sweden and Austria the tendency to develop explicit forerunner positions may thus, in the longer term, come to overhaul the constructive approach, Finland and The Netherlands seem to be more genuine constructive pushers. For Finland at this time, this can mainly be related to a wish to avoid any conflict that might endanger its crucial economic and security interests. How these factors will develop in the long run, as well as how they are perceived in the Finnish domestic context, remains difficult to predict. For The Netherlands, an open economy in the polluted core of the Continent, the constructive approach is based on the conviction that, in the end, both the domestic environment and the national economy benefit more from international compromises than from unilateralism.

The remaining state on the tableau is Germany, the most important but at the same time the most ambiguous of the 'green' Member States. Owing, among other things, to severe economic problems and an inability to catch up fully with the shift in EU environmental policy from a standard-oriented to a more processual approach (Pehle, 1997), Germany has gradually lost the position of pusher-by-example that it had built up during the 1980s. What is left is not always clear. In some cases, such as climate policy, Germany appeared as the most reluctant 'green' Member State. In other cases, including many of the more 'traditional' environmental issues, Germany is still among the forerunners, but the willingness to make active use of this in the EU context, for instance by (threatening) *Alleingang,* has diminished. This situation may lead Germany increasingly to behave as a defensive forerunner, concerned primarily with maintaining its own standards.

By moving from activist to more defensive strategies, Germany appears to have changed places with Denmark. Obviously, this has profound implications for the group of 'green' Member States. Germany's participation is crucial for the formation of a successful 'green' alliance. The remaining five, if they are at all able to hold together, lack both the formal voting power and the political and economic impact to maintain pressure on EU environmental policy-making.

The German case makes it very clear that having strict domestic policies is not sufficient to be a 'leader' in EU environmental policy. While general strategic considerations prevent the formation of a standing environmental coalition, as discussed above, differences in the ways in which 'green' positions are articulated in the EU context may seriously thwart the building of 'green' alliances on an issue-by-issue basis.

Acknowledgements

We are grateful to the EU for funding this research under the 'Environment and Climate' programme (contract number EV5V-CT94-0385) and to the officials at various national ministries and in Brussels who agreed to be interviewed. We would also like to thank the editor of the *JEPP* and three anonymous reviewers for helpful comments on an earlier version.

Notes

1. Greece, Spain, Portugal and Ireland are usually counted among the 'laggards'. In several studies, in fact, a middle category of 'neutrals' is also distinguished, consisting of the UK, France, Luxembourg and, in most cases, Belgium and Italy (Krämer, 1992; Sbragia, 1996; Johnson and Corcelle, 1995).

2. In each country either the Head of the Division for International Environmental Affairs or the EU co-ordinator (or in some cases both) at the Ministry for the Environment was interviewed, with the exception of Denmark where the Environmental Protection Agency (Miljøstyrelsen) was visited instead. In Sweden, both the Ministry and the Agency (Naturvårdsverket) were covered. At the Ministries of Foreign Affairs, internal organization showed more variation. Interviews were therefore held with either Heads or environment experts from the International Trade or Internal Market Divisions or with officials responsible for general European integration matters (and in two cases with both). For five countries, moreover, environment attachés at the Permanent Representations to the EU in Brussels were interviewed. All interviews were carried out between October 1995 and January 1996.
3. Article 100a was amended and clarified in the Amsterdam Treaty, concluded in June 1997. After ratification, Member States will be explicitly allowed not only to *apply* but also to *introduce* stricter national measures. The new Article 100a(5) seems to suggest, furthermore, that this is possible regardless of whether the Member State originally voted against or in favour of the harmonization measure. These changes are not pertinent to the present discussion, however.
4. It is interesting to note that in February 1996 a Danish ban on PCP, which had in fact been in force already for some years, was authorized by the Commission (cf *Europe Environment*, No.472, pp1–10).

References

Aguilar Fernández, S. (1997) 'Abandoning a Laggard Role? New Strategies in Spanish Environmental Policy', in Liefferink, D. and Andersen, M. S. (eds) *The Innovation of EU Environmental Policy*, Copenhagen: Scandinavian University Press, pp156–72.

Andersen, M. S. (1997) 'Denmark: The Shadow of the Green Majority', in Andersen, M. S. and Liefferink, D. (eds) *European Environmental Policy: The Pioneers*, Manchester: Manchester University Press, pp251–86.

Andersen, M. S. and Liefferink, D. (1996) *The New Member States and the Impact on Environmental Policy. Draft Final Report to the Commission*, Aarhus: Aarhus University, Department of Political Science.

Andersen, M. S. and Liefferink, D. (eds) (1997a) *European Environmental Policy: The Pioneers*, Manchester: Manchester University Press.

Andersen, M. S. and Liefferink, D. (1997b) 'Introduction: The Impact of the Pioneers on EU Environmental Policy', in Andersen, M. S. and Liefferink, D. (eds) *European Environmental Policy: The Pioneers*, Manchester: Manchester University Press, pp1–39.

Arp, H. A. (1992) *The European Parliament in European Community Environmental Policy*, Florence: European University Institute, EUI Working Paper EPU No.92/13.

Axelrod, R. (1997) 'Environmental Policy and Management in the European Union', in Vig, N. J. and Kraft, M. E. (eds) *Environmental Policy in the 1990s*, 3rd edn, Washington, D.C.: CQ Press, pp299–320.

Det svenska miljöarbetet i EU – inriktning och genomförande (1994–1995) Stockholm: Riksdagen, Regeringens skrivelse 1994/95: 167.

EU, EES och miljön, betänkande av EG-konsekvensutredningen – miljö (1994) Stockholm: Miljö- och naturresursdepartementet, Statens offentlige utredningar SOU 1994: 7.

Haas, P. M. (1993) 'Protecting the Baltic and North Seas', in Haas, P. M., Keohane, R. O. and Levy, M. A. (eds) *Institutions for the Earth: Sources of Effective International Environmental Protection,* Cambridge, MA: MIT Press, pp133–81.

Héritier, A. (1994) '"Leaders" and "Laggards" in European Policy-making: Clean Air Policy Changes in Britain and Germany', in Waarden, F. van and Unger, B. (eds) *Convergence or Diversity. The Pressure of Internationalization on Economic Governance Institutions and Policy Outcomes,* Aldershot: Avebury, pp278–305.

Héritier, A. (1996) 'The Accommodation of Diversity in European Policy-making and its Outcomes: Regulatory Policy as a Patchwork', *Journal of European Public Policy,* Vol.3, No.2, pp149–67.

Héritier, A. et al (1994) *Die Veränderung von Staatlichkeit in Europa. Ein regulativer Wettbewerb: Deutschland, Grossbritannien, Frankreich,* Opiaden: Leske & Budrich.

Holzinger, K. (1994) *Politik des kleinsten gemeinsamen Nenners? Umweltpolitische Entscheidungsprozesse in der EG am Beispiel der Einführung des Katalysatorautos,* Berlin: Edition Sigma.

Holzinger, K. (1997) 'The Influence of New Member States in EU Environmental Policy-making: A Game Theory Approach', in Liefferink, D. and Andersen, M. S. (eds) *The Innovation of EU Environmental Policy,* Copenhagen: Scandinavian University Press, pp59–82.

Johnson, S. P. and Corcelle, G. (1995) *The Environmental Policy of the European Communities,* 2nd edn, London: Kluwer Law International.

Judge, D. (1992) 'Predestined to Save the Earth: The Environment Committee of the European Parliament', *Environmental Politics,* Vol.1, No.4, pp186–212.

Koppen, I. J. (1993) 'The Role of the European Court of Justice', in Liefferink, J. D., Lowe, P. D. and Mol, A. P. J. (eds) *European Integration and Environmental Policy,* London and New York: Belhaven, pp126–49.

Krämer, L. (1992) *Focus on European Environmental Law,* London: Sweet & Maxwell.

Kronsell, A. (1997) 'Policy Innovation in the Garbage Can: The EU's Fifth Environmental Action Programme', in Liefferink, D. and Andersen, M. S. (eds) *The Innovation of EU Environmental Policy,* Copenhagen: Scandinavian University Press, pp111–32.

Liefferink, D. (1996) *Environment and the Nation-state: The Netherlands, the European Union and Acid Rain,* Manchester: Manchester University Press.

Liefferink, D. and Andersen, M. S. (forthcoming) 'Greening the EU: National Positions in the Run-up to the Amsterdam Treaty', *Environmental Politics.*

Naturvårdsverket (1993) *Sverige och den europeiska miljöpolitiken,* Solna: Naturvårdsverket.

Nielsen, K. (1994) *Gröna stjörnor eller blå dunster. Om EU och miljön,* Göteborg: Miljöförbundet/Bokskogen.

Pehle, H. (1997) 'Germany: National Obstacles to an International Forerunner', in Andersen, M. S. and Liefferink, D. (eds) *European Environmental Policy: The Pioneers,* Manchester: Manchester University Press, pp161–209.

Pellegrom, S. (1997) 'The Constraints of Daily Work in Brussels: How Relevant is the Input from the National Capitals?', in Liefferink, D. and Andersen, M. S. (eds) *The Innovation of EU Environmental Policy,* Copenhagen: Scandinavian University Press, pp36–58.

Putnam, R. (1988) 'Diplomacy and Domestic Politics: The Logic of Two-level games', *International Organization,* Vol.42, No.3, pp427–60.

Sbragia, A. (1996) 'Environmental Policy: The "Push–Pull" of Policy-making', in Wallace, H. and Wallace, W. (eds) *Policy-making in the European Union,* Oxford: Oxford University Press, pp235–55.

Van As, C. (1995) *EU-waterrichtlijnen in beweging – een tussenstand,* Wageningen: Wageningen Agricultural University, Department of Sociology, unpublished paper.

Weale, A. (1996) 'Environmental Rules and Rule-making in the European Union', *Journal of European Public Policy,* Vol.3, No.4, pp594–611.

Weiler, J. H. H. (1991) 'The Transformation of Europe', *The Yale Law Journal,* Vol.100, pp2401–83.

Wurzel, R. K. W. (1996) 'The Role of the EU Presidency in the Environmental Field: Does it Make a Difference Which Member State Runs the Presidency?', *Journal of European Public Policy,* Vol.3, No.2, pp272–91.

National Environmental Policy-making in the European Framework: Spain, Greece and Italy in Comparison

Geoffrey Pridham

Introduction

This chapter examines the contribution of EU policy pressures to the development of national policy in southern Europe. While it is supposed that the three southern Member States of Italy, Spain and Greece are broadly similar in their position on environmental questions – they are all, for instance, included in the category of 'cohesion countries' (recipients of the EU's new Cohesion Fund) – differences between them are also significant. These differences tend to be emphasized by the effect that Brussels has on the motivation and coherence of their environmental policy as well as on their policy style and implementation.

Confronting Southern Europe over the Environment: Problems and Issues

The capacity of individual countries to respond to the challenge of ecological modernization and, more recently, sustainable development – an outlook that has come to influence EU policy-making – cannot be assessed without reference to national systemic factors. As Weale notes, cross-national difference here 'is deeply rooted in policy styles and organizational structures', comprising a mix of institutional and ideological factors, and as such 'is likely to be difficult to change' (Weale, 1991, p21).

The reputation of these southern countries for ineffectiveness and corruption, administrative lethargy and defective policy co-ordination clearly has profound implications for their capacity to respond to what Weale refers to as the 'new politics of pollution'. These are all countries in which the State has been over-developed, playing a dominant part in the economy. Furthermore, the prevalence of consumerist values in these recently modernized countries presents a powerful obstacle to environmental values. Moreover, traditional features of a country's culture may affect response to the environment, such as national pride in *'putrimonio'* – to use the term widely employed in both Italy and Spain – which is often idiosyncratic. An example of this would be the particular Greek concern for national monuments. To add to this, there is a strong pattern of localistic cultures in the South, introducing a territorial dimension to environmentalism. Public feelings might become sensitized over a location-specific environmental issue or event and exert pressure on parties and their leaders. Indeed, there are signs of environmentalist values gaining ground in southern Europe in recent times.

In terms of broad characteristics, there is a case for considering Member States in the Mediterranean region as a group – bearing in mind climate, physical features and, of course, the common problems relating to the Mediterranean Sea. The physical peculiarities of that sea, including its low volume of water, make it especially vulnerable to environmental damage through pollution – such as industrial and chemical waste, domestic sewage and oil pollution. The total human population in the area has increased and is increasing rapidly. Around the coast there are 537 cities with populations of 10,000 or more, 70 per cent of them in EU countries (*The Economist*, 21 December 1991). Italy, Spain and Greece are also countries which have been modernizing fast. Greece, for example, has experienced rapid urbanization (notably in the Athens area) and the expansion of tourism (elsewhere in Greece), which have combined with weak infrastructure and the failure of planning controls to produce considerable disruption (OECD, 1983, pp20, 30, 720).

Destructive consequences for the environment have been exacerbated through EU membership, notably by the application of Structural Funds to the south. The Commission's Task Force report on the Single Market and the Environment (1989) noted the severe problems of environmental degradation in southern Europe and expressed alarm over the environmental consequences of the Single Market for the region, especially given the predicted growth in tourism (EC Commission, 1989, 4.7–4.8, 3.21–3.25). There is a general sense that the southern Member States are markedly behind the most advanced Western countries in the environmental field. The Ministry of the Environment in Rome has admitted that:

> *The Italian government certainly finds itself, in certain respects, behind compared with the principal Western countries, which many years before Italy created structures assigned to the management of environmental problems in their respective public administrations* (Ministero dell'Ambiente, 1989, 1.1–1.2).

At the same time, it is important not to ignore ecological diversity in the region. This warns against too rigid a distinction between countries from the south and the north and requires that we take account of cross-national, not to mention intra-national, differences within southern Europe. These differences may be summarized as follows:

- *Environmental administration:* there are differences at both national and sub-national levels. These countries follow different models, with Italy opting for a small ministry responsible for environmental policy while Spain and Greece have larger ministries comprising other areas (notably public works) as well as the environment. Accordingly, conflict of policy interests, notably between development projects and the environment, are in the first instance (Italy) inter-ministerial and in the other cases intra-ministerial. The three countries also vary subnationally in that Greece has centralized control over environmental affairs, while Spain and Italy respectively have quasi-federal and devolved structures.
- *Length of EU membership:* the three countries joined the Union at different stages – Italy was a founder member from the early 1950s, Greece acceded in 1981 and Spain in 1986. Italy was therefore involved in shaping EC environment policy from the start in the early 1970s, while the other two countries joined when the EC was expanding its activity in this area.
- *Implementation deficit:* while the southern states have a reputation for being tardy in transposing EU directives into national law (though they are not unique in this respect), they have shown some differences. Italy has by far the worst record of the three (and the worst in the EU), while Spain's record is among the best. There is often, however, a big gap between enactment and enforcement of EU legislation: Greece has a much better record than Italy on the first count but on the second is notoriously ineffective.
- *Socio-economic development:* these countries developed in different periods and in somewhat different ways. Italy urbanized earlier in the post-war period, while Spain and Greece did so mainly from the 1960s. Spain and especially Italy are generally more industrialized than Greece, whose industry is rather localized – especially in the Athens area. These differences have predictably influenced the nature and degree of environmental impacts in these countries.
- *Environmental awareness:* it is possible to note some broad differences between the three countries. For instance, the EC Commission Task Force report of 1989 recorded that Italy and Greece were high up among EU states in perceiving environmental problems as urgent. It also noted an above-average level of 'don't knows' in southern Europe, except for Italy, reflecting possibly the limited degree of environmental education (EC Commission, 1989, 7.9–7.70).
- *Regional differences:* there is a pronounced divide between north and south in Italy as to degrees of industrialization and urbanization, not to mention culture; in Spain, there are regional differences, with Catalonia and the Basque Country having a high degree of industrialization not met elsewhere; while in Greece the main divide is between the two main cities (Athens and Thessaloniki) with high population density and the rest of Greece. Predictably, apart from determining the incidence of environmental problems, these differences have influenced the response to environmental issues.

- *Differences of specific environmental concern:* Spain has a particular interest in desertification and soil erosion, not to mention natural habitats; Italy and Greece are rather more concerned about the state of coastal water quality, with the latter generally more successful in maintaining such quality. Both countries are increasingly concerned about urban air pollution. This is especially true in the north and the centre of Italy, while in Greece, Athens forms the main focus of attention in matters relating to air quality.

The similarities and differences among the three southern European countries are elaborated in the following sections. In particular, changes arising from new environmental pressures at the national and European levels will be identified. We look in turn at national governmental structures and whether these facilitate or hinder environmental policy, at southern European responses to EU policy on the environment and then at different actors and influences under the heading of 'society'. It is hypothesized that the first (national governments) are more likely to give priority to environmental policy and to embrace new directions when there is combined pressure from the second (the EU) and the third (society).

The State Dimension: Institutional Lethargy or Policy Adaptation?

Policy Structures

In a recent study, Lopez Bustos presents a range of organizational models for environmental policy (Lopez Bustos, 1992, Chapter 7). These include: the concentration of competences in an environmental ministry; partial concentration of such competences in the same (with the environment ministry playing a co-ordinating role); partial clustering of competences in an already established (non-environment) ministry; the dispersal of competence between various ministries; and, hyper-sectorialization, whereby each ministry incorporates an environmental division. Italy, Spain and Greece fall into the second and third groups in terms of policy structures. Various points about these structural distinctions help to put the southern European countries into comparative perspective.

First, given the relatively recent importance of environmental policy, there is a general difficulty in introducing effective environmental administration into traditional bureaucracies as logically that involves some radical restructuring of ministerial responsibilities; and this is bound to encounter bureaucratic resistance because of established interests in the government machinery. Of the three, the most fragmented is the Greek case. The Ministry of Environment, Physical Planning and Public Works in Athens has a number of limited functions, but many other ministries have environmental functions too: Merchant Marine covers protection of the marine environment; Health tests sea water quality and classifies beaches; Agriculture is responsible for protecting forests and monitors rivers; and Transport monitors car emissions (Commission of the EC, DC XI, 1993, pp57–8, 66). Institutional fragmentation is to some degree inevitable in a policy area that is itself cross-sectoral, but this is not, however, peculiar to southern Europe.

Second, these problems can in part be neutralized by effective co-ordination at both horizontal (inter-ministerial) and vertical (centre-periphery) levels, but it is here that the southern European countries are notably deficient. Ministerial rivalry and bureaucratic lethargy have proved powerful, as has the weakness of efficiency values and professional competence (as distinct from cliental practices). For instance, the Italian Ministry of the Environment attempted to introduce a national agency for environmental protection, 'with offices located territorially, and to which would be attributed the chief task of proposal, planning, control and verification of technical environmental standards' (Ministero dell'Ambiente, 1992a, p74). But, within a year of this being announced, the draft law was blocked because of objections from other ministries involved, especially the Ministry of Industry which was strongly opposed to its creation. As to vertical co-ordination, this is crucial in such systems as the Spanish and Italian where environmental administration is not centralized. But inadequate procedures have magnified considerably the problem of vertical policy co-ordination. This has only begun to change in Italy with efforts by the Environment Ministry to centralize procedures through control over finance and impact assessment and the use of triennial plans (Lewanski, 1993, pp22–4).

Third, the different organizational models and their functioning raise the related problem of political weight. Thus, Italy has concentrated some tasks in the Ministry of the Environment, but its staff is extremely small compared with the larger and older ministries. It has only 300 employees, while Interior has 140,000, Labour 16,000 and Agriculture 4000 (Hine, 1993, p232). Its report on its first five years of existence complained of its not being given an effective administrative structure, in particular with respect to adequate personnel, territorial articulation (field agencies) and resources (Ministero dell'Ambiente, 1992a, pp7–8). It also has logistical problems as its offices are located in four different parts of Rome. In Spain, national environmental responsibilities are partially concentrated in the large and powerful Ministry of Public Works and Transport, but the former have usually been subordinate to the concerns highlighted in the Ministry's title.

The outcome is that problems of environmental management experienced by the southern European countries are not as a whole unique, but there are special difficulties, particularly in relation to administrative procedure and competence. At the same time, the EU has created a consistent pressure on these countries to consider and even implement certain new procedures. These point to a possible new trend in institutional adaptation. For instance, Spain has, as the most recent entrant of the three, felt under compulsion to consider environmental planning for the first time and also the creation of a proper Ministry of the Environment (Ministerio de Obras Publicas, 1990, Chapter 9).

Policy Style and Policy Patterns

While institutional history accounts partly for the problem of introducing effective environmental management, a low priority has often been accorded environmental policy by the governments of these countries, as reflected in their approach to problem-solving, policy outlook and degree of activism in this area. This is not entirely surprising since we are talking about countries – Italy is a partial exception – which have arrived late on the environmental policy scene, compared with countries in northern Europe. There have, however, been some recent signs of a more preventive or strategic approach, especially in Italy, but also at the regional level in Spain.

Evidence of low policy priority is either explicit, such as in public statements from key government leaders, or implicit, as in the priority given to policy which commonly conflicts with environmental concerns; in Spain's case, Gonzalez's dismissive approach to the environment and greater stress on the habitual Spanish preoccupation with water provision. This was on the occasion of the tenth anniversary of the Spanish Socialist Workers' Party's (PSOE) accession to power in 1992 and illustrated the line that had characterized his government over the previous decade. In Spain, the possibility of a new direction in environmental policy is also inhibited by a policy style that is closed and bureaucratic and without institutionalized channels for consultation with interest groups (Aguilar, 1991, pp1, 7).

In Italy, the traditional policy approach has been dominated by response to crisis or emergency, leading invariably to a flurry of hasty legislation via decree. It is only in this ad hoc manner, responding to such temporary pressure, that bureaucratic lethargy has been overcome. It is indicative that Italian governments have invariably favoured detailed EU regulation of environmental matters which has then simply been incorporated into national law without undergoing the lengthy business of processing their own legislative proposals (Rehbinder and Steward, 1985, p140).

Generally, these countries exhibit at best incrementalist rather than rationalist styles. Changes occur slowly and are usually of a minimal kind; but the absence of environmental policy strategy has usually meant traditional and especially economic concerns have remained predominant. Giorgio Ruffolo, Italian Minister of the Environment 1988–1992, in his statement accompanying the first national report on the state of the environment in Italy (1989), spoke bluntly of his country's obsession with the gross national product and of 'basic cultural resistance to accepting the idea of sustainable development'. He goes on to argue that:

> *Environmentalist policy is conceived still, to a large degree, as something external, peripheral and sectoral with respect to the production and consumption processes. Its actions are principally understood as ex-post facto, for repairing damage and reducing destructive and polluting effects. The concerns and resources of scientific and technological research are oriented predominantly towards progress in work productivity and product competitiveness* (Ministero dell'Ambiente, 1989: Nota Aggiuntiva: 37).

Italy has a high proportion of environmental laws, but, as Capria has noted, '... their production is strongly conditioned by the economic situation: only when market reasons and decisions of energy policy favour them and don't hinder their promulgation, then they are published' (Capria, 1991, p13). Similarly, in Spain, the overriding concern with high unemployment has made it difficult to break the traditional view that environmental protection and employment generation stand in an antagonistic relationship to each other (Ministerio de Obras Publicas, 1989a, p22). Such resistance to the ideas of sustainable development in policy thinking has been revealed also at the European level, where Spain has been virulently opposed to the idea of a carbon tax while Greece has resisted Commission proposals on chlorofluorocarbons (CFCs). Greek governments have placed a priority on acquiring EU resources for development, as from the Structural Funds, irrespective of their environmental consequences. Of the three countries, only Italy has shown a readiness of late to consider seriously policies promoting sustainability.

In these countries the main exception to the pattern of reactive response is to be found in the Italian attempt at the start of the 1990s to act strategically on environmental matters. Ruffolo's insistence on shifting to a preventive approach led to the development of three-year and even ten-year programmes to back up his intention. He also argued for increasing environmental expenditure, enlarging environmental legislation and for a more activist line by Italy at the international level to confront problems of ozone depletion and the greenhouse effect (Ministero dell'Ambiente, 1992, preamble). The government has also begun to think about eco-taxes and to promote recycling schemes and voluntary agreements with major industrial groups (Lewanski, 1993, 13). In southern Europe, such initiatives have been linked more to individual ministerial commitment than to a collective redirection of approach towards integrating environmental concerns into other ministerial portfolios. In the early 1980s and early 1990s the Greek environment ministers, Antonis Tritsis and Stefanos Manos, respectively, pushed for new environmental legislation, especially over air pollution in Athens. At the same time, they suffered from institutional constraints as did Ruffolo – above all, fragmented responsibility for the environment – so their activism did not produce permanent effects in terms of policy priority. The policy change in Italy may, however, be a new trend, linked as it has been to greater public concern.

At the subnational level the idea of sustainable development, specifically in tourism, has, however, begun to affect policy thinking, albeit in a few regions rather than as a general phenomenon. This may suggest that the periphery in some cases is ahead of the centre. In Italy, the region of Emilia-Romagna has been in the forefront of pilot schemes to make the environment an integral part of land-use and industrial development planning (Nanetti, 1990, pp145–70). This is also true of Catalonia and Andalusia, with their more activist line over environmental affairs. Andalusia has one of the largest environmental administrations in Spain, including an environmental agency (Commission of the EC, DG XI, 1993, p72). A notable case is the island of Majorca, where the regional administration has introduced new quality regulations and laws controlling traffic and the building of tourist facilities (*Financial Times*, 5 August 1992). Majorca's exclusive dependence on the tourist trade combined with a sensitivity to changing attitudes among up-market tourist families and a traditional appreciation of nature conservation have encouraged this policy line. It is now being used by the International Federation of Tour Operators (IFTO) as a model for upgrading the tourist industry in the Greek island of Rhodes as well as in Ireland

(*Financial Times*, 5 August 1992). According to the IFTO president, 'there is no altruism of any kind involved; it's absolutely straightforward – unless something is done we won't even have business' (*The European*, 30 July–2 August 1992). It goes without saying that environmental degradation, albeit in part a consequence of mass tourism, hits at the heart of the tourist industry's interests; and that in southern Europe there is a compelling need for tourism policies that respond to growing demands for sustainable development.

Policy Infrastructure

Policy facilities or resources of expertise may well strengthen the competence of policy-making in the environmental field. They include planning and monitoring mechanisms, efficiency of data collection and regularity of environmental information and the availability of expertise and environmental research. It is in this respect that the southern European countries are distinctly behind those of northern Europe.

Changes are beginning to occur at a basic level, such as the appearance of regular official reports on the national state of the environment. These have drawn on committees of experts both within ministries and those allied to national research councils. In Italy, the first such report was published by the Ministry of the Environment in 1989, with the second following – with a certain delay – in 1992. The Ministry of Health in Rome also now publishes detailed reports on the state of water quality at all Italian beaches; and the results – beach by beach – are reproduced in the press in the early summer. Clearly, that is an issue that arouses public interest. The Spanish Ministry of Public Works has, since 1984, published yearbooks on the state of the environment and legislation in addition to special volumes on such matters as environmental education and the principles of environmental law. In Greece, there have only been occasional reports. In 1983, the Organization for Economic Co-operation and Development (OECD) published a short though useful report on environmental policies there (OECD, 1983), but it has not been updated since; and Greece, like other countries, issued a somewhat generalized report for the Rio conference in 1992 (Minister of Environment, 1991).

The southern European countries have in this respect been following an international trend; but in other ways they are weak in policy infrastructure. Within the EU, they are usually the states with the least developed systems of planning control and with limited capacity for judging the potential damage done by investment in development projects (*The Economist*, 14 October 1989). This deficiency has been notorious in the case of Greece, where the lack of planning was highlighted by the controversy over the Prespa National Park, a pilot scheme for the Integrated Mediterranean Programmes which went wrong environmentally (Baldock and Long, 1987, pp17–19). Greece has some infrastructural mechanisms, such as the Athens Environment Pollution Control Programme (PERPA), the agency which daily tests air quality in the Athens area for the Environment Ministry and the monitoring stations of the Ministry of Merchant Marine which is responsible for the quality of sea water. Spanish laws on environmental protection have traditionally been marked by their lack of planning, although

Madrid has increasingly come under pressure from the EU for changes in this respect (del Carmen, 1986, p13). As the Ministry of Public Works has admitted, the EU has been crucial in launching the process of data collection on the environment as a necessary precondition for policy planning (Ministerio de Obras Publicas, 1990, p11).

Italy has a relatively extensive system of monitoring, but, as the Ministry's report of 1989 admitted, has problems with the reliability of estimates and completeness of information (Ministero dell'Ambiente, 1989a, pp152–3). Some improvement had occurred by the time of the 1992 report following a greater recognition of the importance of hard environmental information for public policy. But there remained insufficient expertise in public administration, according to the head of the environmental impact division:

The analysis of the environment, whether for getting to know the Italy in which we live, or for defining the programmes for action and estimating their success, is not now considered an option, but is recognized – by all and in each institutional office – as a laborious necessity; however, we are not endowed with suitable personnel and the capacity for linking the world of public administration with the technical contribution of different indispensable disciplines (Ministero dell'Ambiente, 1992, p8).

As a recent survey of air pollution control in EU Member States showed, the establishment of a monitoring service in Italy was not followed by adequate financing, thus making implementation difficult. For example, no systematic sampling and analysis programme could be undertaken and the data collected was not sufficient for a complete picture (Bennett, 1991, p32). In Spain, research and development is especially lacking in the environmental field, as a study sponsored by the Ministry of Industry has noted. It argued the need for Spanish scientific participation in the EU and other international organizations as a way of overcoming this infrastructural deficit (Estevan, 1991, pp518–19).

In short, the southern European countries do not always fully deserve their reputation for backwardness in the environmental field. In some respects they are not entirely different from northern Member States. However, they stand somewhat apart with their limited professionalism and infrastructural facilities and, to some extent, in their traditional concern for the economic imperative. If changes have begun to occur, the EU has been a significant although not sole or isolated influence; and it is to this we now turn.

The European Union Dimension: Pressure for Policy Change or Recipe for System Overload?

The EU has become a real pressure for environmental policy change both in principle and in practice. In principle, this is evident from the Single European Act's emphasis on integrated pollution control and the preference for the precautionary principle and preventive action in the Maastricht Treaty. One study, looking at air quality standards, for instance, noted the 'radical challenge' EU environmental strategy could represent for national approaches to pollution control (Elsom, 1987, pp210–14). At the same time, various features of EU policy and procedure have tended to exacerbate the problems for southern European countries in responding to EU environmental initiatives.

The stimulus to environmental legislation from Brussels has affected even Italy, a long-standing Member State. As Capria concluded, 'what distinguishes Italian legislation from others' legislation, above all in Northern and Central Europe, is the absolute prevalence of rules which owe their inspiration to the EC rather than the national level', for before the EC's first action programme Italian legislation on the environment was thin and 'first generational', meaning basic and inadequate (Capria, 1991, p1). Spain, which joined more than a decade after EC legislation began, spent the first couple of years of membership enacting a whole backlog of EC environmental laws. Unlike Portugal, Spain did not request a delay in this enactment requirement because, basically for political reasons, it wished to be seen as participating fully in Europe (Ministerio de Obras Publicas, 1989b, p245). For Spain therefore the effect of EC policy was more sudden and disruptive than for Italy or Greece.

Government leaders in the south have recognized that more adaptation is required of them than of their northern counterparts. Jose Borrell, Spanish Minister of Public Works, noted that the southern Member States – including Spain 'will have to make a greater effort than those of the North' in view of their climatic characteristics and their tourist industries (*Pais Internacional*, 2 March 1992). His government's Industry Ministry acknowledged this was due to the 'lack of preventive and corrective measures in the last 15 years' (Estevan, 1991, p183). The southern countries have therefore in recent years felt increasingly on the defensive over the growing pressure for environmental improvement in the EU. The debate over such issues has also tended to exacerbate the sense of a north–south dichotomy over environmental issues. As one Spanish official put it in reference to a dominance of particular northern concerns, this is:

a policy which has concentrated more on problems of industrial pollution and measures to combat it, than on programmes on the assessment, protection and recovery of soil, flora and fauna, and of making proper use of resources to avoid the progressive impoverishment and waste of nature (Baldock and Long, 1987, p59).

For some time, contrary pressures have been evident between the legislative or standard-setting approach, urged by certain northern countries like Germany (concerned that their own advanced standards might be weakened at the European level) and the tendency of other Member States to look to the EU for resources in dealing with particular environmental hazards. Meanwhile, the Single Market and the prospect of monetary union have injected new urgency into pressure for economic development at the periphery, while at the same time, demands for environmental policy harmonization have increased.

This situation has produced, not surprisingly, contradictory policy responses. The EU has thus acted as both a catalyst and a resource for environmental improvement in the south. This dual response has created special problems for the southern Member States. These problems arise partly from the fact that the EU's own policy has in a particular sense been contradictory. Its developmental policy, in the form of the Structural Funds, has not harmonized well with its environmental policy. This lack of harmonization may arise partly from institutional fragmentation in the EU decision-making process and partly from the fact that the principle (in the Single European Act) of an environmental dimension to different EU policy areas had not yet been officially adopted when the Integrated Mediterranean Programmes (IMPs) were launched in the mid-1980s. In fact, the regulation establishing them (2088/85) refers to environmental protection as a subsidiary activity to be achieved largely through other sectoral programmes. It did not encourage the submission of proposals which made environmental objectives their principal goal, nor did it specify the general balance between development aims and environmental constraints (Baldock and Long, 1987, p25).

The particular method adopted by the EU Commission, of issuing directives, requires their incorporation into national legislation before they become effective, allowing a certain discretion over the form of detailed application. Thus, the EU has a potential for shaping, even modifying, national policy styles, while leaving room for flexibility or possibly national foot-dragging. It is easy to see that the kind of institutional and policy-infrastructural problems, discussed in the previous section, have complicated the process of applying and especially enforcing EU legislation at the national level.

It is against this background that southern European difficulties in adapting to increasing EU environmental legislation become more understandable, although they are not necessarily unique in the European context. A report on the success rate of Member States in transposing EU directives into national laws up to the end of 1991 gave Italy 59 per cent compared with 93 per cent for Spain, 94 per cent for Portugal and 76 per cent for Greece. The figures for selected northern Member States were: Germany 92 per cent, The Netherlands 95 per cent, Denmark 98 per cent, and Britain 85 per cent (*Financial Times*, 3 November 1992). Thus, there was no clear north–south divide on this basis. Italy clearly has the worst record among Member States of applying EU directives on the environment, although recently things have improved with the *legge comunitaria* tightening up parliamentary procedure on EU legislation. As to infringements, Spain has been at the top of the list of Member States against which proceedings have been taken concerning EU environmental laws (*The European*, 26–28 October 1990; *Pais Internacional*, 9 February 1990).

There is a noticeable feeling in the south that EU environmental policy is rather northern in outlook and specifically German in its emphasis on uniform standards. This concern has been expressed over car emission standards and more recently the directive on recycling packaging (Arp, 1991, pp17–18) (see Chapters 13 and 15). Philosophical differences also surfaced in 1992 over the debate about introducing a carbon tax, arousing southern fears about what this might do to economic growth and unemployment in weak economies struggling to keep pace with the drive towards a single currency (*The Times*, 3 March 1992). There was strong opposition from Spain, concerned about the cost effects particularly on its languishing coal industry (*Financial Times*, 28 January 1992). Admittedly, though, this was not a straightforward south versus the rest problem, for the proposal – pushed fervently by Commissioner Ripa di Meana – was deeply divisive, such as in the Commission itself over the rival claims of economic growth and environmental rescue (*The Times*, 3 March 1992).

One increasing problem facing the southern countries is the costs incurred in applying EU environmental directives. These costs hit them severely both because they tend to be the poorer Member States, but also they have to make greater strides to keep pace with European environmental policy. It is for this particular reason that Spain blocked the extension of majority voting on the Council of Ministers in this area (*The Economist*, 16 November 1991). This special problem has now become officially recognized in the new Cohesion Fund.

More recently, the EU has begun to develop special programmes for assisting environmental progress, such as MEDSPA, LIFE and ENVIREG, so that the Cohesion Fund follows a certain pattern. EU assistance, such as under the STEP programme, has undoubtedly been important in furthering environmental research in the poorer countries. Furthermore, environmental considerations have begun to be incorporated into the criteria for approval of projects under the Structural Funds. At the same time, there are more regular warnings from Brussels over the environmental impact of construction projects; while Italy has come under more persistent pressure from the Commission for flouting EU drinking water standards on pesticide levels (*The European*, 31 January 1992).

There are two problems that may be observed in southern Europe: governmental incapacity and overload, magnified by policy pressure from Brussels; and some reservations about the pace if not the content of EU environmental policy, particularly from Spain. However, the Union has in effect adopted the carrot and stick approach, and, very gradually, this has started to have limited results.

The Society Dimension: Towards Ecological Modernization?

'Society' as employed here is a collective term for a variety of influences and actors – political, economic and social – which are seen as normally playing a significant part in policy debate and input at the national level. They include political parties as social actors, economic interests, environmental organizations and the media. For most of these actors the EU has in recent years acquired more political salience and impact. The impact of the EU on wider public opinion is more diffuse and more difficult to estimate. It is essentially transmitted via the kind of actors just listed.

We are probably looking at gradual societal response to the demand for greater environmental commitment. It is unlikely therefore that the three southern European countries will have moved far along the road of ecological modernization. However, dramatic events can shift opinion, this clearly being the case with the Chernobyl crisis of 1986. For reasons of geographical proximity this had a noticeable effect on Italy, in particular mobilizing elite and informed opinion especially in the northern areas.

How the EU fits into this scenario is obviously complex. But we are not as such concerned with whether the EU has any deeper impact or is out of touch with public opinion – an issue raised in the debate over the Maastricht Treaty –

but with how the different actors listed above interact with the EU and among themselves to encourage, or otherwise, policy movement in a more environmentally friendly direction.

The main *political parties* in these countries have tended not to give a priority to environmental policy or concerns, save on an ad hoc basis. This is blatantly the case in Spain where 'politicians are convinced green measures do not win votes' (*The Economist*, 27 April 1991). The same is broadly true of Greece (except when one or other party has made a passing issue of air pollution in Athens); while in Italy the parties have not traditionally been any more responsive, although the situation has now begun to shift. That is because of the political arrival of *I Verdi*, the Greens, who have been in the Parliament since 1987 – always a sure indicator of a likely response by political rivals. Growing environmental sensitivity has occurred at a time of widespread political protest and general disaffection with established parties in Italy. Traditionally, political parties were often allied with economic interests and pandered to consumer values. Even in 1990, one study of the Italian environment noted that 'the country's main political forces still regard environmental protection as external, peripheral or only partially relevant to the production-distribution-consumption function of society' (Alexander, 1991, p106).

Shifts in the balance of forces in a party system or in the outlook of individual parties may as a rule prove the decisive factor in bringing about change on environmental matters. Apart from that, movement is likely to occur as a result of the following: environmental organizations becoming more effective in lobbying or provoking policy-makers; a gradual sea-change coming from the spread of environmental information or education; adoption by the media of the environment as a regular rather than spasmodic concern; public opinion developing greater environmental awareness in response to these influences or simply environmental events; or a change of attitude on the part of business and industry. Clearly, there is a potential interlinkage between these different factors, but we examine them briefly in turn.

Environmental organizations are fairly numerous in these countries, there being around 700 in Spain according to a 1989 survey (La Calle Dominguez, et al, 1991), but their political impact has usually been very limited and they have often appeared as less aggressive than their German and British counterparts (*The European*, 26 March–1 April 1992). Admittedly, the closed decision-making process on the environment, in Spain and Greece particularly, has left only limited scope for lobbying. The passivity of these organizations has otherwise been illustrated by the link between private complaints about environmental problems and activism on the part of such organizations; that is, the latter perform a mobilizing function with respect to the former. Complaints are noticeably infrequent in the south which may also owe something to basic public scepticism towards or mistrust of state authorities. However, an opportunity has been opened up at the European level, for the EU Commission has come to rely considerably on environmental organizations for concrete information on environmental defaults which is then used against member-governments. Those in southern Europe have also begun to respond to this channel for influence.

As to *public information,* the environmental organizations clearly have a part to play as do governmental authorities. The relevant ministries in Rome and Madrid, while issuing reports and publicity on environmental matters for some years, have also invested in environmental education (the Greek government has been rather less active). More recently, environmental education in schools has developed in Italy and to some extent in Spain. The ministry in Rome has promoted this as well as vocational training in environmental matters (Ministero dell'Ambiente, 1989, Part III). It is difficult, however, to establish whether any gradual sea-change is occurring, as the effects of these relatively new activities are likely to be slow. Some clues may come from the role of the media and changing patterns of public behaviour.

The *media* have their own sensationalist way of interpreting issues, as in Italy, where headline news has concentrated on major emergencies and crises such as the problem of the algae in the Adriatic or the affair of the 'Karin B' waste disposal ship. The press has nevertheless served an important purpose in persistent coverage of scandals, such as the death of thousands of wild birds in the Donana nature reserve in south-west Spain. Since the mid-1980s there has been a distinct growth in regular press coverage in Italy of environmental matters outside emergencies; 'urban smog' has been a regular for several years, and informative background reports ('dossiers') have occasionally featured, for example on drinking and coastal water. By comparison, the national press in Spain has been less assiduous in its coverage. Since one of the problems there has been access to hard information, Spanish journalists have come to rely more on environmental organizations than on government sources (Aguilar, 1992, pp18–19). As a whole, television has usually been much more neglectful of environmental matters than the quality press. The 1992 Ministry report on the state of the environment in Italy quoted a survey on the state radio and television network (RAI) during 1986–1990, showing that environmental problems counted for only 1.7 per cent of news items (Ministero dell'Ambiente, 1992, p26). There is of course an environmentalist press in these countries, but that tends to reach only the converted.

One feature remarkable in southern Europe is the strong *localistic focus* on environmental problems, suggesting a link between territory and environmental awareness. This is noticeable in Spain in that, in several areas, the regional press is often more interested in such problems than is the national press. The Italian ministry carried out a survey on the selected local press during 1989–91 (Ministero dell'Ambiente, 1992, pp450–1). It emerged that waste disposal was the most itemized issue, clearly one of particularly local concern. In 1989, there was, for instance, a major local scandal at Montalcino, Tuscany, where the proposal to establish a large waste disposal facility aroused intense local opposition, concerned that it would contaminate the soil in this famous Brunello wine-growing area. The localism in southern Europe was also evident in the campaigns conducted for the 1987 European Year of the Environment. In Spain, they included ambitious regional programmes financed by several autonomous communities, especially on nature protection; in Italy, there were numerous local projects (monuments of Rome, green areas in Naples, pollution in La Spezia); while in

Greece, the 'campaign in general was far more local and national rather than European', including much activity by small groups and NGOs at local level.

Undoubtedly, the various actors discussed above have an influential role in sensitizing people to the environment, but whether this has any deeper impact is less clear. The signs from southern Europe are mixed, with some evidence of growing environmental consciousness, but hardly – as yet – any overall 'remaking' of public attitudes over the environment, save possibly in Italy. Even there, consumerist attitudes have dominated, as the familiar attachment to the automobile in Italian life testifies:

> *The car is a consumer good surrounded by a mythical halo, as an imaginary collective that has a consistent part in influencing the level of demand ... the point of attack on the culture of the car is precisely its role as a status symbol (and bad habit) ...* (Lega per l'Ambiente, 1990, p30).

From the late 1980s, there were signs of some change with a growth in Italy of the use of lead-free petrol (though not in Spain and Portugal), the appearance of bottle banks in rural towns as elsewhere and the institution in some Italian cities of traffic-free zones (*Die Zeit*, 17 June 1988). Local authorities played an important part in such changes, and they seemed to form part of some attitudinal transformation. One report in 1989 noted that 'nowhere in Europe is the environmental pendulum swinging so fast, from neglect to acute concern, as in Italy' (*Financial Times*, 24 April 1989). But this was regionally variable, for 'environmentalism is strongest in the North of Italy and weakest in the south' (Alexander, 1991, p105), which may be explained in terms of greater proximity to central and northern Europe, where environmental values are generally more developed. Familiar socio-economic differences between the north and south of Italy are also likely to have been influential here.

Environmental awareness is rather less advanced in Spain than in Italy for several reasons: a lack of environmental education in schools, the overwhelming emphasis on economic growth, and the lack of participatory mechanisms combined with traditionally hierarchical relations between public administration and society (Aguilar, 1992, pp22–4). Others have noted that Spaniards see their country as largely empty, so that dumping rubbish in the countryside is hardly regarded as offensive (*The European*, 28–31 May 1992). However, opinion polls have in the last few years detected some signs of an increase in ecological sensitivity. A *Demoscopia* survey in late 1990 identified a growing awareness but, at the same time, a firm reluctance to accept more taxes on cars and petrol (*Pais Internacional*, 8 October 1990). In Greece, on the other hand, the 1980s have seen a gradual rise in awareness from the time the OECD report noted that 'public concern about environmental problems is fairly recent in Greece but is an increasingly important force' (OECD, 1983, p12).

Turning to *business and industry*, the Commission's Task Force report of 1989 noted the low level of environmental markets in southern Europe (EC Commission, 1989, 9.3). Clearly, business and industry are more likely to adapt when both the global markets and national publics demand more environmentally-friendly products. In Italy, on other counts the most environmentally advanced of the three countries, the evidence so far has not been encouraging. One recent survey of four European countries recorded that the Italian market was far less ready to follow tighter norms over car emissions than the German, and that this affected the attitude of companies (Arp, 1991, p13). A 1990 report on environmental policy in relation to socio-economic planning noted a conflict between growing environmental consciousness and industrial secrecy in Italy, especially over soil protection (Lega per l'Ambiente, 1990, p510). Such conflict seems to be under increasing pressure of EU legislation. Changing attitudes is not the only problem. There is also the question of capacity for environmental adaptation. Much of industry in these countries has neither the skills nor resources to meet changing international demands, particularly the high proportion of small and medium businesses with very limited investment scope and weak technology (Estevan, 1991, p475). Until recently, Spanish industry 'considered the protection of the environment as an extra cost, without any productive yield', however, attitudes have begun to change and the environment variable is being viewed as a means for introducing improvements in products (Estevan, 1991, p476). FIAT, in Italy, is exceptional in having responded more clearly since the mid-1980s to European markets. Greece has a less complicated experience since it is less industrialized and has no car industry. Also, an initiative was taken in the mid-1980s to regulate its shipping industry to protect the marine environment of the Mediterranean (Rehbinder and Steward, 1985, p212).

Overall, then, the southern European countries have, to differing degrees, evidenced greater mass-level interest and activity by interest and pressure groups. But this is a recent departure. It is one that may well continue, and if so could lead to a change of policy direction, although the impact of the recession has to caution any judgement about the immediate future.

Conclusion

Discussion of the three southern Member States of Italy, Spain and Greece has certainly demonstrated the complexities of EU policy-making. In particular, the EU's policy process is crucially dependent on national institutions and procedures – which in these countries have serious weaknesses – and these may have a profound effect on policy outcomes in the EU.

We have hypothesized that national governments are more likely to lend the environment a priority and to change their policy approach when there is combined pressure from outside (the EU) and from below (society). In the three cases examined, these pressures are real and indeed stronger than ever before, but they are also limited and vary cross-nationally.

Policy in the southern Member States has tended to be reactive towards EU policy demands on the environment, perceived by them like a cold if bracing wind from the north. However, it is undeniable that the EU is responsible for a considerable amount of the environmental legislation in these countries as well as for modest moves towards environmental planning. The EU has thus been significant in the content of, and to some extent the motivation behind, environmental policies in the south. The record is less clear as to the priority and coherence of their policies, for EU membership has rather acerbated conflict between economic concerns and environmental ones. The southern importance attached to the economic imperative has remained, although there are recent signs of policy innovation, especially in Italy and in some regions there and in Spain. These have combined with signs of greater public, media and even interest and pressure group sensitivity to environmental concerns.

The idea of there being a 'north–south divide' between Member States over the environment can be overrated. The southern countries do have particular problems of administrative procedure and competence and they are notably short of infrastructural facilities in this policy area. They also face difficulties in meeting environmental costs. But, in other respects, they stand less apart from the northern states. This is certainly true of the problem of fragmented policy structures, whether at national or centre-periphery level. Furthermore, environmental policy priority may vary among Member States irrespective of such a 'divide' (it has conceivably been stronger in Italy than the UK in the past half-decade).

Moreover, there are also limits to regarding the southern three as simply one group. There are some significant differences among them, over not only policy priority, but also policy structures, enactment of EU legislation and environmental awareness, not to mention policy content, given differing environmental concerns. If anything, recent changes in the environmental field have tended to highlight such differences. Apart from policy innovation, these are most evident at the societal level, with Italy again more advanced than the other two. It is difficult, however, to attribute all these changes simply to that country's longer membership of the EU. The impression gained from this study is that deeper change will come about more as a result of general secular processes – such as European or other influences of a vaguer transnational kind – than of policy initiative from Brussels. That reminds us not to be too deterministic about the direct effects of EU policy on Member States.

Acknowledgements

This chapter is part of a research project, Environmental Standards and the Politics of Expertise in Europe, funded under the Single Market Programme of the Economic and Social Research Council (ESRC). The author wishes to thank Albert Weale for his comments on a draft version.

References

Aguilar, S. (1991) 'Policy Styles and Policy Sector Influence in Pollution Control Policies', paper presented at the ECPR Joint Session of Workshops, Essex.

Aguilar, S. (1992) 'Environmental Monitoring and Environmental Information in Spain', in Weidner, H., Zieschank, R. and Knoepfel, P. (eds) *Umwelt-Information*, Berlin: Sigma.

Alexander, D. (1991) 'Pollution, Policies and Politics: The Italian Environment', in Sabetti, F. and Catanzaro, R. (eds) *Italian Politics: A Review*, Vol.5, London: Pinter.

Arp, H. (1991) 'Interest Groups in EC Legislation: The Case of Car Emission Standards', paper presented at the ECPR Joint Session of Workshops, Essex.

Baldock, D. and Long, T. (1987) *The Mediterranean Environment Under Pressure: The Influence of the CAP on Spain and Portugal and the 'IMPs' in France, Greece and Italy*, London: Institute for European Environmental Policy.

Bennett, G. (1991) (ed) *Air Pollution Control in the European Community*, London: Graham and Trotman.

Capria, A. (1991) 'Formulation and Implementation of Environmental Policy in Italy', paper presented at the 12th International Congress on Social Policy, Paris, 8–12 October 1991.

del Carmen, M. (1986) 'Spain's Accession to the European Community: Repercussions on Spanish Environmental Policy', *European Environment Review*, Vol.1, No.1, pp13–17, October.

La Calle Dominguez, J., et al (1991) *On The Origins of the Environmental Question in Spain*, Madrid: October.

EC Commission (1989) *Task Force Report on the Environment and the Single Market*, Luxembourg.

EC Commission, DG XI (1993) *Administrative Structures for Environmental Management in the European Community*, Luxembourg.

Elsom, D. (1987) *Atmospheric Pollution*, Oxford: Basil Blackwell.

Estevan, M. (1991) *Implicaciones Economicas de la Proteccion Ambiental de la CEE: Repercusiones en Espana*, Madrid: Ministerio de Economia y Hacienda.

Hine, D. (1993) *Governing Italy: The Politics of Bargained Pluralism*, Oxford: Clarendon Press.

Lega per l'Ambiente (1990) *Ambiente Italia 1990*, Giovanna Melandri (ed), Milan: Arnoaldo Mondadori.

Lewanski, R. (1993) 'Environmental Policy in Italy: From the Regions to the EEC, a Multiple Tier Policy Game', paper presented at workshop 'Environmental Policy and Peripheral Regions of the EC', ECPR Joint Session of Workshops, Leiden.

Lopez Bustos, F. (1992) *La Organizacion Administrativa del Medio Ambiente* Granada: Editorial Civitas.

Ministerio de Obras Publicas (1989a) *Medio Ambiente en Espana, 1988*, Madrid.

Ministerio de Ohras Publicas (1989b) *El Derecho Ambiental y sus Principios Rectores*, Madrid.

Ministerio de Obras Publicas (1990) *Medio Ambiente en Espana, 1989*, Madrid.

Ministero dell'Ambiente (1989) *Rapporto al Ministro sulle Linee di Politica Ambientale a Medio e Lungo Termine*, Rome.

Ministero dell'Ambiente (1989a) *Rapporto sullo Stato dell'Ambiente*, Rome.

Ministero dell'Ambiente (1992) *Relazione sullo Stato dell'Ambiente*, Rome.

Ministero dell'Ambiente (1992a) *Bilancio di un Quinquennio di Politiche Ambientali*, Rome.

Minister of Environment, Athens (1991) *National Report of Greece*.

Nanetti, R. (1990) 'Social Planning and Environmental Policies in a Post-industrial Society', Leonardi, R. and Nanetti, R. (eds) *The Regions and European Integration: The Case of Emilia-Romagna*, London: Pinter.

OECD (1983) *Environmental Policies in Greece*, Paris.

Rehbinder, E. and Steward, R. (1985) *Environmental Protection Policy,* Vol.2, Berlin: Walter de Gruyter.

Weale, A. (1991) 'Ecological Modernization and the Integration of European Environmental Policy', paper presented at conference on 'European Integration and Environmental Policy' at Woudschoten, The Netherlands, November.

Williams, A. (ed) (1984) *Southern Europe Transformed,* London: Harper and Row.

7

The Role of the European Court of Justice

Ida J Koppen

Introduction

The decisions of the European Court of Justice (hereinafter 'the Court') have had a significant impact on the development of environmental policy in the European Community. The Court has consistently supported the view that the Community should have a broad legislative competence in this domain, notwithstanding the fact that such a competence originally did not appear in the Treaty of Rome, the source of all Community powers. It might seem rather exceptional for a court to take such an activist stance. The Court, however, is known for its judicial activism in this and other areas of Community policy. In the field of human rights, for instance. Community policy developed entirely on the basis of a judicial inference of powers not mentioned in the Treaty. Similarly, in the field of external relations, the case law of the Court has been decisive in determining the scope of Community powers.

The active role of the Court in interpreting Community law and promoting Community policies is generally recognized as a driving force behind the process of European integration. Although most authors have been appreciative of the Court's attitude (Dauses, 1985, p418; Kapteyn and Verloren van Themaat, 1989, p169 and authors cited therein), some have criticized it, arguing that the Court's decisions trespass the boundary of judicial powers and run the risk of losing authority (especially Rasmussen, 1986).

The nature of the environmental issues addressed by the Court has changed through time. Two phases can be distinguished, with a potential third phase in prospect. The first phase lasted until 1987, when the Single European Act came into force, giving environmental policy a legal basis in the Treaty of Rome (hereinafter 'the Treaty'). Until then, the Courts role was largely confined to arguments about the legitimacy of Community environmental measures in view of the lack of attributed powers in the Treaty. The second phase concerns the situation that has arisen after the coming into force of the Single Act. The new provisions about environmental policy have created numerous legal uncertainties which the Court still has to resolve.

In this chapter the historical development of the Court's environmental case law is discussed as well as some general aspects of the functioning of the Court. We will start by looking at the different procedures before the Court and the Court's judicial activism in the field of human rights and with respect to external relations. This short excursion serves to put the discussion of the Court's case law concerning environmental issues in perspective. First, an overview is presented of the early case law of the Court, specifically addressing the legitimacy of Community environmental measures. Then, the important changes that were introduced by the Single European Act are described, followed by a discussion of the Danish bottle case and the Cassis de Dijon doctrine. The last Court case we will discuss concerns the different decision-making procedures to adopt environmental measures. The final section draws some conclusions and speculates about the future role of the Court in promoting European integration vis-à-vis European environmental policy.

The Different Court Procedures

The task of the Court is to ensure the uniform interpretation and application of the Treaty. Proceedings in front of the Court are contentious or non-contentious. Contentious procedures can be initiated by a Community institution, by one of the Member States and, to a lesser degree, by private persons, ie individuals and legal persons. The non-contentious procedure is a matter of co-operation between the Court and the national courts in the Member States.

The Non-contentious Court Procedure

One non-contentious procedure exists, the so-called *preliminary ruling* or *preliminary judgement* (Article 177 of the Treaty), in which the Court interprets a specific rule of Community law (Kapteyn and Verloren van Themaat, 1989, p311ff; Hartley, 1988, p64). National courts can ask for a preliminary ruling whenever they have to apply a Community rule; if deciding in last instance, national courts are required to do so. A preliminary ruling is binding on the national court hearing the case and is intended to secure the uniform interpretation and application of Community law in all the Member States. No formal hierarchy exists, either between the Court and national courts or between Community law and national law. The priority of Community law over national law stems from the fact that the transfer of certain powers from the Member States to the Community has created a new legal order in which sovereign national competences are restricted (Kapteyn and Verloren van Themaat, 1989, p36ff).[1] Thus, a preliminary judgement is recognized by the national legal order of each Member State as if it were issued by a national court (Articles 187 and 192 of the Treaty).

The Contentious Court Procedures

Contentious proceedings before the Court can be divided into four categories: proceedings between Member States, proceedings between Community institutions, proceedings between the Commission and a Member State and proceedings between private persons and Community institutions (Kapteyn and Verloren van Themaat, 1989, p152ff). Other procedures exist that are of little relevance to our subject (see Articles 178–81 of the Treaty). A schematic overview of the different contentious proceedings is given in Table 7.1.

The Court procedure that is applied most frequently to environmental cases is the *infringement procedure,* initiated by the Commission against a Member State that fails to fulfil its obligations under the Treaty (Article 169 of the Treaty). An infringement procedure is brought before the Court after a mandatory round of consultation with the incriminated Member State. During the phase of consultation, a Member State is given the opportunity to voluntarily adjust the alleged infraction. It is the discretionary power of the Commission to decide whether or not to file suit if a Member State persists in its non-compliance. The Court

Table 7.1 *Plaintiffs and defendants before the European Court of Justice (All articles refer to the Treaty of Rome)*

| | Defendant | | |
Plaintiff	Member State	Commission	Council
Member State	Inter-state infringement procedure (Art.170)	Action for annulment (Art.173) Action against failure to act (Art.175)	Action for annulment (Art.173) Action against failure to act (Art.175)
Commission	Infringement procedure (Art.169)		Action for annulment (Art.173) Action against failure to act (Art.175)
Council		Action for annulment (Art.173) Action against failure to act (Art.175)	
European Parliament		Action against failure to act (Artl75)	Action against failure to act (Art.175)
Private parties		Action for annulment (Art.173) Action against failure to act (Art.175)	Action for annulment (Art.173) Action against failure to act (Art.175)

hears the parties before it delivers its judgement, often accompanied by an opinion of the Advocate General. If a Member State is convicted, its punishment is mostly restricted to political embarrassment, since the executive enforcement powers of the Court and the Commission are very limited (but see Chapter 3).

With respect to environmental measures, infringement procedures are typically directed at the failure of a Member State to adopt national legislation implementing EC directives. In most cases, directives must be implemented within two years after the date of their issuance, but sometimes another time period is indicated in the directive itself. The number of infringement procedures in the area of environmental policy has recently increased dramatically (see Chapter 17): in 1990, 362 cases were pending (EC Commission Directorate General XI, 1991). We must keep in mind, however, that the effect of a preliminary ruling, addressed to the judiciary of the Member State in question, although limited in scope, since it only affects the outcome of the instant case, might be more direct than the impact of an infringement procedure directed at the legislature. It often takes a Member State years to adjust its legislation to the changes required by a condemnation in an infringement procedure.

Member states can initiate infringement procedures in the so-called *inter-State complaint* (Article 170 Treaty). In that case the Commission gives a reasoned opinion about the case. Member States, however, are usually hesitant to file a complaint against other Member States, in implicit recognition of the principle that those who live in glasshouses should not throw stones.

The other two procedures mentioned in Table 7.1 are the *action for annulment of Community acts* and the *action against the failure to act in violation of the Treaty*. The first is a typical judicial review procedure in which the Court tests the legitimacy of decisions of the Council and the Commission (Article 173 Treaty) and annuls decisions that violate the Treaty (Article 174 Treaty). Although the Treaty does not mention decisions of the European Parliament, the Court has accepted on several occasions to review decisions of the Parliament.[2] Each Member State, the Council and the Commission can ask for the annulment of a Community act. Private parties have a limited right of action, confined to decisions with an individual character which directly affects them. The same restriction applies to private parties in the case of an action against a failure to act by Community organs (Article 175 Treaty). In the latter procedure, the European Parliament is granted an equal position as the Member States, the Council and the Commission; each of them can resort to the Court to ascertain the failure of the Council or the Commission to fulfil their obligations under the Treaty and to adopt the necessary measures (Article 175 Treaty).[3]

The Role of the Court in Other Policy Fields

The Court's role in the field of environmental policy must be assessed against the background of its contribution to other Community policies. Indeed, a brief review of the origins of the Court's judicial activism is indispensable to frame the role of the Court's jurisprudence in the shaping of the Community's environmental policy.

The Community's Human Rights Policy

The lacuna in the Treaty of Rome with respect to human rights protection has been the subject of much academic and political debate. The suggestion that the Community joins the European Convention on Human Rights was given serious attention (Clapham, 1991, p84ff) and the Commission formally proposed accession in 1979 (Dauses, 1985, p414). The proposal, however, failed and the Treaty was never amended on this point. Thus, the Court did not seem competent to apply human rights.

After an initial period of 'judicial reticence' (Weiler, 1986, p1114), beginning in 1969 a series of decisions were issued in which the Court progressively established its power to apply fundamental human rights notwithstanding the constitutional omission in the Treaty. In its first judgement, the Court decided that human rights were enshrined in the general principles of Community law which the Court has to apply (Case 29/69, *Stauder* vs *City of Ulm*, ECR, 1969). Respect for human rights forms an integral part of the general principles of law protected by the Court, and has to be ensured within the framework of the structure and objectives of the Community (Case 11/70, *Internationale Handelsgesellschaft GmbH* vs *Einfuhr- und Vorratsstelle fur Getreide und Futtermittel*, ECR, 1970). In protecting human rights, the Court, moreover, draws inspiration from the constitutional traditions common to the Member States as well as from the international treaties for the protection of human rights of which the Member States are signatories (Case 4/73, *Nold* vs *Commission*, ECR, 1974 and Case 44/79, *Hazier* vs *Rheinland-Pfalz*, ECR, 1979).

The Court, in other words, applies human rights as if they were incorporated in the Treaty. The absence of a written bill of rights has been offset by the Court's judicial activism creating additional guarantees for the individual citizen (Weiler, 1986, p1117). The question whether this activism is driven by concern for human rights or by the interest of market integration recently surfaced again in two decisions reported by Clapham (1991, pp48–9). Contrary to other legal systems, the Court does not grant human rights the sense of absoluteness normally associated with rules that enjoy the highest rank within the legal order. The Court stated explicitly that restrictions may be imposed on the exercise of fundamental rights 'in the context of the common organization of the market' (idem). Thus, we may conclude that the activist role of the Court in the field of human rights protection must be seen in the light of the Court's continuous contribution to European integration.

The External Relations Competences of the Community

Clear Community competences regarding external relations exist only in the area of foreign commercial policy (Articles 110–16 of the Treaty). In most other fields, competences are derived from the general provisions in the Treaty concerning the legal personality of the Community and its competence to conclude international agreements with third countries and international bodies (Articles 210, 228–31, 238). Besides the case law of the Court, the process of European

Political Cooperation and the activities of the Commission have had a significant role in this development.[4]

The first important decision of the Court in the famous ERTA case (Case
22/70, *Commission* vs *Council,* ECR, 1971) was to abolish the principle of enumerated powers, *compétences d'attribution,* with respect to external relations, and
to adopt the doctrine of implied powers. Contrary to the prevailing doctrine and
contrary to the opinion of the Advocate General, the Court ruled that Community treaty-making powers concerning transport were to be inferred from its internal powers in this field. The Court determined that the Community had the
power to enter into external relations in all the fields for which it held internal
competence. No separation must be created, according to the Court, between
the system of internal Community measures and external relations (ECR, 1971,
p274). The adoption of certain internal measures necessarily confers on the
Community the authority to enter into international agreements relating to the
subject matter governed by that measure, to the exclusion of concurrent powers
on the part of the Member States (idem, pp275, 276). Implied powers exist, in
other words, for external relations with respect to all fields in which the Community has internal competences. This is referred to as the doctrine of 'parallel
powers'. The implied power doctrine was upheld in the *Kramer* case concerning
agricultural policy (Joint cases 3,4 and 6/76, *Cornelis Kramer and others,* ECR
1976). Here, the competence to enter into an agreement on the conservation of
ocean fishing was derived from the power to adopt a common agricultural policy and from an internal Council regulation on fisheries conservation in the
Member States (ECR, 1976, pp1309, 1310).

An issue not clarified in these decisions was to what degree external competences could only be derived from the existence of a specific internal measure, or
could also be based on a general competence to adopt internal measures in a certain
field. This question was addressed in a subsequent case which the Court heard in
1976. In Opinion 1/76 (*Draft Agreement establishing a European laying-up fund for
inland water vessels,* ECR, 1977), the Court stated that treaty-making powers do
not necessarily depend on a prior internal measure but may flow from the general provision creating the internal competence if the participation of the Community in the international agreement 'is necessary for the attainment of one of
the objectives of the Community' (ECR, 1977, p755).

The Court's interpretation of the limited Treaty provisions concerning external relations has expanded the overall competences in this field considerably.
In principle, the implied power doctrine applies equally to the Community's
external environmental policy that has recently become an increasingly important aspect of Community foreign affairs (Nollkaemper, 1987) (see Chapter 16).

The First Environmental Cases and the Single European Act

The beginning of the Community environmental policy can be traced back
to 1972. In 1973, the Commission published its first Environmental Action
Programme and issued proposals for several environmental directives (Koppen,
1988). Some Member States were slow in implementing the Community measures

and by the end of the 1970s the Commission had started infringement procedures against several countries. In the cases against Italy and Belgium that are discussed below, the Court addressed the issue of the legitimacy of environmental measures in the absence of an explicit reference in the Treaty. By interpreting the general provisions in the Treaty, the Court determined that environmental policy fell within the sphere of competence of the Community as an implied power. In a preliminary ruling a few years later, the Court went even further, by stating that environmental protection was one of the Community's essential objectives. Considering the fact that environmental protection was not yet included in the Treaty, this was a bold statement, reminiscent of the Court's judgements in the fields of human rights and external relations (see Chapter 2).

Infringement Procedures Against Belgium and Italy

The Commission filed suit against Italy for not implementing a Council directive on the approximation of the laws of the Member States relating to detergents as well as a directive on the approximation of the laws of the Member States relating to the sulphur content of certain liquid fuels.[5] The first provided for an 18-month implementation period, which expired on 27 May 1975, the second gave the Member States until 26 August 1976 to adopt the necessary internal measures. The Commission started the infringement procedures in May 1979 and the Court issued its judgements in March of the following year (Cases 91 and 92/79, *Commission* vs *Italy*, ECR 1980, p1099 and p1115). Against the claim of the Commission that it had failed to fulfil its obligations under the Treaty, Italy stated that it would not raise the question whether the directives were 'valid in the light of the fact that combating pollution was not one of the tasks entrusted to the Community by the Treaty' (ECR, 1980, p1103 and p1119). However, Italy did maintain that the matter lay 'on the fringe' of Community powers and that the contested measures were actually an international convention drawn up in the form of a directive (idem). The argument Italy was trying to make was weak. First of all, as was pointed out by the Advocate General, if Italy really wanted to challenge the validity of the directives it should have brought an action for annulment under Article 173 of the Treaty (ECR, 1980, pp1110–11). Moreover, the directives were not only adopted as part of the Environmental Action Programme but also under the General Programme for the elimination of technical barriers to trade, adopted by the Council in 1969. The Court ruled that the directives in question were both validly based on Article 100 of the Treaty, which authorizes the Community to adopt all measures necessary to eliminate trade barriers resulting from disparities between provisions in the national legislation of the Member States. Article 100, in other words, was recognized as the legal basis for environmental measures which were adopted in order to harmonize national provisions. 'If there is no harmonization of national provisions on the matter', according to the Court, 'competition may be appreciably distorted' (ECR, 1980, p1106 and p1122). Thus, the legitimacy of Community environmental measures was recognized to the extent that the harmonization of national measures was necessary to eliminate trade barriers.

A few years later, in a series of six cases against Belgium, the Court broadened the legal basis of environmental directives by interpreting Article 235 of the Treaty which authorizes all Community action which is not explicitly included in the Treaty, but proves to be 'necessary to attain, in the course of the operation of the common market, one of the objectives of the Community' (Cases 68–73/81, *Commission* vs *Belgium*, ECR, 1982, pp153, 163, 169, 175, 183 and 189). The cases were similar to those against Italy. Belgium had failed to implement a number of environmental directives and the Commission brought an action against it for failure to comply with its obligations under the Treaty.[6] All six directives were based on Articles 100 and 235 of the Treaty. The Court accepted this dual basis, repeating that environmental measures may on the one hand be required to 'eliminate disparities between the laws of the Member States likely to have a direct effect upon the functioning of the common market' (ECR, 1982, p171) and, on the other hand, may be necessary 'to achieve one of the aims of the Community in the sphere of protection of the environment and improvement of the quality of life' (ECR, 1982, p191). By adding the second phrase, the Court established environmental measures as one of the implied powers of the Community, similar to the case law regarding external relations competences. As far as the relevant objectives of the Community are concerned, they were to be found in the Preamble and in Article 2 of the Treaty. *Inter alia*, such objectives include the constant improvement of living and working conditions and an accelerated raising of the standard of living.

Preliminary Judgements About the Directive on the Disposal of Waste Oils

The French association of waste oil incinerators contested the validity of some provisions in the EC Directive of 16 June 1975 on the disposal of waste oils (OJ No L 194/23) in a national case before the Tribunal de Grande Instance de Creteil. Since the matter regarded the interpretation of Community law, the Tribunal asked the Court for a preliminary judgement (Case 240/83, *Procureur de la Republique* vs *l'Association de Défense des Bruleurs d'Huiles Usagées*, ECR, 1985, p531). The question put before the Court was whether the Directive, by empowering Member States to create restrictive systems of waste oil collection and treatment, violated the principles of freedom of trade, free movement of goods and freedom of competition (ECR, 1985, p548). Articles 5 and 6 in particular, concerning the assignment of exclusive zones to waste oil collectors and the prior approval and licensing of disposal undertakings, were under scrutiny.

In an earlier judgement about the same directive, the Court had ruled that the directive did not authorize Member States to prohibit the export of waste oils to other Member States since this would constitute a barrier to intra-Community trade. France had adopted national legislation to implement the directive which had this effect (Case 172/82, *Fabricants raffineurs d'huile de graissage* vs *'Inter-huiles'*, ECR, 1983, p555).

In its 1985 judgement, the Court referred to the earlier decision, adding that the legitimacy of the restrictions to the freedom of trade, adopted by France on the basis of the directive, had to be interpreted in the light of its aim 'to ensure that the disposal of waste oils is carried out in a way which avoids harm to the environment' (ECR, 1985, p549). 'The principle of freedom of trade,' according to the Court:

> *is not to be viewed in absolute terms but is subject to certain limits justified by the objectives of general interest pursued by the Community [...]. The Directive must be seen in the perspective of environmental protection, which is one of the Community's essential objectives* (idem).

Restrictions posed by environmental measures may be justified, according to the Court, as long as they are not discriminatory nor disproportionate. The Court concluded that the directive had not exceeded these limits (idem).

Two aspects of the judgement deserve particular attention. First of all, we observe that the Court digressed to state that environmental protection was one of the Community's essential objectives. The phrase was added to strengthen the line of reasoning of the Court, but it was not indispensable. It was, moreover, not true. Environmental protection was not yet mentioned in the Treaty as a Community policy, let alone as a Community objective. Why then did the Court choose such a strong formulation? Undoubtedly, the judgement had an impact at the time on the discussions that were being held about the proposed Treaty changes. The Court took a position in these discussions, by showing its support for the proposal to include environmental protection among the objectives of the Community. This is indeed a typical instance of judicial activism of the Court. The Court ruled according to what it thought the law ought to be and not according to what the law was (Hartley, 1988, pp77–8).

Having put environmental protection on an equal footing with other Community objectives, the Court was then able to make a relative assessment of the different interests at stake. It was the first time that the Court undertook to balance the interests of environmental protection against the interests of the internal market, applying the principles of non-discrimination and proportionality. A few years later, the Court applied this method again and developed it further (see the discussion of the Danish bottle case, below). It must be kept in mind, however, that this was after environmental protection had been included in the Treaty. In 1985, the Court's reasoning was certainly beyond the limits of legal interpretation. With its activism, the Court made up for some of the political and legislative inertia of the Community, just as it had done in other policy areas (Rasmussen, 1986, p416; Weiler, 1986, pp1116–17).

The Amendments Introduced by the Single European Act

With the coming into force of the Single European Act on 1 July 1987, environmental protection was included in the Treaty as one of the Community policies (Articles 130r, 130s and 130t). Environmental protection is also mentioned in Article 100a, a provision inserted in the Treaty by the Single Act, which authorizes the adoption of all harmonization measures necessary for the establishment of the Internal Market. Thus, a dichotomy is created between environmental measures that are part of the Internal Market programme and action that is not related to the functioning of the Internal Market. The distinction has several important consequences.

First of all, Article 100a establishes that all harmonization measures adopted in the context of the Internal Market are adopted by qualified majority, whereas measures based on Article 130s require a unanimous vote in the Council. The difference in the voting procedure is furthermore reflected in different roles for the European Parliament (see Chapter 3). This particular aspect will be discussed separately, in the light of recent case law of the Court.

Another difference that needs to be considered regards the margin of discretion of Member States to enact national legislation after the adoption of a Community measure. If a measure is adopted on the basis of Article 130s, this 'shall not prevent Member States from *maintaining or introducing* more stringent protective measures compatible with this Treaty' (Article 130t, italics added). Measures adopted on the basis of Article 100a, however, allow a Member State to *apply* a national provision after notifying the Commission who must verify that the national provision is not 'a means of arbitrary discrimination or a disguised restriction on trade between the Member States' (Article 100a, para 4). The different wording of the two articles – 'maintaining or introducing' as opposed to 'applying' – is generally interpreted as follows. If a measure is adopted on the basis of Article 100a, Member States can continue to apply already existing national provisions, to the extent that they have been approved by the Commission. In the case of measures based on Article 130s, Member States are free to adopt new national legislation on the same topic as long as it contains more stringent standards. The requirement that the national provisions must be compatible with the Treaty means that they have to fulfil the same general requirements that apply to national environmental legislation in the absence of Community rules. Therefore the choice of the legal basis of a proposed environmental measure has significant ramifications and it is one of the issues addressed by the Court in its case law after the Single Act (see below).

Among the principles that underlie Community environmental policy, enumerated in Article 130r, one deserves special attention. The 'integration principle' requires that environmental considerations be an integral part of all other Community policies. This principle gives environmental policy a unique status in the Community since it is the only policy field for which such a requirement is formulated. Although many were sceptical at the time about the implementation of the new principle, five years later we must acknowledge that some results have been attained. Recent initiatives in the transport sector might serve as an example (EC Commission Directorate General VII, 1992). Moreover, the principle has served the Court as a guidance in interpreting other aspects of Community environmental law.

With respect to Community external relations in the field of environmental protection, the Single Act has created an ambiguous situation. Article 130r, paragraph 5, determines that the conclusion of international agreements by the Community 'shall be without prejudice to Member States' competence to negotiate in international bodies and to conclude international agreements'. The provision seems to imply that Community competence in this field never excludes concurrent powers on the part of the Member States. This interpretation, however, would be contrary to the general case law of the Court on external relations. It would especially come into conflict with the Court's decision in the ERTA case. A partial solution to the dilemma can be found in a Declaration that was added to the Final Act of the Intergovernmental Conference where the Single Act was adopted, which states that the provisions of Article 130r, paragraph 5, 'do not affect the principles resulting from the judgement handed down by the Court of Justice in the ERTA case'. From this we can deduce that the ERTA doctrine of implied external competence is applicable to environmental policy. Obversely, this would mean that the other relevant decisions of the Court in this matter, most notably the *Kramer* case and Opinion 1/76, do not apply to environmental policy. External powers could then be legitimately based on an existing internal measure, excluding concurrent powers of the Member States. They could not, however, be deduced from the existence of the general competence to adopt internal measures concerning a certain subject matter. The Court has not yet had occasion to clarify the situation. It is doubtful that the Court would limit itself to applying the ERTA doctrine to international environmental agreements without reference to the other aspects of the jurisprudence it developed about external relations competences. For the moment we can observe that in practice the Community assumes exclusive powers only concerning matters for which internal rules have been adopted. For all other issues the Community participates in international negotiations alongside the Member States (see Chapter 16). Most international environmental agreements are so-called mixed agreements, signed by the Community and by the Member States (Nollkaemper, 1987, p70ff; Haigh, 1991, p173).

Towards 'Diversified Integration': The Freedom to be Cleaner than the Rest

The judgement of the Court in the Danish bottle case (Case 302/86, *Commission vs Denmark*, ECR, 1988, p4627) is one in a series of decisions about the scope of admissible exceptions to the general prohibition of quantitative import restrictions and all measures having equivalent effect in the Community (Article 30 of the Treaty). The Treaty itself lists a number of acceptable reasons, including public morality, public security, public health and the protection of national monuments (Article 36). Member states have extensively tried to exploit these categories of exceptions to try and convince the Court of the necessity to apply a national rule that created an obstacle to free trade. The argument of consumer protection, for instance, was used on a number of occasions, and the case law thus developed served as a precedent for the first decision about environmental protection as a legitimate exception.

French Liqueur, Belgian Margarine and German Beer

The first relevant case law of the Court dates back to 1979, when the Court issued its Cassis de Dijon decision (Case 120/78, *Rewe-Zentral AG vs Bundes-*

monopolverwaltung fur Branntwein, ECR, 1979, p649). Germany had banned the import of the French liqueur Cassis de Dijon on the grounds that its alcohol content, 15–20 per cent, did not satisfy the German requirements for the import of spirits contained in the Law on the Monopoly in Spirits of 1922, which required a minimum wine-spirit content of 32 per cent. The Court observed dryly that the fixing of a minimum wine-spirits content for potable spirits could certainly not be justified by reasons related to human health, as the German government had maintained, and obliged Germany to adjust its national legislation in order to allow for the marketing of the French liqueur. A similar decision was issued in 1982, when the Court ruled that Belgian legislation concerning the shape of the packaging of margarine constituted an obstacle to free trade unwarranted by the need to protect or inform the consumer (Case 261/81, *Walter Rau Lebensmittelwerke* vs *De Smedt PvbA,* ECR, 1982, p3961).

Two years later, the Commission brought an action against Germany for its restrictive legislation on the quality of imported beer. German legislation prohibited any additives in beer. The Commission observed that this resulted in limited imports of beer into Germany while favouring the export of German beer. The German government emphasized that its legislation, referred to as the 'Reinheitsgebot', the purity requirement, dating back to 1516, was a measure to protect public health, and was thus acceptable as a legitimate exemption from the prohibition of Article 30. The Commission maintained that this was merely a pretext, since additives were allowed in Germany in other products. In its judgement (Case 178/84, *Commission* vs *Germany,* ECR, 1987, p1227), the Court repeated the arguments it had put forward in the two cases mentioned above, also referred to as the 'Cassis de Dijon formula':

> *In the absence of common rules relating to the marketing of the products concerned, obstacles to free movement within the Community resulting from disparities between the national laws must be accepted in so far as such rules, applicable to domestic and to imported products without distinction, may be recognized as being necessary in order to satisfy mandatory requirements relating inter alia to consumer protection. It is also necessary for such rules to be proportionate to the aim in view. If a Member State has a choice between various measures to attain the same objective it should choose the means which least restricts the free movement of goods.*
> (ECR, 1987, p1270)

It was with respect to the last requirement that the Court deemed the German legislation excessive. An absolute prohibition on additives was not necessary, according to the Court, since it was 'contrary to the principle of proportionality' (idem, p1276).

Recapitulating, we can say that the Court has been reluctant in recognizing consumer protection as a legitimate argument to justify the application of national rules that create obstacles to intra-Community trade.

The Danish Bottle Case

In view of the Court's restrictive interpretation of consumer protection as a ground to justify quantitative import restrictions, the Commission must have been quite

certain of its case when it filed suit against Denmark for the packaging requirements it had issued for beer and soft drinks. It was certainly a test case, and the
Commission made it clear that it was of great importance to establish:

> *whether and to what extent the concern to protect the environment has precedence*
> *over the principle of a common market without frontiers since there is a risk that*
> *Member States may in future take refuge behind ecological arguments to avoid*
> *opening their markets to beer as they are required to do by the case-law of the Court*
> (ECR, 1988, p4611).

In Denmark, legislation had been enacted requiring that beer and soft drinks be
marketed in reusable containers approved by the National Agency for the Protection of the Environment. A limited number of 23 containers had so far been
admitted. The number was kept small since that was the only way to make sure
that each container would be taken back by every retailer of beverages, irrespective of the place where the product had been purchased. This, in turn, greatly
enhanced the effectiveness of the mandatory system, ensuring a return rate of
99 per cent, a figure that could never be reached with any other deposit-and-
return system. Beverages in non-approved containers were allowed up to a yearly
quantity of 3000 hectolitres per producer, provided that a deposit-and-return
system was established by the producer. Non-approved containers would only
be taken back by the retailer who sold the beverages. No form of metal container was allowed. The rationale behind the system, according to the Danish
government, was to protect the environment and to conserve resources and
energy as well as to reduce the amount of waste.

Allegedly, the Danish requirements made it very difficult to import beer
and soft drinks into Denmark and the Commission questioned whether this
trade barrier was justified on the grounds put forward by the defendant. The
Commission did not question the general principle that environmental protection was one of the Community's essential objectives and, as such, one of the
mandatory requirements recognized by Community law that could justify certain
import restrictions. The Commission questioned the sincerity of Denmark's
ecological concerns, just as it had challenged Germany's concern for consumer
protection in the case concerning beer additives, noting that the severe packaging requirements only applied to beer and soft drinks and not to other products
like milk and wine which were not subject to competition between foreign and
domestic producers. If Germany was not allowed to invoke its 'Reinheitsgebot'
to justify import restrictions on beer, then Denmark could not hide behind
mandatory recycling requirements that had a similar effect. The Advocate General supported the Commission's claim and expressed the opinion that the
judgement of the Court had to be similar to the judgement in Case 178/84:
the Danish requirements were disproportionate in view of their aim (ECR,
1988, pp4619–26). But the Court took a more subtle stance. First of all, the
Court referred to the Cassis de Dijon formula: obstacles to the free movement of
goods within the Community must be accepted in so far as 1) no common rules
relating to the marketing of the products in question exist, 2) the national rule
in question applies equally to domestic and imported products and 3) the rule is

necessary to satisfy mandatory requirements of Community law. The national rules must, moreover, be proportionate to the aim in view. Then the Court repeated its decision in Case 240/83: environmental protection is one of the Community's essential objectives which may as such justify certain limitations of the principle of the free movement of goods. Thus the Court recognized that environmental protection is one of the mandatory requirements which may limit the application of Article 30 of the Treaty and extended the Cassis de Dijon doctrine to include environmental protection. This was the first important pronouncement in the case.

The Court then went on to interpret the proportionality of the Danish measures in view of the alleged aim of environmental protection. In full support of the Danish arguments, the Court stated simply that the establishment of an obligatory deposit-and-return system with a limited number of containers was indispensable to ensure the reuse of containers and therefore necessary to achieve the aim. Only one aspect of the rules was disproportionate, according to the Court, namely the fact that a maximum marketing quota of 3000 hectolitres was established for beverages sold in non-approved containers in addition to the requirement that the producer set up a deposit-and-return system for the containers. This aspect of the Danish rules was considered in violation of Article 30 of the Treaty.

Determining where to draw the line between disproportionate and proportionate measures is hardly a matter of juridical interpretation. It is a subjective assessment of advantages and disadvantages and an allocation of responsibilities. In this case, the Court tried to strike a balance between the economic interests of the Community and the increasing concern for environmental values. The decision shows that the Internal Market does not preclude differences between environmental standards in the Member States. From an environmental point of view this is an important achievement. The situation is still more complex if Community measures on the same topic exist. In that case the freedom of the Member State to adopt divergent national standards depends on the legal basis that was chosen for the Community rule (see above). This is one of the topics that will certainly be brought before the Court in the near future.

Different Procedures to Adopt Environmental Measures

As we have seen, since the coming into force of the Single European Act, two different procedures exist to adopt environmental measures. The Single Act introduced the so-called *Cooperation* procedure which grants the Parliament the power to put forward amendments to proposed measures. This procedure applies to all measures related to the Internal Market that are adopted by the Council with qualified majority. Instead, if a measure is based on Article 130s, the Council must decide unanimously, after *Consultation* of the Parliament. In the consultation procedure, the opinion of the Parliament does not have any binding effect. In both cases proposals must come from the Commission since in the legislative system of the Community, the Commission has the exclusive right of initiative.

The ambiguous system thus created left a major question unanswered: how to determine when an environmental measure has to be adopted on the basis of Article 100a as part of the Internal Market programme and when a measure should be based on Article 130s. The Court addressed this question in a case in which the Commission, the Parliament and the Council disagreed about the legal basis of an environmental directive. Before looking at the Court decision itself, we will briefly examine the role of the Parliament in the different procedures. A final section describes the situation that will arise when the Maastricht Treaty on European Union comes into force.

The Role of the European Parliament

The cooperation procedure introduced by the Single European Act enlarged the role of the Parliament in the Community legislative process. Although Parliaments powers are still limited and the democratic content of Community decisions remains questionable, a slight increase in influence was achieved (see Chapter 8). The cooperation procedure basically adds a phase to the procedure followed in the case of consultation. When the Commission issues a proposal, the proposal is first sent to the Parliament for its opinion. The Commission is free to adjust the proposal to the changes suggested by the Parliament. The proposal and the Parliament's opinion are then forwarded to the Council. If the procedure of Article 130 is followed, the Council at this point takes a final decision and the proposal is adopted if the Council reaches unanimity. In the case of the co-operation procedure, however, the Council adopts a common position about the proposal. The common position is returned to the Parliament. If the Parliament agrees with the common position, the Council can adopt the proposed action by qualified majority. If the Parliament rejects the common position, the Council can adopt the action only by unanimity. If the Parliament proposes amendments, these are reviewed by the Commission who sends a revised proposal to the Council. At this stage the Council can adopt the second Commission proposal by qualified majority. If the Council wants to make any further changes these have to be adopted by unanimity. The main effect of the second phase is that the Parliament's opinion can force the Council to decide unanimously which sometimes means that a decision actually gets blocked. Another effect of the enlarged procedure is that Parliament is kept better informed of the considerations and arguments of the Council. Communication between the institutions is therefore intensified.

Commission and Parliament Versus Council: Majority Versus Unanimity Voting

A little more than a year after the coming into force of the Single European Act, the first dispute arose between the Council and the Commission about the different procedures envisaged to adopt environmental measures. In June 1991, the Court passed its first judgement about the issue (Case 300/89, *Commission* vs *Council,* ECR, 1991, pp1–2867).[7] The Commission, supported by the European Parliament, asked for the annulment of Directive 89/428/EEC of 21 June 1989 about the harmonization of programmes to reduce waste from the titanium di-oxide industry (OJ L No 201/56). Contrary to the Commission's proposal, the directive had been adopted unanimously by the Council on the basis of Article 130s. The Commission had suggested Article 100a as the basis for the directive since its principal objective, its 'centre of gravity', according to the Commis-sion, was to improve the conditions of competition in the titanium dioxide in-dustry, which made it clearly an Internal Market measure.

In its judgement, the Court stressed that the legal basis of a proposed mea-sure has to be chosen according to objective criteria like the aim and the con-tent of the measure (ECR, 1991, pI–2898). The aim and the content of the directive under scrutiny, however, did not result in a clear answer since the directive is as much related to environmental protection as it is related to the Internal Market (idem, pI–2898/2899). A dual legal basis was excluded by the Court, arguing that the two Articles in question require different and incompat-ible decision-making procedures. If Articles 100a and 130s were to be applied simultaneously, this would force the Council to decide unanimously. This, in turn, would exclude the cooperation procedure and limit the role of the Euro-pean Parliament In that context the Court recalled the importance of the stronger role of the Parliament emphasizing that the cooperation procedure was added to the Treaty:

> to strengthen the participation of the European Parliament in the legislative process
> of the Community. ... This participation is the reflection, at the Community level,
> of a fundamental democratic principle, by which the people participate in the exercise
> of power through the intermediary of a representative assembly (idem, pI–2900).

Besides the emphasis placed on the role of the European Parliament, three ele-ments can be discerned in the Courts decision to annul the directive. First of all, the Court argued that the integration principle implies that measures to protect the environment do not always have to be adopted on the basis of Arti-cle 130s (idem, pI–2901). Second, the Court referred to its early judgements in the cases against Italy, to recall that the harmonization of national environmen-tal measures is often necessary to prevent the distortion of competition. This type of harmonization measure thus contributes to the establishment of the In-ternal Market and falls within the scope of Article 100a. Finally, the Court pointed to the fact that Article 100a itself requires that harmonization measures concerning environmental protection take as a base a high level of protection. This provision is a guarantee, according to the Court, that environmental ob-jectives can be effectively pursued on the basis of Article 100a.

The consequences of the decision are rather complex. From now on, most environmental measures are likely to be based on Article 100a, which makes environmental protection more closely related to the Internal Market policy of the Community. This is a realistic solution in view of the fact that the two pol-icy fields need to be integrated. The Court's favourable attitude towards the co-operation procedure and the role played by the European Parliament is certainly positive in view of the democratic content of Community legislation. The poten-tial danger of the decision concerns the fact that majority decisions have been shown to facilitate the adoption of low standards. Member States are, moreover, prohibited from adopting more stringent national standards, an option they have if a Community rule is adopted on the basis of Article 130s. Until now there is little reason to have much confidence in the requirement that proposed harmonization measures take as a base a high level of protection. The conclusion, then, must be that the Court's judgement was primarily inspired by considerations of integration; not the integration of environmental requirements into other Community policies, but the integration of the European market, a Community objective that continues to have priority over environmental protection.

Conclusions

It would be too simple to characterize the case law of the Court concerning Community environmental policy as merely pro-integrationist. The cases described above show a more complex picture/a line of reasoning in which a twofold orientation can be discerned. Besides elements of traditional judicial activism in favour of market integration, we also notice an increasing concern for the protection of the environment in Europe.

A strong element of market integration was present in the first environmental cases (Cases 91 and 92/79, *Commission* vs *Italy,* ECR, 1980, p1099 and p1115) in which the Court recognized environmental measures to the extent that they harmonized national provisions which would otherwise create trade barriers and distort competition. Two years later, the Court slightly adjusted this reasoning by adding that environmental measures may also be necessary to achieve one of the aims of the Community (Cases 68–73/81, *Commission* vs *Belgium,* ECR, p153ff), thus establishing a broader legal basis for Community action. In the preliminary judgement issued in 1985 (Case 240/83, *Procureur de la Republique* vs *l'Association de Défense des Bruleurs d'Huiles Usagées,* ECR, 1985, p531), the Court started to challenge its own concern for market integration by first of all stating that environmental protection was in itself one of the Community's essential objectives and second, upholding the contested French measures even though they created obstacles to trade in the field of the treatment and disposal of used oils. The argument is a matter of simple deduction: environmental protection is a Community objective, all Community objectives are equal and may pose limits to each other's application, environmental protection may therefore pose limits to the application of other Community objectives. The same construction was applied again in the Danish bottle case with respect to intra-Community trade. The Court upheld Danish packaging requirements even though they did, in fact, create an obstacle to the import of beer and soft drinks into Denmark. The Court accepted the Danish argument that the requirements were justified by reasons of environmental protection and ruled that, as one of the Community's essential objectives, environmental protection was one of the mandatory requirements of Community law which may limit the scope of the general prohibition of quantitative import restrictions of Article 30 of the Treaty.

It is beyond doubt that the objectives of market integration and environmental protection are at times hard to reconcile. In this respect it is important to note that the Court in its most recent case law seems to have given priority to the imperative of market integration. Faced with the question of which legal basis must be chosen for environmental measures, the Court insisted on linking environmental protection closely to the Internal Market programme (Case 300/89, *Commission* vs *Council,* ECR, 1991). Although the Court stressed in its judgement that the provision contained in Article 100a, paragraph 3 – that all Commission proposals must take as a base a high level of protection – should function as a guarantee, the fear remains that the harmonization measures adopted by the Community will force several Member States to lower their national standards.

It seems to us, however, that the best guarantee for a high level of environmental protection, is the freedom for Member States to adopt their own national measures, a freedom that does not exist if a Community measure is adopted on the basis of Article 100a. If most environmental measures are based on Article 100a, this may indeed hamper the progressive development of environmental protection in Europe.

So far, the Court has not passed any judgements about the extent to which national measures may diverge from Community rules. This is likely to be one of the first issues which the Court will address in its future case law. Once the Court discovers that the guarantee contained within Article 100a does not always lead to the desired effect, the Court might very well review its decision in Case 300/89 and rule that more environmental measures must be based on Article 130s, thus leaving Member States the freedom to adopt more stringent national rules. Such a revirement in the jurisprudence of the Court is all the more needed when one realizes that the different realities existing in Member States require decentralized environmental action. If the Court wants to continue to support environmental protection it will then have to elaborate the doctrine of 'diversified integration', the basic tenets of which were set forth in the Danish bottle case.

Notes

1. The special features of Community law vis-à-vis national law were established by the Court in a series of cases, the most important of which are: Case 26/62, *Van Gend en Loos* vs *Nederlandse administratie der belastingen,* ECR 1963; Case 6/64, *Costa* vs *ENEL,* ECR 1964; Case 106/77, *Amministrazione delle Finanze dello Stato* vs *Simmenthal SpA,* ECR 1978. Other relevant case law is cited in Kapteyn and Verloren van Themaat, 1989, p38ff. See also Hartley, 1988, p219ff.
2. The most important cases are: Case 230/81, *Luxembourg* vs *European Parliament,* ECR, 1983; Case 108/83, *Luxembourg* vs *European Parliament,* ECR, 1984; Case 294/83, *Parti Ecoligiste Les Verts'* vs *European Parliament,* ECR, 1986; 34/86, *Council* vs *European Parliament,* ECR, 1986.

3. The Parliament did so once, in a famous case regarding the (lack of a) Community transport policy: Case 13/83, *European Parliament* vs *Council*, ECR, 1985. For a detailed discussion of the peculiar position of the Parliament in both procedures, see Barnard, 1987; Hartley, 1988, pp77–8, 374–5; Kapteyn and Verloren van Themaat, 1989, pp143–5 and pp281–90.

4. It is not possible here to analyse these complex processes in any detail; I refer to the overview article by Stein (1991) and the literature cited there for further reading. See also Kapteyn and Verloren van Themaat, 1989, pp21–8 and Hartley, 1988, pp153–76.

5. Council Directive No.73/404/EEC of 22 November 1973 on the approximation of the laws of the Member States relating to detergents (OJ L No.347/51) and Directive No.75/716/EEC of 24 November 1975 on the approximation of the laws of the Member States relating to the sulphur content of certain liquid fuels (OJ L No.307/22).

6. The following directives had not been implemented: Directive No.75/439/EEC of 16 June 1975 on the disposal of waste oils (OJ L No.194/23); Directive No.75/440/EEC of 16 June 1975 concerning the quality required of surface water intended for the abstraction of drinking water in the Member States (OJ L No.194/26); Directive No.75/442/EEC of 15 July 1975 on waste (OJ L No 194/39); Directive No.76/160/EEC of 8 December 1975 concerning the quality of bathing water (OJ L No.31/1); Directive No.76/403/EEC of 6 April 1976 on the disposal of polychlorinated biphenyls and polychlorinated terphenyls (OJ L No.108/41); Directive No.78/176/EEC of 20 February 1978 on waste from the titanium dioxide industry (OJ L No.54/19). See the Opinion of the Advocate General (ECR, 1982, p159) and Koppen (1988) for a description of the cases.

7. References to the titanium dioxide case apply to the French documents, because the English versions had not been published at the time of writing.

References

Barnard, J. (1987) 'The European Parliament and Article 173 of the EEC Treaty', EUI Working Paper No.87/290, Florence: European University Institute.

Cappelletti, M. (1987) 'Is the European Court of Justice "Running Wild"'?, *European Law Review*, Vol.12, pp3–17.

Clapham, A. (1991) *Human Rights and the European Community: A Critical Overview*, Baden-Baden: Nomos Verlag.

Dauses, M. A. (1985) 'The Protection of Fundamental Rights in the Community Legal Order', *European Law Review*, Vol.10, pp398–419.

EC Commission DG VII (1992) *Green Paper on Transport and Environment*, COM (92) final.

EC Commission DG XI (1991) *Implementation of Community Law in the Field of Environmental Protection*, COM (91) 321 final.

Haigh, N. (1991) 'The European Community and International Environmental Policy', *International Environmental Affairs*, Vol.3, pp163–80.

Hartley, T. C. (1988) *The Foundations of European Community Law* (2nd edn), Oxford: Clarendon Press.

Kapteyn, P. J. G. and Verloren van Themaat, P. (1989) *Introduction to the Law of the European Communities: After the Coming into Force of the Single European Act* (2nd edn by Gormley, L. W. (ed)), Kluwer Law and Taxation Publishers: Deventer.

Koppen, I. J. (1988) *The European Community's Environment Policy: From the Summit in Paris,* 1972, *to the Single European Act,* 1937, EUI Working Paper 88/328, Florence: European University Institute.

Krämer, L. (1987) 'The Single European Act and Environmental Protection: Reflections on Several New Provisions in Community Law', *Common Market Law Review*, Vol.4, pp659–88.

Nollkaemper, A. (1987) 'The European Community and International Environmental Cooperation: Legal Aspects of External Community Powers', *Legal Issues of European Integration,* Vol.2, pp55–91.

Rasmussen, H. (1986) *On Law and Policy in the European Court of Justice: A Comparative Study in Judicial Policymaking,* Dordrecht: Martinus Nijhoff Publishers.

Stein, E. (1991) 'External Relations of the European Community: Structure and Process', *Collected Courses of the Academy of European Law*, Vol.1, pp115–68.

Weiler, J. H. H. (1986) 'Eurocracy and Distrust: Some Questions Concerning the Role of the European Court of Justice in the Protection of Fundamental Human Rights Within the Legal Order of the European Communities', *Washington Law Review*, Vol.61, pp1103–42.

Weiler, J. H. H. (1987) 'The Court of Justice on Trial', *Common Market Law Review*, Vol.24, pp555–89.

8

'Predestined to Save the Earth': The Environment Committee of the European Parliament

David Judge

That the influence of the European Parliament (EP) in the decision-making process of the EU has increased in recent years is generally acknowledged, but the exact extent of that increase remains the subject of significant controversy. This chapter examines the contribution of one part of the EP – the Environment Committee – to one part of EU policy – environment policy.

Legislative Role: Formal Powers and Informal Processes

It is often asserted that the EP's legislative role in relation to environmental policy began with the Single European Act (SEA), and moreover that this role is essentially negative as conceptualized in the 'co-operation' procedure. Such assertions are inaccurate on both counts: first, the EP performed a 'legislative' role in environmental policy *before* 1987, a role that was *enhanced* and not initiated by the SEA; and, second, the EP performed a positive legislative role of initiation which again predated the SEA.

Initiation of Legislation

Under Article 155 of the Treaty of Rome the Commission alone is empowered to formulate recommendations for legislative action. In the 1957 Treaty it was not envisaged that the 'Assembly' would have anything other than consultative status (Lodge, 1989, p59). Nonetheless, and especially since the introduction of direct elections to the EP in 1979, Members of the European Parliament (MEPs) came to adopt procedures which enabled them to forward draft proposals for legislation to the Commission.[1] Any MEP may table a short, 200-word, motion for resolution on any matter falling within the sphere of EC competences. These resolutions are then referred to the appropriate EP committee for consideration whether or not to produce a report or an opinion. Only a minority of individual resolutions become the subject of a committee report and an even smaller number become the basis of 'Rule 63' reports proposing legislation. In addition, committees themselves may independently seek to draw up a report on an particular issue. In these circumstances the committee concerned must seek authorization from the Bureau of the parliament to draw up an 'own-initiative' report.[2] The first point of significance therefore is that, although there is no mention in the treaties of an EP involvement at the initiation stage of EC legislation, the EP has established procedures to insert its ideas into the formulation stage of legislation. The second point is that, even before the SEA, 'own-initiative' reports constituted 'a major source of Community initiatives' (HL 226, 1985, p167). And the third point of significance is that the Environment Committee is exceptional among the major 'legislative' EP committees in continuing to produce a considerable flow of 'own-initiative' reports (Jacobs and Corbett, 1990, p106).[3] Indeed, the Environment Committee has had several notable successes in prompting the Commission into legislative action. Again, it is important to make the point that several of these successes *pre-date* the SEA. Thus, before 1987, initiatives taken within the EP contributed to the genesis of directives on major industrial hazards (82/501/EEC), the lead content in petrol (82/884/EEC), the importation of seal pup skins (83/129/EEC), and transfrontier shipment of waste (84/631/EEC). Since 1987 the Environment Committee has also been able to claim 'parentage' of the proposals, among others, on a Financial Instrument for the Environment (LIFE) (COM (91) 0028 final; for details of inception (PE 146.246/fin., 31 July 1991, pp25–9)), and on minimum standards for keeping animals in zoos (COM (91) 0177 final).

Agenda-setting

In addition to overtly 'legislative' initiatives the EP has used 'own-initiative' and 'Rule 63' reports to 'bring up a new issue on the policy agenda, to give a view on a Commission Communication on which Parliament has not been formally consulted' (Jacobs and Corbett, 1990: 106). Indeed, the Environment Committee has consistently sought to involve itself at the *pro-legislative* stage through a conscious strategy of agenda setting. There are several dimensions to this strategy. One is to use 'Rule 63' reports to encourage action on the part of the Commission. On many occasions the Commission might already be considering such action, and so the intention of the committee is either to accelerate this process, and so advance the issue up the Commission's overcrowded agenda, or to focus the Commission's attention upon an issue and so determine the priorities and relative policy-weighting of the Commission.

Indeed, since 1989 it is apparent from the 'Rule 63' reports emanating from the Environment Committee that it, or its presidency at least, has a clear vision of what the priorities of the Commission should be in the early 1990s. Aware, for example, that the Commission was formulating proposals on waste management, the Environment Committee initiated its own investigation into the subject (PE 144.1351/fin., December 1990) with the intention of 'guiding' the Commission's own internal deliberations. The influence of the Committee's report is partially observable in the Commission's eventual proposals on the incineration of hazardous waste (COM (92) 9 final, 19 March 1992) and on landfill of waste (COM (91) 102 final, 23 January 1992). Similarly, since 1989, the Committee has launched a series of its own reports on the issues of Economic and Fiscal Instruments (PE 145.367/fin., 13 May 1991), eco-labelling (PE 152.137/fin., 5 November 1991), and the implementation of EC environmental law (PE 152.144, 28 August 1991). Clearly, in this exercise the Environment Committee has been engaged in a pro-active strategy of articulating its own policy concerns to the Commission, rather than simply waiting to react to formal Commission proposals as part of the consultation process (see below). Equally clearly it is difficult, if not impossible, to assess the direct influence of this strategy upon the final Commission proposals, and, indeed, the Committee itself would probably claim no more than that it seeks to get the voice of the EP heard as part of the chorus of interests considered by the Commission at the formative stage of legislation.

There are, however, notable examples where EP initiatives are openly acknowledged by DG XI itself as prompting action or changing its own priorities. Perhaps the clearest, and most publicly acknowledged, example is the genesis of the Commission's *Green Paper on the Urban Environment* (EUR 12902 EN, 1990). In the preface to the *Green Paper* Commissioner Ripa Di Meana openly records that the paper is 'a practical response to the resolution tabled in December 1988 by a Member of the European Parliament, Mr Ken Collins, urging that the problems facing the urban environment be studied in greater detail' (EUR 12902 EN, 1990, p5). Moreover, the DG XI official responsible for drafting the paper was in no doubt as to the 'importance of the Collin's report', and was willing to attribute to the EP 'a considerable share of responsibility' (alongside Ripa di Meana's own commitment to putting urban issues on the environmental agenda) for the introduction of the *Green Paper* (interview, Brussels, 20 May 1992). As the Commission official went on to state: 'the Commission could have easily ignored the Collin's report, but chose not to do so. It is a good example of the coming together of interests within two institutions to advance policy'.

A less publicly documented recent example of EP influence over the Commission's pro-legislative agenda concerns the Environment Committee's reports on tropical rainforests (PE 139.166/fin., 5 July 1990). A member of the Directorate of DG XI noted in interview (Brussels, 19 May 1992) that:

> *The EP has been pressing very hard for a ban on all tropical hardwoods. As a result, it is true to say that thinking within the Council and Commission has developed on tropical forests. There is no Commission legislation yet, but the EP has been in early pushing this item up the agenda.*

The problem in assessing the precise impact of the EP's agenda-setting and initiation roles is that they are largely unquantifiable.[4] As such they are often overlooked in standard texts on, and 'guides' to, the EC decision-making process (see, for example, Budd and Jones, 1990 and de Rouffignac, 1991, which make no mention of the EP's informal contributions to the initiation stage of legislation). Nonetheless, as more perspicacious commentators have observed 'astute interpretation of the Treaty and its own rules allowed the EP to find, for itself, a right of legislative initiative' (Lodge, 1989, p66), and the 'Commission pays a great deal of attention to the views of the Parliament in its preparation of draft legislation' (Pinder, 1991, p37).

Indeed, the transmission of information between Commission and EP at the pro-legislative stage is not simply a one-way process. Nugent (1991, p256) points out that Commission officials may informally 'sound out' EP committees on draft legislation. This process has to remain informal because as one senior member of the Directorate-General of DG XI commented:

> *You have to remember that there is an institutional relationship: the Commission proposes, the Council accepts and the EP adopts. In which case there cannot be formal consultation with the EP until the Commission announces its proposal. National parliaments are already critical of the Commission for not consulting them; it we don't talk to the EP then we shouldn't talk to national parliaments* (interview, Brussels, 20 May 1992).

Another DG XI senior official was even willing to acknowledge informal 'soundings' at the pro-legislative stage and stated categorically that, 'The Commission does not want to get involved with the EP at the preparatory stage of legislation' (interview, 19 May 1992). Nonetheless, the same official held the personal belief that there was a case for providing the chairman of the Environment Committee with a copy of draft proposals circulated by the Commission.

The Committee's chairman understood the Commission's reluctance to include the EP in the formal process of consultation. Indeed, he argued that the Committee itself did not wish to be a part of this process as it would 'reduce Parliament's pre-legislative contribution to that of merely another lobby'. Instead, what the committee sought to maintain was informal contact whereby 'the Commission was well aware of what was likely to be acceptable to Parliament. So that when the Commission sought the opinion of Parliament it was already running with the tide' (interview, Brussels, 21 May 1992).

Consultation, Conciliation and Co-operation

Consultation

The founding treaties of the EC allowed for the involvement of the EP in the legislative process only to the extent that the Council was required to consult Parliament on Commission proposals (relating to 33 Treaty articles) before their adoption. As is well documented (Jacobs and Corbett, 1990, pp162–6; Lodge, 1989, pp65–6; Nugent, 1991, pp130–31) the EP successfully maximized the significance of the consultation procedure, both formally and informally. Informally, in response to pressure from the EP, the Council in successive steps in the 1960s and 1970s committed itself to consulting Parliament on all important matters whether or not required to do so by the treaties. In addition, by the early 1970s the Council had agreed, when adopting community legislation that departed from an EP opinion, to inform Parliament of its reasons for doing so.

Formally, the right of the EP to be consulted in designated areas was upheld by the Court of Justice's ruling on the celebrated 'isoglucose' case in 1980 (Kirchner and Williams, 1983). This ruling made it clear that the Council of Ministers could not adopt a Commission proposal without awaiting the EP's opinion. In 1981, in the wake of the 'isoglucose' ruling, Parliament amended its procedures to enable its committees to postpone a vote on a Commission proposal until the Commission had taken a position on Parliament's amendments. Under the present rule 40 (EP Rules of Procedure, 1992) a committee is enabled to postpone a vote if the Commission does not adopt all of Parliament's amendments. The significance of this rule is that without a positive vote for a motion for resolution an opinion of Parliament cannot be expressed. In turn, in the absence of an opinion the Council cannot act upon a Commission proposal and so the legislative process stalls on that particular issue. As the chairman of the Environment Committee noted in his evidence to the House of Lords' Select Committee on the European Communities (HL 226, 1985, p168) this rule 'enables the EP to move beyond a formal right to be consulted and propels Parliament into something more akin to a bargaining relationship'. The Commission rapidly recognized the potential of this delaying power, so making it more receptive to EP views and more willing to engage in a dialogue with the relevant parliamentary committee to avert later delay (Lodge, 1989, p64) (also see below).

Conciliation

A further formal extension of the EP's contribution to the legislative process has been the development of the 'conciliation procedure' between the Council and Parliament. The stated aim of the procedure is to reach 'an agreement between the EP and the Council' on 'acts of general application which have appreciable financial implications' (Joint Declaration of EP, Council and Commission, 1975). However, the deficiencies of the procedure were illustrated in 1985 when the Environment Committee sought to activate the conciliation procedure in response to the EP's opinion on the car exhaust emissions proposal. The chairman and rapporteur of the Committee met with the President of the Council and expressed the Committee's disquiet over the Council's decision on this proposal. As the Committee's chairman noted at the time: 'At that meeting the President did not concede the principle that the Committee should be informed of the grounds for Council's decision nor that Parliament had the right to a conciliation procedure on general legislative matters' (HL 226, 1985, p171). If anything, since 1985, the position has worsened with the increased propensity of the Council to adopt resolutions on the basis of papers presented by the Council presidency or on the basis of Communications from the Commission, upon neither of which is the EP formally consulted. In February 1991 the Environment Committee unanimously requested the renegotiation of the 1975 joint declaration. This specific request met with no direct positive response, though it is notable that the Maastricht Treaty embodies, in Article 189b, a new co-decision procedure which incorporates conciliation between Council and Parliament (see Chapter 3).

Co-operation

Concern with the restricted formal legislative powers of the EP, and the Council's often cavalier attitude even to those powers, was one of the stimuli for the EP's draft Treaty on European union and subsequently for the SEA itself (Pinder, 1991, p37). The SEA introduced a new 'co-operation' procedure for ten articles of the EEC Treaty dealing with harmonization measures necessary for the completion of the single market, regional fund decisions, some social policy matters and specific research programmes. In the case of environmental legislation the SEA distinguishes between measures introduced under Article 130s of the new Title VII on the environment, and those introduced under Article 100a (see Chapter 2). The former are subject to the established consultation procedure, where the Commission proposal is considered by the EP in a single reading in which amendments are voted upon and an opinion formally delivered (with recourse if necessary to the de facto delaying powers noted above). Measures dealing with the harmonization of environmental standards necessary for the completion of the internal market under Article 100a are subject however to the new co-operation procedure.

Given the different 'legal base' available to the Commission in the introduction of environmental proposals under the SEA, the EP has been anxious to ensure that Article 100a is used wherever possible. As Jacobs and Corbett (1990, p170) note 'the Commission has usually been willing to co-operate closely with the Parliament on this'. Indeed, since 1989, of the 29 environmental directives proposed by the Commission, 15 have been based on Article 100a. Hence the Commission has already demonstrated its willingness to invoke the co-operation procedure on major environmental proposals. The quantitative significance of the co-operation procedure in both the volume of environmental and related public health and consumer legislation and in the work of the Environment Committee itself can be gauged from Table 8.1.

The Environment Committee alone accounted for 27 per cent of co-operation procedures up to November 1991, and in combination with the Energy, Economic and Legal Affairs Committees accounted for 90 per cent of the total.

Table 8.1 *Total co-operation procedures begun by the EP by Committee (July 1987–November 1991)*

Environment	80
Energy	72
Economic Affairs	66
Legal Affairs	52
Social Affairs	11
Other Committees	18
Total	299

Source: EP Dossiers d'études et documentation, Series 4-A. Jan. 1992

The fact that the majority of environmental proposals have been adopted under Article 100a has not prevented the Environment Committee from pressing the Commission for still further use of the cooperation procedure. One of the first and most dramatic disagreements between the Commission and the EP arose out of the Environment Committee's insistence that the regulation (3954/87) laying down maximum permitted radioactivity levels for foodstuffs after Chernobyl should come under Article 100a. The Commission chose instead to use Article 31 of the Euratom Treaty which required only consultation with the EP. In response the Committee sought to amend the legal base. When the Commission refused to accept this amendment, the Committee then delayed giving its opinion. And at the December 1987 Plenary session the EP finally rejected the Commission's proposal. The Council then acted on the basis of the Commission proposal and Parliament responded by taking the Council to the Court of Justice on the grounds of an incorrect legal base (Corbett, 1989, pp361–2; Jacobs and Corbett, 1990, p172). The outcome was that in October 1991 the Court ruled that the contested regulation was correctly based on Article 31 of the Euratom Treaty. In the interpretation of the EP's Directorate General for Committees (PE 200.380, 22 March 1992) this simply means that: 'This judgement should not however be regarded as limiting of the scope of Article 100a except in respect of health protection measures against radioactive contamination'.

Despite the occasional public disputes between the EP and the Commission over the appropriate legal base to be adopted (and the innumerable informal disputes – as one senior Commission official commented 'one thing you can be sure of is that the Environment Committee wants 100a as many times as is possible'), nevertheless, the EP has consistently supported the Commission in its own battles with the Council over the legal base of proposals. This was demonstrated in 1991 when the Commission, supported by the EP, took the Council to the European Court for its adoption of Directive 89/428/EEC on pollution reduction measures in the titanium dioxide industry. The Commission had proposed Article 100a as the legal base for the directive on the grounds that its proposal was essentially concerned with the harmonization of pollution control standards. The Council changed the legal base to Article 130s maintaining that the main aim of the measure was 'environmental' in that it sought to eliminate pollution (PE 200.380, 25 March 1992; Wilkinson, 1992, pp10–11).

In June 1991 the Court ruled in favour of the Commission pointing out that under the SEA the Commission was obliged under Article 100a to take as its basis a high level of environmental protection when proposing measures for approximating the laws of Member States. Equally Article 130r stated that environmental protection should be a component of the Community's other policies. In which case the court ruled that the removal of market distortions and the goals of environmental protection could not be separated in this case (the Court talks of *la double finalité*). The decision has been greeted by one commentator at least as a 'benchmark ruling' (Wilkinson, 1992, p11), and the expectation is that 'the Commission (will) make a generous interpretation of the applicability of Article 100a'. Nonetheless, disputes between the Commission and Council over the appropriate legal base still continue. Thus, in mid-1992, the two institutions disputed the legal base of the proposal for a regulation on the supervision and control of shipments of waste (Corn (90) 0415 final). The EP was consulted under Article 100a, the Environment Committee produced a report in November 1991 (PE 151.226/A/fin. 5 November 1991; rapporteur Florentz), and the proposed regulation received its first reading in the EP in March 1992. At the Environment Council of 23 March, however, ministers failed to reach agreement on the key issues on the export of waste to certain developing countries and on the movement of waste within the EC. In asking the Commission to bring forward an amended text, the Council also argued for the new text to be dealt with under Article 130s. If the proposal is reintroduced in late 1992 under Article 130s then there is every probability that the Environment Committee, on being reconsulted, would seriously question the text's legal base under the SEA. The intriguing prospect therefore is that in taking its time in considering the amended proposal the committee knows that if the Maastricht Treaty is ratified in 1993 then even regulations introduced under Article 130s will be subject to a co-operation procedure (see below).

At the same time as the EP (and its Environment Committee) has been actively promoting a creative interpretation of the SEA to maximize the use of Article 100a, it has also sought to maximise, through informal means, the formal legislative influence conferred upon it by the cooperation procedure. In other words, the true significance of the SEA rests not merely in the specification of a formal legislative role for the EP but in the enhanced capacity of its committees and individual MEPs to negotiate and bargain informally with other EC institutions. An increase in formal legislative power has thus served to enhance the informal influence of the EP to a cumulatively greater degree than can be gauged simply by looking at the Treaty-prescribed institutional relationship.

The co-operation procedure itself is specified in the revision to Article 149 of the EEC Treaty enacted by the SEA. The elaborate details of the procedure need not detain us here (SEA, 1986: Article 7; Jacobs and Corbett, 1990, pp169–71; Nicoll and Salmon, 1990, pp38–40; Nugent, 1991, pp131–4). In essence the co-operation procedure accords to the EP two legislative readings linked to deadlines, so breaking the 'rolling non-decisions and deliberations extending over many years that typified traditional decision-making' (Lodge, 1989, p70). While much academic attention was initially focused upon the novelty of the second reading, the real significance of the second reading is the enhancement of parliamentary power *before* legislation reaches that stage. As much is recognized in the EP's changed rules of procedure in the wake of the SEA. Hence under current rule 51 (EP Rules of Procedure, 1992) amendments to Council's 'common position' are only accepted at second reading if they seek to restore some or all of the position adopted by the parliament at the first reading;[5] if they are compromise amendments based on agreement between the Council and the EP; or if they seek to amend content changes in the common position not included in the original text at first reading. The main focus of parliamentary attention remains therefore the first reading; with second reading providing spectacular, if ultimately limited, examples of EP influence over the Council. Generally, there is far less chance of parliamentary amendments being accepted at second reading than at first reading (see Table 8.2).

Table 8.2 *Co-operation procedure: acceptance of EP amendments by the Commission and Council (July 1987–September 1991)*

	First reading		Second reading	
	n	%	n	%
Amendments adopted by EP	2734	–	716	–
Amendments retaken by Commission	1626	60	366	48
Amendments retained by Council	1216	45	194	27

Source: EP dossiers d'études et documentation, Series 4-A, Jan. 1992

Only rarely has the parliament sought to reject a common position, and only on three occasions has it succeeded. Significantly, two of these rejections involved the Environment Committee. Indeed, the first rejection came in November 1988 after the Commission refused to accept the Environment Committee's amendments to the common position on a proposed directive on the protection of workers from benzene in the workplace (OJ C 290/36 14 November 1988). Most recently in May 1992 the EP, on the advice of the Environment Committee, rejected the common position on a proposal for a Directive on Artificial Sweeteners (Earnshaw and Judge, 1993). In both instances the Environment Committee was at the forefront of procedural innovation and the testing of the formal powers of the EP.

More routinely, but ultimately perhaps more importantly, the Committee has used the formal powers conferred by the co-operation procedure to strengthen its informal negotiating position with both the Commission and Council in the stages of the legislative process *prior* to second reading. In terms of its relationship with DG XI, the Committee has benefited from the existence of something resembling a shared inter-institutional ethos. Indeed, four senior officials from within the Directorate General and Ripa di Meana's cabinet (interviews, Brussels, 19 May, 20 May, 16 June and 17 June 1992) readily identified the EP and its Environment Committee as allies of the Commission in the legislative process. One member of the Commissioner's cabinet noted how Ripa di Meana 'sees the parliament as a natural ally, they are both supranational bodies against the Council'. In the next breath he went on to observe that 'Ripa also sees the Parliament as an ally against the Commission itself. Parliament is much greener than the Commission and offers a surprising degree of support for Ripa and DG XI'. Similarly, a member of the Directorate-General noted:

> *You have to remember that environment policy within the community was very much seen as a 'bolt-on' policy. For a long time DG XI wasn't taken too seriously within the Commission. In this context DG XI would lobby the EP to act on its behalf... In fact the Council still sometimes thinks that there is an incestuous relationship between the EP and DG XI, with the Environment Committee used to turn the screw.*

One commonly used tactic in jointly 'turning the screw' on the Council is for officials in DG XI to assist committee rapporteurs in the drafting of reports and resolutions on legislative proposals. Indeed, Commission officials in interview could only recall one recent incident of an Environment Committee rapporteur rejecting outright the offer of informal assistance. The flow of influence between Commission and EP at this stage of the legislative process is apparent from the statement of an official in the Directorate-General:

> *We will ask Parliament to do things, to look at things. If we need things to be changed in the Council then we might ask the EP to take an amendment on board. We then go back to Council and say 'look this is what parliament is pressing for' ... This is a legitimate tactic on our part* (interview, 20 May 1992).

Equally, officials within DG XI will seek the support of the Committee in internal Commission negotiations:

> *In helping draft a report, Commission officials who have been involved with the proposal from the outset, and who may have seen their own pet proposal skinned at third and fourth floor levels at the Commission, will attempt to get their initial active proposal back in play as an amendment in the Parliament* (interview, 17 June 1992).

The capacity of the EP to amend legislative proposals is of course recognized by other organizations beyond the Commission and parliament itself. Organized interests – industrial, environmental, and consumer groups alike – acknowledge the significance of the Environment Committee in the promotion of their specific interests (see Chapter 9). This acknowledgement takes several forms. The first is the sheer number of lobbyists who regularly attend and monitor the Committee's meetings. The second is the opinion of members of the Committee themselves. In interviews and discussions with nine leading members of the Environment Committee (interviews, Brussels, May and June 1992) all could point to instances where lobbyists had drafted amendments for them to include in their reports as rapporteurs and all recorded that contact with lobbyists was a daily occurrence. Indeed, most MEPs actively sought the opinions of lobbyists in drafting reports. As one EP member stated:

> *MEPs need a network, we all need information, and, as a rapporteur, groups will come to you. Of course they don't provide disinterested information. All information is biased. But what some of them do provide is good analysis of what the proposal is about, and all provide ideas for change* (interview, Brussels, 22 May 1992).

Carlos Pimenta as Liberal Group Coordinator on the Committee, and ex-environment minister in Portugal, brought a comparative dimension to the assessment of lobbying:

> *In Portugal, as national environment Minister, I wasn't lobbied very often, and when I was it was only by small national groups. Now in the European Parliament I am lobbied all the time, every day, by multinational groups, by energy groups, by environmentalists, by industry: you name it. What this reflects is the lobbyists' own view of the influence of the Environment Committee. It does have a legislative impact* (interview, 22 May 1992).

This view was indeed confirmed by one consultant from a UK-based lobbying company:

> *The Environment Committee is a high profile activist committee. The commission is always our first port of call when we want something done; but the EP provides an extra wing to our activities ... The Committee is particulary useful for inserting into a proposal what we failed to get inserted at the drafting stage. On some resolutions you can see chunks of it written by groups and lobbyists* (interview, 16 June 1992).

Clearly therefore in the perceptions of those members of the Commission, of MEPs and of lobbyists interviewed for this study, the EP is of some significance in its potential for affecting the content of EC legislation. But how, and how often, is this potential realized? Table 2 has already revealed the overall success rate of EP amendments under the co-operation procedure. The simple proportion of amendments accepted by the Commission and Council does not, however, indicate the magnitude of change effected by the EP upon the initial legislative proposal. A large number of amendments might be accepted to little substantive effect, or vice versa. In this respect the influence of the EP can only adequately be assessed through detailed case studies. While bearing in mind the methodological difficulties involved in such an exercise what is offered below is a summary of documented cases from within the EP itself.[6] No claims are made that these cases are necessarily 'typical' (as there is no such thing as a typical legislative environmental proposal in the EC). Instead, these cases point to the diversity of policy issues covered by the Environment Committee and the differential impact achieved on these issues. At most, all that is claimed here is that the Committee and its resolutions has *some* impact, and that in many instances, its influence upon EC legislation is far from marginal.

The first case concerns exhaust emissions for small cars. The changes wrought by the EP to the draft directive on small-car emissions in 1987 provide the exemplar, to date, of how parliament can use its powers of amendment (Jacobs and Corbett, 1990, p170; Arp, 1992, p31; Peters, 1992, p92). The genesis of the legislative proposal and its specification of emission standards are both convoluted and complex, and need not detain us here (Johnson and Corcelle, 1989, pp127–34) (see Chapter 15). The important point is that the emission standards initially specified in the 1984 draft directive of the Commission, of 30 grammes/test of carbon monoxide and 8 grammes/test of unburnt hydrocarbons and nitrous oxide combined, were far from exacting in comparison with standards enforced in the USA since 1983. The proposed standards were blocked in the Council by Denmark in 1985 for being too lenient. It was not until the introduction of the SEA and qualified majority voting under Article 100a that the Council was able to adopt a 'common position' (against the votes of The Netherlands, Denmark and Greece) on 24 November 1988. The EP provided its opinion on 14 September 1988, and proposed far more stringent emission standards in accordance with the 1983 US norms and the introduction of catalytic converters to all classes of cars (OJ C 262/89, 10 November 1988). In reaching its common position in November the Council ignored the opinion of the EP.

With the EP threatening to reject the common position at the plenary session in April 1989, and with the Dutch government's introduction in January 1989 of tax breaks on cars which met the US standards, followed immediately by the Commission beginning formal infringement proceedings against The Netherlands under Article 169 EEC, Ripa di Meana seized the opportunity to convince the Commission of the desirability of revising the common position on the draft directive to take account of the Environment Committee's preference for the 1983 US standards. In addition, DG XI was also aware that many car manufacturers in Europe were capable of meeting the new standards, and with the weakening of the main source of resistance within the industry, Peugeot in France, DG XI was able to gain acceptance within the Commission, 'over many meetings and protracted discussions' (interview. Commission official, 17 June 1992) of the stricter emission standards. In return, the Environment Committee compromised by dropping two amendments unacceptable to the Commission. And so the amended common position was returned to the Council, where it was adopted by a qualified majority in June 1989 (Directive 89/458/EEC). This outcome was evidence, in Ripa di Meana's view, of the capacity of Commission and EP to 'co-ordinate their action in order to establish the necessary conditions to reach the objectives they have in common' (Europe Bulletin, 14 April 1989, p8). It was a *'résultat remarquable'* in the opinion of the Directorate-General for Research of the EP (WIP 91/071/176, 1991, p14), and was 'to be seen as a victory both for the growing environmental movement and for the European Parliament' according to Johnson and Corcelle (1989, p132).

The second case was that of the European Environment Agency. On 7 May 1990 the Council adopted a regulation (1210/90, 7 May 1990) on the establishment of the European Environment Agency and a European Environment and Observation Network. Agreement was only reached, however, after months of protracted argument between the EP, the Commission and the Council. The intention was to create an agency as a source of reliable, objective and comparative – cross-EC – information on the basis of which the EC institutions, Member States and other third countries could make 'scientifically' informed decisions. To this effect, in June 1989, the Commission proposed the creation of an Environmental Agency (Corn (89) 303 final). By November the Council had agreed a compromise proposal on the agency, based upon the original Commission text. As the Environment Committee chairman observed:

> *Not surprisingly, the European Parliament which had only been elected four months before and whose Committees were not formed until two months before that Council decision, did not find this acceptable. We had not even discussed it properly and a rapporteur had only been in place for about eight weeks. We were frankly appalled at the insensitivity of the Council in agreeing a proposal as important as this without any real critical evaluation of it* (Collins, 1991, 2).

Between November 1989 and February 1990 the Environment Committee's rapporteur, Beate Weber, drafted an opinion which sought the extension of the role of the Agency far beyond that envisaged by the Commission or the Council. Indeed, subsequent efforts by the Committee to force its opinion on the

Commission were not welcomed by the Environment Commissioner. As one of his closest advisers put it:

> *The case of the European Environment Agency is, if you like, an example of the negative side of the relationship between the EP and the Commission. From Ripa's view this was a case where the ambivalent relationship with the Environment Committee had a minus sign in front of it. It was felt that the EP was playing a demagogic role* (interview, Brussels, 17 June 1992).

Nonetheless, the Committee pressed its case remorselessly. Having prepared and agreed a parliamentary opinion, the decision was then taken to suspend the final vote for one month. In this period the rapporteur and Committee chairman engaged in discussions with national ministers in order to effect a compromise. Although there is no institutional provision for such direct contact between Council members and EP Committee chairmen, this did not dissuade the Environment Committee chairman:

> *In February 1990, I toured a number of Community capitals and was in practically daily and certainly weekly discussion with Carlo Ripa di Meana ... In March 1990, the Parliament gave its formal Opinion and Commission and Council eventually accepted, and then incorporated in the Regulation itself, word for word, three crucial so-called 'compromise amendments', which had been negotiated with the Irish Presidency and with other ministers during the previous month* (Collins, 1991, p3).

These three compromise amendments (OJ C 96/112–3, 17 April 1990) incorporated vital parliamentary demands. First, that the agency should work at Community level to guarantee the implementation of EC law. Second, that the EEA should develop 'uniform assessment criteria' for the measurement, recording and evaluation of data, and produce reports on the quality, sensitivity of, and pressures on the Community environment. The ultimate objective, however, was to guarantee the effective implementation of Community law in the environmental sector and so open the door for the co-ordination of national environmental inspection. In this respect the EP did not entirely get its way. The Council refused to award inspection competences to the Agency outright, but did concede, nevertheless, that within two years of the adoption of the regulation it would consider proposals for the enlargement of the Agency's tasks. Particular attention was to be paid in this review to the 'granting of powers of inspection with regard to the implementation of Community environmental legislation' and the 'development of criteria for the environmental impact assessments necessary for the application of Directive 85/337/EEC' (OJ C 96/112–3, 17 April 1990).

Hence, the case of the EEA provides another example of the capacity of the EP to influence EC legislation.[7] What it also shows is the 'creative use of procedure'. As the EP's Directorate-General for Research (WIP 92/01/142, 1992, p25) concludes:

> *On the whole this (example) demonstrates considerable parliamentary influence on the content of the regulation. This is remarkable, because, in accordance with the*

underlying Article 130, the Parliament need only be consulted and not given the
authority of the co-operation process according to Article 149(2) EC.

Furthermore, this case also underscores the tenacity of the Environment Committee in pursuit of 'green' policy resolutions. Policy issues are conceived in a dynamic way in the Committee. Thus, not satisfied with the compromise reached on the allocation of functions to the Agency, the Committee has already indicated its intention to operationalize Article 20 in the regulation – to review the Agency's tasks after two years – and so to influence the precise form of 'the enlargement of the Office's tasks'. 'In other words, the Agency is not to be a static phenomenon at all. It is expected to be dynamic' (Collins, 1991, p4).

The third case concerned genetically modified micro-organisms. In 1988 the Commission, strongly influenced by OECD guidelines of 1986, proposed a directive aimed at harmonising the regulation of recombinant biotechnology in the EC (COM (88) 160 final; for details see Lake (1991)). One obvious impact the Environment Committee had upon this directive was that it decided that the original draft directive would better be considered as two separate proposals: one dealing with the 'contained use of genetically modified micro-organisms' (GMMOs) and the other concerning the 'deliberate release of genetically modified organisms' (GMOs). Thereafter this division was maintained by the Council. In essence the 'contained use' directive sought to establish a regulatory regime where GMMOs would be classified according to risk, and establishments operating with GMMOs classified according to size and purpose (whether operations are research-based or commercially-based prototype/production). National competent authorities would have to be informed of the contained use and where necessary explicitly authorize such use. The 'deliberate release' directive on the other hand is concerned with the intentional release of GMOs into the environment.

In its detailed assessment of the impact of the EP upon the final directive on 'deliberate release' the Directorate General for Research (WIP 92/01/142, 1992, p22) found that 10 of the 17 amendments put forward by Parliament at first reading were worked into the revised Commission proposal and that in turn the Council, in adopting its common position, 'substantially adopted the draft of the Commission'.

At the outset it should be noted, however, that the Environment Committee had little success in contesting the definition of key terms in the directive such as 'registration', 'registrant' and 'authorization'. Similarly it had no success in trying to incorporate into the directive questions of legal liability and compensation which were absent from the original proposal. Nevertheless, Parliament managed to convince the Commission of the need for residents in the vicinity of a planned release to have advance notification, but the Council did not incorporate this into the final directive. Likewise, the Commission was also willing, but the Council was not, to meet the EP's demand for the alteration of a technical specification (of hydrologic characteristics) contained in the technical appendix.

Parliament did succeed, however, in influencing both Commission and Council on the necessity for adequate practical testing of the effects on other eco-systems prior to the lifting of controls on GMOs (Amendment 7). Equally the EP had some success in ensuring that a deliberate release might only take place with the agreement of the responsible authority; and that a prerequisite for authorization was adequate proof that the environment and human health was not endangered (Amendment 9). The final directive also reflected the EP's demand for a more exact definition of a GMO. Amendment 30, that release should not take place without the written authorization of the responsible authority was reproduced in slightly different wording in Article 6(4) of the directive; Amendment 29, on the obligations of notification of changes in the release was included in Article 5(6); and Amendment 78, on the prohibition of the transmission of confidential information to third parties was reproduced as Article 19(1) of the directive.

What this example shows is the differential impact the EP has upon certain parts of directives: making outright changes to some Articles, modifying others, and having no impact whatsoever on others. Overall, however, the verdict of the Directorate-General for Research (WIP 92/01/142, 1992, p22) is that 'the influence of the Parliament was considerable'. Similarly, Lake (1991, p12) concludes that the 'EP did have the satisfaction of seeing amendments (on explicit authorization and penalties for infringement) included in the final Council text'. But Lake then proceeds to make the wider point that:

> *A significant impact of the EP's deliberations has not so much been on the legal detail of the directives, but rather on the prevailing consensus within the Commission. Thus (the Environment Committee's) concerns over the mobility of genetic elements are now reflected by increased funding for further studies in these areas from DG XI and DG XII, which will be significant in the development of working guidelines for national competent authorities ... Indeed, it is in the practical implementation of these directives that the real efficacy of this European legislation will be established, and the EP has been concerned for some time about what its own role should be (in this process)* (Lake, 1991, p13).

Before examining the role of the EP in the implementation process, however, one further point about the EP's legislative role, an issue raised above in the discussion of agenda setting, is worthy of note; and this concerns the ability of the Environment Committee to signal its aspirations for future policy while reporting on current legislation. One example will suffice here. In February 1990 the EP was requested to deliver an opinion on a proposal from the Commission for a Directive amending Directive 76/464/EEC on 'pollution caused by certain dangerous substances discharged into the aquatic environment of the Community'. Without going into the details of the resolution itself (PE 143.032/fin, 18 July 1990) the important point is that the Commission's 1990 draft proposal was a direct response to the Environment Committee's earlier demands voiced in its resolution on Corn (87) 457 on limit values for discharges (PE 119.413, 18 February 1988). As much was gleefully pointed out by the Committee's rapporteur:

> *The rapporteur congratulates the Commission wholeheartedly for submitting this proposal along the lines first suggested by Parliament .... The rapporteur proposes that Parliament approve the Commission's proposal without amendment. The proposal submitted by the Commission reflects entirely the commitment made by the Commission to Parliament* (PE 143.032/final, 18 July 1990, pp6–9).

Despite the obvious successes noted above of the EP and its Environment Committee influencing legislation, an accurate audit of the Committee's activities would also reveal instances where the effects of its attempts 'to guide' the Commission's internal deliberations were not particularly apparent (for example, recently on eco-labelling); where its legislative amendments were largely ignored by the Commission (for example, trans-shipment of hazardous waste); or where its recorded influence on the final Council directive was. marginal (for example, 88/609/EEC on large combustion plants). This is hardly surprising, for, in the context of institutional fluidity and legislative substantive complexity in which the Environment Committee operates, it is only to be expected that in the words of its chairman: 'You win a few and you lose a few. The important point is that the Committee continues trying to win' (interview, 22 April 1991).

Implementation

One stage of the legislative process at which the Committee considers that it (along with the EP and the Commission) has traditionally 'lost' is that of implementation. The importance of the implementation stage in the EC policy process is dealt with more fully by Jordan in this volume (see Chapter 17), but it is worth highlighting the specific contribution of the Environment Committee at this point. Quite simply the Environment Committee has been perhaps the collective memory and conscience of the Community on the subject of the implementation of EC environmental legislation (the Legal Affairs Committee can also claim such a role). Thus as one member of DG XI's Directorate General observed:

> *The Environment Committee sits on our backs and watches things. It is concerned with the systematic enforcement and application of legislation, and consistently reminds us of our own role in this respect* (interview, 20 May 1992).

This concern is of relatively recent origin and dates back essentially to the Committee's 1988 reports on the implementation of EC legislation relating to water and to air (OJ C 94/151–8, 11 April 1988).[8] These reports coincided with the introduction of the Fourth Action Programme and the Commission's stated objective of securing the implementation of environmental directives. The report on water was particularly transparent in its intent: 'Parliament ... has a responsibility to assist the Commission in this (implementation) exercise, as well as ensuring that each aspect of the Commission's work is subject to democratic supervision' (PE 116.085/fin, 14 February 1988, p14). The report examined the EC implementation process as it related to three specific directives on the quality of bathing water, the quality of drinking water and the discharge of dangerous substances into the aquatic environment. In detailing the deficiencies of the implementation process the rapporteur concluded that 'the implementation of environmental legislation should henceforth be assessed systematically by Parliament's Committee on Environment, Public Health and Consumer Protection (PE 116.085/fin., 14 February 1988, p54). Since the first reports the Committee has produced further reports including an overview of the implementation of environmental legislation (OJ C 68/183–4, 19 March 1990), and most recently a major report on the application of environmental legislation by Jacques Vernier (PE 152.144, 28 August 1991).

The consistent theme of these reports from the Environment Committee, and one elaborated by its chairman in his evidence to the House of Lords Select Committee on European Communities (HL 53–11 1992, pp27–38), is that more attention needs to be paid to the implementation of EC legislation. In practical terms this means: less secrecy where the Commission has recourse to Article 169 EEC; the systematization of reporting requirements under environmental directives; the introduction of an environment inspectorate; enhancement of DG XI's monitoring role; and the 'democratization' of the EC's legislative process.

Undoubtedly the Committee has been of some importance in raising the profile of the issue of implementation, as the creation of the European Environment Agency partially testifies, but as its chairman observed in November 1991: 'we are perhaps a little bit clearer about why implementation is a problem, but we have not solved the problem by any stretch of the imagination' (HL 53–11 1992, p33). While reaffirming the importance of monitoring both the legal and practical dimensions of compliance and of addressing the issue of enforcement, he proceeded to argue that:

> *The Environment Committee is necessarily the best place to do that. The Environment Committee is the right place to do it ... I would like to think that [the] Committee at least once every five years will do a general report on implementation, but will also do individual reports on the implementation of specific Directives* (HL 53–11 1992, p36).

Given its concern with the problems of implementation, it is not perhaps surprising that the Environment Committee reacted angrily in mid-1992 to suggestions from within the Commission, most particularly from Jacques Delors and Leon Brittan, that 1992 might be an appropriate time to reconsider the competences of the EC institutions in regard to environmental policy. The concerns of the Committee were forcibly expressed through the medium of a letter from its chairman to the President of the European Parliament. The contents of this letter were agreed unanimously at the Committee session of 25 June 1992:

> *In our view subsidiarity does not entail a zero-sum ('or winner take all') trade off over the allocation of power to different levels of government ... implementation is, of course, primarily the responsibility of Member States. However, Member States must examine honestly their own records of implementation ... the Community should, of course, retain powers to scrutinize implementation and in exceptional cases have the possibility, as at present, of recourse to the Court of Justice. This is essentially the philosophy agreed by the Council in the regulation establishing the European Environment Agency, itself an idea proposed by President Delors.*

Clearly, the Committee will have to work hard in the aftermath of the May 1992 Danish referendum to ensure that the concept of subsidiarity is not redefined to legitimate the dilution of standards and control of environmental policy by returning 'competence in this area to national parliaments' (Brittan, 1992, p18).

Conclusion

One role traditionally performed by the Environment Committee has been the promotion of 'environmentalism' within EC policy and institutions. As one member of the Committee commented:

> *The Environment Committee is different from most other committees, it sees itself as a crusader, at the cutting edge of one of the most important policy areas of our time ... Occasionally you get the impression that some of its members feel that they are predestined to save the earth* (interview, Brussels, 21 May 1992).

This zeal, some might say zealotry, has not always endeared it to other committees within the EP (interviews, Brussels, 15 and 17 June 1992, with members of the Secretariat of two other Committees) nor to other Directorate-Generals within the Commission (interview, official of DG VI, 22 May 1992). Within the Committee, however, there appears to be a fundamental consensus, universally acknowledged by all of the Committee members interviewed for this study, which basically transcends political groupings and nationalities. Indeed, a typical response was: 'You have a look at the (political) groups: the Liberals are pro-environment, the socialists are pro-environment; the Christian Democrats are pro-environment; even the British Conservatives are!' (interview, Brussels, 22 May 1992). A shared recognition of the importance of environmental issues has undoubtedly assisted the Committee in its efforts to influence EC policy. As a result, the practical legislative impact of the Committee stands in stark contrast to the academic assessment which still maintains that the 'European Parliament itself is not very powerful, lacking true legislative capabilities ... MEPs have so little structural influence in their own policy domain' (Thomas, 1992, pp4–5). Environmental policy is one policy domain where this assessment sits uneasily with current reality.

Acknowledgements

The author's especial thanks to Ken Collins MEP and David Earnshaw, without whose generous assistance this study would not have been written. Thanks also to Dr Hans Herman Kraus of the EP's DG IV for providing research documents; and also to Jane Aitken, and Dr Tricia Hogwood. To those members of the Commission, MEPs, parliamentary consultants, and EP committee secretariats who gave so generously of their time in interview the author hereby expresses his gratitude. The Nuffield Foundation provided a grant to enable these interviews to take place.

Notes

1. Currently Rules 63 and 121, *Rules of Procedure*, 7th edn, February 1992.
2. Since 1989 the Environment Committee has not sought approval from the EP's Bureau for legislative initiatives under Rule 121, preferring instead to use Rule 63, which does not require authorization by the Bureau.

3. 'Legislative' in the sense of having a heavy legislative burden. The Environ-
    ment Committee is presently the most heavily burdened committee.
4. The statistics that are available are largely inconclusive (Arp, 1992, p14).
5. Under the co-operation procedure, once the EP has given its opinion the pro-
    posal then goes to the Council with the Commission's views on the opin-
    ion. The Council then adopts by a qualified majority a 'common position'
    which it then transmits to the EP.
6. Not least the selection of case studies, the problems of assigning causality,
    the degree of receptivity of the Council and Commission to amendments
    on specific issues and so on.
7. By mid-1992 the European Environment Agency had still not been estab-
    lished. The Council, having agreed to the regulation on the creation of the
    Agency, has been unable to reach agreement as to where the Agency's head-
    quarters should be located.
8. The EP passed a resolution in 1983 (OJ C 68/32, 14 March 1983) calling
    upon the Commission to submit an annual report on the monitoring of the
    implementation of EC law. In turn the Legal Affairs Committee based its
    monitoring of Member States' legal compliance upon these annual reports.

References

Arp, H. A. (1992) 'The European Parliament in European Community Envi-
    ronmental Policy', *EUI Working Papers,* No.92/13, Florence: European Uni-
    versity Institute.
Brittan, L. (1992) 'Subsidiarity in the Constitution of the EC', Robert Schuman
    Lecture, 11 June, Florence: European University Institute.
Budd, S. A. and Jones, A. (1990) *The European Community: A Guide to the Maze*
    (3rd edn), London: Kogan Page.
Bouguignon-Wittke, R., Grabitz, E., Schmuck, O., Steppat, S. and Wessels, W.
    (1985) 'Five Years of the Directly Elected Parliament: Performance and Pros-
    pects', *Journal of Common Market Studies,* Vol.24, No.1, pp39–59.
Capotorti, F., Hilf, M., Jacobs, F. G. and Jacque, J. P. (1986) *The European
    Union Treaty,* Oxford: Clarendon Press.
Collins, K. (1991) 'The European Environment Agency: The Opinion of the
    European Parliament', *Proceedings of the 32nd/IPRE Symposium,* Brussels:
    International Professional Association for Environmental Affairs.
Corbett, R. (1989) 'Testing the New Procedures: The European Parliament's
    First Experiences with its New "Single Act" Powers', *Journal of Common
    Market Studies,* Vol.27, No.4, pp359–72.
de Rouffignac, P. D. (1991) *Presenting Your Case to Europe,* London: Mercury.
Earnshaw, D. and Judge, D. (1993) 'The Sweeteners Directive: From Footnote to
    Inter-Institutional Conflict', *Journal of Common Market Studies,* Vol.31, No.2.
EP (1985) *A New Phase in European Union,* Luxembourg: European Parliament
    General Secretariat.
EP Rules of Procedure (1992) *Rules of Procedure* (7th edn), Luxembourg: Euro-
    pean Parliament.

EUR 12902 EN (1990) *Green Paper on the Environment,* Brussels: DG XI Commission of the European Communities.

Haigh, N. and Baldock, D. (1989) *Environmental Policy and 1992,* London: Institute for European Environmental Policy.

HL 226 (1985) *European Union,* House of Lords Select Committee on the European Communities, Session 1984–5, London: HMSO.

HL 53-11 (1992) *Implementation and Enforcement of Environmental Legislation,* House of Lords Select Committee on the European Communities, Session 1991–2, London: HMSO.

Jacobs, F. and Corbett, R. (1990) *The European Parliament,* London: Longman.

Johnson, S. P. and Corcelle, G. (1989) *The Environmental Policy of the European Communities,* London: Graham & Trotman.

Kirchner, E. and Williams, K. (1983) 'The Legal, Political and Institutional Implications of the Isoglucose Judgments 1980', *Journal of Common Market Studies,* Vol.22, No.2, pp173–90.

Lake, G. (1991) 'Biotechnology Regulations: Scientific Uncertainty and Political Regulation', *Project Appraisal,* Vol.6, No.1, pp7–15.

Lodge, J. (1984) 'European Union and the First Elected European Parliament: The Spinelli Initiative', *Journal of Common Market Studies,* Vol.22, No.4, pp377–402.

Lodge, J. (1986) 'The Single European Act: Towards a New Euro-Dynamism?', *Journal of Common Market Studies,* Vol.24, No.3, pp203–23.

Lodge, J. (1989) 'The European Parliament', in Lodge, J. (ed) *The European Community and the Challenge of the Future,* London: Pinter.

Nicoll, W. and Salmon, T. C. (1990) *Understanding the European Communities,* London: Philip Allan.

Nugent, N. (1991) *The Government and Politics of the European Community* (2nd edn), London: Macmillan.

PE 116.085/fin. (1988) 'Report of the Committee on the Environment, Public Health and Consumer Protection on the Implementation of European Community Legislation'.

PE 119.413 (1988) 'Report of the Committee on the Environment, Public Health and Consumer Protection on Limit Values and Quality Objectives for Discharges of Certain Dangerous Substances', Luxembourg: European Parliament Session Documents.

PE 139.166/fin. (1990) 'Report of the Committee on the Environment, Public Health and Consumer Protection on Measures to Protect the Ecology of Tropical Rainforests', Luxembourg: European Parliament Session Documents.

PE 140.600 (1990) *Fact Sheets on the European Community,* Luxembourg, Office for Official Publications of the EC.

PE 143.032/final (1990) 'Report of the Committee on the Environment, Public Health and Consumer Protection, Commission Proposal for a Council Directive Amending Directive 76/464/EEC on Pollution Caused by Certain Dangerous Substances Discharged into the Aquatic Environment of the Community', Luxembourg: European Parliament Session Documents.

PE 144.135/fin. (1990) 'Report of the Committee on the Environment, Public Health and Consumer Protection on a Community Strategy on Waste Management', Luxemburg: European Parliament Session Documents.

PE 145.367/fin. (1991) 'Report of the Committee on the Environment, Public Health and Consumer Protection on Economic and Fiscal Instruments on Environment Policy', Luxembourg: European Parliament Session Documents.

PE 146.246/fin. (1991) 'Report of the Committee on the Environment, Public Health and Consumer Protection on the Commission Proposal for a Council Regulation Establishing a Financial Instrument for the Environment', Luxembourg: European Parliament Session Documents.

PE 152.137.fin. (1991) 'Report of the Committee on the Environment, Public Health and Consumer Protection on the Commission Proposal for a Council Regulation on Eco-Labelling', Luxembourg: European Parliament Session Documents.

PE 152.144 (1991) 'Report of the Committee on the Environment, Public Health and Consumer Protection on the Implementation of Environmental Legislation', Luxembourg: European Parliament Session Documents.

PE 151.226/A/fin. (1991) 'Report of the Committee on the Environment, Public Health and Consumer Protection on the Commission Proposal for a Council Regulation on the Supervision and Control of Shipments of Waste within, into and out of the European Community', Luxembourg: European Parliament Session Documents.

PE 200.380 (1992) 'Committee on the Environment, Public Health and Consumer Protection, Notice to Members, Judgement of the Court of Justice of 11 June 1991 – Titanium Dioxide', Luxembourg: European Parliament, Directorate-General for Committees and Delegations.

Pinder, J. (1991) *European Community: The Building of a Union,* Oxford: Oxford University Press.

SEA (1986) *Single European Act,* Bulletin of the European Communities, Supplement 2/86, Luxembourg, Office for Official Publications of the EC.

Thomas, S. T. (1992) 'Assessing MEP Influence on British EC Policy', *Government and Opposition,* Vol.27, No.1, pp3–17.

Vandermeersch, D. (1987) 'The Single European Act and the Environmental Policy of the European Economic Community', *European Law Review,* Vol.12, pp407–429.

Wilkinson, D. (1992) *Maastricht and the Environment,* London: Institute for European Environmental Policy.

WIP 91/071/176 (1991) 'Evaluation de l'impact du Parlment sur les politiques communitaires dans les dernières années', Luxembourg: European Parliament Directorate General for Research.

WIP 92/01/142 (1992) 'L'influence du Parlement européen dans la procédure legislative à la lumiére de l'adoption de quatre directives ou réglements dans les secteurs des affaires sociales et de l'environnement', Luxembourg: European Parliament Directorate General for Research.

9

Environmental Groups and the EC: Challenges and Opportunities

Sonia Mazey and Jeremy Richardson

Lobbying and Policy-making in the EC: Some Special Characteristics

While the environmental sector exhibits some special characteristics – not least of which is the currently very high political salience of environmental and green issues and the almost unique cross-sectoral nature of the environmental issue – groups lobbying in this sector face the same range of opportunity structures as other groups in the EC. Indeed, we argue elsewhere (Mazey and Richardson, 1993a, 1993b, 1992c) that the fundamental rules of the game for lobbyists at the European level are much the same as at the national level. Although politics in Brussels is not yet akin to the 'village life' which is thought to exist, say, in Whitehall in Britain, there are nevertheless some basic cultural norms that are not so dissimilar to those of more tightly integrated and unified national bureaucracies.

Thus, the successful groups are those that exhibit the usual professional characteristics – namely resources, advance intelligence, good contacts with bureaucrats and politicians, and above all an ability to provide policy-makers with sound information and advice. Reputations for expertise, reliability and trust are key resources in lobbying in Brussels as elsewhere. A respondent from DG XI, for example, stressed the need for groups to be 'responsible' – by which was meant a willingness to be involved in the policy-making process without publicity. This means that lobbying *styles* may be as important as the content and objectives of the lobbying itself. The way that business is conducted will affect policy outcomes, as it plays a significant part in shaping the perceptions of participants and therefore their willingness to listen to each other, and to make concessions during the processing of issues. As another respondent remarked to us, there was a marked difference in the degree of professionalism of groups that approached the Commission and hence in the weight that was attached to their views. As we will suggest in the next section, perceptions may be especially relevant to a consideration of the politics of the environment in the EC, as the three main groups of interests – bureaucrats, environmentalists and industrialists – have particular perceptions of each other which may affect their effectiveness in the policy-making process.

Even though the 'basic rules of the game' may be familiar, however, the EC policy process is in many ways unique. Its multinational, neo-federal nature, the openness of decision-making to lobbying, and the considerable weight of national politico-administrative elites within the process, create a rather unstable and multidimensional environment (see Chapters 12 and 18) to which all pressure groups must adapt if they are to achieve their objectives.

A major problem for all groups in the EC policy process is the comparative instability and unpredictability of the agenda-setting process. In the UK, to take what may be an extreme example, significant policy change is usually preceded by a rather slow and well-known process, in which the 'affected interests' are given early warning of the possibility of policy change. Moreover, once the policy process is underway, it is unusual for there to be abrupt changes once basic agreement within the 'policy community' has been achieved (Richardson and Jordan, 1979; Jordan and Richardson, 1987). The existence of these well-defined policy communities at the national level (especially in the Northern European democracies) is possibly the greatest contrast between national and EC policy-making at present. The European Commission is not yet sufficiently mature as an organization for it to have developed widespread 'standard operating procedures' for processing policy issues. Of particular relevance to the lobbying strategies of groups trying to influence the EC is the fact that the Commission is still in the process of developing its consultation and co-ordination procedures. (For a discussion of the early development of the Commission see Mazey (1992).)

As two DG XI officers described the process to us, it can still appear 'far too haphazard' and something of a 'free for all ... [leaving] the door open for any groups wishing to contact Commission officers, rather than a selective grouping'. Yet there is an apparent contradiction in this characterization of the consultation process, possibly explained by the fact that the Commission is an 'adolescent bureaucracy'. Thus a mixed style of consultation appears to exist. For example, there is some evidence that something like standard operating procedures are emerging in some sectors. Thus, in social policy there is a quite developed framework for negotiation and consultation, and in the environmental sector itself there are now plans to set up an official environmental forum (see conclusion below). There may now be sufficient examples of institutionalized and regularized consultation to suggest at least the existence of a 'procedural ambition' on the part of Commission officials to achieve a more stable (though possibly informal) set of policy actor relationships. Arp (1991, p14) cites the example of car emission regulations which are translated into the language of engineers and discussed as technical questions. These discussions are chanelled through the Motor Vehicle Emissions Group composed of Commission officials, national experts, the car industry, and consumer and environmental organizations. Similarly,

the issue of how to respond in practice to the EC's international treaty obligations regarding the depletion of the ozone layer was processed with the advice
and participation of a group of industry representatives which the Commission
convened.

In contrast to most national policy-making systems, policy-making power
in the EC is dispersed and there are several informal policy initiators. Though
the Commission announces its own legislative programme at the beginning of
each year, other more pressing items may be added as a result of European
Summit decisions. In addition, every national government uses its six-month
presidency of the Council of Ministers (during which period it also chairs and
sets the agenda of all Council working groups) to push favoured projects to the
front of the agenda (for example, the promotion of the 'social dimension' of the
internal market by the French government) while MEPs, individual commissioners, ambitious ministers and interest groups all seek to push the Commission
in certain directions. The multiplicity of 'opportunity structures' for groups is
often perceived to be an advantage by all groups, but particularly by those denied
access to national policy-makers. Yet this permeability of the system is also a
disadvantage to groups. With few exceptions (agriculture may be the only one)
no one set of groups – and certainly no individual group – can rely on *exclusive*
access.

Thus, the process is best described as policy-making through loose, open
and extended issue networks, rather than through well defined, stable, and exclusive policy communities. Participation in the policy process is unpredictable,
and policy ideas may appear suddenly and from little known sources (see Chapter 12). In practice therefore keeping track of EC policy initiatives is a major
undertaking for groups, many of which lack sufficient resources to perform this
task on their own. Our own research to date suggests that the need to monitor
EC policy developments is now widely acknowledged by national lobbies and is
often cited as an important factor in their decision to form and join Euro-groups,
however ineffective those groups might be. For example, one British company
told us that it joined virtually every relevant trade association, at both the national
and European level, as part of its information gathering system and in order to
demonstrate to its peers that it was a good corporate citizen within the various
industrial sectors in which it operated. In practice, it often did not rely on the
relevant Euro-group and preferred to lobby Brussels directly itself.

A second reason for the uncertain agenda is the existence of different national
political agendas, which in turn leads to a degree of competitive agenda-setting
within the EC itself (see Chapter 11). Again, our industrial contacts have suggested
to us that this is their main weakness – an inability to influence, let alone control, the agenda-setting process within Brussels and Strasbourg. This produces a
reactive style of lobbying. More often than not, firms and industries are conducting rearguard or fire-brigade campaigns in response to agendas set by others –
often by the environmentalists. While many Community issues are common
across national boundaries, others are country specific; in other cases there are
cross-national variations in the position of common issues or differing ideological stances, or both. Environmental policy is an example of the differing
emphases found in EC states and of the EC's own agenda being pushed along

by certain enthusiastic actors. For example, domestic 'green' pressure in West Germany played a part in encouraging its government to take the initiative in pressing for limits on car exhaust emissions, as did the interests of the German car industry. In the event, the issue soon became more complicated than a simple conflict between environmentalists and polluters (Jordan and McLaughlin, 1993). The controversy, in 1991/92 over possible EC controls on packaging is also a case of a national agenda impinging on the EC's agenda (see Chapter 13). The German 'Packaging Decree', implemented in January 1992, placed responsibility upon manufacturers and distributors to the German market for the collection and disposal of all packaging materials, with further restrictions coming into force in April 1992 and January 1993. The German interest in the issue had a knock-on effect at the EC level, where a draft Directive on Packaging was being prepared. Fear that something like the German legislation would be introduced at the EC level caused consternation in the European packaging industry. For example, a representative of the Euro-federation – The Industry Council for Packaging and the Environment (INCPEN) – commented on the German proposals as follows: 'Never mind the Nimby factor (Not in My Back Yard), they seem to be suffering from the Banana syndrome – Build Absolutely Nothing Anywhere Near Anyone'. (*The Independent*, 10 September 1991). Significantly perhaps, INCPEN is a relatively new and predominately British actor at EC Level.

This particular example is illustrative of another general phenomenon of relevance to any discussion of environmental politics in the EC – namely that national action in the environmental field can soon be caught up in broader questions relating to the Single Market. There is an increasing fear that environmental action at the national level can be used as back door trade restrictions or to give special market advantages to firms that are launching new products or that have perfected a particular innovation (Sargent, 1993) The environmental field may be especially rich in cases of a close link between innovation and regulation and we must therefore be cautious in portraying the politics of the environment as a straightforward conflict between two blocks of interests groups – polluters and environmentalists. We suspect that, as the sector becomes more stable (in the sense that competing interests, and interested bureaucrats, may all tend to seek stability of processes and structures) we may see the emergence of rather unusual and complex coalitions of interests around particular policy problems. For example, the exhaust emissions issue was not a simple case of polluters versus environmentalists because of the different anti-emission technologies being developed by different car manufacturers, who soon came into conflict with each other over the preferred solution to the problem.

As suggested above, stability and predictability have certainly not yet arrived – if only because the basic formal processes of EC policy-making (and *implementation* mechanisms) are still in a state of flux. Also in the environmental sector, the legal competence of the Commission is relatively new. In that sense, all players are involved in a game in which the goal posts are bound to move. Yet, as Majone suggests, in the 20 years from 1967 to 1987 almost 200 directives, regulations and decisions were introduced by the Commission. This is despite the fact that environmental protection is not even mentioned in the Treaty of Rome and that the Commission's authority in this area was not recognized until the passage of the Single European Act (SEA) (see Chapters 1 and 2). Moreover, as he notes, the rate of growth of environmental regulation appears to have been largely unaffected by 'the political vicissitudes, political crises, and recurrent waves of Europessimism of the 1970s and early 1980s' (Majone, 1989, p165). Thus, environmental policy-making is now relatively well developed and in some cases the appropriate 'constituencies' of interests have been organized and mobilized and to some degree integrated into the policy process. More recently, the possibility of a 'partnership' between the interested parties has been emerging as an important concept presenting the opportunity to produce a greater degree of stability and predictability than described by the officers cited above (see conclusion below).

In fact, very little detailed research has been done on the subject of how groups generally have responded to the shift in policy-making power away from national capitals to Brussels, although much research is now under way. It is very clear, however, that the nature of the interface between the EC and interest groups generally is in a state of flux and is recognized by the Commission and the Parliament as a problem to be addressed. It is also clear that the constant shift in power to Brussels has resulted in increased pressures upon national groups to co-ordinate their lobbying activities through the European Federations. This trend has been encouraged by European Commission officials who are currently trying to rationalize the growing problem of group consultation and who have an official preference for dealing with Euro-groups. Preliminary findings suggest, however, that many European Federations (especially industrial sectoral federations) are beset by internal cleavages along national, ideological, organizational and policy lines (Collie, 1993).

Moreover, the European community, despite its growing importance, is not a sovereign state. Legislative power is shared between national Member States and the Community. In consequence, groups must maintain existing national lobbying strategies while developing new strategies in response to the growing legislative competence of the EC. They must do this in a way which does not undermine existing relationships at the national level. Thus, 'playing the Brussels card' against a national administration may work on any given issue, but it may have serious long-term consequences in undermining relationships at the national level which have taken a very long time to build. This is especially relevant to environmental groups, many of which have worked hard over many years to achieve the respectability and consultative status at the national level which industrial associations have traditionally enjoyed.

A further problem for groups is that they have to contend with the fact that within the European Commission, policy-making is highly compartmentalized with little horizontal co-ordination between different Directorates-General which have a shared interest in an issue. Despite the fact that the Commission is a collegiate body, there is nevertheless a risk that once a legislative proposal has become the property of a particular DG and the particular constellation of interests surrounding it, other groups may find it difficult to be consulted effectively. Conflicting policy proposals relating to the same issue can emerge from different parts of the Commission. In order to avoid being taken by surprise, groups must be able to monitor and respond to policy developments in more than one DG.

For environmental groups, for example, this task is rendered more difficult by the high turnover of people employed by the Commission on temporary contracts and the considerable variation in the internal organization, culture and working methods (including consultation procedures) of different DGs, and different divisions within the same DG.

Another important feature of the Commission is its small size. Despite the popular image (especially in Britain!) of the Commission as a bloated bureaucracy, it is in fact very small when compared with national administrations. If we take an environmental example, there are approximately 15 staff in DG XI concerned with the control of chemicals yet in the USA the Environmental Protection Agency has over 500 staff. The small size of the Commission has two important consequences for lobbying – it leaves the Commission very dependent upon outside sources (both pressure groups and national administrations) for expertise and information and it leaves the Commission very weak in terms of the oversight of EC directives once they have been incorporated into national legislation. (The European Court is, of course, also involved in the oversight of implementation and the Commission is involved in cases which come before the Court.)

The Commission's aspiration is to be able to deal with Euro-groups which are at the same time *representative* and *expert*. In practice Commission officials regularly depart from this procedural ambition and consult not only national groups but individual firms. There is also a tendency to bypass representative structures altogether as, for example, in the establishment of the Industrial Round Table in 1983. This horizontal Euro-Grouping brings together the heads of the leading European companies and multinationals. Significantly, membership of the ERT is by invitation only. (It currently consists of approximately 44 members drawn from individual companies and is chaired by Wisse Dekker from Philips, with Vice-Chairmen from Siemens and La Compagnie Lyonnaise des Eaux-Dumez.) Similar groupings include the European Information Technology Round Table created in the late 1970s at the initiative of the Commission and the Association for the Monetary Union of Europe, established in 1987. Those companies denied access to these groupings are under further pressure to join forces with their EC counterparts in the various Euro-groupings. Commission attempts to 'rationalize' the process of interest intermediation may mean that the EC policy-making process becomes corporatist in nature in those areas which have hitherto been more pluralist. The corporatist ambitions of the Commission are widely acknowledged. The key issue, however, is the extent to which the deregulatory thrust of the Single Market Programme, the internal characteristics of key interest groupings and the EC decision-making structures will permit such a development (Gorges, 1991; Rhodes, 1990). In the case of the environment, there are very specific problems with the SEA. As Huelshoff and Pfeiffer (1997, p145) argue, 'the ambiguity of the SEA and the opposition of some Member States to higher environmental standards have led to market goals being put before environmental goals in the EC'.

Since all legislative proposals are drafted by the Commission, it tends to be the focus of EC lobbying. Of particular importance in this respect are the 1000 or so advisory groups and consultative committees some of which can play an important role in the initial drafting of EC proposals as well as being involved in the implementation of policy. Not surprisingly, membership of these groups is highly valued by groups. Since the adoption of the SEA, the European Parliament has also become a more important focus of lobbying activities and if the Maastricht Treaty is adopted, it looks set to increase further its role in environmental policy. However, within the EC the final decision on all policies is taken by *national* officials and politicians in the Council of Ministers. Groups at this stage must rely principally upon the negotiating skills and support of national civil servants and government ministers. Thus, somewhat paradoxically, the growing importance of EC legislation may sometimes reinforce the dependency which exists at the national level between groups and 'their' ministers. The degree of co-operation between groups and national administrations in this respect varies considerably, both between countries and between groups – not all of which enjoy the same degree of political legitimacy. In the environmental sector, groups at the national level are often in conflict with their own national administrations and hence see the EC as an alternative arena in which to excercise influence.

Finally, any assessment of the techniques of Euro-lobbying must examine the use of the courts by groups. The European Court of Justice, which is responsible for interpreting and enforcing EC law, is of crucial and increasing importance for EC lobbyists concerned with *implementation* of EC law (see Chapter 7). Since the 1970s, environmental organizations and women's groups especially, have used the Court (whose appellate powers resemble those of the US Supreme Court) as a means of forcing recalcitrant national governments to implement EC legislation concerning, for example, the quality of drinking water and equal treatment between working men and women (on the latter see Mazey (1988)). Under Articles 169 and 170 of the EEC Treaty the Court rules on whether Member States have failed to uphold their Treaty obligations. Actions may be brought by the European Commission or by other Member States. More generally, the principle of direct effect means that individuals and groups can rely upon EC law in national courts.

Environmental Groups in the EC: A Preliminary Analysis

If we set the ambitions and activities of environmental groups in the context of the characteristics of EC policy-making, as described in the first section, how might the groups be rated in terms of their likely efficacy as lobbyists? What are their strengths and weaknesses?

It appears that environmental groups have at least three fundamental strengths in the context of the EC at present[1] (although as we shall argue, these advantages may be eroded over time). They are in no particular order of priority:

* a capacity to build European level coalitions in the form of Euro-groups, umbrella organizations, or through the creation of cross-national Euro-level networks;
* through these coalitions, an ability to contribute to European integration in the manner predicted by neo-functionalist theory and hence, in a manner likely to be attractive to the Commission;

- an ability to set the political agenda in the environmental sector and to structure the content of issues in ways which place other interests at a disadvantage. In contrast, environmental groups may have certain fundamental weaknesses;
- these groups may be too dependent upon good relations with one part of the Commission, namely DG XI, and upon the European Parliament;
- they may lack the resources or will to participate within the policy process *intensively* from the initiation phase right through to policy decision and beyond, up to implementation;
- other interests are becoming more effective in their mobiliatizon around the environmental issue, presenting much more competition for the attention and consideration of policy-makers;
- notwithstanding the first point, above, the environmentalists may be subjected to some of the competitive and entrepreneurial tendencies to which all pressure groups are subject, and this may ultimately limit the effectiveness of their coalition-building capacities;
- their lobbying style may limit their capacity to influence policy-making, yet if it changes, they may face problems in maintaining support within their own constituencies.

We shall deal with these strengths and weaknesses in turn, although it should be emphasised that they are, of course, interrelated.

All researchers have emphasized the weakness of Euro-groups, essentially because these groups are usually composed of very diverse interests, often in fierce competition with each other in the market place. The Euro-federation representing the chemical manufacturers is usually cited as one of the few really successful Euro-federations. This alleged success has much to do with the fact that CEFIC is dominated by a few large manufacturers within European and worldwide interests and that the structure of the European Chemical Industry does not vary as much as, say, the financial services sector in Europe (Knight et al, 1993). The most common criticism of Euro-federations representing industry is that they are understaffed (Collie, 1993) and that in so far as they have anything to say, it is characterized by the label 'lowest common denominator' – that is, the internal divisions are such that their policy statements are more like peace treaties designed to keep the federations together, than well argued technical proposals on which EC officials can act. Thus many, if not most, peak and sectoral associations representing industry are not highly regarded, are under-resourced with small (but increasing) staffing, and subject to unwitting undermining by the actions of the Commission itself – namely by the Commission regularly consulting individual firms and national organizations. Moreover, it is often the case that these federations are often not staffed by people who have a long-term future in their own industries, in that it is relatively common for them to be staffed by personnel who are nearing retirement. Thus, it appears that few companies see sending their young or middle managers to Euro-federations as part of a programme of long-term career development.

Following the EC's increasing involvement in international affairs (the EC is currently involved in the negotiation of over 20 international treaties) (see

Chapter 16), environmental groups and other non-governmental organizations (NGOs) are present in large numbers whenever and wherever international negotiations take place and are of increasing influence in these negotiations, albeit that they are not *directly* involved in them. There is also, of course, a widespread and genuine recognition within the environmental movement that problems are cross-national and worldwide and that there is little point in trying to redistribute environmental costs between one country and another through the lobbying process. Few *industries* are capable of taking a co-ordinated industry-wide European – let alone a worldwide-view – of their long-term interests (for example, in such industries as telecommunications, the concept of national champions dies hard). The big conflicts of interest which arise within European industry (and between European industry and the Americans and Japanese) generally do not arise between environmental groups. They have different interests and emphasize different issues, but they are essentially on the same side fighting the same cause and have a common interest in better environmental regulations. There is not the kind of competition to use regulatory regimes to gain comparative advantage in which industrial and commercial interests are engaged.

This relative lack of conflict of interest enables environmental groups – and other NGOs (Harvey, 1993) – to construct large networks of interests which link Euro-level organizations and national level organizations. These *are potentially* powerful if they can be managed successfully. The European Environmental Bureau (EEB) is one example of such a network, consisting of over 120 NGOs in the environmental field. It was founded 16 years ago, in part because the Commission (particularly DG XI) needed an NGO movement as a counterweight to the industrial lobby. Consequently, the EEB receives significant amounts of the EC funding to hold seminars (for example, on eco-labelling) and round tables on specific issues, although opinions on EEB's actual policy impact differ considerably. The mobilization and management of these networks (there is a proliferation of them) is a problematic task, but they represent a considerable resource – both in political and expertise terms – if they can be made to work, and there are few if any permanent equivalents on the industrial and commercial side.

The networks do also possess the potential predicted for groups by the neo-functional theorists such as Haas (1958), who suggested that groups would play a central role in European integration. They would turn to supranational means when this course appears profitable to their members. He argued that this process of group formation would be purely *tactical* as organized employer interests in a pluralistic setting outgrew the nation state (Haas, 1958, p354). This lack of 'ideological cohesion' which he saw in industrial and commercial interests is not however, as we have argued, really a problem within the environmental movement, which is much more often able to express a genuinely European view. This is, of course, attractive to the Commission which is particularly anxious to see all lobbying presented in European terms. (All commercial lobbying firms advise their commercial clients to present arguments in European and not national terms, for example.) In this sense, the environmentalists have reached a much more advanced stage in the Europeanization of lobbying and have already adopted the ideals of European integration. They are much more integrated in their behaviour than are the groups with whom they normally compete, and do not find the adoption of a European perspective nearly as problematic as industrial and commercial groups (for an example see Knight et al, (1993)).

The ability of environmental groups to set the political agenda is perceived by the industrialists to whom we have spoken as perhaps the greatest current asset of the environmentalists. Indeed, one leading European environmental campaigner told us that he saw his organization as very much at the 'ideas level' and rather less involved in the very specific technical details of policies. Indeed, he argued that his organization has eschewed the 'expertise' approach. It saw itself as dealing in the currency of ideas and in creating the conditions under which the level of detail could then be decided. The strategy appeared to be to place issues on the agenda and to define the issues sufficiently clearly so that technical detail could safely be left to others. We might qualify this view by suggesting that the environmentalists are in fact rather effective in translating scientific findings of a complex kind into more generally comprehensible political issues (for example, global warming, or heavy metal pollution) to which policy-makers and other interests have to respond. Indeed, environmental groups might be said to be one of the key links in modern society between science and politics, often being responsible for some kind of 'megaphone' effect transmitting scientific ideas from the private world of professional science into the world of public policy. The fact that many of the groups have especially good links with the European Parliament also lends support to the thesis that agenda setting is their forte; in so far as the Parliament has influence, it is better at raising issues than in processing them. The downside of this power on the part of groups is that it may be heavily dependent on what Gregory (1977) termed the 'halo effect' of the environmental issue. Currently (as in the 1970s) the environment is high on the political agenda and all interests are inclined to take it seriously. But if the environment were again to enter the downward sector of the Downsian issue attention cycle (Downs, 1972), the environmentalists might find greater difficulty in exercising what Schattschneider (1960) terms the supreme exercise of political power – determining what politics is actually about.

Turning now to the possible weaknesses of the environmental movement at the EC level, perhaps the most obvious is their relative dependence on DG XI. Indeed, one Commission official suggested to us that the task force which preceded the formation of DG XI was originally so weak that it sought the support of the NGOs and mobilized and supported them in order to defend itself. He believed that without NGO support DG XI might have died in its early years. This suggests that the Directorate is possibly an example of a phenomenon described by Downs as being common to all bureaucracies – namely that in the early stages of their life, they deliberately cultivate external clients who then come to depend upon them and will defend them in times of crisis faced by the agency (Downs, 1967). It is certainly the case that the NGO movement generally (including environmental groups) receives financial support from the Commission (directly or via various contracts) and it can be argued that as a result, there is an unhealthy degree of dependency (indeed one Commission official described some of the environmental groups as having been 'tamed'; however, groups like Greenpeace deliberately avoid Commission funding, and the World

Wide Fund for Nature (WWF) has set a limit of between 10 and 15 per cent on funding from public agencies). Gradually, the environmentalists are gaining more access to other Directorates General – quite successfully on some specific issues – but most environmental respondents reported what we would see as 'skewed' access to the Commission, with much better access to DG XI than elsewhere. Some (rival) interests see this ready access as 'agency capture' by the environmentalists and argue that it is extremely difficult to represent an alternative (industrial) view to most of DG XI. They therefore seek representation at levels higher than the service level and attempt to mobilize other Directorates General to fight their corner on environmental issues. Of much more importance to the environmentalists is the fact that so many other Directorates General are responsible for policies which have major environmental implications. This means that the task of lobbying the Commission is that much more difficult (say compared with that for interests in the IT field) and demands vast resources if the 'environmental waterfront' (in lobbying terms) is to be covered properly. Even in those areas where the environmentalists have especially good contacts, Commission officials have the ability to 'close' the issue without much difficulty, unless the group can mobilize pressure in the European Parliament. There is no doubt, however, that there is a degree of 'greening' of the Commission as a whole, reflecting European-wide pressure on all national governments and parliaments to pay greater attention to environmental issues.

The question *of resources* and its impact on the efficacy of environmental groups is quite difficult to assess. The European level environmental groups may seem quite well resourced when compared with sectoral business associations at the European level. For example, Greenpeace has 12 full-time staff in its European office compared with a typical sectoral federation such as The European Association of Textile Polyole-firms (EATP) which has only four staff yet represents 60 members drawn from 15 European countries (Peckstadt et al, 1992), or indeed with a peak business association such as UNICE (Collie, 1993). Moreover, Greenpeace claims to have access to over 1200 environmental and scientific experts worldwide and feels able to compete with industrial groups in terms of specialist advice, as well as in the more political arena for which it is best known through its publicity-seeking activities. Our own interviews with officials within DG XI also suggest that environmental groups (and indeed the NGO movement generally in other fields such as poverty, housing and health) are rather well regarded by many (though not all) officials for their groups' expertise in environmental matters. Groups like WWF can also claim considerable field expertise and have a degree of legitimacy from their direct involvement in the *implementation* process. Thus, WWF currently spends 19.5 million ECUs per year on conservation work in Europe. By no means all of the work is in Western Europe as WWF has recognized the growing importance of environmental problems in Eastern Europe, for example, and is involved at a very practical level in developing schemes for better environmental management of resources (WWF, 1991). It is not simply an advisory group, raising issues and helping to define the agenda, but it also has the resources (a limited proportion of which, unlike Greenpeace, came from the EC) both to devise and implement practical solutions. This is particularly important in certain areas of the EC where local administrations may not be the best agents for service delivery – for example, in Spain. In these contexts, WWF can actively devise and deliver field projects.

Groups such as WWF, Gteenpeace and Friends of the Earth can also mobilize the resources of their *national* organizations to lobby individual national administrations, thus influencing deliberations in the Council of Ministers. Yet, there still remains a doubt concerning the group's ability to stay with an issue from A to Z of the EC policy process. Two important rules of lobbying in Brussels are that groups need to get in *early* – when the issue is but a gleam in an official's eye (Hull, 1992) and to *stay* with the issue at every stage throughout the whole process. Our interviewees suggest that the environmentalists do not really have the capacity to stay with the detail of an issue through its life cycle in the policy process. (Thus, the view cited above, to the effect that agenda setting may be sufficient, is a high risk strategy; the devil may be in the details!) Alternatively, they may not have the deep-seated *interest* that, say, a company whose very survival is threatened by EC legislation would have. Sargent's (1993) study of trade associations points out that firms are often reluctant to commit resources to a trade association (at either the national or the European level) but are more willing to set up specific, ad hoc, well resourced organizations, on issues that are of special significance to them. It is therefore misleading to compare the resourcing of environmental groups with equivalent Euro- and national trade associations. Firms both devote resources to ad hoc, one issue, organizations and do a lot of direct lobbying with Commission officials and MEPs. Our evidence suggests that in those areas of environmental policy where industry has a really keen and vital interest, the resources mobilized are very considerable indeed and usually far outweigh those of any of the environmental groups. This is because, although industrial Euro-associations have very small staffs, they are able to call upon both the personnel and the expertise of their member firms.

In fact, key firms are probably the first port of call for some EC officials wanting particular types of data and information. The firm's national and Euro-association will be 'consulted' but often only after prior 'testing' of problems and ideas at the level of the firm. A related weakness for environmental groups, in terms of resources, is that – as one environmental group official put it to us – 'we can't follow *every* issue of relevance to the environment – they are too many – and we have to choose on which of the many issues we can concentrate our resources'. One consequence of this is that there appears to be a degree of 'product specialization' (itself an advantage in terms of expertise) by the main Euro-level environmental groups, which may be leaving significant tracts of 'environmental policy space' to the lobbying activities of industrial and commercial groups (IT policy and R&D policy may be examples). Thus, Greenpeace has a strategy of concentrating in four areas of campaigning – ocean ecology; toxics; nuclear; and atmosphere and energy, and WWF is especially interested in the EC Structural Fund's relationship between trade and the environment, and in the Common Agricultural Policy.

Perhaps the greatest long-term threat to the influence of environmental groups is that other interests are becoming much more active in this sector. Essentially, industrial interests are now taking the environmental issue much more seriously and are beginning to devote the lobbying resources needed if their voice is to become more effective and if they are to become less 'reactive' in their lobbying styles. There is increasing pressure on DG XI, for example, to talk to industrial interests. Also, the industrial interests can be expected to defend their existing relationships with other DGs as the environmentalists try to expand their sphere of influence. Moreover, we should not underestimate the capacity of industry to take on board the environmental issue at the company level, partly in response to their perception of public pressure and in part out of purely commercial self interest. As one participant put it to us, he had not come across very many environmental issues that really were life and death to a particular company or industry. He was surprised how often legislation was originally opposed because it would be 'the end of the industry', only for the industry to absorb the extra costs (or pass them on to its consumers) with relative ease once the legislation was in place.

Thus, 'delay' rather than 'stop' may well be the slogan more appropriate to industrial lobbying in the environmental sector, with the more sophisticated industrial actors being aware that being pro-active (preemptive strikes) may be the best lobbying stategy of all. Whether or not this is true, there is little doubt that industrial interests are becoming much more active in presenting technical and well researched arguments when faced with challenges, and in actually *anticipating* possible challenges. Nor should it be assumed that industrial interests necessarily seek to obstruct the introduction of EC environmental legislation. Within the internal market, a competitive advantage accrues to environmentally progressive companies. This may gradually improve the bad public image of industrialists and enable them to engage in political dialogue more effectively. Also, they may be more willing to enter into a direct dialogue with the environmental interests, forcing the latter to rethink their own lobbying strategies, too.

Finally, we may speculate that, in practice, the environmental sector is not quite as 'uncompetitive' as we have earlier suggested. There is broad ideological agreement and generally an absence of conflicts over policy – yet in one sense there is a degree of competition within the environmental sector. True, there is much collaboration and co-ordination at the European level – for example, the main Euro-level organizations have regular meetings every four to six weeks in order to exchange information and ideas. Similarly, as we have suggested, there is a degree of 'product specialization' or 'niche marketing' – to use two commercial analogies. Yet it is also possible to characterize the leaders of environmental groups – and of other NGOs – simply as essentially entrepreneurs who wish to expand the influence of their organizations just as firms wish to expand their markets – and whose own success to some degree depends on their organization's achieving some special status in the policy process. They may also be in competition for members and financial support and need to demonstrate 'action' and 'success' (not always synonymous) to their members as well as to the broader policy network as a whole. This is especially true at the national level, where the organizational representation of the environmental issue may well be beyond saturation point in some of the Northern democracies. However, it is not at all certain that there is a total absence of competition at the European level or that some organizations might not be squeezed by a degree of over-representation of interests at the European level.

Conclusion: Lobbying Styles and Long-term Success

By way of brief conclusion we now turn to the difficult concept of 'lobbying styles', as this does still present a problem to the environmentalists. The sometimes confrontational styles of environmental groups – and the increased use of legal actions (see below) – may be perpetuating an image which at least some of the groups might wish to shed. For example, one environmental respondent told us that his organization was working hard to create a rather different image because some EC officials saw environmentalists as obstructionist, anti-growth and heavily reliant on the use of the media to attack both decision-makers and companies alike. His ambition was to emphasize a new perspective, which was to engage in a political and economic discussion in those policy areas 'hitherto regarded as more centrally economic than environmental. (Significantly one official, dealing with this group, commented to us that he had indeed found the group considerably more useful and better informed of late.)

If our underlying assumption is correct – namely that the Commission will gradually seek to establish a more regularized and structured form of group participation in the policy process (whether by the establishment of policy communities or even corporatist structures, or by structures that are peculiarly European, remains to be seen) – then this will present a serious challenge to the environmentalists. This is because confrontational and challenging styles of lobbying may well be incompatible with the unwritten rules of the game implied by the policy community model or its variants. Essentially, policy communities are about the private management of public business (Richardson and Jordan, 1979). However, the nature of the EC policy process, with increased use of the Court and an increased role for the Parliament, may mean that it will be difficult to confine the processing of issues within the bounds of well defined policy communities. Whether resort to more public and openly conflictual arenas of decision-making is conducive to the development of stable long-term relationships between decision-makers and groups is, however, open to doubt.

A particular problem may arise because of the increase in 'whistle-blowing' by environmental groups who now play an important role in warning the Commission of implementation failure at the national level. Thus the number of complaints by individual citizens (often encouraged by pressure groups) and the number of legal actions by groups themselves is showing a rapid increase. For example, a number of British groups, including the UK branch of FoE, have been involved in complaining to the Commission about the British government's handling of various road schemes – notably the M11 link road and the East London river crossing – resulting in Carlo Ripa di Meana's challenging the UK government in October 1991.

In the short term, national groups are gaining considerable benefit from this type of activity and the Commission seems anxious to maintain this unofficial monitoring function by groups, as it is increasingly conscious of the 'implementation gap'. Yet it does risk placing the groups in what at the national level would be regarded as the 'outsider group' category and this process may be counterproductive in terms of their developing a more co-operative dialogue with national governments (still of central importance in the implementation of environmental policy, despite the growth of EC influence). It may also affect the perception that Commission officials have of the Euro-level environmental groups. The temptations of demonstrable success now – of considerable importance in maintaining membership support and media coverage – may be at the price of a more fundamental influence in the policy process in the long run. The trade-off may be between maintaining a high public profile through an action-oriented approach to lobbying, and sacrificing a chance of long term influence in the *processing* of issues.

Acknowledgements

This study is part of a project on lobbying in the EC funded by the ESRC. The authors wish to thank David Judge and Laura Cram for their comments on an earlier draft, and the many Commission officials and environmental groups and firms who agreed to be interviewed.

Note

1. For the purposes of this study the term 'environmentalists' is used to describe individuals **or** groups whose primary objective is the introduction of policies beneficial to the environment. In contrast to firms and industrial federations which may promote environmentally friendly products, environmentalists have no direct material interest in EC environmental policy.

References

Arp, H. (1991) 'European Community Environmental Policy: What to Learn From the Case of Car Emission Regulation?', paper presented to Conference on European Integration and Environmental Policy, Woudschoten, Netherlands, 29–30 November.

Collie, L. (1992) 'Business Lobbying in the EC: The Union of Industrial Employers' Confederations of Europe', in Mazey and Richardson (1992c).

Downs, A. (1967) *Inside Bureaucracy*, Boston, MA: Little, Brown.

Downs, A. (1972) 'Up and Down with Ecology: The "Issue Attention Cycle"', *The Public Interest*, Vol.28, pp38–50.

Gorges, M. J. (1991) 'Euro-capitalism? The System of Interest Intermediation in the European Community', paper delivered to the Annual Meeting of the American Political Science Association, Washington, D.C., 29 August–1 September.

Gregory, R. (1971) *The Price of Amenity*, London: Macmillan.

Hass, E. B. (1958) *The Uniting of Europe: Political, Social and Economic Forces*, Stanford, CA: Stanford University Press.

Harvey, B. (1992) 'European Lobbying: The Experience of Voluntary Organisations', in Mazey and Richardson (1993b).

Huelshoff, M. G. and Pfeiffer, T. (1991) 'Environmental Policy in the EC: Neofunctionalist Sovereignty Transfer or Neo-realist Gatekeeping', *International Journal*, Vol.47, No.1, pp136–58.

Hull, R. (1992) 'Lobbying in Brussels: A View from Within', in Mazey and Richardson (1993b).

Jordan, A. G. and Richardson, J. J. (1987) *British Politics and the Policy Process*, London: Alien & Unwin.

Jordan, A. G. and McLaughlin, A. M. (1992) 'The Rationality of Lobbying in Europe: Why are Euro-groups So Numerous And So Weak: Some Evidence from the Car Industry', in Mazey and Richardson (1993b).

Knight, J., Mazey, S. and Richardson, J. (1993) 'Groups and the Process of European Integration: The Work of the Federation of Stock Exchanges in the European Community', in Mazey and Richardson (1993b).

Majone, G. (1989) 'Regulating Europe: Problems and Prospects', *Jarbuch zur Staats- und Verwaltungswissenschaft*, Baden-Baden.

Mazey, S. (1988) 'European Community Action on Behalf of Women: The Limits of Legislation, *Journal of Common Market Studies*, Vol.27, No.1, pp63–84.

Mazey, S. (1992) 'The Administration of the High Authority 1955–56: Development of a Supranatural Bureaucracy?', in Morgan, R. and Wright, V., *The Early Principles and Practice of the EC (European Yearbook of the History of Administration)*.

Mazey, S. and Richardson, J. J. (1992) 'British Pressure Groups in the European Community: The Challenge of Brussels', *Parliamentary Affairs*, Vol.45, No.1, pp92–127.

Mazey, S. and Richardson, J. J. (1993a) 'Interest Groups in the European Community', in Richardson, J. J. (ed) *Pressure Groups*, Oxford: Oxford University Press.

Mazey, S. and Richardson, J. J. (eds) (1993b) *Lobbying in the EC*, Oxford: Oxford University Press.

Peckstadt, J.-P., Mazey, S. and Richardson, J. J. (1992) 'Defending and Promoting a Sectoral Interest Within the European Community: The Case of the Textile Polyolefins Industry', in Mazey and Richardson (1993b).

Rhodes, M. (1990) 'The Social Dimension of the Single European Market: National vs Transnational Regulation', *European Journal of Political Research*, December.

Richardson, J. J. and Jordan A. G. (1979) *Governing Under Pressure*, Oxford: Martin Robertson.

Sargent, J. (1993) 'The Corporate Benefits of Lobbying: The British Case and its Relevance to the EC', in Mazey and Richardson (1993b).

Schattschneider, E. E. (1960) *The Semi-Sovereign People: A Realist's View of Democracy in America*, New York: Holt, Reinhart & Winston.

WWF (1991) *Focus in WWF in Europe*, Brussels.

Part 3
POLICY DYNAMICS

10

Task Expansion: A Theoretical Overview

Anthony Zito

Introduction

Despite the initial lack of an explicit treaty basis, the European Union (EU) nevertheless has constructed a very wide-ranging set of. regulations that cover the critical environmental media (water, air and soil) and a range of products and industrial processes. From Table 10.1 the tremendous expansion of environmental policies between 1957 and 1994 is evident, although the 1995 Figures raise interesting questions about the future trajectory of EU environmental policy.

In this chapter I investigate how well current theories explain 'task expansion' in the sphere of EU environmental policy over the past 40 years. Pollack (1994, p96) defines 'task expansion' as 'the initial expansion of the Community agenda to include new policy areas' and the subsequent growth of substantive policies in these new areas. A study of task expansion is primarily focused on the outputs – the laws, regulations and policy documents – of the EU policy process rather than on measuring the relative influence of national and supranational authorities in bringing that process about, which is the primary concern of European integration theory. This chapter is a stocktaking exercise. I will be asking two basic questions: (1) How well do five popular theories explain the scope and level of policy outputs in the EU environmental arena? and (2) What are the critical empirical issues that might allow us to adjudicate between the different perspectives?

The analytical perspectives included here frequently appear in EU studies: namely, neofunctionalism, intergovernmeritalism, 'new' institutionalism, ideational – epistemic approaches and policy networks. Peterson (1995) provides a useful framework for ordering these theories, distinguishing between macrotheories (for, example, traditional integration theories such as neofunctionalism that examine the international state system in which the EU operates), systemic analysis (theories explaining political behaviour in the context of the EU), and mesolevel perspectives (showing the linkage between the EU macro-structure and micro-interests within the larger European society). Peterson notes that the macrotheories

Table 10.1 *The expansion of European Union environmental policy*

	Period				
	1958–72	*1973–86*	*1987–92*	*1993–95*	*1995 alone*
Number of laws adopted[a]	5	118	82	60	5
Average number of laws adopted per annum	0.3	8.4	13.7	20	5
Total number of laws adopted[b]	9	195	192	144	28
Average number of new and amended laws adopted per annum	0.6	13.9	32	48	28

[a] Regulations, directives, and decisions only
[b] Including amendments and elaborations
Source: McCormick, 1998, p195

are better equipped to explain the broad historical trends in integration, but that these perspectives are less well equipped to explain the choices made by specific actors operating within the EU structure. Nevertheless, although such perspectives are more oriented towards the broader question of EU integration in a larger context, neofunctionalism and intergovernmentalism do provide insights into task expansion in particular sectors (for example, Cram, 1993; Golub, 1997). At the same time, scholars are increasingly studying the EU as a comparable polity, using traditional political approaches to study factors such as institutions that shape policy outcomes (Hix, 1994). 'New' institutional and ideational perspectives provide important systemic insights into how the EU operates, whereas policy network analysis reveals what occurs in policy sectors within the EU structure.

One cannot simply fuse the theories described above together because they operate at different levels. Some are macrotheories whereas others operate at a mesolevel. However, they all contain interesting explanations of task expansion. In this chapter I explore these different perspectives in the context of four time periods defined by the following four key events: (1) the creation of the Common Market in 1957; (2) the Paris Summit of 1972; (3) the enactment in 1987 of the Single European Act; and (4) the adoption in 1993 of the Maastricht Treaty (see Chapter 2).

Theoretical Approaches

Neofunctionalism

In this chapter I examine only the basic neofunctional programme (Haas, 1958), recognizing that later versions either addressed many of the deficiencies noted here (for example, Lindberg and Scheingold, 1970) or adopted slightly different perspectives yet borrowed key assumptions (for example. Marks et al, 1996). Original versions of neofunctionalism hypothesise that successful supranational policy-making can induce people to learn to reorient their national identities towards European institutional structures. The key agents of change are held to be actors in the European institutions and external socio-economic interests who seek to expand the scope of supranational policy. When national populations witness the benefits of integration occurring in one policy sector, they will embrace the extension of supranational control into other sectors. This 'spillover' process gradually embraces an ever-increasing set of issue areas (Haas, 1958, pp514–18).

The neofunctional perspective contains a clear and parsimonious explanation of why change occurs. It focuses not only on the independent role of entrepreneurial institutions, particularly supranational bodies such as the Commission and the European Court of Justice (ECJ) (Burley and Mattli, 1993), but also on national interests such as the business sector. This entrepreneurial activity tends to be technocratic. The more entrepreneurial EU organizations, such as the Commission and the European Parliament, exert influence by helping to define agendas and initiating policy proposals (see Chapters 8 and 9). Such powers fit more in the realm of influencing the interests of other actors than of having the ultimate power to pass and veto legislation (Golub, 1996a, p332). Neofunctionalism explains task expansion by asserting that EU institutions and societal actors seize opportunities to promote common environmental policies.

Despite these insights, a number of analytical problems dissuade most researchers working in EU environmental studies from relying solely on a neofunctionalist framework. Neofunctionalism implies a unidirectional progression for task expansion when empirical evidence from the environmental sector, notably the recent emergence of the subsidiarity principle, emphasizes the likelihood of policy reversals (or what neofunctionalists might term policy 'spillback') (Corbey, 1995). This deterministic outlook reflects the inadequate theorizing of national governments and popular loyalty (Pentland, 1973, pp85–6) and of the often significant internal politics within the supranational institutions (Peters, 1992, pp115–21). National governments may fear that regulatory task expansion erodes national interests, and non-environmental Commission directorate generals (DGs) may resist the intrusion of environment regulation into their policy sector. Consequently, the neofunctional expectation that achievements in more technical environmental policy will 'spill over' into more politically contested environmental issues is questionable. The assumption that environmental areas are easily separable from the political realm is itself debatable. Last, neofunctionalism suffers from a tendency to presume the naturalness of outcomes when reality is far more contingent on varying choices of conscious actors (Tsebelis, 1990, p102).

Intergovernmentalism

Like neofunctionalist approaches, recent versions of intergovernmentalist theory also contain more sophisticated accounts of the domestic political process shaping national preferences and other factors (for example, Moravcsik, 1993, pp486–7, 514–5). A realist-intergovernmental approach highlights national governments and interests seeking integration on certain issues and pushing the process forward yet also notes the importance of external pressures, particularly interdependence, and the national governments' ability to learn to co-operate to protect national interests (Taylor, 1975, pp338–47).

Intergovernmentalism remains a powerful, relatively parsimonious explanation of EU environmental task expansion because it recognizes the importance of external pressures such as economic interdependence; the critical influence exerted by Member States in the EU process (especially in the Council of Ministers); and the linking of the national political process to the EU system. For intergovernmentalists, task expansion occurs because the Member States agree that co-operative environmental policies are mutually beneficial, based on an assessment of their own domestic political concerns and transnational environmental pressures. Consequently, task expansion is tightly constrained to reflect those domestic concerns.

Few EU environmental policy studies rely solely on intergovernmentalism for their explanation. Current versions of intergovernmentalism emphasize the policy impact of treaty renegotiations (for example, Moravcsik, 1993, pp496–9), although they have been applied to the day-to-day process of environmental policy-making (Golub, 1997, p4). However, intergovernmentalism underestimates the role of actors in defining problems and shaping agendas. It also plays down the influence of non-state actors and small EU states in furthering task expansion (Peters, 1994). Although one should not ignore the ultimate Council veto, many key moments in the policy-making process occur before the decision to act has been taken, which constrains national actors later in the process. Even when the Member State governments make a determined effort to control the process, they may not be able to manage the future implications of these decisions, because of such factors as the restricted time horizons of actors and because of unintended consequences (Pierson, 1996, pp131–43). Moreover, autonomous EU institutions (for example, the European Parliament, under the co-operation and co-decision procedures) constrain the Member States' ability to control the processing of specific items of legislation (Garrett and Tsebelis, 1996, pp285–94; Golub, 1996a, pp330–5).

'New' Institutionalism

A common criticism of integration theories derived from international relations is that they cannot anticipate the EU outcomes shaped by the independent, unique EU institutional structures. EU scholars, such as Pierson (1996) and Pollack (1996), have returned to institutional analysis to interpret European integration. 'New' institutionalism is a mid-range theory that can explain specific policy outcomes and task expansion. Accordingly, EU institutions provide structures that shape how EU actors define their roles, interests and relations to other actors, and that frame the general context for acting and making choices. The EU structures consist of rules and norms that embody certain identities, interests, and values and therefore define appropriate actions for policy-makers (March and Olsen, 1989, pp159–61). Weale (1996, pp606–9) argues in favour of an institutionalist approach to studying EU environmental policy.

A 'new' institutional approach clarifies the complex relationships between EU actors at the supranational, national and subnational levels and how those relations shape environmental policy. Such an approach accepts the importance of agenda-setting as well as the ability to veto actions. The perspective explains task expansion in terms of organizations enhancing their institutional mandates, which define their worldviews (Peters, 1992, pp115–21). Therefore a 'new' institutionalist explanation of EU environmental task expansion suggests that institutional actors in the European Parliament and other organizations seek to fulfil their mandates and carve out a larger role for themselves by expanding the quantity of environmental regulation (Judge, 1993). Another institutionally based explanation of the EU policy process, principal-agent analysis, suggests that these motivations will lead to complex relationships between the institutions (Pollack, 1997). In creating the EU treaties the Member States delegate power to the Commission to perform certain regulatory tasks, such as protecting the environment, that are better performed at the EU level than within the individual Member States. These institutional interpretations differ from neofunctionalism in that they do not presume an integrationist motivation on the part of EU actors; it may be that institutions work against task expansion in several key respects.

Although institutionalist perspectives provide necessary insights into the EU political system their ability to explain EU task expansion remains limited. Although institutional structures shape many of the important opportunities that policy actors face they do not determine those interests. Institutional analysis also emphasizes the role of formal institutional bodies as opposed to equally significant informal networks. Last, although institutional approaches are good at explaining why certain decisions recur over time, they are less able to explain non-incremental policy change (Pollack, 1996, pp453–4). The institutional explanation focuses on how EU institutions channel external pressures for change and how new decisions will tend to follow the course set by previous decisions.

Ideational-Epistemic Accounts

The need to understand why policies change has led scholars to turn increasingly to the realm of ideas. Ideational perspectives contend that ideas and knowledge influence actors into redefining their interests and seeking policy change. Ideas serve as a road map for determining actor interests, prescribing the choices and values of actors (Goldstein and Keohane, 1993, pp12–3). In order to infuse some agency into the ideas argument, scholars have suggested that epistemic communities, a policy network organized around shared causal beliefs, shape policy-making, especially in areas involving a high degree of policy complexity and uncertainty (Haas, 1992, p3). Ideas, and the communities that wield them, gain influence when proponents secure positions of authority within decision-making processes (Haas, 1990, pp226–31).

Because they focus on the formulation of actor interests in times of uncertainty, ideas or epistemic approaches better explicate the EU problem-definition and agenda-setting stages of the EU policy process as opposed to the subsequent institutional bargaining (Raustiala, 1997, pp507–8). Nevertheless, ideational approaches clarify how substantial policy change occurs and how interests evolve over time. Important scientific knowledge about pollution and new ideas such as sustainable development may alter actor interests, convincing them to incorporate more EU regulation which in turn sparks further task expansion.

The role of ideas is beginning to gain some prominence in European environmental studies (for example, Lenschow and Zito, 1998; Weale, 1992). Nevertheless, the perspective faces difficulties, particularly the ambiguous distinction between ideas and interests: do interests follow ideas or vice versa? The receptivity of policy actors to ideas may remain a function of their perceived interests (Litfin, 1994, pp186–8). Policy uncertainty may lead policy-makers to interpret the knowledge in different ways, as opposed to following one approach – again raising the question of actor agency and individual interest. The epistemic community approach is one attempt to explore the question of agency in policy analysis. It also recognizes the potentially international scope of ideas. However, the narrow criteria of what constitutes an epistemic community suggests that other vehicles also translate ideas into the EU policy process (Zito, 1998).

Policy Networks

Institutional and ideational-epistemic perspectives present a difficult challenge in that their frameworks emphasize abstract concepts that are difficult to link to actual actor behaviour and policy outcomes. Policy network analysis is attractive because of its inherent focus on the actors operating in the network. These actors make calculations of interest in the context of the policy network, which in turn shapes their worldview.

The policy network approach provides a mesolevel analysis because it links specific actors to the larger EU institutions and structures (Peterson, 1997). This linkage between societal groups and public organizations mirrors neofunctionalism. The internal characteristics of the network, namely the resource dependencies between individual actors, is said to shape the political outcome of this interaction (Rhodes, 1988, pp77–8). An epistemic community is a very cohesive knowledge-driven policy network in which the independent impact of ideas is crucial.

Policy networks are a popular means of understanding the day-to-day process of deciding and implementing EU environmental policies (for example, Héritier et al, 1996; Richardson, 1994). Their advantages include the ability to recognize the importance of less formal relationships and multilayered processes operating in the EU. Networks also fit the fluid structure of environmental policy structure brought about by actors attempting to expand the competence of the EU (Bomberg, 1994, pp47–8). It is especially concerned with the alliances that develop between pro-environment actors in different organizations (for example, the commission DG XI for the environment and the European Parliament's environment committee) as they battle to set the EU-wide agenda and introduce new EU environmental policies (Mazey and Richardson, 1993, pp120–25). To achieve such changes, this environmental network must overcome other actor coalitions with less green sectoral and/or organizational interests (for example, agricultural interests that seek to control issues within their respective network).

Network analysis faces the difficulty of cleanly differentiating actor interests from ideas and institutions. Moreover, the approach focuses on EU policy-making in specific sectors; it was not intended to explain the broader EU process of integration. Networks form only one part of the structure that determines task expansion. The approach illuminates the agenda-setting phase before the Member States make their final decision in the Council of Ministers, but the intergovernmental decision-making remains (Rhodes et al, 1996, p382). Policy network explanations also have difficulty explaining why substantial EU policy change occurs (Richardson, 1996, pp34–7).

The Founding Period: 1957–1972

Having set out the theories, let us turn to reconsider the history of task expansion. The slow rate of adoption during the period 1957–1972 (see Table 10.1) suggests the intermittent nature of EU environmental regulation building during this first period. Nevertheless, this era raises several theoretical issues. As the founding Treaty made no explicit reference to environmental priorities, a wide range of legal justification, particularly Articles 235 and 100, provided the basis for the infrequent regulations with environmental implications (also, see Hildebrand, 1993, pp17–20). A pattern of embedding environmental issues in the building of the European Common Market emerged: policy-makers used Article 100 to give the European Economic Community (EEC) institutions the power to protect the construction and operation of the Common Market, thereby fulfilling indirectly some of the broad objectives contained in Articles 2 and 3 of the Treaty of Rome (Rehbinder and Steward, 1985, pp16–28). Article 100 provided the basis for regulations of dangerous substances and noise and exhaust emissions – the foundation for future legislation in these areas.

Given the rather creative interpretation of an environmental mandate, this period appears to bear all the hallmarks of functional spillover, or what Weale (1999) describes as 'integration by stealth' (see Chapter 18). Commission officials had the opportunity to link the functioning of the Common Market, protected by Article 100, to other policy issues when national legislation impinged on the market (Pollack, 1994, pp123–5). The Commission's ability to harmonize national legislation in different economically related areas suggests it seized the opportunity to extend the Community's scope and protect the objectives of the market.

Although the case for neofunctionalism during the agenda-setting stage of the EU policy process is highly suggestive, individual Member States continued to hold a veto in the Council of Environment Ministers. An intergovernmental interpretation argues that this arrangement allowed Member States and national interests to retain control over the overall direction of task expansion. Certain national governments took the initiative by creating legislation. The Member States responded by permitting the Community process to harmonize environmental legislation as long as it was mutually beneficial. However, the Commission's exclusive right of initiative grants it a gate-keeping role, enabling it to define problems in particular ways. More research is needed into the motives of the Community institutions during the foundational period to judge whether the neofunctional or the intergovernmental perspectives best explain the spill-over process.

The application of the mid-range approaches is more clear-cut. The influence of institutions is particularly salient: ideas, centred around the economic goals of the Common Market which are embedded in the EU institutional structure, played an indirect role. After all, developing a Common Market is the Community institutions' raison d'etre. Even without the drive to extend supranational control over environmental policy, other, more powerful, parts of the Commission such as DG III (at the time covering the internal market and industry) would have watched for issues that threatened the common market and diluted them. An alternative interpretation based on principal-agent theory is also plausible: the technical nature of regulations, such as the classification and handling of hazardous substances, and the uncertainty of what is happening in all of the Member States, creates incentives for the Member State governments to delegate regulatory functions to the Commission. Thus institutionalist analysis, which focuses on how organizations seek to fulfill their tasks and protect their mandate, can reinforce either the neofunctional or the intergovernmental interpretations.

In terms of the ideas and policy network approaches, the intermittent appearance of environment-related regulation underlines the absence of powerful clearly focused political groups capable of defining the environment as a distinct political issue. More often than not, 'environmental' measures often were ushered through under the guise of 'health' or 'safety' matters (Vogel, 1993, pp244–50). In these circumstances, the historical record prior to 1972 offers little evidence either of a united coalition of environmental interests or of an influential set of environmental ideas capable of progressing task expansion.

The regulatory record for the era suggests that the key question is to define whether the Commission or the Member States set the EEC agenda and spurred spillover. The degree to which the policy issue is technical is an important angle to this question. The more technical and less salient the issue is to the general public, the more tenuous the linkage between the regulation and distinct national interests (and the less the pressure on national politicians to intervene). There is also a dimension that gives intergovernmentalism an analytical edge over neofunctionalism and the mid-range theories: intergovernmentalism acknowledges that external factors can have an impact on the EU. For example, the Community institutions-based Directive 70/157 (noise emissions from cars, buses and lorries) on a United Nations Economic Commission for Europe regulation (Haigh, 1997). Policy emulation such as this emphasizes the importance of international factors in EU policy-making.

The Institutionalization of Environmental Concern: 1972–1987

The impact of rising levels of environmental awareness during the 1970s is reflected in the upsurge of environmental legislation adopted by the EEC in the period following the adoption of the first action programme (see Table 10.1).

Nevertheless, task expansion followed the paths laid down during the foundational era because of the continuing lack of an explicit treaty basis.

The speed and scale of expansion, and the increasingly prominent role of supranational institutions, would appear to confirm early neofunctional predictions: namely that institutions such as the Commission and European Parliament expanded the presence of the EEC in national affairs. The creation of dedicated environmental organizations such as the European Consumer Protection Service was significant in reinforcing task expansion. The European Parliament created a dedicated environmental committee in 1972 (see Chapter 8). The establishment of Commission Directorate General for the Environment (DG XI) in 1981 created both an institution dedicated to promoting environmental priorities in the larger EEC arena and a focus for environmental coalition building (Mazey and Richardson, 1993; Sbragia, 1993, pp345–8). Pro-environment actors in the Commission used their mandate to propose a battery of new regulations.

On the surface, these developments seemed to follow neofunctionalist predictions. Nevertheless, the empirical question remains of how much problem-definition and agenda-setting influence is attributable to the Commission when it comes to the actual *output* of new regulations. Supranational actors cannot claim the entire role in agenda setting, as the presence of intergovernmental actors is also discernible. The Commission's attempts to harmonize national legislation induced a large portion of the expansion in legislation in this era. But national policy priorities and interests of certain pro-environment states were also critical in pushing task expansion forward (Sbragia, 1996). The enormous impetus given to EEC environmental policy by West Germany's conversion to green thinking is mentioned by Jordan (1999a). The German government's primary objective was to define the EU legislation in such a way as to minimize its own legal adjustment costs and reduce the economic burden on its industry (see Chapter 11).

Germany's role in the adoption of the landmark Directive on Large Combustion Plants (Sbragia, 1996; Weale, 1996) broadly confirms an intergovernmental perspective. Nevertheless, the sequence of events which culminated in the adoption of the directive also contains some special features: acid rain was an issue at the top of political agendas in a number of key Member States because of the visibility of its effects and the potentially very high economic cost of remedial measures. The issue was not completely dominated by scientific or technical argumentation. In other words, the circumstances were precisely those in which one would expect intergovernmental forces to be strong. Low-visibility issues are more likely to engage officials in the lower echelons of the Commission and national ministries, and those interests directly affected by control measures. In this scenario, the Commission's agenda-setting role and ability to act as a mediator may have given officials the leeway to guide the agenda.

Although the large-combustion-plant outcome broadly fits an intergovernmental view of European environmental policy, institutions helped shape the precise pathway of task expansion. Significantly, the German government used its Council presidencies and the Commission's agenda-setting and brokering roles to make headway on the directive (Héritier et al, 1996, pp200–2; Sbragia, 1996, pp238–9). The UK found itself in a minority of one. This gave DG XI, which at the time was headed by a German official, room to mediate between national positions. The influence of institutions is likely to be even stronger in other less salient issues. Acting not as a neofunctional body seeking to expand the EU role but rather as an organization seeking to enhance its own position, the European Parliament helped define the agenda in such areas as the trade in hazardous waste (Zito, 1995).

Idea-based explanations also present a rather equivocal picture during this era. At a basic level, the knowledge about the impact of human processes placed tremendous pressure on EEC policy-makers to respond with concrete policies. Unprecedented levels of environmental awareness pushed EEC leaders to give the Commission an institutional mandate to propose large quantities of regulation. However, this was a general, regionwide movement shaping EEC actions rather than a specific set of ideas spurring task expansion. However, the presence of specific new ideas capable of reshaping EEC interests and expanding the EEC role are noticeable in the three environmental action programmes (EAPs). For instance, the third EAP contained the new policy idea of focusing environmental policy on prevention and of integrating environmental factors into other sectors (Johnson and Corcelle, 1989, pp17–9). Nevertheless, despite the requirement that the Council adopt these programmes, the actual regulatory influence of EAPs is fairly indirect; they raise issues for discussion rather than promulgate specific legislative actions.

It is more difficult to assert that policy networks played a consistently important role in EU task expansion during this period. Although networks of interested parties do surround the environmental policy process they are more likely to be fluid because of the novelty and openness of the EEC environmental policy structure (see Chapter 9). There was no solid green coalition pushing for, task expansion across the entire environmental policy sector. The Commission looked to producer groups to help on technical details on relevant legislation, but these interests would concentrate their efforts there. Although organizations such as Greenpeace focus on highly visible issues such as nuclear power, climate change, and acid rain they do not have sufficient resources to mount a sustained campaign across a range of issues. There does not seem to have been an organized coalition pushing the EEC into new environmental areas. It is only when the EEC expanded into new areas that policy networks became prominent, supporting a particular aspect of task expansion such as a legislation on emissions of a particular type of chemical.

The analysis above suggests that supranational (neofunctional or 'new' institutionalism) and intergovernmental theories provide the most convincing account of task expansion in the period 1972–1987. In order to determine more decisively the relative influence of institutions versus Member States a comprehensive overview of EEC policy output during this time period is necessary. The difficulty of penetrating actor motivations across such a huge spectrum of cases can be overcome by examining how far Community policy has moved beyond pre-existing Member State laws (see Chapter 13). If Community policies move significantly beyond those found at the national level, this might imply that external ideas or institutions have pushed the majority of Member States beyond the lowest common denominator of state preferences (as predicted by intergovernmentalism).

A study of particular types or cases of regulation in the 1972–1987 period may provide a more rapid resolution of these questions. A regulatory typology indicates the cases that present a strong challenge to the intergovernmental thesis. First, technical issues of low political salience provide a stiff test for inter-governmentalism. Second, process-oriented legislation seems a more difficult test for intergovernmentalism than does product regulation. Both Pollack (1994, pp125–6) and Gehring (1997, pp342–5) argue that the EU's efforts to reconcile the tension between protecting environment policy and promoting an internal market led to two distinct categories of intervention: process-related regulation and product-related regulation. Product-related regulation creates relatively high minimum standards across all Member States, whereas process-related regulations, which typically rely on more indirect incentives, have had greater difficulty gaining Member State acceptance.

A substantial portion of EU regulation in the 1972–1987 period falls under the product harmonization rubric (for example, vehicle emissions regulations). The Commission proposed the basic waste framework directives to deal with the consequences of national legislation. Although this case highlights Commission entrepreneurship and activity by the European Parliament, the legislation that was finally adopted amounted to a basic compromise between the legal characteristics of the Member State legislation (Zito, 1995). Product standards suggest a stronger presence of national interests in pushing task expansion and setting the agenda.

Process standards regulation provides a clearer test of the intergovernmental thesis because the linkages between industrial competitiveness (often a national priority) and environmental protection may be less clear-cut. Although many of the air-pollution directives were strongly influenced by pre-existing national legislation in some of the most environmentally concerned northern states (Golub, 1997), EU water policy presents a slightly different picture (Sbragia, 1993, pp342–3). Water legislation, such as the Bathing and Drinking Water Directives, offers a case where a less 'green' UK government went along with Community proposals without realizing some of the long-term regulatory costs (Golub, 1996b, pp708–9; Jordan, 1999b). Nevertheless, the presence of national governments shaping the details of Community legislation is evident in many of the water directives in this process-oriented environmental sector (Haigh, 1997).

A third likely area for investigation is wildlife conservation (Pollack, 1994). Popular interest in protecting endangered species often outweighs the concerns of economic actors dependent on the species. Both the European Parliament and the Commission achieved Council acceptance for the Wild Birds Directive (EEC/79/409) despite Member State haggling. The process forced concessions from certain Member States, and protecting certain aviary categories has caused particular states unanticipated problems and costs (Haigh, 1997, section 9.2, pp5–7). The need to find regulatory characteristics that favour environmental priorities is important given that the economic logic found in the typical EU environmental regulation often reflects (and therefore is difficult to distinguish from) national economic priorities.

Comparing the prior Member State positions with actual EU regulation enables one to extrapolate from limited research material, but it has some drawbacks. It is difficult to isolate what shapes state preferences. Non-state actors may have convinced Member States that a Community approach was important to their national interests and minimized the perception of negative costs. Furthermore, decision-makers may not realize the long-term consequence of supranational control; unforeseen circumstances may make the legislation more important in the future (Pierson, 1996, pp135–44).

1987–1992: the High-water Mark?

Although the second phase created the regulatory foundation for EU environmental policy, one can see from Table 10.1 the enormous rate of task expansion in the third period as the EU created new directives and amended old legislation. The period before the ratification of the Maastricht Treaty reveals the increase in pressures towards constraining new environmental proposals. The long, conflictual discussions about subsidiarity, enshrined in Article 3b of the Maastricht Treaty indicate the challenge to continued policy task expansion. The UK used its presidency of the EU in 1992 to push the subsidiarity principle in the environmental arena (Maddox, 1992).

Neofunctionalism provides a general explanation for the sheer number of new policies and the effort to link environmental priorities to other EEC policies during this period. The goal of completing the Common Market by 1992 presented a huge challenge to proenvironment actors (TFEIM, 1990). This policy linkage strongly suggests the neofunctionalist notion of spillover between issue areas. However, neofunctionalism suffers from a teleological view of continued supranational expansion and integration. Both Jordan (1999a) and Lenschow (1999) show that, by 1992, task expansion had become more focused on consolidating the *acquis communautaire* (that is, better implementation, more policy consultation and co-ordination, and greater integration) rather than expanding it into new areas. Furthermore, neofunctionalism does not explain why some Member States eagerly endorsed the subsidiarity principle. Nor does it specify the directions that the EU took (that is, developing new environmental instruments such as voluntary agreements and eco taxes). To answer these questions we need to turn to the mid-range theories.

The increasing level of rhetoric about subsidiarity perfectly fits intergovernmentalist expectations. This interpretation emphasizes the ability of Member States to control and shape the EU according to their preferences. Countries such as the United Kingdom have used subsidiarity as a means of shifting the Commission's organizational direction and of constraining task expansion. This action occurred despite the greater institutional recognition of environmental priorities and the extension of qualified majority voting in the SEA and Maastricht Treaties (Golub, 1996b). National business interests have been extremely effective at pushing the theme of competitiveness and deregulation (Collier, 1997). Two prominent examples of relatively strict EU legislation, the Packaging Waste Directive (see Chapter 13) and the Automobile Emissions Directive (see Chapter 15), are product- oriented regulations and are Commission responses to externalities triggered by national regulations.

Although intergovernmentalism explains the general shift in direction, it is less successful in explaining the nature and specific impetus of this change. The evolution of regulatory policy seen from 1992 onwards has not necessarily reduced regulatory costs for national businesses. A 'new' institutionalist perspective suggests that the policy leadership did not consist merely of national interests. The Commission recognized the need to create environmental policy which was more effective and to enhance implementation to fulfil its organizational aims; this motivation is not the supranational expansionism suggested by neofunctionalism. To some extent one must credit this change of thinking to Member State pressure to accept the subsidiarity principle and to economic hardship. The Maastricht Treaty negotiations and the critical reaction from the public to the final agreement appear to have changed the Commission's outlook.

'New' institutional analysis also provides a slightly different explanation for the task expansion witnessed before 1992. It highlights the changing dynamics between the various EU actors in this time period. Specifically, the explicit Treaty references strengthened the organizational mandate of 'pro-environment' actors such as DG XI. By using the explicit organizational mandate of the Member States, DG XI then developed a wide range of proposals and looked at new instruments, such as an energy carbon tax, which gave Europe (and the Commission) a stronger international profile on global issues such as climate change (see Sbragia, 1999). Because the tax was a fiscal measure, certain states opposed it in principle. Nevertheless, the Member States have had to adapt to protect their interests by sustaining a blocking coalition in other issue areas. Perhaps even more important, Member State governments were forced to pursue different strategies to protect their interests in this setting: they must seek to define the environmental problem and solution far in advance of the Council stage in areas where qualified majority voting applies (Héritier et al, 1996, pp160–1).

This behaviour argues strongly for the importance of an institutional approach, which also recognizes the increasing impact of the European Parliament and the ECJ in a way not fully captured by neofunctionalism (see Chapter 15). Jordan in his introductory paper (1999a) records how the Court supported informal integration against the wishes of individual states. The Court ruled in favour of the Parliament and the Commission in the titanium dioxide case (see Chapter 7), and it has directly supported the environmental *acquis* by ruling against the Commission when it argued that a Wallonian law on wastes violated the free movement of goods (Lenschow and Zito, 1998).

In evaluating the direction the EU institutions have taken towards constructing new environmental regulations, the ideational-epistemic literature provides a different set of insights. However, the call for new ideas in this time period is as much a question of justifying political options as opposed to trying to understand complex issues within the context of a high degree of problem uncertainty (policy uncertainty being the favourable condition for epistemic communities). The subsidiarity principle is a good case in point.

During the rapid expansion of environmental regulation prior to 1992–1993 new ideas were prominent and arguably helped actors to promote EU task expansion. The fourth and fifth action programmes reflect the ideas that national and EU actors were considering. A key theme of the fifth programme was sustainable development. This has three critical elements: (1) integration of the environmental priorities into other societal activities; (2) greater participation of all relevant actors; and (3) greater internalization of external costs (Collier, 1997, p5). All three principles suggest a recalibration of EU environmental policy, leading to an expansion in the EU's role. Policy integration expands the scope of EU environmental policy actors to participate in the decision-making for other areas such as the Regional Development Fund (see Lenschow, 1999; see also Lenschow, 1997, pp111–3).

Even if one accepts the intergovernmentalist premise, the ideas explanation illuminates how the discourse led to policies that did not always reduce regulatory burdens. For example, the shared-responsibility theme suggested the need for new kinds of legislation and policy instruments that would increase private actors' regulatory role as long as minimum EU standards were met. The importance of getting private actors to regulate themselves and the subsidiarity concept are all ideas tied to the emphasis of sustainable development on actor involvement and shared responsibility (Collier, 1997; Lenschow and Zito, 1998).

The policy networks approach also has a greater analytical utility in this period, although it is difficult to identify policy networks consistently pushing task expansion. Much of the important expansion into new regulatory areas occurred prior to 1986 – for example, the creation of the waste and water framework directives. Nevertheless, the elaboration and amendment of substantive policies within these areas is more likely to preoccupy the technical experts in DG XI, the national environmental ministries, and interested private groups than involve substantial intergovernmental decision-making – unless the issue is of such vital national interest that it requires top-level political involvement (Peterson, 1997).

The greater prominence of pro-environment institutions also spurs the creation of policy networks. The European Parliament's environment committee has become part of an institutional alliance and network of interests promoting stronger environmental EU regulations (see Chapter 8). Economic interests are also devoting greater attention to DG XI's activities and are trying to exert more influence within these admittedly fluid networks (Mazey and Richardson, 1998). This greater attention partially explains the change in regulatory philosophy witnessed at the end of the period. Moreover, the Commission and national environmental ministries have changed their focus on what constitutes effective environmental regulation and are seeking to create conditions that favour the appearance of networks. The Commission has tried to use private organization and public awareness to prevent Member States violating EU standards (Héritier et al, 1996; Jordan, 1999a). Ward and Williams (1997, pp448–53) note how DG XI has pushed an innovative green paper to build networks with regional and local authorities in the area of urban environment. Although not binding on Member States, this document nevertheless constitutes task expansion.

Finally, the struggle to integrate environmental priorities into other EU sectoral areas suggests very strongly the utility of the policy network approach, which helps to gauge the opposition to pro-environment forces. Environmental interests are trying to insert themselves into comparatively stable policy sectors where stronger, more identifiable networks among Commission, national ministry, and interest-group officials are likely to exist. In sectors such as the Common Agricultural Policy there are more cohesive economic and producer networks seeking to resist the incursion of proenvironment interests (Lenschow, 1997, 1999).

Post-1993: Task Expansion or Retrenchment?

Although the data in Table 10.1 are suggestive of continued regulatory expansion, many of the important trends discernible in the early 1990s have carried over in the current era. The 1995 data show a considerable decline in task expansion; the expansion witnessed in the period 1993–1994 may be a function of a backlog of proposals that the EU process has since eliminated. Of course, one should not extrapolate too far on the basis of one year's results. In fact, the latest edition of Haigh's (1998, Section 2.2) handbook suggests that 1995 (only 22 items adopted) was an anomaly, with 43 and an unprecedented 51 items of environmental legislation adopted in 1996 and 1997, respectively (see McCormick, 1998; Mazey and Richardson, 1998). Jordan (1999a) identified the Santer Commission's preference for using green and white papers to stimulate environmental action, backed up by regulation when it is absolutely necessary (McCormick, 1998, p194; Mazey and Richardson, 1998). Nevertheless, a number of recent developments may yet spark further environmental task expansion, such as the Amsterdam Treaty provisions (see Chapter 4). The increased Scandinavian presence in the Council of Environment Ministers may also encourage the EU to expand its environmental scope, particularly if important external 'shocks', such as international negotiations and high-profile environmental disasters, trigger a sudden demand for concerted action.

Neofunctionalism, as traditionally defined, struggles to account for the changing momentum, typified by the current decline in Commission proposals. With its supranational expectations the approach cannot capture fully the fact that Commission activity may not be decreasing but rather channelled into new areas. This reality of continued Commission activity geared towards new aims also presents difficulties for intergovernmentalism. Elements of this change do highlight the importance of national preferences. The perspective that Member States have taken on subsidiarity and the impact of environmental regulation on economic competitiveness has altered the strategy of environmental regulators.

Nevertheless, a 'new' institutional analysis presents a more complicated picture of this process, with institutions such as the Parliament having a more autonomous role. The new Council decision-making rules have forced actors to pay attention to how the agenda is shaped; the Commission has retained its ability to influence and even guide this agenda through discussion papers and new instruments. Environmentally progressive actors in the Commission can only hope that increased information about how well Member States are addressing environmental problems (see Jordan, 1999a) will induce the public and environmental organizations to seek change.

The shift in direction towards regulatory expansion is consistent with an ideational explanation. The Commission may still seek to promote its organizational objectives of protecting the EU environment, but the means of doing so have had to be adapted to fit the real politik. The Auto-oil programme, which involves the Commission, fuel producers, and car manufacturers in a tripartite negotiation process shows how task expansion continues without recourse to command-and-control instruments. Policy networks, oriented towards individual sectors, do not capture the overall nature of this change although the discussions in the policy networks probably are shaping the utilization of the available ideas.

Conclusions

Under which conditions do the five analytical approaches work best? I suggest that their explanatory power varies across the different stages of the task expansion process. It is therefore worth differentiating between the two broad phases of task expansion: (1) the initial period when regulatory parameters and frameworks are being set out for the policy area; (2) a subsequent period during which the *acquis communautaire* is fleshed out and amended. Macrolevel theories seem better suited to the period 1957–1972, whereas the ideational-epistemic and policy network approaches come into their own in the second period (1972–1987). However, even in this second phase one cannot abandon international explanations – much of EU environmental policy continues to be shaped by external international actors, forces and problems, and by the preferences of particular states. Mid-range theories have difficulty encompassing these factors although ideational explanations, such as those concerning epistemic communities, recognize that the ideas may have an international origin.

If one takes the theoretical approaches in turn, neofunctionalism remains a plausible theory for the period of task expansion up to 1991–1992. However, it makes a key assumption, namely that the Member State governments are willing to let the Commission take the lead in setting the agenda and defining the scope of EU activity. It is more likely that the Commission will do so when the issues are very technical, have low saliency among the national publics, and involve wildlife conservation and process regulations. Nevertheless, it is unwise to rely solely on neofunctionalism because it cannot explain the slackening pace of task expansion, the change in regulatory philosophy in the 1990s, or highly politicised cases of policy-making.

The intergovernmentalist approach, especially when supported by principal-agent analysis, suggests that the Commission's agenda-setting role may be conforming to national preferences; it thus offers a plausible explanation of pre-1992 task expansion. This is most likely to be true in highly politicized issues and product regulations where Member State economic interests are clearly defined and forcefully articulated. The more technocratic policy areas present the difficult cases. Intergovernmentalism does not allow for the independent impact of the European Parliament and the ECJ on legislative outputs, such as the Auto-oil programme and the philosophical switch to less regulatory forms of intervention.

As Weale (Chapter 12) argues, the role of institutions is critical throughout the history of a policy area. Institutional structures have defined the way in which EU actors have expanded the EU policy scope. Nevertheless, a 'new' institutionalist approach seems most appropriate during periods of institutional stability. Institutionalist accounts can explain how actors reacted to the non-incremental change which was operative in the early 1970s and early 1990s, but they struggle to explain instances of sudden change.

On the whole the ideational-epistemic perspective seems to explain how many of the regulatory outputs were framed, but there is no one idea (or overarching epistemic community) that accounts for the ebb and flow of task expansion since 1957. Individual ideas, such as sustainable development and subsidiarity, explain some of the changes since the SEA. However, it is difficult to tell how much the change is the result of independent ideas, and much is related to actors seizing on ideas as rhetorical weapons to protect bureaucratic, national, or other pre-existing interests. Ideas are likely to be powerful when causal beliefs come under challenge – owing, for example, to the challenge of new, unknown problems – and when policy-makers have to choose between several different and contentious policy directions.

The policy network framework has similar limitations. It can explain the course of action taken in specific issue areas, especially where policy networks are present, but no single policy network seems to have provided the momentum to drive EU task expansion over the four time periods. For this reason, we should not completely dismiss either the policy network of the ideational approaches. Given the inherent limitations of international relations theory, we should take our cue from Corbey (1995) and Peterson (1995) and explore *combinations* of theories. An explanation of EU task expansion requires the ability to explain the stability or instability of policy-making in the system and to explore specific outcomes. To illustrate some possibilities, when there is little pressure on the EU system to change the nature of its environmental policy, an institutionalist analysis of the EU system combined with policy networks may explain the task expansion periods. When Member States are strongly divided on key issues, an intergovernmentalist approach helps to explain the systemic constraints whereas ideational explanations explain the specific policy direction. This theoretical strategy lacks parsimony, but it does provide the means for explaining task expansion and the absence of a single theory of task expansion.

References

Arp, H. A. (1993) 'Technical Regulation and Politics: The Interplay between Economic Interests and Environmental Policy Goals in EC Car Emission Legislation', in *European Integration and Environmental Policy,* Liefferink, J. D., Lowe, P. D. and Mol, A. P. J. (eds) Belhaven Press: London, pp150–171.

Bomberg, E. (1994) 'Policy Networks on the Periphery: EU Environmental Policy and Scotland', *Regional Politics and Policy,* Vol.4, pp45–61.

Burley, A. and Mattli, W. (1993) 'Europe before the Court: A Political Theory of Legal Integration', *International Organization,* Vol.47, pp41–76.

Collier, U. (1997) 'Sustainability Subsidiarity and Deregulation: New Directions in EU Environmental Policy', *Environmental Politics,* pp61–23.

Corbey, D. (1995) 'Dialectical Functionalism: Stagnation as a Booster of European Integration', *International Organization*, Vol.49, pp253–284.

Cram, L. (1993) 'Calling the Tune without Paying the Piper? The Role of the Commission in European Union Social Policy', *Policy and Politics*, Vol.21, pp135–146.

Garrett, G. and Tsebelis, G. (1996) 'An Institutionalist Critique of Intergovernmentalism', *International Organization*, Vol.50, pp269–299.

Gehring, T. (1997) 'Governing in Nested Institutions: Environmental Policy in the European Union and the Case of Packaging Waste', *Journal of European Public Policy*, Vol.4, pp337–354.

Goldstein, J. and Keohane, R. O. (1993) 'Ideas and Foreign Policy: An Analytical Framework', in *Ideas and Foreign Policy: Beliefs, Institutions, and Political Change*, Goldstein, J. and Keohane, R. O. (eds) Cornell University Press: Ithaca, NY, pp3–30.

Golub, J. (1996a) 'State Power and Institutional Influence in European Integration: Lessons from the Packaging Waste Directive', *Journal of Common Market Studies*, Vol.34, pp313–339.

Golub, J. (1996b) 'British Sovereignty and the Development of EC Environmental Policy', *Environmental Politics*, Vol.5, pp700–728.

Golub, J. (1997) 'The Path to EU Environmental Policy: Domestic Politics, Supranational Institutions, Global Competition', paper presented at the 5th Biennial ECSA Conference, Seattle, WA; copy available from the European Community Studies Association, Pittsburgh, PA.

Haas, E. (1958) *The Uniting of Europe: Political, Social, and Economic Forces 1950–1957*, Stanford University Press: Stanford, CA.

Haas, P. (1990) *Saving the Mediterranean*, Columbia University Press: New York.

Haas, P. (1992) 'Introduction: Epistemic Communities and International Policy Coordination', *International Organization*, Vol.46, pp1–35.

Haigh, N. (1997) *Manual of Environmental Policy: The EC and Britain*, Longman: Harlow, Essex.

Haigh N, (1998) *Manual of Environmental Policy: The EC and Britain*, Longman: Harlow, Essex.

Héritier, A., Knill, C. and Mingers, S. (1996) *Ringing the Changes in Europe*, De Gruyter: Berlin.

Hildebrand, P. (1993) 'The European Community's Environmental Policy, 1957 to "1992": From Incidental Measures to an International Regime', in *A Green Dimension for the European Community: Political Issues and Processes*, Judge, D. (ed), Frank Cass: Portland, OR, pp13–44.

Hix, S. (1994) 'The Study of the EC: The Challenge to Comparative Politics', *West European Politics*, Vol.17, pp1–30.

Johnson, S. P. and Corcelle, G. (1989) *The Environmental Policy of the European Communities*, Graham and Trotman: London.

Jordan, A. J. (1998) 'Step Change or Stasis? EC Environmental Policy after the Amsterdam Treaty', *Environmental Politics*, Vol.7, pp227–236.

Jordan, A. J. (1999a) 'The Construction of a Multilevel Environmental Governance System', *Environment and Planning C: Government and Policy*, Vol.17, pp1–17.

Jordan, A. J. (1999b) 'European Community Water Standards: Locked in or Watered Down?', *Journal of Common Market Studies*, Vol.37, No.1, pp13–37.

Judge, D. (1993) '"Predestined to Save the Earth": The Environment Committee of the European Parliament', in *A Green Dimension for the European Community: Political Issues and Processes*, Judge, D. (ed), Frank Cass: Portland, OR, pp186–212.

Koppen, I. (1993) 'The Role of the European Court of Justice', in *European Integration and Environmental Policy*, Liefferink, J. D., Lowe, P. D. and Mol, A. P. J. (eds), Belhaven Press: London, pp126–149.

Lenschow, A. (1997) 'Variation in EC Environmental Policy Integration: Agency Push within Complex Institutional Structures', *Journal of European Public Policy*, Vol.4, pp109–127.

Lenschow, A. (1999) 'The Greening of the EU: The CAP and the Structural Funds', *Environment and Planning C: Government and Policy*, Vol.17, pp91–108.

Lenschow, A. and Zito, A. R. (1998) 'Institutional Linkages Across EC Economic and Environmental Policy Realms', *Governance*, Vol.11, pp415–441.

Lindberg, L. and Scheingold, S. (1970) *Europe's Would be Polity: Patterns of Change in the European Community*, Prentice Hall: Englewood Cliffs, NJ.

Litfin, K. (1994) *Ozone Discourses*, Columbia University Press: New York.

McCormick, J. (1998) 'Environmental Policy: Deepen or Widen?', in *The State of the European Union Volume 4: Deepening and Widening*, Laurent, P. H. and Maresceau, M. (eds), Lynne Rienner: Boulder, CO, pp191–206.

Maddox, B. (1992) 'UK Threat to European Green Laws', *Financial Times*, 9 July, p8.

March, J. and Olsen, J. (1989) *Rediscovering Institutions: The Organizational Basis of Politics*, The Free Press: New York.

Marks, G., Hooghe, L. and Blank, K. (1996) 'European Integration from the 1980s', *Journal of Common Market Studies*, Vol.34, pp341–378.

Mazey, S. and Richardson, J. (1993) 'Environmental Groups and the EC: Challenges and Opportunities', in *A Green Dimension for the European Community: Political Issues and Processes*, Judge, D. (ed), Frank Cass: Portland, OR, pp109–128.

Mazey, S. and Richardson, J. (1998) 'Framing and Re-framing Public Policy in the EU: Ideas, Interests and Institutions in Sex Equality and Environmental Policies', paper presented at the annual ECPR Joint Sessions of Workshops, Warwick University; copy available from ECPR Central Services, University of Essex, Colchester, Essex.

Moravcsik, A. (1993) 'Preferences and Power in the European Community: A Liberal Intergovernmentalist Approach', *Journal of Common Market Studies*, Vol.31, pp473–522.

Pentland, C. (1973) *International Theory and European Integration*, The Free Press: New York.

Peters, B. G. (1992) 'Bureaucratic Politics and the Institutions of the European Community', in *Euro-politics*, Sbragia, A. (ed), The Brookings Institution: Washington, D.C., pp75–122.

Peters, B. G. (1994) 'Agenda-setting in the European Community', *Journal of European Public Policy*, pp19–26.

Peterson, J. (1995) 'Decision-making in the European Union: Towards a Framework for Analysis', *Journal of European Public Policy*, Vol.2, pp69–93.

Peterson, J. (1997) 'States, Societies and the European Union', *West European Politics*, Vol.20, pp1–23.

Pierson, P. (1996) 'The Path to European Integration: A Historical Institutionalist Analysis', *Comparative Political Studies*, Vol.29, pp123–163.

Pollack, M. (1994) 'Creeping Competence: The Expanding Agenda of the European Community', *Journal of Public Policy*, Vol.14, pp95–145.

Pollack, M. (1996) 'The New Institutionalism and EC Governance', *Governance*, Vol.9, pp429–458.

Pollack, M. (1997) 'Delegation, Agency, and Aagenda Setting in the European Community', *International Organization*, Vol.51, pp99–134.

Raustiala, K. (1997) 'Domestic Institutions and International Regulatory Co-operation: Comparative Responses to the Convention on Biological Diversity', *World Politics*, Vol.49, pp482–509.

Rehbinder, E. and Steward, R. (1985) *Environmental Protection Policy, Volume 2: Integration Through Law: Europe and the American Federal Experience*, De Gruyter: Berlin.

Rhodes, R. A. W. (1988) *Beyond Westminster and Whitehall: The Sub-central Governments of Britain*, Unwin Hyman: London.

Rhodes, R. A. W., Bache, I. and George, S. (1996) 'Policy Networks and Policymaking in the European Union: A Critical Appraisal', in *Cohesion Policy and European Integration: Building Multi-level Governance*, Hooghe, L. (ed), Oxford University Press: Oxford, pp367–387.

Richardson, J. (1994) 'EU Water Policy: Uncertain Agendas, Shifting Hetworks and Complex Coalitions', *Environmental Politics*, Vol.3, pp139–167.

Richardson, J. (1996) 'Actor-based Models of National and EU Policy-making', in *The European Union and National Industrial Policy*, Kassim, H. and Menon, A. (eds), Routledge: London, pp20–51.

Sbragia, A. (1993) 'EC Environmental Policy: Atypical Ambitions and Typical Problems?', in *The State of the European Community: Maastricht Debates and Beyond*, Cafruny, A. and Rosenthal, G. (eds), Lynne Rienner: Boulder, CO, pp337–352.

Sbragia, A. (1996) 'The Push–Pull of Environmental Policy-making', in *Policy-making in the European Union* (3rd edn), Wallace, H. and Wallace, W. (eds), Oxford University Press: Oxford, pp235–255.

Sbragia, A. (1999) 'From Laggard to Leader: The EU, Institution Building and the Politics of Climate Change', *Environment and Planning C: Government and Policy*, Vol.17, pp53–68.

Taylor, P. (1975) 'The Politics of the European Communities: The Confederal Phase', *World Politics*, Vol.27, pp336–360.

TFEIM (1990) *'1992' The Environmental Dimension: Task Force Report on the Environment and the Internal Market*, Task Force Environment and the Internal Market, Economica: Berlin.

Tsebelis, G. (1990) *Nested Games: Rational Choice in Comparative Politics*, University of California Press: Berkeley, CA.

Vogel, D. (1993) 'Representing Diffuse Interests in Environmental Policy-making', in *Do Institutions Matter? Government Capabilities in the United States and Abroad*, Weaver, R. K. and Rockman, B. A. (eds), The Brookings Institute: Washington, D.C., pp238–271.

Ward, S. and Williams, R. (1997) 'From Hierarchy to Networks? Sub-central Government and EU Urban Environment Policy', *Journal of Common Market Studies*, Vol.35, pp439–464.

Weale, A. (1992) *The New Politics of Pollution*, Manchester University Press: Manchester.

Weale, A. (1996) 'Environmental Rules and Rule-making in the European Union', *Journal of European Public Policy*, Vol.3, pp594–611.

Weale, A. (1999) 'European Environmental Policy by Stealth: The Dysfunctionality of Functionalism?', *Environment and Planning C: Government and Policy*, Vol.17, pp37–51.

Zito, A. R. (1995) *European Union Environmental Policy-making: Contending Approaches to Institutional Decision-making*, unpublished PhD thesis, Department of Political Science, University of Pittsburgh: Pittsburgh, PA.

Zito, A. R. (1998) 'Epistemic Communities and European Integration', paper presented at the annual ECPR Joint Sessions of Workshops, Warwick; copy available from author.

11

The Accommodation of Diversity in European Policy-making and its Outcomes: Regulatory Policy as a Patchwork

Adrienne Héritier

European regulatory policy-making unfolds in the context of the diverse regulatory interests and traditions of Member States. The latter meet in the European arena, have to be balanced and brought to a compromise. As a result, European regulation often acquires features of a 'policy patchwork' in which diverse regulatory approaches are linked under the roof of the same directive. Alternatively, one European measure may be modelled after the regulatory style of one Member State, while the next follows the regulatory approach of another. Thus, in the field of clean-air policy, some directives are shaped according to the German tradition geared towards technology-based emission control while others are patterned after the British model of regulating ambient air quality. The distinctive regulatory elements are not systematically linked in a comprehensive European policy scheme, but simply added to one another.

The patchwork character of European regulatory policy is the result of a process of interest accommodation which shows specific patterns of co-ordination. The latter and their results are the object of investigation here. The analysis starts with two assumptions: first, it is assumed that Member States have diverse national regulatory traditions and diverse economic interests. Second, we assume that they seek to maximize their utility in European policy-making in the context of existing institutions.[1] Against the background of these assumptions the questions to be dealt with are: What typical informal process patterns (under the given institutional framework) emerge and what types of policies do they produce? The process of accommodation of interest diversity in Europe varies according to the institutional conditions of the specific phase of policy-making, ie problem definition, agenda-setting, drafting of legislation and policy formulation (see also Richardson, 1996). Thus, it makes a difference that there is a right of initiative by the Commission, or that qualified majority voting (QMV) may be used in the Council, etc. It is hypothesized that, depending on the specific stage of European policy-making and its institutional setting, typical patterns of informal co-ordination among actors evolve: first, a strategic 'first move' is used in problem definition and agenda-setting; second, a phase of 'problem-solving' in the early stages of drafting; third, the linked pattern of 'negative co-ordination, bargaining and compensation' (Scharpf and Mohr, 1994, p37) dominates the formal decision process.

New initiatives in European regulatory policy-making are, to a significant extent, engendered by the competition among highly regulated Member States which seek to influence European policy-making in order to shape it according to their own traditions (see also Richardson, 1994, p140). This competition gives rise to the first pattern of co-ordination of interest diversity which is characterized by the strategic 'first move' of one country and 'unilateral adjustment'[2] of all others during problem definition and agenda-setting. A 'first mover' is successful only if the Commission, which functions as a 'gate-keeper', adopts the policy proposal of the 'first mover'. The initiator then has a chance to define the scope and nature of problems dealt with by European institutions and shape the European policy agenda, whereas the other Member States are forced into a reactive mode. In defining the problem, the 'first mover' also suggests a practical approach to solving the problem which he has defined. Consequently, he may carry his 'initiator' advantage into 'problem-solving', the second co-ordination pattern, and anchor its regulatory approach, its 'frame' (Tversky and Kahnemann, 1981) in drafting European legislation. If not seriously challenged by an opposing approach by another highly regulated state, problem-solving subsequently proceeds within the regulatory 'frame' defined by the 'first mover'. This provides him with a considerable advantage in policy definition. During the final political decision-making phase, the third informal patterns of 'negative co-ordination, bargaining and compensation' (Scharpf and Mohr, 1994, p37) emerge.[3] At this point it is most difficult for the 'first mover' to maintain his structural advantage because distributional questions are centre stage.

It is further hypothesized that specific paths of co-ordination emerge at the different stages, depending on the nature of the issue at hand, its complexity or easy accessibility, its distributive or redistributive character. From the viewpoint of the 'first mover' and his relative success in pushing through an initiative, one may distinguish between four different paths of co-ordination: the 'clear home run', the 'moderated home run', the 'saddled home run' and the 'thwarted home run'. Each path in turn has a specific impact on the basic features of the policies produced, especially with respect to their homogeneity. If the 'first mover' has to make considerable concessions with respect to the policy principle proposed, the final policy often contains diverse national principles, as in the case of the 'thwarted home run'.

In the section on 'Process Patterns in European Regulatory Policy-making', the hypothetical patterns and their results will be analysed at a general level. Then in the section on 'Combatting Industrial Emission', they will be illustrated by key directives in the field of clean air policy, namely industrial emissions.[4]

Process Patterns in European Regulatory Policy-making

'First Mover' Advantage and 'Unilateral Adjustment'

The expansion of regulatory policies[5] in Europe can often be traced to the initiative of one Member State.[6] It is generally countries with a strong regulatory tradition that approach the Commission with a policy proposal for a problem which, in their view, calls for Community measures. Needless to say, the proposal put forward by the 'first mover' corresponds to its economic interests and regulatory traditions. In doing so, the initiator seeks to widen the scope of European policy-making according to its own preferences, and to transfer its own regulatory style to the European level. The reasons why highly regulated Member States engage in such a step are as follows: first, they seek to avoid the costs of institutional and legal adjustment caused by European legislation. Second, they try to establish favourable competitive conditions for their own industry by raising European environmental standards to their own national level. Third, suggesting more stringent technology-oriented environmental rules enhances the market for national environmental technology industries. Fourth, by preventing more lenient European regulation, national authorities seek to maintain their bargaining power with their own industries because the latter cannot point to more lax European standards when required to implement national standards. These reasons explain why European regulatory policy-making often amounts to regulatory competition among highly regulated Member States.

In addition to the motives of Member States outlined above, an institutional rule, typical of European environmental policy-making,[7] favours regulatory competition. An environmental policy framework decision of the 1970s obliges Member States to inform the Commission about all community relevant drafts of national primary and secondary legislation (notification). Member states are to suspend their decision processes until the Commission has decided, within a given timespan, whether European legislation will be undertaken in the same area. If so, the Commission has to submit a legislative draft within five months (Weinstock, 1984, p310). Because of this, national and European policy initiatives are automatically linked, encouraging the diffusion of national regulatory measures by means of European legislation.

Whether or not a Member State is successful in shaping the European regulatory agenda by using the 'first-mover strategy' depends on the response of the Commission. The Council cannot take any policy measures unless the Commission has put forward a corresponding proposal. The Commission functions therefore as a 'gatekeeper'. In this role the Commission is confronted with a variety of regulatory proposals by Member States of which the individual countries might be unaware.[8] From the multitude of policy proposals the Commission chooses the ones which it wants to put on the legislative track. The highly regulated Member States, for their part, may be regarded as innovative policy entrepreneurs in the European regulatory market, offering their 'products' to the Commission:

> *The Commission officials listen (in the committee as in informal preconsultations) to everybody, but are free to choose whose ideas and proposals they adopt. This*

> *behaviour opens up great chances of influence for certain individual experts who,*
> *because they present ideas which are in line with the Commission's interests, may*
> *thus act as 'partisans'* (Eichener, 1992, p54)

The Commission's responsiveness to such policy proposals is no act of generosity. Having relatively few personnel of its own, it depends on Member States to provide policy expertise. Also, the Commission as a corporate actor is interested in expanding regulatory policies in order to enhance its own power, reflecting the limited financial resources of the European Community (Majone, 1994). However, whether or not the Commission responds favourably to the policy initiative of a 'first-mover' Member State ultimately depends on whether this proposal fits into the overall policy-making philosophy of the European Community as such. Currently, this means that it has to be compatible with the subsidiarity principle.

If the 'first mover' is successful in winning the support of the Commission, its policy proposal – along with the national problem-solving approach – gains access to the European political agenda. The initiator 'anchors' his problem definition and policy approach in the subsequent drafting phase and offers a 'frame' for 'problem-solving' (Tversky and Kahnemann, 1981)[9] which is underpinned by special expertise in this field. A successful first move in problem definition and agenda-setting may be regarded as an attempt to secure a positional advantage (Hirsch, 1978): once one Member State has shaped a policy proposal and – in collaboration with the Commission – defined the problem-solving approach and the policy agenda, respective opportunities for the other Member States automatically decrease. In what follows, they merely respond initially and to some extent adapt unilaterally to the policy proposal advanced by another Member State.

However, considering an entire field of regulatory policy-making, a pattern of first moving *à tour de rôle* emerges. Yet, being the 'first mover' once does not mean always being so. In view of the diversity of the Community, the Commission carefully avoids adopting the proposals of one and the same Member State. In other words, there is no 'structural first mover'. This is partly because Member States watch each other carefully and suspiciously during the drafting stage, when an issue has once left the secluded dialogue between one Member State and a division of a Directorate General and has come out into the open. As a result, taking environmental legislation covering a number of directives and regulations as an example, the benefits gained by being the 'first mover' and shaping European policy-making as well as the costs of institutional and legal adjustment spread quite evenly among the regulatory ambitious Member States. As a consequence, a picture of diffuse reciprocity of benefits and costs[10] emerges in which 'actors expect to benefit in the long run and over many issues, rather than every time on every issue' (Caporaso, 1992, p602).

The attempts by Member States to act as 'first movers' in problem definition and agenda-setting are facilitated by one recent change in institutional rules and, at the same time, are made more difficult by another new institutional development. While, on the one hand, under the unanimity rule the regulatory wishes of other Member States can be fended off easily and the need to bargain is pronounced, under the qualified majority rule the 'danger' of being subject to an 'alien' regulatory style has increased. Hence, the motivation for Member States to act as 'first movers', to play an active role in regulatory competition and to put forward policy proposals of their own, has increased under the qualified majority vote. Of course, one could argue that making the first move does not necessarily imply a policy advantage, but may immediately trigger the formation of an opposing coalition seeking to obstruct the 'first mover's' policy proposal. Yet, under the given institutional conditions of problem definition and agenda-setting in European regulatory policy-making, this is unlikely. The reason is that these first steps in problem definition and agenda-setting are taken under circumstances of exclusiveness and secrecy. The Commission (or, more precisely, a division of a Directorate General) is confronted with various policy proposals and has considerable latitude in choosing from among the policy options of the European 'policy market' (Peters, 1992, p75ff). It is not obliged to inform the other Member States at this point about who has suggested what, why and when. Nor is the Commission obliged to discuss the consequences of a policy proposal in a central arena and to point out the costs and benefits implied for Member States.[11] This relative insulation of problem definition and agenda-setting follows from a central institutional aspect of the political architecture of Europe. The activities of the Commission do not have to follow a general legislative programme of a popularly elected European government which is held accountable by a majority in parliament (see also Hull, 1993).

However, owing to the institutional ambitions of the European Parliament the conditions of seclusion have recently come under attack. Members of Parliament demand to be informed about all planned measures of the Commission at an early stage so that the costs and benefits of these measures may be debated publicly and extensively in the European Parliament.[12] This would imply a much earlier politicization of European policy-making and would reduce the chances of securing a 'national home run' by making the first move and 'anchoring' a particular regulatory approach in the early drafting phase.[13] Bargaining processes and compensation mechanisms would emerge much earlier in the decision process.

From the perspective of less regulated Member States, applying the Strategy of the first move is not so attractive. A complete absence of European regulation is considered to be the most favourable solution because lower standards in their production processes constitute a competitive advantage in an integrated European market. As a consequence, they tend to 'sit on the fence', watch the development of the policy debate, and jump on the bandwagon later on and/or have their vetoes 'bought off', ie accept compensation for acquiescing to the proposed legislation. Also, at times, calculated non-implementation makes it easier to support a new regulation in policy formulation.

Considering both highly and less regulated Member States and their preferences, the following priorities emerge: for highly regulated countries, the greatest benefits accrue from solutions which follow their own national regulation. The second-best solution is when European legislation incorporates at least a substantial part of their own policy concept, although some concessions must be made. The worst outcome is non-regulation of production processes (the default condition) since in an integrated market this involves a competitive disadvantage. Conversely, in the eyes of the less regulated states, no solution is the most favourable 'solution'. A mixed solution is second best and, finally, a measure which corresponds to the proposal of the highly regulated states is the most expensive option.

Problem-solving

After a 'first mover', jointly with the Commission, has defined the problem, suggested a way of dealing with the latter and set the agenda, a co-ordinative pattern emerges in the early drafting process – what has been termed 'problem-solving' (Mayntz, 1994; Scharpf, 1991; Scharpf and Mohr, 1994). It links to the preceding pattern of 'first moving' in so far as a successful 'first mover' is able to define the broad 'frame' in which subsequent problem-solving takes place. In 'problem-solving', actors concentrate on joint production and – at least temporarily – put aside distributive issues.

> *The point of departure ... of a problem-solving process is, first, a situation in which changes are called for, as opposed to a situation which offers only an opportunity for utility maximization. Typically, second, analysis of the problem, and definition of the objective of action which is considered to be the problem solution, are constitutive parts of the decision process in problem-solving, whereas in rational decision-making models the objectives (as types of benefit to be realized) are given. Third, and finally, there is an initial uncertainty in problem-solving as to the methods of achieving the defined objective so that – in contrast to the model of rational decision-making – the emphasis is not on comparing costs and benefits of given alternatives but on finding possible solutions, a procedure which includes multiple attempts and trial-and-error behaviour* (Mayntz, 1994, p22; translated by A.H.)

Thus, there are generally no 'diplomatic behavioural patterns' and 'no hidden power games' (IEP 1989, p107). Rather, a 'denationalization' (Bach, 1992, p92) of regulatory policy-making occurs. Technical, scientific and legal experts, who are more interested in pragmatic problem-solving (Majone, 1994, p91), dominate the debates. The more complex and the more technically oriented a regulatory question, the more easily an insulation from distributive questions may be achieved, the more the discussions develop into a discourse of regulatory national experts. What was found to be true in the field of health and safety (Eichener, 1995; 1992) also holds good for environmental policy:

> *The debates tend to move quickly to a level of technical details (about what is technologically possible and at what cost) so that technical expertise is a crucial condition for effective participation... The interest in the matter is an important corresponding variable, because the higher the interest is, the more resources will be invested in the committee work. Members report that delegates from low-level countries frequently prefer to listen to discussions to get early information on regulatory acts than to actively contribute* (Eichener, 1992, p52).

Specific institutional conditions of European decision-making render problem-solving easier. For example, if working groups and committees sit over a longer period, a learning process evolves which facilitates the development of 'epistemic communities' and a mutual learning among national experts (Haas, 1992). They tend to share problems, professional knowledge and a professional language. Consensus-building across diverse national interests becomes easier. Two other institutional aspects facilitate problem-oriented discussions among national experts in the preparation of legislative drafts. The first is the role of the Commission as a process manager, able to choose between policy proposals and set the agenda for the Council.[14] Second, the fact that committees do not make decisions, but have only a consultative function,[15] makes problem-solving easier. Often, proposals for solving problems are collected, but not selected by members of the working group (Eichener, 1992). However, also in the case of this co-ordination pattern, recent institutional developments may 'disturb' problem-solving in the future. If the European Parliament obtains the right to be fully informed at the outset about the work of committees (Lodge, 1994: *The European*, 29 December 1994–4 January 1995), distributive aspects will emerge much earlier and a politicization of the debate will ensue.

Negative Co-ordination, Bargaining and Compensation

When a problem solution has been elaborated by a working group, it is put forward for a decision in the Commission as a whole and, subsequently, in the Council and European Parliament. The linked co-ordinative patterns of 'negative co-ordination, bargaining and compensation' become preponderant. Now actors focus primarily on specific costs and benefits. If an issue is perceived as redistributive, the decision process rapidly becomes polarized and clear-cut conflict lines emerge. The actors consider whether they are favourably or adversely affected by the measure (negative co-ordination). Those adversely affected fend off expected costs and signal their rejection of the proposal. Once the relative positions are clear, a bargaining process begins and possible compensations are proposed to overcome the resistance of the 'losers', provided that the nature of the issue allows for such compromises (Benz et al, 1992; Scharpf, 1992, p68). If there is only a choice between 'yes' and 'no' and/or monetary compensations do not seem acceptable (Scharpf, 1992, p70), a package deal may be struck in which a trade-off of benefits is sought over different issue areas. The larger the number of issue areas involved in such a deal, the higher the political level at which negotiations are conducted.

If a compensation to 'buy off' the threatened veto has been found and a package deal struck, the question arises of whether the compromise is considered to be fair, ie whether costs and benefits accruing to the various actors from different issue areas are perceived as well balanced. Given the incommensurability of various kinds of costs and benefits involved over several issue areas (Scharpf, 1992, p77), this is not an easy matter. However, since there is no need for single-issue reciprocity, each actor making a concession can expect that, in return, others will make concessions in the (near) future. In other words, since specific reciprocity cannot be reached in every case, diffuse reciprocity becomes more and more important (Schmidt, 1995, p4). How is it possible that such a diffuse reciprocity comes about?

Of course, there is no institutional centre in the European Union which serves the explicit purpose of ensuring mutual fairness and equity, and guaranteeing diffuse reciprocity above and beyond the turmoil of conflicting Member State interests. The Commission, as the actor which comes closest to an overview of the distribution of costs and benefits across issue areas and time, is itself not a unified actor. Rather, beneath the surface of a formal independence from national interests, divergent national and sectoral loyalties quickly re-emerge.[16] Yet, there are informal mechanisms which again are rooted in the competition among Member States that work to balance costs and benefits over issues and time. Member states jealously keep a record of when and to whom concessions have been made. Since the number of involved actors is relatively small, mutual control of the approximate reciprocity of measures and their balance over a longer period is possible. Thus, the institutional memory of the Council, or rather the Committee of Permanent Representatives (COREPER) with its permanent representatives, functions very well when it comes to keeping track of concessions made by individual Member States. In short, bargaining takes place 'under the shadow of the future'. Participants know that their relationship is not merely a temporary one, but meant to be durable. They therefore think twice before ruthlessly seeking to maximize their individual interests.

Within a stable institutional framework such as the European Community, the willingness of a Member State to make concessions is also enhanced by the fact that Member States have to be 'economical' in their opposition to proposed measures. Bearing in mind the 'economics of vetoing', every actor is aware that he cannot constantly oppose all kinds of issue (Peters, 1992). There is a 'conflict among conflicts', and obstruction has to be used 'economically' across policy fields and time. As a consequence, each country tends strategically to support issues which are closest to its heart and which offer the highest economic and regulatory pay-off. In preparing negotiations in the Council, Member States therefore carefully decide on which issues they are not willing to make concessions, which are negotiable and which can be 'sacrificed' altogether.

Specific institutional rules, such as the unanimity principle or qualified majority decisions, affect the extent to which actors are willing to make concessions. The qualified majority rule tends to enhance the anticipation of possible opposing coalitions, at the same time functioning as a 'shadow of hierarchy' speeding up negotiations (Scharpf, 1992, p25).[17] Member states may also use institutional resources in order to enhance their position in the bargaining process. A case in point is the Council presidency. The country holding the presidency can influence the decision agenda, give specific issues priority over others and, by arranging the list of items to be discussed, prepare possible package deals. Another increasingly significant institutional resource consists of collaborating with the European Parliament. Member states, in the attempt to defend their position in the Council, seek the support of their co-nationals of different political parties. Also, domestic institutional resources may be used to strengthen their own position at the European level. Since the political arenas are interlinked (Benz et al, 1992), Member States may point to restrictions imposed on them by their national parliaments in order to increase their weight. European restrictions may also be used at home in order to gain more room for manoeuvring in dealing with national parliaments.

Patterns of Co-ordination: Long-term Perspective

Four possibilities present themselves when one considers the informal patterns of co-ordination through the entire cycle of problem definition, agenda-setting, policy drafting and formal decision-making. The first hurdle for an actor, of course, is to bring an issue to the attention of the Commission, to induce the latter to perceive the problem as a policy problem, and to have the issue put on the European agenda. If this is achieved by a 'first mover' it is in itself an important step in European policy-making. This holds good even if a Member State does not succeed in imposing all its national views on how the problem should be solved at the European level, but has to accept minor or major modifications. Once this threshold is passed, the co-ordinative patterns may follow four paths, which are distinguished from the viewpoint of the relative success of the 'first mover' in maintaining his initial advantage.

In the first scenario, the 'clear home run', the 'first mover' convinces the Commission that a specific problem calls for legislative action at the European level, and that it should be dealt with in the manner proposed by the initiating Member State. The advantage of the 'first-mover' strategy can be upheld because the policy problem is narrowly defined, highly complex and of a technical nature requiring considerable expertise. The costs and benefits involved are not easy to assess. Under the second scenario, the 'saddled home run', the 'first mover' is equally successful in pushing through its policy initiative. It even causes a 'bandwagon effect', in the course of which the Commission and other Member States try to saddle it with additional – similar – proposals. In the end a comprehensive piece of legislation is enacted. In the third scenario, a 'moderated home run' materializes. The initiating state realizes its basic policy principles, but has to make a number of concessions which, however, do not jeopardize the basic policy approach. In the fourth scenario ('thwarted home run' plus 'policy mix'), the policy proposal of the 'first mover' meets with the full-scale resistance of another Member State. An opposing policy approach is suggested, possibly early on. This may be because of conflicting national regulatory traditions and/or the redistributional impacts of the original proposal. If the issue is easily accessible and has redistributional impacts, it quickly becomes a subject of wider concern and 'negative co-ordination, bargaining and compensation' set in at an early stage. Compromises have to be sought. Either a third joint solution is developed or, alternatively, additional policy instruments are included from which Member States can choose in order to reach a broadly set policy objective.

Which particular scenario emerges, always assuming that the Commission is willing to share the problem definition of the 'first mover' and adopt the issue, depends on the specific features of the policy issue at hand. If an issue is technically and legally complex, if it is not easily accessible to the public at large, if political saliency and the potential for mobilization are low, the chances that it will be contested at an early stage are small. Epistemic communities tend to prevail for longer, unless a community with conflicting expertise materializes during 'problem-solving'. If, by contrast, the issue at hand involves the redistribution of costs and benefits in a way which can be easily perceived, its potential for political mobilization is considerable. The odds that it will not run through smoothly are high.

Regulatory Competition and its Outcomes: Policy Features

Since regulatory policy-making is driven by competition between highly regulated Member States, it produces specific policy results. First, one expects that the inevitable outcome of regulatory competition is an ever-increasing and thickening network of European regulations. This is because Member States are keen to transfer their own regulatory traditions to the European level and the Commission itself has a vested interest in expanding regulatory activities. Although this expectation is to some extent corroborated by the empirical development of European regulatory legislation, especially in the field of the environment, there are also countervailing tendencies. Counter effects originate in the subsidiarity principle and the lack of support among Member States for ever-increasing and detailed European regulation. Recognizing the changing tides, the Commission, in devising legislation, has recently deliberately given more latitude to Member States in policy implementation. Often only policy objectives are laid down while the choice of instruments to reach these is left to Member States.

A second important feature of regulatory policy outcomes, under the condition of regulatory competition, arises from the fact that there is no structural 'first mover'. As a consequence, no particular tradition dominates European regulation across the board. Rather, it resembles a colourful patchwork composed of various instruments and national regulatory styles derived from distinctive regulatory backgrounds.

Yet even mere framework legislation may be a first step 'on the slippery slope' of growing detailed European regulation, for the framework legislation is often only the 'mother'-directive from which 'daughter'-directives follow. Whereas the 'mother' defines the general principles of action and the overall objectives, the 'daughters' provide details of action to be taken. In this pattern of sequential self-commitment 'the reasons for the consent to each subsequent measure are given by pointing out that an obligation has been created by taking the preceding decision' (Eichener, 1995, p38).

In the following section, the different patterns of co-ordination, the typical paths along which they develop, and their policy consequences will be discussed by using the examples of key directives on clean air policy.

Combating Industrial Emissions

Emission Standards and Best Available Technology: Germany as a Pace-setter

It was the Federal Republic which, during the 1980s, was successful in imposing its own regulatory style at the European level. It approached the Commission proposing to enact European emission standards for specific pollutants, such as sulphur dioxide, nitrogen oxide and dust particulates from stationary plants. It suggested incorporating its own problem-solving approach, established under the German Large Combustion Plant Regulation of 1982, into European legislation. Although Germany acted as a 'first mover' in the European decision process, it was the Scandinavian countries which – pointing out the problem of acid rain – had triggered off international measures (Geneva Conference and Helsinki protocols) in order to reduce long-range trans-boundary air pollution. As a consequence, the European Community, some members of which had signed the protocols specifying implementation measures, had to join in. Initially, the Federal Republic had resisted the Helsinki protocols. However, having come under strong domestic pressure owing to the debate over the dying forests, it developed national measures to reduce pollutants deemed to cause acidification. After national legislation, with relatively stringent emission-oriented standards based on Best Available Technology (BAT) and precautionary action (Large Combustion Plant Regulation), was enacted in 1982, it was only rational for Germany to carry its domestic solution to the European level in order to avoid competitive disadvantages for its own industry and the costs of institutional adjustment to a likely 'alien' European solution. The Commission, in its turn, was unhappy with the lack of implementation of the previous air-quality control measures in Member States. Therefore it welcomed the German proposal with its emission- and BAT-oriented approach. Strong opposition was voiced in particular by Britain, which wanted to use an air-quality oriented practice based on sound scientific evidence, before any further action. In order to reduce political opposition, more framework legislation, a 'mother-directive' (Framework Directive on Industrial Installations), was enacted in 1984 which followed the German model. It defined the new approach as a general principle without imposing specific emission standards. Political conflicts did not ensue because costs and benefits were not specified. The 'mother'-directive therefore, as far as its basic principle is concerned, may be considered a German 'home run'. Anticipating that controversies would arise once precise emission standards were proposed, the UK acquiesced in the Framework Directive on condition that the emissions limits were to be decided only under the unanimity rule.[18]

As expected, the decision process concerning the 'daughter'-directive, the Large Combustion Plant Directive prescribing Community-wide emission standards, proved to be difficult. While the Federal Republic, in collaboration with the Commission, was able to 'anchor' its basic policy approach, that is combating emissions at source on the basis of BAT, a prolonged and bitter conflict ensued in the Council of Ministers between the Federal Republic, The Netherlands and Denmark, on the one hand, and Britain and Spain, on the other, in the Council of Ministers. Finally, after five years of negotiations the Large Combustion Plant Directive was enacted in 1988. The compromise struck upheld the general approach of problem-solving proposed by the Germans.[19] However, inasmuch as the absolute reduction of emissions was concerned, both the amount and speed of rebatement were substantially moderated. Hence, the path of interest co-ordination typical for the Large Combustion Plant Directive may be classified as a 'moderated home run' by Germany.

Similar conflicts between the German-influenced emission and BAT orientation and the British-inspired air-quality orientation are typical for other Directives in the field of European air pollution control; eg in the case of the Volatile Organic Compounds (VOC) and the Hazardous Waste Disposal Directives. The latter is an emission-oriented and BAT-based measure proposed by the Germans and supported by the Commission. It was enacted according to the concept originally proposed by Germany. The path of co-ordination which it followed may therefore also be classified as a clear German 'home run'.

Similarly, the Directive on VOC started out as a German initiative, using its typical approach. However, owing to its specific features, this policy proposal was contested from the beginning. It affects a wide variety of small and medium-sized plants and operations which call for distinctive regulation, producing a multiplicity of new proposed standards. This detailed regulation, in turn, provoked the opposition of the UK, which demands the use of an air-quality approach and recently went even further in suggesting that all Member States with existing relevant legislation should be exempted from the European VOC regulation. The outcome of the negotiations which have followed the path of a 'thwarted home run' is a policy mix.

In all three instances, the Large Combustion Plant Directive, the Hazardous Waste Disposal Directive and the VOC Directive, the Germans used the 'first-mover' strategy successfully, defined the policy problem to be dealt with, and influenced European agenda-setting. However, their ability to maintain the initial structural advantage varied.

Self-regulation of Operators, Access to Information and Integrated Pollution Control: The UK as a Pace-setter

Eco-audit and Access to Information

In other areas of the same policy field, it was the British who successfully moved first, defined the policy problem to be dealt with, and urged the Commission to place a specific problem on the European agenda, and to follow their national problem-solving approach. Thus, the European legislation on eco-management and the self-regulation of operators (Eco-Audit and Management Regulation), the European legislation on public access to information (Access to Information Directive), as well as integrated pollution control, followed the British example. Britain acted as a 'first mover' for the same reasons that the Germans had pushed the legislation mentioned above. Legislation on eco-auditing and eco-management, as well as access to information, was already in place in Britain. By transferring it to the European level, the costs of adjustment to corresponding European legislation could be avoided. Also, the British did not want their industry to be the only one subject to the costs of such procedures. In the case of eco-audit, the British Standards Institution had developed a standard which was subsequently offered to the Commission as a policy model for European legislation. Under the impact of the subsidiarity principle, the Commission was eager to go along with the 'new' approach. The latter was in absolute contrast to German regulatory philosophy and therefore met with vehement opposition. However, Germany was outvoted in the Council and had to accept the new regulation. Eco-audit clearly was a British 'home run'.

Policy-making developed along similar lines in the case of the Access to Information Directive. Although problem definition and pressure to take action in this field originated in the European Council, which urged the Commission to increase the transparency of European administrative decision processes (Lodge, 1994), simultaneously there was an endogenous development in Britain pushing for access to information and the opening-up of administrative processes. With its Environmental Protection Act the UK had introduced extensive rights for the public to inform itself on administrative authorization procedures. Not surprisingly therefore Britain emphatically supported the proposal of the Commission to introduce an Access to Information Directive on a community-wide basis, and sought to shape the policy contents of the proposal according to their own notions. The Commission in turn was eager to realize this policy principle in order to gain more insight into national implementation practices and their effectiveness at local and regional levels. 'Problem-solving' in this case was clearly dominated by the British and their support of the new openness. Apart from strong opposition from Germany, the formal decision process was not controversial among Member States. Germany opposed the proposal on two grounds: the traditional secretiveness of its authorization procedures and the reluctance of its industry to disclose information. The compromise which was finally reached in the phase of 'negative integration, bargaining and compensation' involved offering wide discretion in the implementation process.

Apart from these concessions, which did not affect the core of the new policy principle, 'Access to Information' and 'Eco-audit' are both clear British 'home runs' in European regulatory policy-making.

Integrated Pollution Control

By contrast, the path of co-ordination emerging in the case of integrated pollution control (IPC) reveals a British 'first move' supported by the Commission, which subsequently was stopped by German opposition. Once more, the German and the British problem-solving approaches clashed with particular vehemence. The British had already enacted IPC for air, water and soil in their Environmental Protection Act of 1990. The Commission used the British statutory expertise for the European drafting process and asked them to send a national expert to Brussels in order 'to write the directive'. Hence, the British in conjunction with the Commission successfully defined the problem and set the agenda. They proposed the introduction of quality standards which should be reached by emission standards set at the national level. However, this proposal was contested by the German government which fought the draft tooth and nail ('German environmental policy and its achievements are at risk' – interview *Bundesumweltministerium*, May 1993). Instead, Germany proposed to enact community-wide emission standards and the use of BAT at every source. Other points of controversy related to the question of how to define 'best available technology', whether economic aspects should be taken into account, and whether and to what extent the public should be given access to the authorization procedures. Owing to this early polarization, a number of drafts seeking to satisfy all interests involved were discussed, leading to a compromise representing a true 'policy mix'. In the final stage, however, Germany used its presidency in the Council to change the draft substantially. At short notice a new proposal was submitted in COREPER which significantly altered the Commission's compromise. It met with the collective indignation of the other national delegations, which accused the German presidency of attempting to hijack the directive, whereupon the proposal was withdrawn (interview, Department of Environment, January 1995). Still, it succeeded in removing the 'BAT escape clause', that is, the possibility of avoiding the best available technology at a given level of environmental quality. Yet, regional quality standards and national emission standards remained and special derogations were introduced for the southern member states.

In summary, the development of this important new directive in environmental protection reveals a clear pattern: in the initial phase of problem definition and agenda-setting, the Commission co-operates with the UK because the latter's problem definition and policy approach is congruent with the dominant problem-solving philosophy of Community institutions. During expert consultations the British successfully anchor their problem-solving approach which is geared towards an integrated approach using environmental quality standards and public access to information, much to the discontent of the Germans who see themselves off-side in the regulatory game. When, during the bargaining process of the formal decision, the actual costs and benefits were taken into account, concessions were made to German demands. As to the 'first mover', the British, they had to realize that what initially seemed to be an easy game ended in a 'thwarted home run' and a 'policy mix' of diverse policy instruments.

Conclusion

European regulatory policy-making is characterized by regulatory competition among the highly regulated Member States which, by influencing European policy-making, seek to enhance their competitive position in the European market and to reduce costs of legal adjustment. The regulatory advances are addressed to the Commission which, under the given institutional conditions of the European Community, functions as a gate-keeper and largely determines the chances of the Member States' regulatory proposal to influence the European agenda. The Commission gains its powers from the fact that the European Union does not have an elected government with a policy programme based on the voters' support and supported by community-wide parties with a majority in parliament. The chances of influencing European policy-making by directly approaching the Commission therefore are relatively high, because the attempt to exert influence does not have to pass the institutional filters of a parliamentary democracy governed by parties. If a 'first-mover' Member State is successful in gaining the support of a division of a Directorate General, it can shape the European problem definition and political agenda. This 'first-mover' advantage, however, may be lost once a policy proposal leaves the institutionally secluded stage of drafting and is put to a decision in the Commission as a whole, the Council of Ministers and Parliament. Distributive issues come to the fore which are the object of extensive bargaining processes, in the course of which compensations are offered to those who perceive themselves as the losers of a proposed new regulation. The need to co-ordinate interests and to compromise explains the patchwork character of regulatory policy-making in Europe.

Notes

1. Of course, Member States also seek to shape institutional rules in order to enhance their national policy interests.
2. Lindblom uses the term parametric adjustment, if 'in a decision situation, a decision-maker X adjusts his decision to Y's decisions already made and to Y's expected decisions; but he does not seek, as a recognized condition of making his own decision effective, to induce a response from Y; nor does he allow the choice of his decision to be influenced by any consideration of the consequences of his decision for Y' (Lindblom, 1965, p37; cited by Scharpf and Mohr, 1994, p8).
3. The co-ordination patterns of 'first-mover strategy', 'problem-solving' and 'negative co-ordination/bargaining/compensation' correspond to the three styles of interaction: 'competitiveness', 'co-operative and individual/egotistic orientation' which (based on Kelley and Thibaut) are discussed by F. W. Scharpf (Scharpf, 1992).
4. The empirical data on 12 directives and regulations in environmental policy were gathered in a research project financed by the Deutsche Forschungsgemeinschaft. See Héritier et al (1995). German version: *Die Veränderung von Staatlichkeit in Europa. Ein regulativer Wettbewerb* (1994) Opladen: Leske und Budrich.
5. New regulatory policies, the subject of our investigation, deal with the negative external effects of producers' and consumers' activities.
6. According to information from DG Environment the largest proportion of regulatory proposals may be traced back to the initiatives of Member States (interview, GD 11, March 1993). Of course, some policy initiatives originate in the environmental action programmes of the Commission, in memoranda of the Council of Ministers, in initiatives of the European Parliament, as well as in obligations derived from international treaties.
7. Article 102 of the Rome Treaty requires that the Commission be notified about all planned measures affecting the integrated market. A French interviewee described the process of regulatory competition as follows: 'La Commission cherche toujours ce qu'il y a de plus sèvére quo tantôt cela soit en Angleterre, que tantôt cela soit en Allemagne... Il y a une compétition du plus sèvére... C'est comme si on était dans une piscine et qu'il fallait arriver le premier d l'autre côté. Ça c'est la compétition administrative' (interview, Confédération nationale de Paironat Français, June 1993).
8. Only in rare instances within our field of research do negotiations among Member States take place before the Commission is contacted. It may be the

case in politically highly delicate matters, such as the recent joint endeavours by Britain and Germany to scale back existing regulations in European water quality standards.

9. The 'frame' of a decision-maker in problem-solving is influenced by his norms, habits and characteristics (Tversky and Kahnemann, 1981, p453).

10. The diffuse reciprocity with respect to less regulated countries is achieved by compensations and package deals.

11. Even later on in the drafting process, Member States tend to complain that they are not informed by the Commission about ongoing progress: 'We are included in the drafting process by the Commission when information and expertise is needed. But the Commission does not feel much obliged to inform us in return on progress' (interview, Department of the Environment, November 1994).

12. In the context of its ratification by the European Parliament, the new Commission presented its work programme in the Parliament (*The European*, 29 December 1994–4 January 1995).

13. In the interlinked national and European policy network, there is always the possibility of regulatory zealots bypassing their own government and addressing the Commission directly in order to promote its policy objectives.

14. 'With my experts I can get this "regulatory draft" done in no time at all' (interview, DG 8, June 1994).

15. The directives and regulations investigated here were the subject of consultation in the committees.

16. Although members of the Commission are pledged to independence from national interests, national interests are short-circuited in cabinet meetings and in contacts with other co-nationals in other cabinets.

17. Out of 233 decisions concerning the integrated market which had been taken by the Council of Ministers in five years, 91 were enacted against the opposition of one or several Member States. Only the latter were put to a formal decision (Brown, 1994).

18. Included in the mentioned bargain between Britain and the Commission was that the latter withdraw a proposal on fuel gas which caused much concern in Britain.

19. The BAT principle, however, was mitigated by changing it to Best Available Technique Not Entailing Excessive Costs. The technique implies that not only the best technological means should be used in order to reduce emissions, but it also includes 'soft' aspects, such as training for personnel dealing with pollutants as well as managerial aspects; further costs involved for industry are always to be taken into account.

References

Bach, Maurizio (1992) 'Eine leise Revolution durch Verwaltungsverfahren. Bürokratische Integrationsprozesse in der Europäischen Gemeinschaft', *Zeitschrift für Soziologie*, Vol.21, pp16–30.

Benz, A., Scharpf, F. W. and Zinti, R. (1992) *Horizontale Politikverflechtung: Zur Theorie von Verhandlungssystemen,* Frankfurt a.M.: Campus.

Brown, K. (1994) 'Light Cast on Secret Manoeuvring of EU Ministers', *Financial Times,* 13 September.

Caporaso, J. A. (1992) International Relations Theory and Multilateralism: The Search for Foundations', *International Organization,* Vol.46, pp599–632.

Eichener, V. (1992) *Social Dumping or Innovative Regulation? Processes and Outcomes of European Decision-Making in the Sector of Health and Safety at Work Harmonisation,* EUI Working Paper SPS Nr 92/28, Florence: European University Institute.

Eichener, V. (1995) 'Die Rückwirkungen der europäischen Integration auf nationale Politikmuster', in Jachtenfuchs, M. and Kohler-Koch, B. (eds), *Europäische Integration,* Opladen: Leske & Budrich.

Haas, P. M. (1992) 'Banning Chlorofluorocarbons: Epistemic Community Efforts to Protect Stratospheric Ozone', *International Organization,* Vol.46, pp187–224.

Héritier, A., Mingers, S., Knill, C. and Becka, M. (1994) *Die Veränderung von Staatlichkeit in Europa. Ein regulativer Wettbewerb: Deutschland, Großbritannien und Frankreich in der Europäischen Union,* Opladen: Leske & Budrich.

Héritier, A., Knill, C. and Mingers, S. (1995) *Ringing the Changes in Europe: Regulatory Competition and the Redefinition of the State – Britain, France and Germany,* Berlin and New York: de Gruyter.

Hirsch, F. (1978) *Social Limits to Growth,* London: Routledge.

Hull, R. (1993) 'Lobbying Brussels: A View from Within', in Mazey, S. and Richardson, J. (eds), *Lobbying in the European Community,* Oxford: Oxford University Press, pp82–92.

IEP (Institut für europäische Politik) (1989) *Comitology – Characteristics, Performance and Options,* Bonn: Selbstverlag.

Lindblom, C. E. (1965) *The Intelligence of Democracy: Decision Making through Mutual Adjustment,* New York: Free Press.

Lodge, J. (1994) 'Transparency and Democratic Legitimacy', *Journal of Common-Market Studies,* Vol.32, No.3, pp343–68.

Majone, G. (1994) 'The Rise of the Regulatory State in Europe', in Müller, W. C. and Wright, V. (eds), *The State in Western Europe: Retreat or Redefinition?,* special issue, *West European Politics,* Vol.17, No.3, pp77–101.

Mayntz, R. (1994) *Deutsche Forschung im Einigungsprozeß. Die Transformation der Akademie der Wissenschaften der DDR 1989 bis 1992,* Frankfurt a.M.: Campus.

Peters, G. P. (1992) 'Bureaucratic Politics and the Institutions of the European Community', in Sbragia, A. M. (ed), *Europolitics: Institutions and Policy-Making in the 'New' European Community,* Washington, D.C.: Brookings Institute, pp75–122.

Richardson, J. (1994) 'EU Water Policy: Uncertain Agendas, Shifting Networks and Complex Coalitions', *Environmental Politics,* Vol.3, No.4, pp139–67.

Richardson, J. (1996) 'Actor-based Models of National and EU Policy-making: Policy Communities, Issue Networks and Epistemic Communities', in Kassim, H. and Menon, A. (eds), *The European Community and National Institutional Policy,* London: Routledge.

Scharpf, F. W. (1991) 'Political Institutions, Decision Styles, and Policy Choices', in Czada, R. M. and Windhoff-Héritier, A. (eds), *Political Choice: Institutions, Rules, and the Limits of Rationality*, Frankfurt a.M.: Campus, pp53–86.

Scharpf, F. W. (1992) 'Einführung: Zur Theorie von Verhandlungssystemen', in Benz, A., Scharpf, F. W. and Zintl, R. (eds), *Horizontale Politikverflechtung: Zur Theorie von Verhandlungssystemen*, Frankfurt a.M.: Campus, pp11–28.

Scharpf, F. W. and Mohr, M. (1994) *Efficient Self-Coordination in Policy Networks: A Simulation Study*, Discussion Paper 94/1, Köln: Max-Planck-Institut für Gesellschaftsforschung.

Schmidt, S. (1995) *The Integration of the European Telecommunication and Electricity Sectors in the Light of International Relations Theories and Comparative Politics*, paper, ECPR Joint Sessions of Workshops, Bordeaux, 27 April–2 May.

Tversky, A. and Kahnemann, D. (1981) 'The Framing of Decision and the Psychology of Choice', *Science*, Vol.211, pp453–8.

Weinstock, U. (1984) 'Nur eine europäische Umwelt? Europäische Umwelt im Spannungsverhältnis von ökologischer Vielfalt und ökonomischer Einheit', in Eberhard Grabnitz (Hrsg.), *Abgestufte Integration: Eine Alternative zum herkömmlichen Integrationskonzept?*, Ergebnisse eines Forschungsprojektes des Instkuts für Integrationsforschung der Stiftung Europa-Kolleg Hamburg, Schriftenreihe Europa-Forschung, Bd. 8. Kehl am Rhein: Engel, pp301–41.

12

Environmental Rules and Rule-making in the European Union

Albert Weale

Introduction

What does the case of environmental policy tell us about the evolution of rules in the EU and what are the implications of the development of European environmental policy mean generally for our understanding of EU rule-making institutions? This chapter advances the argument that environmental policy displays the policy-making process of the EU as a decision system characterized by the principle of concurrent majorities. A system of concurrent majorities exists when agreement is needed by a high proportion of participants in a set of decision-making institutions before a policy is adopted. Thus, in the case of environmental policy, agreement needs to be secured both within and between key institutional actors (the Commission, the Council, the Parliament and the Court), as well as with the functional constituencies of important interest groups. The result is a 'joint-decision trap' (Scharpf, 1988) in which the status quo is given privileged place and policy *lourdeur* (Wallace, 1994, p80) is the result: important policy measures are not adopted, or adopted only in sub-optimal form.

Such institutional arrangements mean that we cannot account for environmental policy in either purely neofunctionalist terms (in which EU rule-making is seen as a consequence of spillover) or in purely intergovernmental terms (in which EU rule-making is seen as a co-ordination device among nations) (see Chapter 10). Thus, contrary to realist views, there is a European governance structure (Bulmer, 1994) that cannot be understood as the operation in the international arena of purely national policy preferences, but has to be understood in terms of its own institutional characteristics. Equally, there is no smooth transition from the Single Market to the development of European policy-making as a supranational set of institutions possessing or demanding jurisdiction over pre-existing national states, as there would be on a neofunctionalist analysis.

If this is true of environmental policy, is there any reason for supposing that it has lessons for European policy-making more generally? Three reasons come to mind for thinking that environmental policy is an important test case in the broader context of European integration. First, many environmental problems are intrinsically cross-boundary or international. Pollution knows no boundaries, and problems such as acidification or global climate change require international action for their solution. Since, on virtually all accounts, the EU exists to solve problems that cannot be solved at the level of the nation state, environmental policy provides a prime example of policy-making in the circumstances of complex international interdependence in which transnational regimes are said to arise (Keohane and Nye, 1989). Since European environmental policy-makers often conceive of their role as dealing with problems that transcend the boundaries of the nation state, the field of environmental policy seems a good case to take to see how far European integration is being driven by a functional logic of international problem-solving.

Second, there are – in purely technical terms to do with spillovers arising from interdependent effects – close links between the outcomes and effects of the internal market and the concerns of environmental policy, These interdependent effects were identified by the Task Force set up to look at the environment and the Single Market (Task Force Report on the Environment and the Internal Market, 1989; compare Haigh and Baldock, 1989), and they included increased pollution as a consequence of higher levels of production and increased traffic, as well as opportunities for less intensive resource use once national barriers to trade were removed.

Third, at various times, depending on fluctuations in the issue attention cycle, environmental problems and policies have been a highly salient issue in the politics of the EU. If we are looking for one area of policy that highlights the conflicts between the strong sectoral interests of producers and the more diffuse interests of citizens in general, it is likely to be found in the field of the environment. Looking at the policy area, then, tells us something intrinsically important about what Bulmer (1994, pp370–5) has called the European 'governance regime' of particular policy sectors and the policy networks to which they give rise.

The overall argument will proceed by elimination. In the next section, the evolution of EU environmental policy is laid out together with a brief account of the policy-making culture and belief system that has accompanied this development. In the subsequent section, it will be argued that neither neofunctionalist nor realist logic can account for some central features of this process of policy development, so that we have to think of the environmental rule-making process itself as a set of institutional rules with its own form and logic that requires measures to secure agreement from a wide range of actors. The resulting joint-decision trap, it will be argued, suffers from certain pathologies.

European Environmental Policy: From Silence to Salience

The 1957 Treaty of Rome did not contain any reference to environmental protection and, until the Single European Act (SEA) came into force, environmental legislation had to be passed either under the Single Market provisions of Article 100 or under the general 'catch-all' provisions of Article 235. Under the SEA, environmental policy was formally recognized as a proper competence to be exercised at European level (subject to the principle of subsidiarity) and, under the 1992 Treaty on European Union (the Maastricht Treaty), it became possible to pass most environmental measures through the Council of Ministers by qualified majority.

Despite this anonymity, EU environmental policy led a tangible, if somewhat marginal, existence from the early 1970s. A directorate-general emerged, which could be traced back to the Environment and Consumer Protection Unit that had been set up in the Commission in 1971. There was also an environment council, representing the ministries of the national governments. Moreover, in successive environmental action programmes the EU began increasingly to elaborate its ambitions for the development of environmental policy (see Chapter 2).

Behind this growth in activity, it is possible to detect the influence of various political pressures, both in the form of public opinion and in the form of international negotiation. Thus, the beginnings of European environmental policy as a distinct sector of policy are normally traced back to the European Council meeting in Paris in 1972, which reflected the surge of public concern about environmental protection that had swept through the developed world in the late 1960s and early 1970s (sec Haigh, 1989, p9; Rehbinder and Steward, 1985, p17; and Würzel, 1993). The inclusion of environmental competences in the SEA, by contrast, can perhaps best be understood as the result of a tacit bargain between northern and southern states over the terms of their future co-operation. The north wanted high consumer and environmental standards along with the Single Market and the south wanted greater structural funds without the Single Market. The bargain that was eventually struck involved both a commitment to high standards of environmental protection and the use of the structural funds to aid southern countries.

Moreover, the growth of policy at the European level has been fostered by the European Court of Justice (ECJ). Arguably, the ECJ is at the 'federal' end of a federalist/intergovernmentalist spectrum of EU institutions (Shapiro, 1992; Wallace, 1994, pp38–9), developing early in its life the doctrine of direct effect and the precedence of EU over domestic law. In the environmental field it has passed down a series of landmark judgements that have affected the character and scope of environmental policy. Thus, in the case of Danish restrictions on bottle imports, it allowed that the protection of the environment is a legitimate ground for restraint of international trade, provided that the means employed are not disproportionate to the purpose in hand (Case C-302/86). It also sided with the Commission against the Council of Ministers in a case concerned with the regulation of titanium dioxide emissions, deciding that a measure should have been taken under Article 100, rather than Article 130s, when there was still a distinction in terms of the use of qualified majority voting between Single Market and environmental protection measures (Case C-155/91). The ECJ has therefore both supported strong environmental measures and made their passage easier.

Judged in legislative terms, the development of environmental policy has been striking. In the 1970s, a number of directives and regulations were passed, beginning in 1975 with a directive on the control of the ambient quality of surface drinking waters. Other early measures, like the directive on vehicle emissions and the common classification, packaging and labelling of dangerous substances, had an obvious rationale in the attempt to create a single European market. After the 'conversion' of the German government to a pro-environment stance in 1982 on the question of acidification, the pace of developments speeded up considerably, notably with the 1984 framework directive on the control of air pollution from large stationary sources and the passing of the environmental impact assessment directive of 1985. The year 1988 saw the passing of the large combustion plant directive and 1990 saw directives on the control of genetically modified organisms, the establishment of a European environment agency and public access to environmental information. All in all, between 1959 and 1992 there were well over 200 measures passed at European level, leaving aside amendments, covering a wide range of environmental problems (see Table 10.1).

The legislative measures not only increased in number, they also increased in scope. Habitat and species protection came on to the agenda in the 1980s following the wild birds protection directive of 1979. During the 1980s, measures to protect whales, seals and environmentally sensitive areas subject to pressure from farming were passed. Similarly, air quality standards were specified and important procedural measures, like environmental impact statements and public access to environmental information, were adopted. These measures go beyond any conceivable standards that would be strictly necessitated by a concern to ensure a single functioning market.

Moreover, the number and scope of the measures were accompanied by an increasing. The example of vehicle emissions illustrates this trend well. The standards of the 1970s lagged behind those of the USA and Japan. During the mid-1980s it looked as though the countries of Europe would divide in their willingness to pursue higher standards, with some countries like Germany threatening to go it alone. However, after a complex series of negotiations and procedural wrangles involving the European Parliament, the 1989 directive introduced stricter second-stage emission limits for smaller cars, effectively requiring the use of three-way catalytic converters, and thereby brought European standards up to US and Japanese standards (see Chapter 15). It also made the implementation dates mandatory rather than optional, as had been the previous practice. Similar stories could be told of bathing waters, urban waste water treatment, stationary air pollution sources and a range of other measures.

One obvious and visible sign of the growing European importance of environmental policy is the substantial growth of organizational resources, notably but not exclusively related to DG XI. In 1987, for example, the full-time permanent professional staff in DG XI numbered between 50 and 60. By the beginning of 1993, their number had grown to some 450. This growth was accompanied by a move to new and improved offices and owed much to the administrative and diplomatic skills of the Director-General throughout the period, Laurens-Jan Brinkhorst. It is true that a significant portion of this growth occurred in temporary, rather than permanent, staff, and to this extent the interpretation has to be qualified. Still, the growth is striking.

Administrative capacity in relation to European environmental protection has also been increased by the establishment of the European Environmental Agency. Although the long-running dispute about the location of various important institutions, including the European Monetary Institute, held up the establishment of the agency, it is now housed in Copenhagen and staff have been appointed and programmes developed. Although its formal remit is primarily concerned with the collection and standardization of data, one could argue that it has the potential to be a powerful force for the Europeanization of environmental policy, not least given the concerns often expressed about poor implementation of international agreements being disguised by the practice of countries collecting the data on their own performance (House of Lords, 1992, p84).

These European developments have implications for Member States and in some cases it is possible to identify clear instances where the environmental policy of the EU has altered the policy position, institutions or practices of Member States. The UK provides a number of examples, despite (or perhaps because of) its reputation as an 'awkward partner'. Much of the UK's 1990 Environmental Protection Act was necessary in order to implement the requirements of the 1984 air pollution framework directive, and it was this directive that led to the creation of air quality standards in the UK for the first time. Similarly, the retrofitting of flue-gas desulphurizarion equipment to power stations was necessary in order to conform with the 1988 large-combustion-plant directive. Directives on water pollution have also led to expensive investments in waste water treatment facilities that otherwise would have occurred later.

The UK is not alone in this regard, however. It is possible to point to instances in all Member States where practices have had to be changed in order to conform to EU legislation. Perhaps the most striking example among the new Member States of the 1980s is provided by Spain. Its dependence on Brussels has been notably marked in the environmental field, with the whole corpus of EU legislation being adopted after entry in 1986. The decision was taken in the atmosphere of high politics in which entry to the EU was seen as confirming Spain's transition to democracy. Despite the strong emphasis in Spain on economic development, no attention was paid in 1986 to the economic implications of the environmental measures it took over, with the result that the whole process took two years and caused considerable administrative blockage (Pridham, 1994, p91) (see Chapter 6).

As well as these developments in terms of substantive policy, there has also been the development of a well-articulated environmental policy discourse among EU policy-makers. This discourse has a number of distinct elements. First, there emerged in the 1980s the perception that new problems of pollution had to be dealt with and innovative approaches were needed to cope with such problems. The issue that came to symbolize this problem for the early part of the 1980s was acidification (Hajer, 1995). Unlike previous examples of pollution, the science of acidification was poorly understood and gave rise to contested hypotheses about cause and effect relationships. Moreover, everyone agreed that if acidification did have significant effects they were long range, cumulative and difficult to remedy once they had occurred. This in turn led policy-makers in the Community to stress the importance of precaution in the development of policies, and in particular to stress that positive action could not always wait for a complete understanding of the pollution problem at hand without risking the neglect of problems until the environmental damage had been done.

A second theme started from the observation that pollution typically had its source in a variety of otherwise legitimate activities, in particular transport, agriculture and industry. The conclusion to be drawn was that environmental protection could not be the responsibility of a separate administrative section but had to be integrated into a wide range of public policies if harmful effects from those policies were to be anticipated and counteracted. This view found expression in the clause of the SEA stating that 'environmental protection requirements shall be a component of the Community's other policies' (Article 132r(2)). At the national level, this theme has been most vigorously pursued by The Netherlands in its National Environmental Policy Plan of 1989 (see Second Chamber of the States General, 1989 and for commentary Weale, 1992, Chapter 5). It is clear that the Community Fifth Environmental Action Programme (Commission of the European Communities, 1992) bears a strong resemblance to the Dutch approach, with its proposals for collaborative working relations between DG XI and other sections of the Commission's administration, and the formalizing of contacts with interested parties outside the Commission through consultation groups.

Along with the observation that pollution problems had their origin in otherwise legitimate activities, policy-makers began to stress that a wider range of policy instruments was needed than the hitherto conventional use of regulation. The most important thinking has concerned the use of voluntary agreements and the growing interest in economic instruments. The greater use of voluntary instruments might be said to be implicit in the Fifth Environmental Action Programme building as it did on its Dutch precedent and therefore drawing on a system in which voluntary agreements have come to play an important part in the repertoire of policy instruments. Thus, in 1993 .the Commission inaugurated the Auto Oil research programme in conjunction with the motor and oil industries to find ways of cutting exhaust emissions. Although its success is mixed (Plaskett, 1996), it represents an important precedent. Moreover, there is continuing general discussion about the conditions and circumstances under which voluntary agreements are suitable policy instruments, and DG III has also commissioned studies of their use (ENDS Report, 1995, No.246, p34).

In terms of economic instruments, two claims may be distinguished. One is that there are existing subsidies and tax advantages that encourage a wasteful use of resources (for example, exemption from VAT of pesticides or subsidies to car use), which need to be phased out. Second, it is argued that only a greater use of economic instruments will be adequate to meet the goals that have been set in the environmental field, a case that DG XI has sought to articulate particularly in relation to the control of greenhouse gas emissions, and which found detailed expression in proposals for a carbon/energy tax.

The final element in the new policy discourse has been to expand the interest in economic instruments to a concern with the ecologizing of the economy. During the 1980s it became common for policy-makers within the EU (though not exclusively within the EU) to argue for the role of environmental policy in promoting a new sort of economic competitiveness. The argument ran that, with the advent of global markets, the standard of product acceptability for international consumers would be increasingly set by the country with the most stringent pollution control standards, so that the future of the post-industrial economy will depend on its ability to produce high value, high quality products meeting high environmental standards. Thus, on this argument, Europe would only be able to take full advantage of economies of scale in globally competitive markets provided that it legislated for high environmental standards on a par with those to be found in Japan and the USA (Weale, 1992, Chapter 3; Weale, 1993).

This argument thus sought to turn on its head the most familiar objection to stringent environmental policy, namely that there was always a trade-off between the imposition of environmental standards and the protection of economic interests, most notably the protection of employment. In the case of environmental policy, it became almost an article of faith that environmental protection was a precondition of the economic success that was associated with the European project. (In conducting interviews in DG XI, one often finds oneself listening to anecdotes about how firms that had reluctantly taken up environmental measures found after a short while that they had profited thereby.)

It is clear that these arguments were developed extensively within DG XI and the Commission at large, and they surfaced in relation to the Commission's White Paper on growth, competitiveness and employment (Commission of the European Communities, 1993). The background to the document is well known. Amid the growing public and political anxiety about recession and rising unemployment in Europe, the Copenhagen European Council in June 1993 invited the Commission to prepare a document on the subject outlining a diagnosis and discussing possible policy solutions. In terms of environmental policy, there is a clear formal recognition within the White Paper of the role of environmental projects and concerns in promoting enhanced growth and competitiveness. It appears that this acknowledgement of the fundamental tenets of ecological modernization was mediated through the work of Dolors' *cabinet* which became convinced during 1992 of the potential of environmental measures in stimulating economic activity. The last section of the Commission's document is entitled 'Towards a new development model', and it advocates fiscal and other policy instruments as devices for moving costs away from the employment of labour and towards the use of resources. Existing policy instruments, the chapter argues, will have to be reoriented to encourage the more efficient use of resources (thus leaving open the possibility of eco-taxes) and priority should be given to environmentally friendly innovation both by mean of subsidies for technical improvement and by funds for research and development.

In summary, then, we can see that there has been both a significant growth in environmental policy activity and the development of an elaborated set of policy principles for European environmental policy. In this way we have a governance regime in Bulmer's sense, involving not just a set of actors and institutions at the European level, but also a collection of norms and procedures for pursuing environmental objectives.

Rule-making Processes and the Limits of Europeanization

Told in the above way, the Europeanization of environmental policy might seem to follow an elegant political logic. Political decision-makers respond to the public's concerns by adapting procedures and institutions that previously did not include an environmental competence, and when the scope of that competence grows, they adapt the institutions and procedures themselves both to cope with an expanded range of problems and to foster the development of policy-learning and development. This is a view that would be consistent with neofunctionalist accounts of European integration, according to which the dynamic effects of spillovers from one aspect of European integration create conditions for integration in others (see Chapter 10). Just as the internal market has a logic leading to a single currency (Cameron, 1992, pp25–7), so it also has a logic leading to environmental policy at European level to counteract market failures. However, this simple interpretation needs to be qualified in certain important respects.

Although EU rule-making institutions can be said to have a life of their own in the field of environmental policy, they still need to be connected to the life-support machine of the nation states if they are to function at all. Indeed, there are strong constraints at the European level limiting the range of measures that can be adopted as well as the scope and character of European environment policy. These stem most notably from a range of factors including: (1) the ability of the Member States to exercise their veto power in areas of special concern; (2) the role of national economic interests in the conduct of environmental policy; (3) the pattern of agenda-setting at European level which still owes much to national preferences; and the persistence of national norm-setting and policy-making.

In terms of national veto power, the clearest effects on environmental policy occur in relation to questions of taxation. The EU is limited in the amount of taxation that it can collect and its principal source of revenue is from VAT proceeds. This means that it cannot impose pollution taxes as an instrument of policy, and under the Treaty on European Union, any environmental measures that involve fiscal considerations have to be agreed by all Member States before they can be passed. By comparison with fully federal systems of governance, like Germany or the USA, it is clear that there is a significant limitation built into the development of environmental policy at the European level.

These constraints were manifested most clearly over the issue of the carbon/energy tax proposals emanating from the Commission in 1992. In the run-up to the United Nations Conference on Environment and Development in that year, the Commission was anxious to secure agreement from Member States on the imposition of a carbon/energy tax that would contribute to the reduction of greenhouse gas emissions. The original proposal would have required a tax on fossil fuels and most sources of electricity, building up to a value equivalent to $10 per barrel by the year 2000. The measure was opposed by a number of Member States, with France objecting to the taxation of nuclear power, Spain, Portugal, Greece and Ireland claiming exemptions on the grounds of their low contribution to overall levels and their need for economic development, and the

UK arguing it was opposed to the extension of tax-making powers to the EU (ENDS Report, 1995, No.244, p39). Current projections by the Commission suggest that the EU as a whole will fall short of its announced target of stabilizing greenhouse gas emissions at 1990 levels by the year 2000, despite the intervening recession (ENDS Report, 1996, No.255, p38). The failure of the measure also shows the political limits of proposals to ecologize the economy by shifting taxes from labour to resources.

Just as the case of the carbon/energy tax shows the constraints imposed by national vetoes, so there are some clear examples where it is difficult to account for developments in European environmental policy without seeing the economic interest of particular countries at stake behind the proposal of an environmental measure. The original draft of the large combustion directive is the most well-known example. Here, the relevant official in DG XI, who was German, was simply given the recently agreed German large combustion ordinance and told to translate it into Euro-speak. The most recent example would be the pressure from Germany to agree a directive on packaging. Similarly, the UK's reluctance to move as quickly as some other countries have wished in terms of higher pollution control standards has sometimes been ascribed to the view that the UK wishes to use its geographical comparative advantage (westerly winds, short fast-running rivers and clay soils) to maintain low-cost production (Haigh, 1989, p22).

Another feature of the European rule-making process is the way in which the agenda is often set by national concerns and perspectives, with individual countries seeking to ensure that their priorities are generalized within the EU. For example, it is the UK – usually regarded as a European environmental policy laggard – that has taken the lead on such matters as environmentally sensitive farming, integrated pollution control and eco-audits, while Germany has certainly resisted the last of these. On this basis Héritier and her colleagues (Héritier et al, 1994) have spoken of a regulatory competition in European which Member States struggle to secure their own regulatory styles in European legislation (see Chapter 11).

On this account, what we are seeing in the formation of EU environmental standards is not a European agenda, but a process by which national concerns are displaced on to a higher level. If this intergovernmentalist account is correct, it would also make sense of the complaints of the Mediterranean countries that their environmental priorities (for example, water supply and forest fires) were regularly ignored in the making of EU policy, as representatives sometimes allege (Pridham, 1994, p93). However, the story is not quite as straightforward as this argument would suggest, as can be illustrated from the development of the directive on integrated pollution prevention and control. Integrated pollution control has been a cause close to the heart of UK environmental policy-makers and advisers for a number of years (Weale, et al, 1991). Although it originally sought to put the issue on to the EU agenda, the UK found that its scope and significance were expanded in the course of the directive's passage through the process of decision-making, in particular to include a wider range of industries, especially intensive livestock plants and food and drink plants. In other words,

the development of the directive took a more stringent direction than had originally been intended and the original initiative was thereby transformed.

The amount, scope and stringency of EU environmental regulation has certainly grown in the 1980s, but this is quite consistent with a great deal of important norm- and standard-setting going on at national level. One clear indication of this is to be found in the fields of product norms and packaging. As
developments have been stalled at the European level, so individual Member
States have been developing their own schemes. In the case of eco-labelling, for
example, national organizations have set different standards for products and,
just as importantly, have identified different products as priorities. Moreover,
even in sectors that are regulated at the European level, like air and water pollution, there are many pollutants where it is still left to individual Member States
to set standards.

It is also worth noting that there is an open question about the extent to
which there is a genuine convergence of interpretation around measures that
have been formally agreed at an international level. Consider, for example, the
principle of 'best available technology not entailing excessive cost', which is to
be found in the 1984 air pollution framework directive. This provision is also
found in the national legislation that followed in the implementation of the
measure, but as Faure and Ruegg (1994, p52) have pointed out, there can be
considerable differences of national interpretation as to what the principle means
in particular cases.

Behind these varying responses to EU policy developments and principles,
there are persistent differences of national environmental policy preference and
principles. To some extent, national differences in policy-making style and priorities are not simply a lagged response by countries at different levels of economic development to a common set of environmental problems, but reflect
the fact that national environments differ and so their policy needs differ. The
most marked contrast here, of course, is between the relatively undeveloped countries of the south (Portugal, Spain and Greece, as well as the Mezzogiorno) and
the industrialized densely populated countries of the north (notably Germany
and The Netherlands). Here the argument is that there are simply objective
differences in the nature of the problems faced by these different countries, and
some of these differences will not be eroded over time. Germany, post-unification,
is not going to acquire a longer coastline and Spain is not going to acquire a
river Rhine. Hence, so the argument goes, it is unrealistic to expect a high
degree of policy convergence and we should be surprised if issues dealt with at
the European level did not reflect the priorities of different countries.

Moreover, there is a fallacy, so it could be argued, in inferring the Europeanization of environmental policy from observations of the policy-making process in Brussels. Such evidence is bound to distort our perceptions since we are
only looking at the cases that countries think are worth arguing about at an international level. What about the times that they are happy to pursue their own
priorities or simply do not bother to kick up a fuss because their own standards
are higher than the Commission is proposing anyway? Liefferink (1996, pp121–3)
provides an interesting example in connection with the development of policy
on the 1980 directive on air quality limit values and guide values for sulphur

dioxide and suspended particulates. Dutch policy had already developed on this issue and there was little interest in seeking to influence the Commission in its drafting process, since it was clear that any standard that was set at the European level would be less strict than had already been agreed in The Netherlands. For this reason, there was no lobbying by Dutch industry at European level. Similar considerations apply, Liefferink argues, in connection with the air quality standards on lead and nitrogen oxides.

Finally, there is not much evidence of convergence in formal structures of environmental policy-making among the Member States (Weale, et al, 1996). If we simply measure the degree of concentration of environmental functions within a single ministry, for example, it is clear that there is more variance between countries than there is over time. These organizational differences reflect different environmental priorities and different priorities given to the environment. In other words, despite the growing common recognition across Europe of the increasing importance of environmental issues, there is little evidence of convergence in the institutional arrangements that different countries use to formulate and implement policy.

Thus, in summary, the functional links between the Single Market and environmental policy are not sufficient to explain the form and character that the policy has taken, and there is no simple transfer of juridiction from the level of the nation state to the European level. Indeed, there remain what look like ineliminable features of national policy-making and interest in the environmental field. What are the implications for the environmental governance regime of the EU?

Concurrent Decision-making among Institutional and Functional Actors

Scharpf (1988, p242) has argued that the EU is one of a class of political systems in which decision-making authority is not allocated in a zero-sum fashion between different levels of government but is instead shared. Thus, just as the German federal government shares authority with the *Länder* through the need to secure a majority in the Bundesrat, so the EU shares authority with national governments through the pivotal role in decision-making of the Council of Ministers. In such systems, decision-making must necessarily take the form of requiring concurrent majorities of actors, and may in practice – whatever the formal rules say – tend to the rule of unanimity.

Some of the implications of this decision-making structure were spelt out in the previous section, where national actors could block certain measures and where there was a constant tendency to wish to displace national agendas on to the European level. National champions are often needed for measures to succeed, and even under qualified majority voting in the Council of Ministers proposed measures need widespread agreement, or at least acquiescence, if they are to be adopted.

However, the principle of shared authority applies not simply to the relations between the EU and the Member States, but also to the relations between different elements of the EU decision-making process itself: the Commission, the Court, the Parliament and the Council of Ministers. The involvement of all these actors in the decision-making process increases the number of 'veto players', that is, actors whose agreement is required for a change in policy (Tsebelis, 1995, p301). The principle of concurrent majorities thus operates both vertically, in respect of the EU and the Member States, and horizontally, in respect of policy actors at the European level itself.

But the complexity of the story does not stop here. In addition to the formal involvement of various actors in the decision-making process, the Commission has also been called a 'promiscuous bureaucracy' (Mazey and Richardson, 1993), because of its tendency to involve interest groups in the making of policy. Moreover, given diminishing marginal returns in the imposition of environmental standards, many apparently small 'technical' changes in the rules can turn out to have major cost or environmental implications, so that the involvement of interest groups in the processes of standard-setting and rule-making should not be regarded as trivial or simply as a matter of courtesy (see Chapter 9). Instead, we should think of it as involving the concurrence of functional groups, in which sectional interests can often have something close to veto power.

What, then, might be the implications of this institutional and functional sharing of rule-making authority? The first consequence is that in a system in which the agreement of so many actors is necessary in order to have any chance of policy change, policy-makers within the Commission have a strong incentive to be opportunistic in their agenda-setting, taking proposals from Member States, safe in the knowledge that there is at least some support at the beginning for a measure. Add to this incentive the organizational disadvantage of having little by way of resources to conduct policy analysis and development, and the stage is set for opportunistic decision-making relying on the initiative of Member States. This is the most obvious way of accounting for the regulatory competition identified by Héritier and her colleagues (see Chapter 11).

However, once inside the process of decision-making, any issue is subject to capture by other actors, so that what eventually emerges at the other end may contain elements uncongenial to its original proponents. Again, given the impact of apparently small 'technical' features of rules on costs and compliance, there is a great deal of scope for a transformation of proposals during the course of their passage: timetables for implementation can be changed, emission limit values altered, new processes brought under control, administrative requirements changed, and so on. Moreover, the need to secure a concurrent majority in the process of decision-making means that there is little incentive for policy participants to point out the full implications of measures to Member States even if they know them. It is much more attractive to secure agreement in principle and then argue later about the extent to which Member States are implementing what they have already signed up to.

European environmental standards, then, are neither a reflection of a dominant coalition of countries pushing their own national style of regulation (as is sometimes suggested by those who see the UK as subject to an alien form of environmental regulation via uniform emission limits imposed from Germany), nor a merry-go-round in which different countries have a go at imposing their own national style in a sector that is of particular importance to them. Instead, they are the aggregated and transformed standards of their original champions modified under the need to secure political accommodation from powerful veto players.

In addition, in a system like that of environmental policy-making in the EU where not only are the rules being made quickly but also the rules for making rules are changing quite rapidly, there are plenty of opportunities for procedural wrangling, as happened between the Commission and the Council over the directive on titanium dioxide, and as also happened over various attempts to repatriate certain environmental competences (Wallace, 1994, p78). Concurrent majority systems are well known to have high transaction costs attached to them, most notably as the decision rule tends to unanimity, but the procedural wrangling adds to such transaction costs by creating disputes not just about the substance of the measure, but also about the terms and conditions under which the measure is to be taken.

The theory of social choice suggests that as actors with diverse policy positions obtain a share of decision-making power, so the chances of policy change go down (Tsebelis, 1995, pp308–13). A clear recent example of this effect is provided by the European Parliament's rejection of the proposed landfill directive (ENDS Report, 1996, No. 256, pp38–9). The Parliament has the general reputation of having a policy position that is more pro-environment than the Council of Ministers. In the case of the proposed landfill Directive, the crucial issue was a provision that enabled Member States to exempt smaller landfills with a low density of inhabitants (an exemption favoured by Portugal and Ireland). Thus, requiring simultaneous agreement between the Council and the Parliament results in a situation in which it is difficult to move from the status quo.

When we turn to the functional component of the concurrent majority one feature in particular is evident, namely that environmental policy involves co-ordination with other policy sectors, most notably industry, transport and agriculture. Thus, an environmental policy taken on its own may secure the reduction in harmful emissions from individual vehicles, but if transport policy is leading to more vehicles being put on the road, the gain at the individual level is offset by the increase in total emissions arising from the volume increase, a phenomenon that has been observed in respect of nitrous oxide emissions from cars, for example. Since, at the European level, DGs are the guardians of their sectoral interests, it is hardly surprising that sectoral complexity makes for difficult decision-making in institutional terms.

By contrast, environmental policy-makers will also want to be seen to be supporting their own functional constituency, a trend reinforced in the case of DG XI by the fact that a number of the officials clearly have a commitment to environmental protection that is personal as well as professional. It may be this tendency which creates the impression among some other officials that DG XI has a limited perspective, as the interviewee quoted by Peterson illustrates:

> *These DG XI people are like the Trappist monks who make Chimay Bleu [a strong Belgian beer]. They don't consult with anyone besides their religious patrons and they cook up very strong stuff, which will always appeal to a certain segment of the*

'beer-drinking public'. They don't ever think about what a ferocious hangover is induced by the stuff they cook up. (Peterson, 1995, p482)

Similarly, there are officials in DG XI who will volunteer the thought that no one in agriculture is willing to talk to anyone about the environmental problems that the Common Agricultural Policy causes.

Can we characterize the decision-making style that emerges from this institutional process? One important feature of it is that it is difficult for policy actors to adopt what Scharpf terms a 'problem-solving' mentality as distinct from a 'bargaining' mentality. In this sense the attempt to create a discourse of ecological modernization, around which policy could be organized and discussed, has failed. There is simply too much heterogeneity of interest (especially arising from different stages of economic development) for there to be a consensus on the priority to be given to environmental measures. Moreover, even if it is true in the aggregate that environmental protection and economic development pull in the same direction, there is too much conflict in the particular case for the tension to be easily eliminated.

One consequence is that over time the development of environmental policy tends to follow a pattern of *immobilisme* punctuated by activism. Between 1982 and 1992 there was an upsurge of activism in which many environmental measures were passed, partly as a consequence of the need to harmonize environmental measures in the context of the internal market and partly because of the high salience that the environment had as an issue among European publics and governments. Despite some consolidation and advance since 1992, the scale and pace of development have slowed down considerably, and some high profile measures have been stalled.

How well overall is the environmental system of governance performing? In particular, how far is it producing high quality decisions that are well adapted to solve the problems at which they are directed? It is difficult to come to a judgement on these questions, not least because the criteria of evaluation will vary according to one's own policy position. But some things are clear. There *is* environmental spillover from the Single Market. It was *not* anticipated in the creation of the internal market. Moreover, in so far as EU environmental policy has transcended the logic of the Single Market, it is not easy to see how rule-making activity has pursued an effective problem-solving strategy. Decision processes operating on the principle of concurrent majorities and sharing authority between nation and Community as well as both functionally and institutionally are not perhaps best adapted to deal with environmental issues.

Acknowledgements

This chapter draws on the research project 'Environmental Standards and the Politics of Expertise' conducted under the ESRC's Single European Market Research Programme (award number W 113 251 025). I should like to thank my co-researchers in the project (Michelle Cini, Dimitrios Konstadakopoulos, Geoffrey Pridham, Martin Porter and Andrea Williams) for discussions and material. In addition I am grateful to Iain Begg, Maarten Hajer, Duncan Liefferink and Geoffrey Pridham for detailed comments and suggestions on earlier versions. Remaining errors are my responsibility.

References

Arp, H. (1993) 'Technical Regulation and Politics: The Interplay between Economic Interests and Environmental Policy Goals in EC Car Emission Llegislation', in Liefferink, J. D., Lowe, P. D. and Mol, A. P. J. (eds), *European Integration and Environmental Policy*, London and New York: Belhaven Press, pp150–71.

Bulmer, S. J. (1994) 'The Governance of the European Union: A New Institutionalist Approach', *Journal of Public Policy*, Vol.13, No.4, pp351–80.

Cameron, D. R. (1992) 'The 1992 Initiative: Causes and Consequences', in Sbragia, A. M. (ed), *Euro-Politics: Institutions and Policymaking in the 'New' European Community*, Washington D.C.: The Brookings Institution.

Commission of the European Communities (1992) *Fifth Environmental Action Programme*, COM (92) 23 final, Luxembourg: Commission of the European Communities.

Commission of the European Communities (1993) *Growth, Competitiveness, Employment, The Challenges and Ways Forward into the 21st Century*, Luxembourg: Commission of the European Communities (two volumes).

ENDS Report, various numbers.

Faure, M. and Ruegg, M. (1994) 'Environmental Standard Setting Through General Environmental Law', in Faure, M., Vervaele, J. and Weale, A. (eds), *Environmental Standards in the European Union in an Interdisciplinary Framework*, Antwerpen and Apeldoorn: MAKLU.

Haigh, N. (1989) *EEC Environmental Policy and Britain*, 2nd edn, Harlow: Longman.

Haigh, N. and Baldock, D. (1989) *Environmental Policy and 1992*, London: Institute for European Environmental Policy.

Hajer, M. (1995) *The Politics of Environmental Discourse*, Oxford: Clarendon Press.

Héretier, A. et al (1994) *Die Veränderung von Staatlichkeit in Europa*, Opladen: Leske and Budrich.

House of Lords, Select Committee on the European Communities (1992) *Implementation and Enforcement of Environmental Legislation, Volume II – Evidence*, HL Paper 53–11, London: HMSO.

Keohane, R. O. and Nye, J. S. (1989) *Power and Interdependence*, London: HarperCollins.

Liefferink, J. D. (1996) *The Making of European Environmental Policy*, Manchester: Manchester University Press.

Mazey, S. and Richardson, J. J. (eds) (1993) *Lobbying in the European Community*, Oxford and New York: Oxford University Press.

Peterson, J. (1995) 'Playing the Transparency Game: Consultation and Policymaking in the European Commission', *Public Administration*, Vol.73, No.3, pp473–92.

Plaskett, L. (1996) 'Airing the Differences', *Financial Times*, Wednesday 26 June, p20.

Pridham, G. (1994) 'National Environmental Policy-making in the European Framework: Spain, Greece and Italy in Comparison', *Regional Politics and Policy*, Vol.4, No.1, pp80–101.

Rehbinder, E. and Steward, R. (1985) *Environmental Protection Policy*, Berlin and New York: Walter de Gruyter.

Scharpf, F. W. (1988) 'The Joint-decision Trap: Lessons from German Federalism and European Institutions', *Public Administration*, Vol.66, No.3, pp239–78.

Second Chamber of the States General (1989) *National Environmental Policy Plan: To Choose or Lose*, 's-Gravenhage: SDU Uitgeverij.

Shapiro, M. (1992) 'The European Court of Justice', in Sbragia A. M. (ed), *Euro-Politics: Institutions and Policymaking in the 'New' European Community*, Washington D.C.: The Brookings Institute.

Task Force Report on the Environment and the Internal Market (1989) *1992: The Environmental Dimension*, Luxembourg: Commission of the European Communities.

Tsebelis, G. (1995) 'Decision Making in Political Systems: Veto Players in Presidentialism, Parliamentarianism, Multicameralism and Multipartyism', *British Journal of Political Science*, Vol.25, No.3, pp289–325.

Wallace, W. (1994) *Regional Integration: The West European Experience*, Washington D.C.: The Brookings Institute.

Weale, A. (1992) *The New Politics of Pollution*, Manchester: Manchester University Press.

Weale, A. (1993) 'Ecological Modernisation and the Integration of European Environmental Policy', in Liefferink, J. D., Lowe, P. D. and Mol, A. J. P. (eds), *European Integration and Environmental Policy*, London and New York: Belhaven Press, pp196–216.

Weale, A., O'Riordan, T. and Kramme, L. (1991) *Controlling Pollution in the Round*, London: Anglo-German Foundation for the Study of Industrial Society.

Weale, A., Pridham, G., Williams, A. and Porter, M. (1996) 'Administrative Organization and Environmental Policy: Structural Convergence or National Distinctiveness in Six European States?', *Public Administration*, Vol.74, No.2, pp255–74.

Würzel, R. (1993) 'Environmental Policy', in Lodge, J. (ed), *The European Community and the Challenge of the Future*, 2nd edn, London: Pinter, pp178–99.

Part 4
MAKING ENVIRONMENTAL POLICY

13

State Power and Institutional Influence in European Integration: Lessons from the Packaging Waste Directive

Jonathan Golub

Introduction

After nearly three years of protracted negotiations between the institutions of the European Community (EC), the Council of Ministers formally adopted Directive 94/62/EC on packaging and packaging waste in December 1994 (OJL365, 31 December 1994). This study traces the development of the directive in order to illuminate the role of various actors in shaping EC environmental policy. Having become the most heavily lobbied dossier in the history of the European institutions, the packaging directive also provides the perfect vehicle through which to assess a number of larger questions surrounding European integration.

Insight into the actual interplay between the Council, Commission and European Parliament allows tentative conclusions to be drawn about the character of the integration process: the ability of the Commission to set and retain control of the agenda, the impact of the European Parliament on the content of directives, and the extent to which qualified majority voting (QMV) produces Council decisions which are at a level above the lowest-common denominator. Ultimately, by tracing the directive through its many versions, assessing the role of various actors and thereby identifying 'winners' and 'losers', this study seeks to contribute to the larger debate about whether EC integration strengthens the state, or rather empowers supranational institutions at the expense of national sovereignty – two competing concepts of the integration process advanced by prominent theorists (Moravcsik, 1993, 1994; Marks et al, 1994).

The chapter proceeds as follows. The first section traces the development of the packaging directive throughout the entire policy-making cycle – pre-draft stage, official Commission proposal, first reading in the European Parliament, common position in the Council, second reading in the European Parliament, adoption by Council. A primary aim of the first section is to identify the key legislative objectives of the Commission and Parliament, as well as to provide a picture of the current and projected recycling plans of the Member States.

The second section examines in more detail the role of each institutional actor. Evidence of how the packaging directive actually developed is used to test a variety of predictions about the role of each institution in the decision-making procedure which stem from the available theoretical and empirical literature. This section uses experience from the case of packaging to test notions of agenda-setting, parliamentary influence and Council bargaining.

The third section uses the packaging case to address broader questions of European integration. It seeks to refine the current debate between scholars who propose state-centric models and those who advocate a view of Europe in which power is diffused at the expense of state sovereignty. The case study of the packaging directive reveals that this debate has a tendency to proceed along effectively unrelated paths, with state-centrist models focusing on the issue of power while diffusion theorists concentrate instead on the issue of influence. It is suggested that a clearer distinction between these two issues demonstrates the strengths as well as the shortcomings of each theory, and provides a useful analytical framework in which to place future empirical studies.

The Problem of Packaging Waste in the EC

Disposing of the nearly 50 million tonnes of packaging waste produced each year and the 'waste mountains' which already exist throughout the Community presents Member States with serious environmental and economic problems. Some Member States have introduced voluntary or compulsory agreements with industry to reduce the production of packaging waste and encourage its reuse or recycling. The most ambitious programmes have been implemented by Denmark, Germany and The Netherlands. Before reuse or recycling can occur, however, packaging waste must be 'recovered', which entails collecting and sorting various materials from the general waste stream. In some cases states require the recovery of most, if not all, packaging waste. This presents a number of disposal problems. Burning or burying such enormous quantities of waste places human health at risk. Recycling of waste may prevent damage to the environment and to health but only after a substantial investment in appropriate technology. Faced with the costs of recycling and the inability to dispose of waste safely within their own borders, some states pay to incinerate, landfill or recycle their used packaging in other EC countries.

Swamped with what are effectively subsidized waste imports, and thus unable to dispose effectively of their own packaging, several Member States began considering plans to restrict landfill, incineration and recycling to domestic waste only (House of Lords, 1993). While this might solve the problems of a few states, it would of course result in even higher waste mountains in countries which relied on exporting used packaging.

Equally important, restrictions on waste imports raised serious questions about the free movement of goods throughout the Community. Although the European Court of Justice (ECJ) has upheld the right of an individual country under Article 36 to enact environmental laws more stringent than those found in other Member States, such exceptions to Article 30 are allowed only under certain circumstances – the national measures must be necessary to improve protection of the environment, impose no disproportionate restrictions on trade, and must not discriminate between foreign and domestic producers (ECJ, 1988, 1992; Krämer, 1993; von Wilmowsky, 1993; Sexton, 1991).

In what has been widely viewed as a product of contorted legal reasoning, the Court's 1992 ruling in the case of the Walloon waste import ban (Case 2/90) allowed considerable scope for national restrictions on certain types of waste, particularly those destined for landfill, refusing to find such measures discriminatory despite the compelling arguments of the Advocate General which upheld the prevailing view that 'any import restriction on waste constitutes an arbitrary discrimination and is therefore incompatible with Article 30' (Krämer, 1993, pp128–9; see also von Wilmowsky, 1993).[1]

Nevertheless, there are several reasons to believe that the Court would not allow general bans of transnational waste shipments, especially those destined for recycling (von Wilmowsky, 1993, pp557–9, 570). The Walloon ban was supported as an acceptable example of the proximity and self-sufficiency principle implied by Article 130r(2) of the Treaty, but the restrictive provisions were 'an exceptional, temporary measure' preventing Wallonia from becoming the dustbin of Europe, rather than a blanket ban (ECJ, 1992, p396). Furthermore, unlike bottle recycling laws or regulations obliging the use of biodegradable plastic bags, bans on waste destined for recycling do nothing to improve the overall quality of the environment, as pollution is merely relocated rather than reduced. The Court has often held that it makes no difference from an ecological point of view which state disposes of waste, as long as disposal occurs. Finally, the ruling did not specify whether waste destined for recycling fell under Directive 75/442 on transboundary waste shipments, in which case the derogations in Article 36 would not apply.

In sum, the existing case law suggests that prior to the packaging waste directive, the ECJ would not have tolerated broad national bans on imported packaging waste because they constituted unjustified barriers to trade (von Wilmowsky, 1993, p558). In other words. Community law did not require states to develop self-sufficient means of recycling their packaging waste but instead allowed them to make use of recycling facilities in neighbouring states.

In order to avert protracted legal proceedings over the legitimacy of 'green protectionism' and to reduce the environmental threats from excessive packaging waste in the Community, the Commission began considering various preventive and harmonizing measures. The Commission's efforts culminated in its proposal on packaging and packaging waste in July 1992, which was made under Article 100a of the Treaty.

The Policy-making Cycle

From Pro-draft to Draft: DG XI Abandons its Bold Objectives

The driving force behind the proposal was to prevent green protectionism from destroying the free movement of packaging waste within the Community without also preventing Member States from finding ways to deal effectively with their own waste. These two objectives are not easily reconciled – one way of dealing with national waste is to export it to neighbouring states for disposal, often at heavily subsidized rates, a practice which undermines the capacity of the receiving state to deal with its own problems of packaging waste. Hence the rising spectre of protectionism to keep out enormous subsidized waste shipments, particularly those arising from the German Duales System Deutschland (DSD) scheme which was introduced in 1991 by environment minister Klaus Topfer (*Financial Times*, 6 December 1991; *Economist*, 29 May 1993; House of Lords, 1993; *Agence Europe*, 5/6 July 1993).

In order to maintain free movement of goods without condemning some states to act as disposal havens and to suffer burgeoning waste mountains, and in line with its emphasis on preventing environmental damage at its source, DG XI of the Commission originally sought to introduce three major elements into its proposal:[2]

1. Freezing the Community's output of waste at current levels by setting a per capita maximum of 150 kg/yr of packaging waste, to be achieved within ten years.
2. Targets: A mandatory minimum 'recovery' rate of 60 per cent (by weight) for all packaging waste within five years, rising to 90 per cent after ten years.[3] A mandatory minimum recycling rate of 40 per cent (by weight) for each type of packaging material within five years; rising to 60 per cent after ten years.[4] Minimization of the final disposal of packaging waste (ie by landfill or incineration without energy recovery) to no more than 10 per cent by weight of packaging waste output after ten years. Thus, after ten years, 60 per cent of packaging waste would have to be recycled, 30 per cent could be recovered but not recycled, and no more than 10 per cent could be disposed of through rubbish tips or incineration without energy recovery.
3. Hierarchy of disposal options: DG XI originally wanted to encourage what it considered to be the most ecologically rational disposal methods by including within the proposal a hierarchy of goals: prevention, reuse, recycling, incineration with energy recovery, incineration without energy recovery, landfill.

As originally conceived, the targets exceeded the existing plans of many EC countries and were modelled to a large extent on the ambitious national recycling achievements and goals of Germany and The Netherlands. Tables 13.1 and 13.2 show recycling rates within the Community for each type of packaging material and the commitment of each Member State to increase recovery and recycling in the coming years.

Table 13.1 *National recycling rates*

	Paper and Board (1990)	Aluminium (1987)	Glass (1993)
Germany	40	31	65
Denmark	35	31	64
The Netherlands	50	47	76
Belgium	36 (1988)	4 (1987)	55
France	46	25	46
UK	31	19	29
Luxembourg	NA	NA	NA
Italy	25	36	52
Spain	51	28	29
Greece	21	25 (1990)	27
Portugal	39	4	29
Ireland	3	NA	29

Source: Compiled from *European Environment*, 28 July 1992, Newman and Foster (1993), UNEP (1991, 1992, 1994), van Goethem (1993)

Table 13.2 *Commission proposal compared with national plans*

Commission Proposal	Recovery Targets 2005: 90% of All Materials	Recycling Targets 2005: 60% of Each Material
Germany	1995: 80% of each material	1995: 64–72% of each material
Denmark	NA	2000: 50% of each material
The Netherlands	2000: 90% of each material	2000: 50–80% of each material
Belgium		1998: 70–80% of each material
– Flanders	2000: 58% of all materials	
– Wallonia	2000: 60–80% of all materials	
France	2002: 75% of all materials	2000: 75% of glass
UK	2000: 50–75% of all material	
Luxembourg	1995: 95% of liquid food containers	1994: 78% of liquid food containers
Italy	NA	1993: 40–50% for each type of liquid container
Spain	NA	NA
Greece	NA	NA
Portugal	NA	NA
Ireland	NA	NA

Source: Compiled from *European Environment*, 28 July 1992, Newman and Foster (1993), UNEP (1991, 1992, 1994), van Goethem (1993)

For most Member States, DG XI's original proposal would have entailed a serious reconsideration of strategies aimed at reducing and recovering certain types of packaging waste. In many cases it would also have involved additional investment in recycling technology. For the less developed and southern states the proposal would have required a complete overhaul of their waste management programmes, forcing the introduction of stringent recycling targets and implementation deadlines, each of which was practically unheard of or limited to individual types of waste such as drink containers.

DG XI immediately came under pressure from various industrial groups to make the proposal more flexible. This pressure was channelled through Member State governments, as well as other Commission departments, particularly DG III and DG VI (Porter, 1995, Chapter 8). Some states, mainly Germany, Denmark and The Netherlands where green groups enjoyed greater political influence and industry already faced ambitious domestic environmental targets wanted either higher Community targets or flexibility which guaranteed that the directive would not prevent them from adopting more stringent standards of their own. Other states worried that the targets were already too high and impossible to meet. The Bureau International de la Recuperation, the Association of Plastics Manufacturers of Europe, the European Organization for Packaging and the Environment, the European Recovery and Recycling Association, the Alliance for Beverage Cartons, along with several other large European peak organizations for packaging and recycling feared that overly ambitious recovery and recycling targets failed to take account of the market for these products.[5]

In response to this pressure, many of DG XI's original goals were abandoned by the time the Commission released the first official draft (OJC263, 12 October 1992; see *Europe Environment*, 4 February 1992, 28 July 1992, 1 December 1992; *Agence Europe*, 16 July 1992, 18 July 1992; Porter, 1995, Chapters 8–9). Gone were the per capita waste provision, the binding intermediary five-year targets and the hierarchy of disposal methods. What remained was a 90 per cent recovery target, a 60 per cent recycling target for each type of material, and a 10 per cent limit on waste which could be burned or buried in landfill, all of which states had to meet within ten years. In a somewhat sanguine note to Commissioner Ripa di Meana, these requirements, which should be seen as the first expression of the Commission's (as opposed to DG XI's) objectives, were portrayed by Director General Laurens Brinkhorst not as a weakening of the text but rather a tightening of initial environmental objectives (Porter, 1995, p176). This erroneous claim clearly ignored the substantial deviations from DG XI's tough pro-draft objectives, but Tables 13.1 and 13.2 demonstrate the profound environmental implications of the provisions which remained in the official proposal: all three targets would have exerted a dramatic ratcheting effect on all but a few Member States. It is therefore not surprising that the ensuing negotiations revealed substantial efforts to relax the targets.

The European Parliament's First Reading

Under the terms of the co-decision procedure the European Parliament (EP) had two opportunities to amend the packaging proposal. Each 'reading' is actually a two-part process: first, the Environment Committee of the EP issues a report suggesting amendments; second, this report is adopted in part or in full by the rest of the EP.

In its report, the Environment Committee put forward 79 amendments. True to its reputation as a source of zealous environmental concern (see Chapter 8), it proceeded to reintroduce most of the provisions originally favoured by DG XI, including the hierarchy of disposal methods and the binding five-year recovery and recycling targets. The Committee also sought to guarantee the rights of individual Member States to opt-up for more stringent domestic standards, balancing admonitions against distorting the market and endorsement of the proximity principle with language clearly designed to allow ambitious national economic instruments and the continued possibility of waste exports (European Parliament, 1993).[6] These amendments suggested that because no precise definition had been given of what constituted a high level of environmental protection, Member States could take 'more rigorous' unilateral measures as long as the goal was to protect the environment. The Environment Committee also sought to require mandatory minimum proportions of recycled material in packaging, to eliminate in ten years all packaging containing certain heavy metals, and to take account of the special conditions affecting islands.[7] This latter concern, although extremely ambiguous, was the first sign that the EC might consider derogations for some regions.

On 23 June 1993, the EP accepted most of the Environment Committee's major recommendations, retaining the hierarchy, the intermediary standards, the minimum content of recycled materials in packaging, and the sensitivity to the needs of islands (OJC194, 19 July 1993). However, while the EP expanded the scope of unilateral national action slightly by accepting the amendments allowing national economic instruments which pursued environmental goals, it rejected all three amendments aimed at allowing broad national opt-ups. It also rejected the mandatory ban on packaging containing heavy metals (*Europe Environment*, 8 August 1993, 6 July 1993; *Agence Europe*, 25 June 1993).

Round Two

Still wanting to maximize the green provisions of the directive, but aware of the Council's concerns about flexibility and having received the results of the EP's first reading, the Commission produced an amended proposal on 9 September 1993 which reintroduced the binding five-year targets but rejected both minimum levels of recycled material in packaging and a total phase-out of packaging containing heavy metals, and abandoned any mention of a hierarchy for disposal methods (OJC285, 21 October 1993). Just as the Parliament had done, the Commission rejected all of the amendments which would have explicitly allowed widespread national opt-ups, but nevertheless adopted provisions which allowed some autonomous national deviation through the use of environmentally minded economic instruments. The balance between uniform EC standards geared towards free movement of goods, and more stringent national action based on environmental considerations was thus left unresolved.

Within the Council two coalitions were emerging. The UK, the less developed Member States – Spain, Ireland, Greece and Portugal – and to a lesser extent France and Italy favoured a lower recovery target and the omission of binding recycling targets for each type of material. Taking the initiative for this group, the UK proposed dropping any mention of recycling but retaining a goal of 50 per cent recovery within ten years. Not surprisingly, this proposal coincided exactly with existing UK plans (*Europe Environment*, 28 September 1993, 12 October 1993; *Agence Europe*, 6 October 1993).

In the event, the opposing coalition of Germany, Denmark and The Netherlands lost the qualified majority vote and the Council adopted a common position on 4 March 1994 which included flexible and less demanding five-year targets: 50–65 per cent recovery, an overall packaging waste recycling rate of 25–45 per cent, a minimum recycling rate of 15 per cent for each type of material (OJC137, 19 May 1994; see *Agence Europe*, 3 December 1993, 17 December 1993; *Europe Environment*, 9 November 1993, 16 December 1993). Binding ten-year targets were dropped entirely. Instead of limiting special considerations merely to islands, the less developed countries were granted derogations giving them ten years to meet these targets. The common position retained only very limited grounds upon which nations could opt-up for higher targets. States exercising this option were not allowed to cause market distortion and were required to possess sufficient domestic recycling capacity. In essence, the common position foreclosed the possibility of enormous packaging waste exports arising from Germany and other states with extremely ambitious domestic recycling standards.

The European Parliament's Second Reading

Faced with a common position which had been considerably weakened from an environmental standpoint, the European Parliament tried again during its second reading to reintroduce some of the provisions originally favoured by DG XI and the Commission, and a few which it had put forward in its first reading. However, the scale and ambition of the Environment Committee's second reading was a token gesture compared with its earlier efforts, consisting of only 38 amendments (European Parliament, 1994). The Environment Committee voted on 7 April 1994 to remove any restrictions on maximum targets and decided nearly to double the requirements for specific materials from 15 per cent to 25 per cent. It also reintroduced the hierarchy of disposal methods which the Council had rejected and reinserted requirements for a minimum level of recycled material in packaging. On 4 May, however, each of these proposed amendments failed to gain sufficient support in the European Parliament, leaving the Council's common position virtually unchanged (OJC205, 25 July 1994; see *Europe Environment*, 19 April 1994, 17 May 1994; *Agence Europe*, 6 May 1994).

Having survived two readings by the European Parliament, all that remained between the proposal and its adoption was a vote in Council. Before this could occur, however, an unforeseen obstacle appeared in the form of Belgian dissatisfaction with the wording of the text, fearing that its provisions on national economic instruments would jeopardize Belgium's ecotax. A Belgian defection would have proved fatal to the proposal by depriving it of the necessary 54 votes which represented a qualified majority. The problem was compounded when Luxembourg threatened to resist the proposal for similar reasons. To make any changes to the proposal at this point would mean altering the text which the Council had received back from the Parliament after its second reading. But some change was necessary to resolve the deadlock, so the proposal passed into the conciliation procedure as provided for in the Treaty. An equal number of MEPs and members of the Council met to hammer out a compromise. Belgium was eventually satisfied with a revised wording of the section on economic instruments designed to reach the recycling targets. Britain, which had also threatened to defect, was equally satisfied that the proposal would not allow national economic instruments which distorted the market, nor would it herald the future widespread imposition of Community ecotaxes on Member States (*Agence Europe*, 9 June 1994, 10 June 1994).

During the three conciliation meetings which were held between July and November 1994, representatives from the Parliament, supported by the minority coalition in the Council, tried unsuccessfully to reopen debate on various amendments which were defeated during the second reading.[8] Putting on a brave face and overlooking the complete failure of the EP to secure many of its specific environmental objectives. Ken Collins declared that, 'Parliament has won everything on packaging waste' (*Agence Europe*, 10 November 1994). Perhaps more revealing, Greenpeace was furious with the outcome and the European Greens called the result 'a bad directive' engineered by the industrial lobby which posed 'a threat to the environment' (*Agence Europe*, 14/15 November 1994).

The saga of the packaging waste proposal came to an end on 20 December 1994 when Denmark, Germany and The Netherlands lost a qualified majority vote in Council. The directive which was adopted contained all the major features found in the common position, along with the vague section on national economic instruments and a commitment to revisit the entire issue of waste again in ten years with a view to substantially increased recycling targets. Table 13.3 chronicles the development of the directive through each phase of the decision-making process, noting the introduction and demise of various key provisions.

Institutional Roles

Commission as Agenda Setter and Policy Entrepreneur

As the formal initiator of all legislative proposals within the EC, the Commission's power stems from its ability to set the agenda (Wallace et al, 1983; Nugent, 1991; Peters, 1994; Majone, 1994; Marks et al, 1994). If in fact that power is more than illusory, one would expect to find that the Commission exercised considerable control over the shape of the packaging waste directive, with a clear resemblance between the Commission's draft directive objectives and the provisions found in the eventual agreement. Alternatively, development of the directive might illustrate the relative impotence or irrelevance of the Commission's agenda-setting powers. In this case there would be little or no relation between the Commission's plans and the content of the directive after it had survived

Table 13.3 *Development of the Directive*

	Comm1	Comm2	EPEC1	EP1	Comm3	Common Position	EPEC2	EP2	Adopted
Per capita limits	Yes	No	No	No	No	No	No	No	No
Minimum use of recycled materials	No	No	Yes	Yes	No	No	Yes	No	No
Hierarchy	Yes	No	Yes	Yes	No	No	Yes	No	No
Opt-ups	No	No	Very broad	Limited	Limited	Very limited	Very limited	Very limited	Very limited
Derogations	No	No	Very limited	Very limited	Very limited	Yes	Yes	Yes	Yes
Five-year targets									
– total recovery rate	60%	No	60%	60%	60%	50–65%	50%	50–65%	50–65%
– total recycling rate						25–45%	25%	25–45%	25–45%
– recycling rate for each type of material	40%	No	40%	40%	40%	15%	25%	15%	15%
Ten-year targets									
– total recovery rate	90%	90%	90%	90%	90%	No	No	No	No
– recycling rate for each type of material	60%	60%	60%	60%	60%	No	No	No	No
– maximum landfill and burning	10%	10%	10%	10%	10%	No	No	No	No
– heavy metals ban	No	No	Yes	No	No	No	No	No	No

Notes: Comm1 = DG XI pre-draft objectives
Comm2 = Commission draft directive (12.10.92)
EPEC1 = First report by the Environment Committee of the European Parliament (8.6.93)
EP1 = First reading by the European Parliament (23.6.93)
Comm3 = Revised Commission proposal (9.9.93)
EPEC2 = Second report by the Environment Committee of the European Parliament (7.4.94)
EP2 = Second reading by the European Parliament (4.5.94)

protracted negotiation between EC institutions and undergone successive rounds of amendment.

The case of the packaging waste directive reveals the ability of the Commission *formally* to set the agenda and the ability of Parliament to affect the pace and content of EC legislation. Stringent recovery and recycling standards, five- and ten-year targets, per capita waste limits and a hierarchy of disposal methods may have been the product of extensive consultation with a variety of interests, including NGOs and technical experts from each Member State, but these provisions could only be put on the formal agenda if the Commission included them in the draft directive.

For many observers of European integration, agenda-setting is synonymous with controlling the shape of first drafts. It is not difficult to find evidence supporting this conception of agenda-setting – the Commission's right of initiative, its direct dialogue with a plethora of actors, its extensive network of technical experts and its role as policy entrepreneur yield considerable control over the timing and content of legislative proposals, including that on packaging waste. However, this study clearly shows the need for a more demanding conception of agenda-setting, one which also differentiates between intra-Commission objectives and influence. Despite the obvious window of opportunity for a packaging waste directive, the Commission, and to an even greater extent DG XI, failed to secure most of its original primary objectives. The per capita and five-year waste targets, as well as the hierarchy of disposal methods, were dropped even before the first draft appeared. The recovery and recycling targets proposed in the Commission's draft directive were then further reduced in order to meet the demands of the Member States.

Even if one assumes a certain amount of gamesmanship, whereby the Commission habitually puts forward extremely ambitious proposals and targets which it knows will be sacrificed during subsequent negotiations with the Council, the weakness of the Commission as an agenda-setter is striking. As shown in Table 13.3, the almost complete removal of its pre-draft objectives from the final text reflects the extreme impotence of DG XI as an agenda setter. Furthermore, while the change in specific targets from the draft directive to the final adoption, consisting of a few percentage points, might appear insignificant and thus a clear case of Commission (not just DG XI) agenda-setting, it was precisely these few points upon which the possibility of expensive state obligations turned. As noted in more detail below, the provisions in the final version of the directive do not reflect a compromise situated in the middle ground between Commission and Council objectives. Rather, the directive represented the lowest common denominator because the Commission was forced to capitulate to a qualified majority in the Council.

Influence of the European Parliament

Evidence since 1987 suggests that the co-operation procedure did indeed bestow significant new powers on the European Parliament (EP) and elevate its role from that of a hapless spectator to an important partner in the EC policy-making dialogue, often working in conjunction with the Commission against the Council

(Jacobs et al, 1992). Under the co-decision procedure introduced by the Maastricht Treaty, the EP enjoys even greater power to amend or block the Council's common position.

This has been particularly apparent in the field of EC environmental policy where the EP has altered or rejected a number of major directives (Arp, 1992; Earnshaw and Judge, 1993; Judge and Earnshaw, 1994). Much of the EP's success has been due to the ideological devotion and tireless efforts of Ken Collins and the other members of its Environment Committee (Judge, 1993). Based on past experience one would expect to see the European Parliament strive to 'green' the packaging waste directive during its two readings of the proposal. It would also not be surprising to find that the Parliament worked with the Commission to maintain or strengthen the environmental focus of the proposal.

In this respect, two lessons emerge from the saga of the packaging waste directive. First, that the 'greening' effect of the Parliament does not necessarily occur. As this study reveals, this is explained by distinguishing between the efforts of the Environment Committee and those of the Parliament itself. Under the leadership of Ken Collins, the Environment Committee acted predictably during both its readings and reintroduced the stringent environmental standards originally proposed by DG XI. But the Parliament did not always follow the advice of its Environment Committee. Amendments supported by the Committee aimed at removing limits on maximum recycling rates, establishing a hierarchy of disposal methods, allowing considerable room for national opt-ups, requiring a minimum amount of recycled material in packaging, and banning heavy metals in packaging were all defeated during either the first or second reading.

Second, and perhaps more significant, the formal powers of the Parliament to shape EC policy were clear – for some amendments the difference between success and failure was a matter of 22 votes at the second reading.[9] It is impossible to construct a perfect counterfactual scenario based on what might have happened if these 22 votes had been forthcoming. However, two possibilities deserve consideration. The qualified majority coalition could have accepted the amendments, in which case Denmark, Germany and The Netherlands would have been free to achieve high recovery and recycling standards despite the effects which this would have had on neighbouring states. In addition, the hierarchy would have made it politically more difficult for states to avoid prevention as a primary objective, and also more difficult for them to pursue less desirable forms of waste disposal, particularly composting and incineration. Alternatively, an undivided Parliament could have blocked Council action by replacing the common position with an amended and unpopular alternative. If either of these situations had occurred it would have demonstrated the very real agenda-setting power of the Parliament, as the unanimous vote in Council required to overturn amendments would certainly have been prevented by Germany, Denmark or The Netherlands.

Taking these two lessons together, the study demonstrates the limits of the partnership between the Parliament and Commission. Needing to muster only a qualified majority vote in the Council under the terms of the Single European Act (SEA), one would predict that by working together – in essence, pooling their formal powers – the Commission and the increasingly powerful EP would achieve a number of their objectives and dictate the shape of EC policy.

As the case of the packaging directive makes clear, the interests of the Commission and the Parliament do not always coincide. During its first reading, the Environment Committee and the Parliament as a whole reintroduced provisions which the Commission had abandoned in order to gain Council support. Commission encouragement was also noticeably absent during the second reading, which left the Environment Committee, already lacking sufficient support in Parliament, alone to press for these amendments. During both readings the Commission also refused to adopt amendments favoured by the Environment Committee or the Parliament which would have strengthened the environmental profile of the directive, including minimum amounts of recycled material in packaging and a ban on packaging containing heavy metals. Furthermore, the Commission never endorsed the greenest amendment favoured by the Environment Committee – that environmentally progressive states be given considerable discretion to opt-up for more stringent national standards.

Council of Ministers

Changes to the structure of the EC policy-making process brought about by the SEA also allow predictions about the Council's role in the packaging directive. First, the SEA altered the dynamics of bargaining within the Council by increasing the use of qualified majority voting. With the formal demise of the national veto one would expect that environmental directives would contain targets and standards significantly above the prevailing lowest common denominator. Although it is debatable which institutions and pressures were primarily responsible for the conception and adoption of the SEA, there is general agreement that Article 100a expedited completion of the common market and unblocked a substantial number of directives which had previously languished under the constraints of the Luxembourg Compromise (Moravcsik, 1991; Garrett, 1992; Sandholtz and Zysman, 1989). And it was the bargaining dynamics inherent to the Luxembourg Compromise which often prevented Community environmental standards from surpassing the lowest common denominator (Weiler, 1991; Golub, 1994, 1996a, 1996b; Rehbinder and Steward, 1985; Haigh, 1992).

In fact, development of the packaging directive confirms the fears expressed by 'green' Member States during the SEA negotiations – that majority voting would remove their veto and allow European environmental standards to be dragged down to the lowest common denominator.[10] I would suggest that the lowest common denominator obtains when a directive requires no Member State to introduce significant changes in order to upgrade their environmental practices (Golub, 1996b). For the purposes of the present discussion, the lowest common denominator consists of combining information from Table 13.1 and Table 13.2, each of which provides a view of prevailing conditions in the various Member States.

At first it appears from Table 13.2 that, under the terms of the directive, many states would be forced to introduce strict recycling laws. However, comparing the requirements set out in the directive with the recycling levels already achieved in the Member States (Table 13.1), which in many cases do not reflect advances already made since 1987, one finds that only Irish paper, Belgian aluminium and Portuguese aluminium present any problems whatsoever. Table 13.2

shows that recycling of Belgian aluminium was already scheduled to increase regardless of the directive. Furthermore, Portugal and Ireland were given until 2005 to meet the required recycling and recovery targets. Thus, in almost all cases, the directive actually approximated recycling rates which already existed or were already planned throughout the Community. In the remaining few instances, it allowed substantial derogations which postponed any required changes to state practice. Thus there is little evidence that 'the grubbier majority will under the directive have to come up with plans to do much more', and considerable evidence that the directive represented the lowest common denominator (*Economist*, 18 December 1993).

The only provision which might have posed problems for the Member States and thus represented a move beyond the lowest common denominator was the target for plastic, a material the recycling of which involves higher cost and more advanced technology. Calculating the rate of plastic recycling raises a number of definitional problems and is further complicated by a general lack of hard data. But even in this area, close inspection of existing and planned plastic recycling in the Member States suggests that the directive is little more than a lowest common denominator. As of 1993, France, Italy and the UK already recycled 17–31 per cent of their plastic packaging material, with plans to increase these rates significantly by 2000.[11] Germany, Belgium, Denmark, and The Netherlands had recycling plans which far surpassed the targets established by the directive. Each of the remaining five states had plans to increase overall plastic recycling and had already started to recover specific items such as bottles for plastic drinks. Ireland, Portugal and Greece particularly benefited from the ten-year deadline.

That the directive basically reflected the lowest common denominator highlights the fact that even with the structural changes brought about by the SEA, power ultimately lies with the national representatives in the Council of Ministers – more precisely, with a qualified majority of these ministers. Although the Council adopted an enormous number of amendments put forward by the Parliament and Commission, which would indicate that the power of agenda-setting resided in these latter institutions, these amendments primarily affected cosmetic changes to the packaging proposal. Even with clear formal powers to set the agenda and control the content of directives, the Commission and Parliament were unable to dictate stringent environmental standards in the packaging directive because, in the end, their objectives were unpalatable to a qualified majority of Member States. Of course things would have been totally different if the Commission or Parliament had exercised their formal powers and dictated the content of the proposal put before the Council for decision. In this case, the fact is that they did not, or could not, because it would have produced unappealing consequences.

The lowest common denominator result also demonstrates the potential for some states, in this case particularly Germany, to lose under qualified majority voting. Instead of uniform and stringent targets favoured by the Commission, Germany, Denmark and The Netherlands, a QMV saw fit to establish easily met targets which the minority coalition was forbidden from exceeding except under strict conditions of national recycling self-sufficiency. By emphasizing national self-sufficiency in waste recycling, as well as the importance of each state being able to meet the agreed targets, the directive provides Britain, France and other states with legal grounds on which to block such exports. As mentioned at the start of this article, prior to the directive, the ECJ would probably have considered such restrictions to be discriminations on trade and therefore contrary to Article 30. It should be noted that, even after harmonization, Germany and the other Member States which lost the QMV could still opt-up for more stringent domestic recycling standards under Article 100a(4), but in so doing they would not regain political options which the directive curtailed because they could not force other states to accept unwanted waste shipments.

Refining Integration Theory

What does this study of the packaging directive tell us about the current debate on the nature of integration? It clarifies the competing claims of those who defend state-centric models and those who characterize integration as an accumulation of supranational powers or a diffusion of power towards multi-level government, and it suggests a method by which these claims may be reconciled or refuted. Multi-level government models posit that power has moved away from national executives and away from the Council as a plethora of actors mobilize and exert influence at various points in the decision-making process (Marks et al, 1994). State-centric models posit instead that the Council has retained a monopoly on real power and that other EC institutions play either a limited or subservient role in the policy-making process (Moravcsik, 1993, 1994).

The packaging case suggests that either of these theories taken alone lacks explanatory power. It suggests further that the dominant theories do not directly confront one another but are in fact talking about different aspects of integration. The diffusion model is not comprehensive because it conflates *influence* with *power*. It is undeniable that the accessibility of the Commission and EP allows mobilization; there is ample evidence that direct dialogue takes place between these two institutions and NGOs, regions, local government, individuals, single firms and the separate governments. The packaging and recycling industries as well as Greenpeace and other environmental organizations obviously affected how members of the Commission and the EP worded the original proposal and its amendments.

Unfortunately, the diffusion literature often equates influence at draft and pre-draft stages with having power over final decisions. This study suggests that the true test of whether power has been diffused is whether or not one can point to legislation which was amended and then adopted in the face of Member State opposition or to proposed legislation which was blocked by the Commission or EP despite Council support. Unless either of these two instances can be demonstrated, then the most one can say is that the dialogue produced by the participation of multiple actors yields ideas which are in turn used as resources by the Council. As Marks correctly points out, on issues that are not highly polarized among Member States, supranational actors and epistemic communities can influence the content and direction of policy through skilful persuasion.

This is indeed one form of agenda-setting and involvement, but, as Marks and others concede, it does not undermine the power of states (instead, the persuasion of analytical arguments replaces the exercise of power) (Marks et al, 1994, p22). If anything it supports those who claim that the variety of actors serves merely a functional role – a reservoir of creative ideas which are sometimes embraced by the Council to advance the agendas of the Member States. To this extent, involvement and influence differ markedly from power. In terms of institutional influence, Parliament and the Commission can provide a repertoire of policy options. But in terms of power, they cannot prescribe specific policy outcomes. The ability to get people thinking about certain ideas constitutes an important but weak form of agenda-setting which does not threaten state-centric models. It has been argued, for example, that the Commission played just such a role in the development of the Single European Act (Dehousse and Majone, 1994). The crucial point is that when Commission and EP ideas are not embraced by the Council, the mobilization of actors to lobby these institutions produces no tangible results and no influence whatsoever, short of preventing Council action and thereby paralysing the entire legislative process.

But as the packaging example illustrates, state-centric models are of equally limited value because they overestimate the ability of the Council to dominate the other institutions, and because they conflate collective Council authority with the preservation of national sovereignty and national autonomy. The first of these limitations becomes clear if we apply the previously mentioned two-pronged test of where power actually lies to the existing empirical evidence. It is difficult to reconcile the expanded formal powers of the EP with the suggestion that the Council retains total control of the integration process. As mentioned earlier in this chapter, even limiting oneself to the field of environmental policy, it is possible to identify several cases where the EP altered or defeated the Council's common position. In the packaging case, the Environment Committee of the Parliament was powerless to dictate anything to the Council, but if the requisite number of votes had been forthcoming in the Parliament, the clear power of that institution would have become apparent. This illustrates an important clarification to the ongoing theoretical debate: when the involvement of multiple actors produces ideas which the Commission and EP then force into the final directive through amendments, diffusion of power away from the Council is undeniable. Of course the onus is on diffusion theorists to demonstrate that their studies identify a shift of power and not merely contributing factors which influenced the Council to vote in a certain way (Sandholtz and Zysman, 1989; Hooghe and Keating, 1994; Hooghe and Marks, 1995).

It becomes clear at this point that the competing theories are actually speaking in different languages. Whereas state-centric models focus exclusively on power, diffusion models focus on influence. Thus Marks sets out to show that, 'supranational institutions ... have independent influence in policy-making that cannot be derived from their role as agents of state executives', while Moravcsik devotes his analysis to assessing the expanded prerogative of national executives (Marks et al, 1994, p8; Moravcsik, 1993, pp514–17, 1994). In cases other than the two scenarios of shifting power mentioned above, these approaches are actually complementary – by generating ideas and policy proposals which the Member States might not otherwise have thought of, the Commission, EP and NGOs demonstrate considerable influence over the integration process without exercising actual power over individual decisions. Supranational organizations are not in-herently subservient to the will of the Member States, but it would be equally simplistic to claim that the technical expertise, organizational capacity or range of policy options available to the Commission and other supranational actors are decisive in shaping the content of each piece of EC legislation (Majone, 1994; Marks et al, 1994, p26). Models such as the one presented by Moravcsik could subsume much of the diffusion evidence by recognizing this distinction and conceding the influence but not the power of bodies other than the Council.

The second weakness of state-centric models is that, by focusing exclusively on inter-institutional relations and the collective power of national executives in Council, they obscure the fact that some individual national executives inevita-bly become 'losers' under QMV. Having lost the fight, these unfortunate states are faced with binding European legislation which curtails their own choice of policies, thus eroding their individual national autonomy and national sover-eignty. Short of pulling out of the EC, individual national executives have no choice but to live with what they regard as unnecessary or misdirected laws. The case of the packaging directive clarifies this point. By adopting a lowest com-mon denominator approach, the directive made it impossible, in fact illegal, for Germany, Denmark and The Netherlands to pursue what they considered per-fectly reasonable environmental objectives – meeting stringent environmental standards by whatever means possible, including the export of large quantities of packaging waste. There is no evidence that these three states were in any way compensated with side payments or concessions in other policy areas, nor that their national governments actually desired laxer standards and secretly welcomed defeat at Community level in a manner similar to the 'slack cutting' (ie collu-sion among national executives designed to escape constraints imposed by domestic actors) found in the Belgian privatization or the Italian monetary disci-pline cases (Milward, 1992, 1993; Moravcsik, 1994). The lesson is clear: for many directives there will always be at least one loser. Some states will either be forced to adopt expensive and presumably unpopular new policies, or to forgo more stringent standards preferred by their own citizens.[12]

Thus Moravcsik's claim that 'where chief executives have divergent goals, we should expect less cooperation' drastically misrepresents Council dynamics (Moravcsik, 1994, p58). A more accurate rule would hold that where executives have divergent goals, those who find themselves on the losing end of a QMV always forfeit the ability to pursue their domestic agendas free from Community constraints, and are sometimes forced to pursue the majority's agenda using pol-icy instruments chosen by the majority. It should also be recalled that if the EP had secured 22 more votes during its second reading and been able to muster a QMV in Council, the situations might easily have been reversed, with environ-mentally progressive states ending up the winners and a different minority co-alition facing unpleasant but nevertheless binding European targets. In either case, these situations – and there may be literally tens of thousands – reveal quite dramatically that national executives do *not* 'bolster their control over domestic agenda-setting by cartelizing international policy initiation' (Moravcsik, 1994, p11; see also Moravcsik, 1993, p507).[13]

The third shortcoming of state-centric models is that they ignore the effects of mutually beneficial collective action by Council on the residual autonomy available to the Member States. Even assuming that the Council produces laws which on the whole satisfy each of the Member States, obligations undertaken at the EC level place considerable restrictions on the autonomy and flexibility of each individual country. Even the lowest common denominator limits the options of Member States by preventing backsliding, setting compliance deadlines and targets which otherwise might have been repealed or amended by the national executive. Thus the current national executive who negotiated the EC law faces a restricted range of policy options at the national level. In the case of the packaging directive, by being forced actually to carry out existing national recycling plans, EC law clearly restricted the autonomy of the British, French, Italian and Belgian governments. This loss of national executive autonomy becomes even more apparent when new national executives are unhappily bound by EC obligations entered into by previous administrations. In the current case, a new government in any of the Member States will have to comply with mandatory EC recycling targets with which it may or may not agree.

It is therefore not only diffusion to other institutions which erodes sovereignty but the diffusion from individual state executives to the collective will of the Council. Moravcsik admits that states lose external sovereignty' but he wrongly equates 'cutting slack' with enhancing the overall manoeuvrability of national executives. In fact, by fostering wider and deeper integration, national executives cut themselves slack at the price of painting themselves into a corner – they gain the luxury of legislating free from domestic constraints, but exercise this freedom in an ever diminishing policy space. Confined by a burgeoning body of EC law, this steadily shrinking policy space is inherited by each successive national administration.

Thus Moravcsik's assertion that 'EC policies tend, on balance, to reinforce the domestic power of national executives' appears unconvincing (Moravcsik, 1994, p52, see also 1993, pp514–15). For it is not the five examples of intergovernmental bargaining over high politics which he, like Milward before him, defends quite convincingly, which are 'broadly representative' of EC institutions and policies, but examples like the packaging waste proposal and the 27,000 EC regulations and directives which were in force by the end of 1995 which constitute the real test of whether or not 'international institutions undermine domestic sovereignty' (Moravcsik 1994, p64). This question can only be answered by considering the full effect of EC law on national autonomy. Although a daunting task, the persuasiveness of state-centric models would be greatly enhanced if they could show that this huge body of EC law, which in some cases is scheduled to account for over 80 per cent of national legislation by the turn of the century, did not restrict the policy options of national leaders.

Nor can examples such as the packaging waste directive be easily dismissed as unrepresentative by claiming that 'few governments have any pre-existing [environmental] policies' which might conflict with EC actions (Moravcsik, 1994, p53). Besides being factually incorrect, this claim is also irrelevant; even if there had been little national environmental law on the books, at one point or another most Member States have adamantly resisted EC environmental proposals because they would have entailed enormous costs. Intense disagreements between the Commission and Council, and within the Council itself, almost always led to watered down directives and lowest common denominator legislation (Golub, 1996b). Nevertheless, since 1967 the corpus of EC law has steadily expanded, with a corresponding constriction of national autonomy.

It is for this reason that the ambiguous concept of 'pooled sovereignty', which conflates preservation of national legislative autonomy with the attainment of national objectives, has been used so effectively to take the sting out of European integration (Keohane and Hoffmann, 1990; Milward, 1992, 1993; Golub, 1994). Pooled sovereignty implies that states sacrifice autonomy in order to attain national political goals which can better be met through Community legislation. National security and trade liberalization are the two examples usually cited. As realist proponents of state-centric models point out, for each state membership in the Community must be a positive sum game on aggregate, or at least prove less costly than secession. But even if pooled sovereignty enables states to attain their desired goals, they must accept a restriction on their legislative discretion and thus a curtailment of executive autonomy which authors such as Moravcsik fail to acknowledge.

Conclusion

This study has traced the development of the packaging waste proposal in order to assess the role of various Community institutions and thereby identify central features of the integration process. The premise of the analysis was that structural changes introduced by the SEA and reinforced by the Treaty on European Union (TEU) eroded the authority of the Council and formally empowered the Commission and the European Parliament. This shift of power should have been apparent in the Commission's and Parliament's ability to set the agenda and exercise substantial control over the eventual provisions of the directive. Moreover, the reputation of these two institutions as considerably 'greener' than the Council should have led to stringent environmental standards well above the prevailing lowest common denominator.

However, an examination of the protracted negotiations and a comparison of the original proposal with the final directive reveal no evidence of a weakened Council or of the supposed agenda-setting powers of the other major institutions. The final directive contained none of the controversial provisions originally favoured by DG XI (and supported by the Parliament), dramatically weakened the targets proposed in the Commission's draft directive, and reflected instead the lowest common denominator of waste recovery and recycling rates in the Member States. In securing the adoption of its common position, the Council met with little effective resistance from the Commission or Parliament. The Commission abandoned the contentious aspects of its proposal early on in the negotiating process, and failed to support their reintroduction during Parliament's two readings. Besides revealing important divisions within the Commission and the limits of partnership between Commission and Parliament, the study also discovered a further level of complexity surrounding the role of the latter; the ineffectiveness of the second reading stemmed from the fact that the Parliament as a whole refused to adopt the amendments put forward by its remarkably determined Environment Committee.

The directive exemplifies the conflict between the Community's attempt to achieve free trade among Member States and its central environmental policy objectives – preventing pollution at source and achieving sustainable development. As such, one would expect that the lessons learned from the development of the packaging directive would be applicable to the study of a wide range of other Community actions in the field of environmental protection.

Although the study focused on the packaging waste directive, lessons from this one example help clarify central issues in the two competing conceptions of European integration. The role of the various actors throughout the development of the directive shows the fundamental difference between influence and power, a distinction which is often lost in discussions of integration. Until advocates of diffusion and state dominance acknowledge the implications which flow from this distinction they will continue to speak at cross purposes instead of directly addressing points of contention.

It is suggested that state-centric models could subsume much of the diffusion literature by conceding the influence but not the power of the Commission and Parliament in the decision-making process. As the packaging case demonstrates, all the technical expertise, agenda-setting and influence of the Commission and Parliament come to nothing unless these two institutions have the determination to risk paralysing the decision-making process, because ultimately power resides with the Council – with a qualified majority in Council, to be more precise.

This suggests that instead of documenting instances where mobilization and dialogue between an expanding array of actors merely influenced eventual Council decisions, diffusion theorists could sharpen their criticisms of state dominance by focusing instead on cases where action was taken or prevented despite Council opposition. State-centric models are particularly susceptible to such criticism because they overlook the expansion of the Parliament's formal powers and how this may lead to amendment or paralysis of Council decisions. Additionally, state-centric models overlook the impact which EC legislation such as the packaging directive, produced through qualified majority voting, has on the residual ability of national executives to control domestic political agendas when it imposes policy objectives and instruments.

Finally, by narrowing their attention to power rather than influence, diffusion theorists can capitalize on what is perhaps the most blatant omission of state-centric models: the failure to recognize that the enormous body of binding EC laws, even if it 'cuts slack' for national executives and fosters the interests of every Member State, essentially leaves individual national executives with more and more control over less and less, until they achieve absolute control over nothing at all.

Acknowledgements

I am indebted to Alec Stone, Andrew Moravcsik, Martin Porter, John Peterson, Renaud Dehousse and two anonymous reviewers for their detailed comments and suggestions.

Notes

1. Besides noting the discriminatory effects of the Walloon ban, Advocate General Francis Jacobs argued unsuccessfully in his opinion that, 'a global, *a priori* ban on imports of waste from other Member States is clearly neither necessary nor proportionate to avert any danger to public health which might be posed by those products' (ECJ, 1992, p381). This would have excluded the ban from the mandatory requirements exception to Article 30, made famous in the Danish bottles case.

2. These elements featured in the seven pre-draft versions of the proposal which were under negotiation within the Commission since 1990.

3. Recovery includes, among other things listed in Annex IIB of the framework Directive 75/442 on waste: reuse, recycling, composting, regeneration and recovery of energy.

4. Recycling includes reuse, composting and regeneration.

5. Industry and trade representatives set up three highly successful pressure groups: the packaged consumer goods industries co-ordination group, the packaging legislation ad hoc group, and the Packaging Chain Forum (see Club de Bruxelles, 1994; Porter, 1995).

6. See amendments No.10, 53, 60, 66, and 70, none of which envisages the strict regime of national recycling self-sufficiency which was later adopted by the Council.

7. See amendments No.9, 17, 28, 37, 42, 66, 76.

8. *Europe Environment* 14 June 1994, 12 July 1994, 25 October 1994 and 22 November 1994; *Agence Europe* 8 June 1994 and 22 October 1994.

9. This was due to the differing positions of the parties in the European Parliament. Most EP Socialists followed the lead of the Environment Committee. The Greens hated the watered down proposal and put forward a substitute. They might have supported the Environment Committee but preferred no action to bad action. The European People's Party and the European Democratic Alliance (RDE) resisted any move towards more stringent standards.

10. As discussed below, in this case the opt-out provisions provided by Article 100a(4) of the Single European Act offered no escape route for environmentally-minded Member States.

11. These rates combine mechanical as well as chemical recycling, and are also based on a survey of each state (see UNECE, 1993).

12. The relative lack of data regarding legislative plans in southern Europe raises the possibility that the directive was not entirely a lowest common denominator outcome – it might have exerted upward pressure on environmental standards in these states despite the derogations postponing the compliance date. If this is indeed the case, it could provide a clear example of how the integration process creates slack for individual ministers rather than strengthening 'the state'. The increased manoeuvrability of environmental ministers to conclude stringent agreements in Brussels, in a policy-making arena relatively insulated from domestic constraints, plays a particularly important

role in southern Member States with highly fragmented bureaucracies (Golub, 1996b; Collier and Golub, 1996).

13. It should be noted that the limitations of liberal intergovernmentalism do not derive solely from the effects of QMV considered here. Bargaining outcomes reached under conditions of unanimous Council voting – whether they produce lowest common denominator or 'ratcheted' regulatory standards – also illustrate a variety of important problems with state-centred models, particularly the need to disaggregate the state and consider the role of *inter-ministerial* slack (Golub, 1996b).

References

Arp, H. (1992) 'The European Parliament in European Community Environmental Policy', EU Working Paper EPU No.92/13, Florence: European University Institute.

Club de Bruxelles (1994) *Business and European Environmental Policies*, Brussels: Club de Bruxelles.

Collier, U. and Golub, J. (1996) 'Environmental Policy and Polities', in Rhodes, M., Heywood, P. and Wright, V. (eds), *Developments in West European Politics*, Basingstoke: Macmillan.

Dehousse, R. and Majone, G. (1994) 'The Institutional Dynamics of European Integration: From the Single Act to the Maastricht Treaty', in Martin, S. (ed), *The Construction of Europe*, Dordrecht: Kluwer.

Eamshaw, D. and Judge, D. (1993) 'The European Parliament and the Sweeteners Directive: From Footnote to Inter-Institutional Conflict', *Journal of Common Market Studies*, Vol.31, No.1, pp103–16.

ECJ (1988) Case 302/86, *Commission* vs *Denmark* [1988] ECR 4607.

ECJ (1992) Case 2/90, *Commission* vs *Belgium* [1993] 1 CMLR 365.

European Parliament (1993) *Report of the Committee on the Environment, Public Health and Consumer Protection*, Doc A3-0174/93, 8 June.

European Parliament (1994) *Report of the Committee on the Environment Public Health and Consumer Protection*, Document A3-0237/94, 11 April.

Garrett, G. (1992) 'International Cooperation and Institutional Choice: The EC's Internal Market', *International Organization*, Vol.46, pp533–60.

Golub, J. (1994) 'British Integration into the EEC: A Case Study in European Environmental Policy', D.Phil thesis, University of Oxford.

Golub, J. (1996a) 'British Sovereignty and the Development of EC Environmental Policy', *Environmental Politics*.

Golub, J. (1996b) 'Why did they Sign? Explaining EC Environmental Policy Bargaining', paper presented at the 37th Annual Convention of the International Studies Association, San Diego, 16–20 April.

Haigh, N. (1992) *EEC Environmental Policy and Britain*, Harlow: Longman.

Hooghe, L. and Keating, M. (1994) 'The Politics of EU Regional Policy', *Journal of European Public Policy*, Vol.1, pp367–93.

Hooghe, L. and Marks, G. (1995) 'Channels of Subnational Representation in the European Union', (mimeo).

House of Lords (1993) *Select Committee on the European Communities, 26th Report (1992–93).*

Jacobs, F., Corbett, R. and Shackleton, M. (1992) *The European Parliament,* Harlow: Longman.

Judge, D. (1993) '"Predestined to Save the Earth": The Environment Committee of the European Parliament', in Judge, D. (ed), *A Green Dimension for the European Community: Political Issues and Processes,* London: Frank Cass.

Judge, D. and Earnshaw, D. (1994) 'Weak European Parliament Influence? A Study of the Environment Committee of the European Parliament', *Government and Opposition,* Vol.29, pp262–76.

Keohane, R. and Hoffmann, S. (1990) 'Conclusions: Community Politics and Institutional Change', in Wallace, W. (ed), *The Dynamics of European Integration,* London: Pinter.

Krämer, L. (1993) 'Environmental Protection and Article 30 EEC Treaty', *Common Market Law Review,* Vol.30, pp111–43.

Majone, G. (1994) 'The European Community as a Regulatory State' (mimeo).

Marks, G., Hooghe, L. and Blank, K. (1994) 'European Integration and the State', paper presented at APSA meeting, New York, 1–4 September.

Milward, A. (1992) *The European Rescue of the Nation-State,* London: Routledge.

Milward, A. et al (eds) (1993) *The Frontier of National Sovereignty,* London: Routledge.

Moravcsik, A. (1991) 'Negotiating the Single European Act: National Interests and Conventional Statecraft in the European Community', *International Organization,* Vol.45, pp19–56.

Moravcsik, A. (1993) 'Preferences and Power in the European Community: A Liberal Intergovernmentalist Approach', *Journal of Common Market Studies,* Vol.31, No.4, pp473–524.

Moravcsik, A. (1994) 'Why the European Community Strengthens the State: Domestic Politics and International Cooperation', Harvard Centre for European Studies, Working Paper Series No.52.

Nugent, N. (1991) *The Government and Politics of the European Community,* Basingstoke: Macmillan.

Peters, G. (1994) 'Agenda-setting in the European Community', *Journal of European Public Policy,* Vol.1, pp9–26.

Porter, M. (1995) 'Interest Groups, Advocacy Coalitions and the EC Environmental Policy Process: A Policy Network Analysis of the Packaging and Packaging Waste Directive', unpublished PhD dissertation, University of Bath.

Rehbinder, E. and Steward, R. (1985) *Environmental Protection Policy,* Berlin: de Gruyter.

Sandholtz, W. and Zysman, J. (1989) '1992: Recasting the European Bargain', *World Politics,* Vol.42, pp95–128.

Sexton, T. (1991) 'Enacting National Environmental Laws More Stringent than Other States' Laws in the European Community', *Cornell International Law Review,* Vol.24, pp563–93.

UNECE (1993) *Management of Plastic Wastes in the ECE Region,* New York: United Nations Publications.

UNEP (1991) United Nations Environment Programme, *Environmental Data Report 1991.*
UNEP (1992) United Nations Environment Programme, *Environmental Data Report 1992.*
UNEP (1994) United Nations Environment Programme, *Industry and the Environment,* Vol.17, April–June.
Goethem, A., van (1993) *Packaging Waste The Regulatory Framework in the Twelve EU Member States,* Brussels: Europe Information Service.
Wilmowsky, P. von (1993) 'Waste Disposal in the Internal Market: The State of Play After the ECJ's Ruling in the Walloon Import Ban', *Common Market Law Review,* Vol.30, pp541–70.
Wallace, H., Wallace, W. and Webb, C. (eds) (1983) *Policy-Making in the European Community,* Chichester: Wiley.
Weiler, J. (1991) 'The Transformation of Europe', *Yale Law Review,* Vol.100, pp2403–83.

14

Integrating the Environment into the European Union: The History of the Controversial Carbon Tax

Anthony Zito

Reacting to the international concern about climate change, the Energy and Environment Joint Council decided to stabilize carbon dioxide (CO_2) emissions in the European Community (EC) as a whole by the year 2000 at 1990 levels. in order to meet this policy goal, the Commission drafted a group of proposals to limit CO_2 and energy usage. The CO_2 tax on carbon emissions was a major tool in that effort.

The tax has had the potential to be the pre-eminent policy weapon in the European Union (EU) environmental policy arsenal, but the proposal has been weakened and blocked by special interests. Nevertheless, the proposal has continued to survive and be resubmitted in the EU policy despite this opposition. To understand this puzzle, this chapter examines the conditions under which policy innovations such as the carbon tax proposal are translated onto the agenda-setting and decision-making stages of the EU process.[1]

Case Selection and Methodology

The carbon tax case serves as a lens that focuses on several issues relating to environmental policy-making and EU decision-making in general. In an era where some Member States are pushing against the integrationist drive of the EU, the carbon tax raises the issue of whether the EU should have any control over tax policies. The carbon tax also represented a foreign policy bid to make the EC a leading political actor in global environmental issues (see Chapter 16).

With regard to the environmental agenda, the carbon tax is a fiscal instrument that shapes environmental goals by altering economic behavior and incentives for polluters. The carbon tax instrument represents a substantial shift in policy-making philosophy, because traditional policy has focused heavily on environmental regulation and emissions standards. Given the wide variety of CO_2 emission sources alleged to cause global warming and the greenhouse effect, supporters of economic instruments argue that the traditional regulations are inappropriate. Therefore instead of using emissions regulations that set fixed standards for all sources, tax instruments provide a constantly adjustable and relatively easily administered system of environmental incentives. However, economic enterprises that would be affected by the tax worried that it would reduce their competitiveness.

For these reasons, many national and European actors challenged the proposal and managed to create a stalemate that has lasted to the time of this writing (mid-2001). Given the interests' intense opposition and the perceived threat to Member State autonomy, the carbon tax case provides a critical test for theories contrary to the conventional wisdom about the EU. Both the ideas and entrepreneurial approaches maintain that substantial policy change can occur despite contrary Member State positions.

Theoretical Argument

In order to analyse both the persistence and the failure of the tax proposal, this chapter tests the relative impact of explanations drawn from three fields of literature. All three interpretations provide plausible explanations of what happened in the carbon tax case. It has to be emphasized that the demands of space limit this chapter to stylized depictions of each argument.

Idea-Centred Explanation

This first approach derives its perspective from the ideas and epistemic community literature prevalent in international relations theory.[2] The causal explanation rests on the impact of ideas and scientific knowledge about environmental problems. The content of these ideas and knowledge drives actors to redefine their interests and to press for change in the policy process. Ideas serve as a road map for determining actor interests and creating policies in conformity to the ideas, thus providing the norms and prescriptions for action.[3]

Ideas become powerful because decision-makers are facing conditions of uncertainty and environmental problems of great complexity. This makes actors receptive to new ideas.[4] Environmental policy is an area where the consequences and the inter-relation of so many variables creates uncertainly, not only because the problem often defies comprehensive understanding but also because numerous complex linkages with other policy issues exist. Also causing uncertainly is the fact that environmental issues may suggest multiple avenues and solutions that are possible for achieving the national interest. Ideas and knowledge help define the interests, choices and goals actors pursue.[5]

Current international relations literature has focused on the role of epistemic communities in helping to promote these ideas. Epistemic communities are networks of professionals with recognized expertise in a particular domain and an authoritative claim to policy-relevant knowledge within that issue.[6] The key to their association is a set of shared ideas. The groups share a common world view about cause and effect relationships used to explain world problems, as well as common methods and shared normative beliefs based on these ideas. Epistemic communities have a larger role in world politics when there are complex problems with ambiguous linkages and outcomes. National and regional policy-makers take substantially new approaches to environmental problems when the presence of an epistemic community is strong within that area and within the national governments shaping regional environmental policy.[7]

Entrepreneurial Coalition Explanation

While international relations theorists have become extremely interested in ideas, some comparative and US public policy scholarship has turned to the idea of entrepreneurship to explain change. Focusing on the US political system, John Kingdon has isolated the key role that policy entrepreneurs play in instigating change within a policy process.[8] Entrepreneurs look for opportunities to promote policy change, and it is most likely to occur when substantial policy problems arise that challenge existing political arrangements. Ideas are again important in this approach because entrepreneurs search through policy solutions that may be advantageous for shaping a policy initiative. However, causal weight in this approach is centred on the act of entrepreneurship and the creation of a coalition of interests to support that entrepreneurial bid, not the ideas and their contents. The impact of the ideas is completely dependent on the ability of the entrepreneurs to promote them. The ideas that persuade and are chosen are not based on some efficient process of finding an appropriate solution – entrepreneurs must convince the other policy actors that the idea is appropriate.[9]

The complex institutional process of US policy-making is a given for Kingdon's model. This chapter's analysis of EU environmental policy likewise takes the intricate EU institutional structure as a given. In this structure, the power to delay or harm initiatives is diffused in several political bodies. In the EU decision-making process, all initiatives must push through decision-making processes and competing interests within the 12 Member States, as well as the EU institutions.[10] The latter category includes the Commission and its various directorates, the European Parliament, and the Council forum, as well as the decision-making processes within the Member States. To become finalized legislation, an initiative must go through the chain of institutions. Each of these EU institutions can be considered 'veto points', with the potential to block or stop the initiative.[11] These institutions also can serve as fora for setting the larger EU agenda.[12] This decision-making structure makes it easier to place issues on the agenda and keep them there, but the structure makes it more difficult to get a preferred solution accepted by all these actors.

Faced with the numerous potential hurdles of the EU process, any efort at policy innovation requires leadership on the part of actors. However, because the decision-making debate within the EU occurs at both the regional and the individual national levels of government, and as such is extremely complex, no one entrepreneur is likely to be successful. Successful entrepreneurs need to build and maintain political coalitions to gain enough public support to overcome the political obstacles to placing new initiatives on the agenda. Therefore, the task of entrepreneurship requires that someone generate, design and implement the new ideas as well as build political coalitions to achieve political support.[13]

This situation necessitates that any group desiring change form an 'entrepreneurial coalition' and have different members of the coalition conduct collective entrepreneurship at all EU institutional levels. Accordingly, like-minded civil servants, politicians and experts operating in all the separate EU institutions have to form entrepreneurial coalitions for a policy to succeed. Such an organized network will share a basic set of goals and policy solutions. In order to be successful in the EU Council, entrepreneurial coalitions will also require the active support of national governments. Success requires the coalitions to penetrate the entire range of organizations to create consensus (see Chapter 11).

Particularistic Interests

The final explanation centres the causal explanation on the role of both particular organizational and Member State interests. This perspective partially derives its basis from recent environmental work by Detlef Sprinz and Tapani Vaahtoranta as well as more traditional intergovernmental theories found in the integration literature.[14] To explain how decisions and policies are made in the EU, intergovernmentalism argues that national governments pursuing national interest are the key variables that shape EU policy. Governments use the powers of critical EU institutions, especially the Council, to create or block new initiatives. Consequently, much as in the entrepreneurial approach, the analytical emphasis is placed on veto points within the EU institutional structure and the ability of specific interests to influence these institutional veto points.

While not specifically an intergovernmentalist, Fritz Scharpf contends that the EC institutional structure is very similar to that of the Federal Republic of Germany (FRG).[15] Both systems have territorial units and interests that form the heart of the decision-making process. While Maastricht has dispensed with the unanimity voting procedure in many cases (see Chapter 3), the tendency of the EU process toward suboptimal solutions is still compatible with Scharpf's analysis. The national governments must agree on joint policies in the face of their individual and varying interesis and goals, and yet the absence of common goals forces the system to resolve problems by bargaining and side payments. Scharpf concludes that the system does not provide a means for dealing with critical issues where simple bargaining fails. Issues like powers of taxation would be a good example of topics not susceptible to horse trading. Following this interpretation, the interests explanation anticipates that change is likely to occur only at the lowest common denominator of Member State positions. Policy may end in stalemate, and any change is likely to be incremental – ie, it will not change the theories, values and interests underlying the policy currently in place (see Chapter 12).

While the interests explanation emphasizes the importance of national interests and the sectoral interests that individual governments emphasize, the approach in this chapter moves beyond traditional inetrgovernmentalism. It contends that actors other than individual Member States pursuing their national interests may block new initiatives. The literature of bureaucratic politics suggests that actors within the Commission and even the European Parliament, in spite of their supranational status, will sometimes act to protect individual Member State interests.[16] Furthermore, individual Bureaus in the Commission and individual parliamentary committees in the Parliament may have organizational interests and relationships to societal actors that guide policy stances.[17] This points to the importance of sectoral interests that may cut across separate national definitions of interests or separate EU institutional definitions. Accordingly, industrial, economic and energy officials in the Commission, as well as legislative committees in the Parliament with similar interests, may seek to block environmental proposals. The tension between economic and environmental priorities may be as prevalent in Britain as it is in The Netherlands.

International Organizations

This chapter discusses certain external international organizations that, while they bear no relationship to the EU structure, are considered to be a significant part of the EU environmental policy process, regardless of the theoretical framework. Recent literature in international environmental policy has emphasized the role of international institutions in fostering co-operation among states and in pushing national governments to take stronger environmental measures.[18] Several international organizations in Europe have dealt with many of the environmental issues that the EU has, and EU Member States are members of the Organization for Economic Co-operation and Development (OECD) and UN Economic Commission for Europe. Given the complexity of many environmental issues, the EU and these organizations share resources and influence each other's policy-making. This role in the EU environmental process has largely been ignored by EU literature. However, international organizations provide an important setting and arena for EU actors at the start of the case.

The Carbon Tax Case:
Agenda-setting and Agenda Maintenance

International Organizations

As has been emphasized in the initial discussion, fiscal instruments are a step away from traditional environmental regulations. The environmental goal of such instruments was to get users of environmental resources to integrate their economic and environmental goals. It is not surprising that the OECD, with its clear interest in economic models and tools, was probably the first international organization in the European region to assert the benefits of taxes as environmental instruments. In a number of meetings and conferences by the early 1980s, the OECD stressed the need to integrate economic and environmental policies into one concern.

The OECD explored the issue of fiscal instruments only in rather academic studies, considering alternatives and previous European experiences. This effort helped to raise the issue as a possibility for EC environmental policy-makers. Several Commission and Member State officials have commented to the author that the OECD provided a useful conceptual forum for EU officials studying ideas about environmental instruments.[19] However, no epistemic community or entrepreneurial coalition appeared on the scene to generate actual policy suggestions. It is clear that OECD efforts did little more than raise the possibilities of environmental taxes for European decision-makers, as did other international organizations such as the World Commission on Environment and Development. The activities of individual Member States provided stronger impetus for a Commission initiative.

Member State Initiatives

Certain Member States, such as The Netherlands, have had a substantial tradition of using economic instruments to implement environmental policy. In the wake of the rising concern expressed about climate change in such UN fora as the Second World Climate Conference, individual Member States started considering their own carbon tax initiatives. In 1988, the Dutch imposed a levy on fuels, including gasoline, oils, various gases and coal.[20] The Danish Parliament passed a statement of intent to create the first EU CO_2 tax in the spring of 1991 and created a CO_2 tax in May of 1992.

It is significant that the Commission attempted to persuade the Danes to drop their independent initiative.[21] The opposition of the Community was centred upon the harmonization difficulties raised by individual Member States taking separate actions that might cause distortions in the Single Market. One of the traditional ways that environmental policy has been brought to the EC agenda has been through individual Member State initiatives that raise harmonization issues (see Chapters 11 and 12). Here one sees how the complex inter-relationships of EC institutional goals have forced changes in attitude and priorities for one issue, the environment, to reflect priorities in another linked issue, the Single Market. With single countries like the Dutch and the Danes creating taxes, the Commission, fearing that these separate taxes with different economic mechanisms would disrupt the EU market, had motivation to consider an EC tax.

On the other hand, those Member States that created taxes had to consider the effects on the economic competitiveness of their industries. This created pressure on these national governments to push for a regional tax covering competing Member States. The traditional intergovernmental emphasis on large states does not explain why small states have the potential, given the EU structure, to create large policy waves and set the agenda for this issue. Because of the large number of important and inter-related goals that the EU pursues, these states had the ability to set the EC agenda and force the Commission to consider other options.

Carbon Tax Case: The Decision-making Process

Commission Discussions

While individual Member States were reacting to global concern about climate change, the Commission was studying the problems and creating interdirectorate groups to examine the issue in the late 1980s. The idea of using a tax as a potential policy solution seems to have taken hold in the Environment Directorate, Directorate-General (DG) XI, in 1988. Concerns about the likely environmental impact of the Single Market's establishment also moved DG XI officials forward.[22] By the summer of 1989, DG XI civil servants had developed the taxation idea further and convinced the Commissioner for the Environment, Carlo Ripa di Meana, to implement it. In considering the scope for such instruments, the DG XI officials looked carefully at individual country tax experiences, and the fact that many of the DG officials were from Northern European countries, which were considering such instruments, contributed to the positive attitude.

Ripa di Meana and his allies acted as the main source of entrepreneurship to get the proposal accepted by the region. By 1990 Ripa di Meana was justifying the tax as a way of getting the EC to take the mantle of global leadership on the important international issue of climate change.[23] The merits of the foreign policy stance attracted the Member State ministers when it came onto the Council agenda. In October 1990, the joint Energy and Environment Council, eager to make a prominent environmental stance, decided to respond to the issues raised in the Second World Climate Conference by agreeing to a common position that the EC, as a whole, would stabilize total CO_2 emissions by the year 2000 at the 1990 level.[24] This wording reflected the acknowledgement that the different economic positions of Member States would have to be assessed in any policy determination. While the joint Council wanted to take a global stand, it also emphasized the national governments' concern that other OECD countries undertake similar commitments.

On the basis of this qualified agreement, Ripa di Meana circulated a Commission working paper at the end of 1990, exploring policy options. The paper mentions a range of possible tools, including fiscal measures such as a mixed energy/carbon tax. The document did not have a more formal status because of the disagreements among the Commission directorates about the appropriateness of these measures.[25] Furthermore, not all the Commission Bureaus shared the desire to have an environmental tax, creating veto points within the Commission that any DG XI proposal would have to overcome. Members of DG XI undertook the entrepreneurial role of promoting the proposal, but a number of directorates were extremely reluctant, including DG XXI, which oversees tax issues.

At this juncture, Commission President Jacques Delors seems to have played a role in tipping the balance among the commissioners.[26] Perhaps the most important development was an alliance between DG XI under Ripa di Meana and the Energy Directorate, DG XVII, under the Commissioner Antonio Cardoso e Cunha, to support the tax.[27] Most of the other commissioners were not enthusiastic about the tax but were not vehemently opposed. Determined opposition over an energy tax by DG XVII would have severely hampered the initiative, but instead this alliance acted as a limited entrepreneurial coalition, pushing the proposal through the Commission. Nevertheless most of the Commission directorates, such as DG XXI, were not convinced that the carbon tax was the best solution or that the proposal used the best arguments.[28] No set of scientific or technical experts, although most of them in this area did have shared research methodologies, were active in trying to push a particular agenda to tackle climate change or to create a carbon tax instrument. The political argument about EC leadership in global environmental strategy, rather than any argument about scientific knowledge or ideas about rational policy instruments, seemed to carry the day.

The Council Veto Points

The Commission finally worked out a draft directive on tools for limiting CO_2 emission and placed it before the joint Energy and Environment Council on 13 November 1991. By being placed before the Environment and Energy Council first, the proposal managed to avoid a tougher veto point in the Council, namely the Council of Economic and Finance Ministers (ECOFIN). ECOFIN has gained the reputation as the tough institutional gatekeeper in the EU policy-making process and for feeling superior to the other Council ministries.[29] It compares to the role that the British Treasury plays in the UK policy-making process. One might describe ECOFIN as a 'super British Treasury' because it is not trying to protect the revenue of its own organization (the EU) but rather the purses of the 12 individual Member States. These national finance ministers, given their sectoral bias, would be naturally predisposed to question any move, like an environmental tax, that might take away national autonomy on fiscal matters.

The Environment/Energy Council agreement to call for concrete measures created some impetus for the later ECOFIN Council to follow suit. In keeping with the goal of making the EC a global leader on climate change, the Commission decided to make the June 1992 Rio Summit of the UN Conference on Environment and Development the deadline for a concrete proposal.

Interest-group Reaction

This attempt to build political momentum for the proposal brought a mixed reaction from the various regional interests. As it was considering policy options and working up a proposal, the Commission solicited the opinions of individual Member State governments as well as various interest groups. While certain energy-intensive industries generally were against any idea of a tax, the actual industry reaction was fairly equivocal before the Commission's final push to Rio. Interviews suggest that the major industries did not really expect the tax proposal's acceptance because there seemed to be sufficient opposition within the full Commission.[30] Even if European industry generally was taken by surprise, how the business interests were organized around the issue is important. The early stages of the carbon tax proposal were focused on general commitments to reduce energy consumption, and the various industries did not perceive this as threatening any specific interest. Also, some industries, particularly in countries like The Netherlands, had an interest in a tax imposed on competitors as well as themselves.

Equally surprising is the fact that the environmental group reaction was also equivocal. There was no sustained drive on the part of these non-governmental organizations (NGOs) to support the CO_2 tax campaign.[31] These organizations were not confident that fiscal incentives could provide the reductions on pollution that they thought were ensured by traditional government regulation. These groups were only willing to support enthusiastically a tax that brought radically higher prices, substantially altering regional economic behavior. This orientation also reflects the NGO tendency to focus more on general policy objectives than actual policy instruments.

The lack of focused expert, industrial, or NGO participation before the Rio summit suggests that the interested actors exerted only a diffuse pressure on the Commission. This favored the DG XI/XVII coalition, as it tried to convince the Commission to embrace the tax in principle, because a more organized business opposition would have been difficult for the coalition to handle. On the other hand, the lack of any effective, region-wide supporting political base limited the Commission's efforts to design a proposal acceptable to the Council. When the Commission moved to design the proposal before the Rio Summit, business interests woke up and pressed what *The Economist* has called the most powerful EC lobbying effort seen so far.[32]

The Commission Proposal and Aftermath

The Commission was mindful of these concerns as it drafted the proposal. The commissioners went beyond the intent of DG XI and made the tax proposal contingent on action by other OECD countries. The commissioners created possible exemptions for specific industries. The commissioners also compromised by making the tax an even 50/50 split between the CO_2 content of the energy sources and the energy value.[33] Many of these and other specific provisions were left ambiguous, because of both the deadline and the utility of leaving knotty issues intentionally vague.

The actualization of this proposal was a significant political achievement in and of itself, given the opposition within and outside the Commission. However, the position of the tax was tenuous because it had not gone through one of the key veto points, the Council. Moreover, by July 1992, little entrepreneurial leadership and support for the proposal remained. The NGOs and technical experts remained passive. The flamboyant Ripa di Meana left the Commission, angry at the compromise tax agreement and the EC's acceptance of the vague language of the Framework Convention on Climate Change at the Rio Summit. Ripa di Meana bowed out of the Commission, and he never did build an adequate entrepreneurial coalition to deal with the blocking points beyond the Commission. The directorate that had the responsibility for the actual proposal, DG XXI, had been one of the least enthusiastic about the tax, and its head, Christine Scrivener, had publicly questioned the merits of the tax proposal. This directorate was not likely to replace the entrepreneurial activism of Ripa di Meana and DG XI.[34]

Council Stalemate

With an actual proposal established, the EU veto points again came into play. Because the tax was a fiscal measure, it was in the ECOFIN Council's province.

While some national finance ministers may have welcomed the idea of raising revenue, ECOFIN was not as concerned with environment and energy-saving merits as was the Environment/Energy Council. The ECOFIN Council also was aware of the qualifications that the Environment and Energy Council had placed on the idea in the first place. Because it was a fiscal measure, the tax was subject to unanimity voting, making the Council veto point more intractable because one Member State could block the issue.

Given this setting, the chances of the tax successfully negotiating the veto point were slender. Indeed, from 1992 to the present (2001), the Council has been unable to achieve an agreement. During that time, the tax proposal's content has changed substantially. While the intergovernmental frameworks can explain this policy failure, they have more difficulty explaining why the proposal has persisted so long on the Council agenda. They cannot explain why the proposal is constantly being resubmitted to the agenda by the Council presidents. Small states, especially Denmark and The Netherlands, have made an unequivocal effort to pass some version of the tax because of the desire for a regional effort to reduce emissions. Belgium and Germany have also felt the need for stricter regional policy. The French were less positive because they wanted a carbon tax without an energy component, given their strong reliance on nuclear energy.[35]

It was not these wealthier, powerful countries but the remainder of the countries that stopped the proposal. Ireland and the other southern countries argued consistently that any acceptance of the tax proposal on their part was contingent on the more-developed (and thus also higher pollution-emitting) states taking a large part of the tax burden. However, the UK expressed the most vocal opposition and acted as the key veto state. While economic repercussions for British industry were certainly an issue, the British opposition seemed to rest more on issues of sovereignty over fiscal matters. The disagreement of the 'Poor Four' was a substantial problem for the tax promoters, but the vehement action of the British deflected attention from their strong opposition and veto position. In 1993, the Danish Presidency managed to create an acceptable compromise for the four poorer states but could not overcome the British refusal.[36]

In the last half of 1993, DG XI and the Belgian Presidency, acting as a loose coalition, tried to use the tax proposal's potential to integrate environment and economic concerns to gain Member State acceptance. Here they followed the final initiative of Jacques Delors: a White Paper on competitiveness, growth and employment. In it, Delors gave a prominent place to environmental taxes as a way of gaining revenue while decreasing taxes on labor.[37] While DG XI was strongly supportive of environmental taxes and lowering labor taxes, many in the Commission were skeptical and suggested other solutions. The Belgian Presidency unsuccessfully tried a burden-sharing compromise to satisfy the poorer states and did not address the British and French concerns. In the discussion of the White Paper, the Member State leadership scuttled the linkage between employment and an environmental tax, specifying that environmental taxes be handled at the national level and not the EU level.[38]

While this would seem to have struck a fatal blow to the CO_2 tax initiative, it was not so. The most recent national discussions have considered an idea prevalent in general EU discussions: namely, having a 'hard core' of Northern

European states create a common energy tax if the EU negotiations fail.[39] With autonomous EU institutions such as the Commission and the institutional opportunities for individual pro-tax Member States, DG XI and favourable Member States can keep the item on the agenda for some time. Furthermore, if a 'hard core' CO_2 tax is created, the issues of market harmonization and economic competitiveness raised at the start of the process may reappear.

Testing the Alternative Explanations

As of the autumn of 1994, the history of the CO_2 tax stands as an EU failure to create policy change in the environmental arena. This leads to different observations about the explanatory power of the three alternative theoretical approaches. The variables that the first approach highlights, namely scientific ideas and epistemic communities, played no substantive role in the case history. While various ideas and perspectives were considered in both the EC and EU, no convincing idea based on scientific knowledge or data ensued.

Entrepreneurs and Agenda-setting

The agenda-setting and maintenance stages of the carbon tax policy supports the entrepreneurial perspective. An entrepreneurial group, led by Ripa di Meana's high profile personal entrepreneurship, came up with a basic political argument that the EC needed to assume some global environmental leadership. The successful placement of the tax on the Commission and larger EC agenda suggests the importance of entrepreneurial factors. Personal entrepreneurial efforts on the part of Ripa di Meana and Delors along with the general alliance between energy and environment directorates-general ensured Commission approval and the placing of the tax on the Council agenda. Equally important, the entrepreneurial perspective explains how a proposal has remained on the Council agenda. The persistent entrepreneurial action of Commission officials and pro-tax states played a key role, one that the intergovernmentalist and ideas approaches do not address. The ability of these actors to maintain the tax on the agenda was due to these actors availing themselves of the EC/EU institutional opportunities.

Particular Interests and the Decision-making Process

On the other hand, the interests approach explains the outcome of the decision-making stage. The specific interests used the very powerful and well-placed veto points of the EU structure to delay and block the tax proposal. It is interesting to note that the recent initiatives to shift the environmental tax back to the Environment Council have faced heavy opposition from ECOFIN, which wants to maintain control of all fiscal policy. No entrepreneurial coalition existed that could create the wide base of support needed to pass the proposal. The entrepreneurial coalition did succeed in getting the tax through the Commission stage of the decision-making process. However, to have an actual outcome, the coalitions needed to penetrate further into the national governments to persuade them to embrace the tax. The closest the tax came to having a coalition's support was within the Commission before 1992 and during the autumn of 1993 when the DG XI and the Belgian Presidency tried to work in the context of Delors's White Paper. These coalitions were not deep enough to overcome the veto point that existed in the Council. The main idea behind the tax was to enhance the EC foreign policy profile. This was a diffuse goal that had no expert knowledge or particular interests to back it. There were no regional or national coalitions of interests, particularly environmental groups, to render effective political support.

Theoretical Notes

If the case history reveals anything, it is the fact that the EU institutional structure is critical for understanding the policy process and the conditions for change. In this case, institutions acted as an intervening variable in both the agenda-setting and decision-making phases of the carbon tax policy. The complex and differentiated nature of the EU policy process is such that a wide range of interests can penetrate the political system at all the multiple access points and put pressure for the veto points within institutions (see Chapter 9). Such diversity is likely to lead to an increase of alternative policies considered on the agenda but also to a stronger opposition to any single proposal.[40] At the same time, these diverse and independent institutions have the ability to propose ideas and to persist in pursuing these proposals over time, whatever the Member State reaction may be.

The carbon tax study also reveals another EU policy-making aspect ignored by traditional EU integration and policy-making literatures: the role of external international organizations in suggesting the tax for the EU agenda. With the limited technical resources available to the EU institutional bodies and the complexity of global problems, international organizations can play an important role. Close co-operation between organizations is possible, and it is important to remember that, when states are members of two organizations, the actions, ideas and obligations of states in one organization will carry into another.

Moving beyond specific conclusions about environmental policy and the conditions necessary for policy change, several general points should be made about the current EU theoretical literature. First, an emphasis on EU institutional complexity helps the observer to move away from the debilitating debate about whether functional or intergovernmental theories possess the key variable explaining EU politics (see Chapter 10).[41] The history of the carbon tax clearly reveals the central role of national governments and their articulation of specific interests in the process, contrary to the functional emphasis. Simultaneously, however, inter-governmentalism cannot explain why the Commission, a coalition of poorer states, or a handful of small proenvironment states can separately manage the following critical elements of EU policy-making: (1) setting the EU agenda; (2) blocking the EU decision-making process; and (3) keeping an issue on the agenda even after the Council has tried and failed to approve the initiative.

The approach explored here emphasizes the need to understand how the EU institutional structure and external organizations like the OECD create special opportunities and incentives for EU actors. The policy study suggests that any policy change in the complex set of EU institutions requires entrepreneurial coalitions that define the problems and push the issues on the agenda. On the other hand, the case history suggests that the EU institutional mechanism gives Member States and other particular interests a decisive role in deciding policy outcomes.

Notes

1. I would like to thank Alberta Sbragia, University of Pittsburgh, and Adele Airoldi, Council of Ministers Secretariat, for their extremely helpful criticisms and suggestions concerning earlier drafts of this chapter. The research for this chapter was funded by a European Community Studies Association (ECSA) dissertation fellowship and funding from the Center for West European Studies, University of Pittsburgh.

2. For examples of the ideas approach, see Judith Goldstein and Robert Keohane (eds) *Ideas and Foreign Policy: Beliefs, Institutions, and Political Change* (Ithaca, N.Y.: Cornell University Press, 1993); and Judith Goldstein, *Ideas, Interests, and American Trade Policy*, (Ithaca, N.Y.: Cornell University Press, 1993). For epistemic communities, see Peter Haas (ed) 'Knowledge, Power, and International Policy Coordination', *International Organisation*, Vol.46 (Winter 1992), pp1–390.

3. Judith Goldstein and Robert Keohane, 'Ideas and Foreign Policy: An Analytical Framework', in Keohane and Goldstein (eds) *Ideas and Foreign Policy*, Vol.12: Goldstein, *Ideas and Interests and American Trade Policy*, pp12–13.

4. Goldstein, *Ideas and Interests and American Trade Policy*, pp12–13.

5. Goldstein and Keohane, *Ideas and Foreign Policy*, p25.

6. Peter Haas, 'Introduction: Epistemic Communities and International Policy Coordination', *International Organization*, Vol.46 (Winter 1992), pp3 and 12–16.

7. Peter Haas, *Saving the Mediterranean*, New York: Columbia University Press, 1990, pp397–398.

8. See John Kingdon, *Agendas, Alternatives, and Public Policies*, (Boston: Little, Brown, 1984), p188.

9. Giandomenico Majone, *Evidence, Argument, and Persuasion in the Policy Process* (New Haven, Conn.: Yale University Press, 1989), pp2–3 and 164.

10. Beginning in 1995 with the accession of Austria, Finland and Sweden, this number increased to fifteen.

11. Ellen Immergut, 'The Rules of the Game: The Logic of Health Policy-Making in France, Switzerland, and Sweden', in Sven Steinmo, Kathleen Thelen and Frank Longstreth (eds), *Structuring Politics: Historical Institutionalism in Comparative Analysis* (Cambridge: Cambridge University, 1992), pp64–65.

12. B. Guy Peters, 'Agenda Setting in the European Community', *Journal of European Public Policy*, Vol.1 (1994): pp9–26; Margaret Weir, 'Ideas and the Politics of Bounded Innovation', in Steinmo, Thelen and Longstreth (eds) *Structuring Politics*, pp192–193.

13. Nancy C. Roberts, 'Public Entrepreneurship and Innovation', *Policy Studies Review*, Vol.11 (Spring 1992): pp56–57; and Terry M. Moe, *The Organization of Interests: Incentives and the Internal Dynamics of Political Interest Groups* (Chicago: University of Chicago, 1980).

14. Detlef Sprinz and Tapani Vaahloranta, 'The Interest-based Explanation of International Environmental Policy', *International Organisation*, Vol.48 (Winter 1994), pp77–105. For an example of recent intergovernmental scholarship, see Andrew Moravcik, 'Negotiating the Single European Act: National Interests and Conventional Statecraft in the European Community', *International Organization*, Vol.45 (Winter 1991), pp19–56.

15. Frilz Scharpf, 'The Joint-decision Trap: Lessons from German Federalism and European Integration', *Public Administration*, Vol.66 (Autumn 1988), pp239–278.

16. Alberta Sbragia, 'The European Community: A Balancing Act', *Public,* Vol.23 (Summer 1993), pp32–33.

17. B. Guy Peters, 'Bureaucratic Politics and the Institutions of the European Community', in Alberta Sbragia (ed), *Euro-Politics: Institutions and Policy Making in the New European Community* (Washington, D.C.: Brookings Institute, 1992), pp262–263.

18. Robert Keohane, Peter Haas and Marc Levy, 'The Effectiveness of International Institutions', in Peter Haas, Robert Keohane and Marc Levy (eds), *Institutions for the Earth: Sources of Effective Environmental Protection* (Cambridge: MIT Press, 1993), pp15–16.

19. Interviews with Commission officials by author, 12 January 1993 and 17 February 1993; and national official interview by author, 1 March 1993.

20. Energy Division, Directorate General for Environmental Protection, 'The Netherlands' Environmental Tax on Fuels: Questions and Answers' (Ministry of Housing, Physical Planning and Environment, August 1992), pp2–3: and OECD, *Climate Change: Designing a Practical System* (Paris: OECD Publications, 1992), pp26–29.

21. Brian Wynne, 'Implementation of Greenhouse Gas Reductions in the European Community', *Global Environmental Change,* Vol.3 (March 1993), p109.

22. Commission interview, 17 February 1993; Task Force Environment and the Internal Market, *'1992' The Environmental Dimension: Task Force Report on the Environment and the Internal Market* (Bonn: Economica Verlag GmbH, 1990), pp208–209.

23. John Hunt, 'Tax on Fossil Fuels Is Urged', *Financial Times,* 13 January 1990; Michael Harrison, 'Carbon Tax Put Back on EC Agenda', *The Independent,* 23 April 1990; and Wynne, 'Implementation of Greenhouse Gas Reduction', pp108–109.

24. Council of the EC, Press Release 9482/90, Presse 167 (Luxembourg: 29 October 1990); *Agence Europe*, 31 October 1990.

25. Interview with Commission official, 13 April 1993.

26. Interview with Commission official, 13 April 1993, 17 February 1993, and with national official, 26 March 1993.

27. Interview with Commission official, 18 March 1993.

28. This was in spite of the fact that during this time various Commission directorates, including both DG XI and DG XVII, conducted studies and called in outside experts. Interview with Commission officials 15 April 1993 and 17 December 1993.

29. Andrew Hill, 'EU Rottweiler Both Petted and Panned', *Financial Times,* 13 December 1993.
30. Interviews with Commission officials, 8 March 1993 and 18 March 1993; with interest representatives, 28 April 1993 and 29 April 1993.
31. Interview with Commission official, 17 February 1993; national official, 4 February 1993; and interest representatives, 18 January 1993 and 28 April 1993.
32. The industries most threatened started paying less attention to diffuse industrial associations and started their own networks. See 'Europe's Industries Play Dirty', *The Economist*, 9 March 1993, p85. Also very active in the lobbying effort were the Gulf states of the Middle East although it is unclear how much influence they had on the actual proposal.
33. Commission of the EC, 'Proposal for a Council Directive Introducing a Tax on Carbon Dioxide Emissions and Energy', COM (92) 226, 30 June 1992.
34. Interview with Commission official, 8 March 1993 and interest representative, 28 April 1993.
35. Interview with national official, 1 March 1993.
36. France accepted on the condition that the tax only cover CO_2. 'Energy/CO_2 Tax: Eleven Member Stales Agree on Need for Tax Instrument', *Europe Environment,* 4 May 1993, p34.
37. Lionel Barber, 'Caution on Brussels Jobless Plan', *Financial Times,* 22 November 1993.
38. 'EC Leaders Give Thumbs Down to Environmental Tax Reform', *Environment Watch: Western Europe,* 17 December 1993, p16.
39. 'Netherlands, Belgium to Introduce Common Energy Tax if EU Talks Fail,' *Environment Watch: Western Europe,* 21 October 1994, p8.
40. Weir, 'Ideas and the Politics of Bounded Innovation', pp192–193; and Desmond King, 'The Establishment of Work–Welfare Programs in the United States and Britain: Politics, Ideas, and Institutions,' in Steinmo, Thelen and Longstreth (eds), *Structuring Politics*, Vol.20.
41. Examples of traditional functional theory and later incarnations are: David Mitrany, *A Working Peace System* (Chicago: Quadrangle Books, 1966); Ernst Haas, *The Uniting of Europe: Political, Social, and Economic Forces 1950–57* (Berkley: Stanford University Press, 1958); and Anne-Marie Burley and Walter Mart 'Europe Before the Court: A Political Theory of Legal integration', *International Organization*, Vol.47 (Winter 1993), pp41–76.

15

Technical Regulation and Politics: The Interplay between Economic Interests and Environmental Policy Goals in EC Car Emission Legislation

Henning Arp

Introduction

A topical research focus on the 'high politics' of European integration should not distract from the more mundane level of the day-to-day business of Community policy-making. It is the underlying assumption of this chapter, that case studies in individual policy areas are the necessary basis for a better understanding of the European Community (EC) as a whole (cf Schumann, 1991). An inductive approach, drawing on empirical evidence, is particularly appropriate for 'the strange animal' that the EC is, and in a research area, such as Community politics, characterized by few theoretical certainties (see Chapter 10).

This chapter aims to contribute to that enterprise. Looking at a specific area of Community regulation – that on motor vehicle emissions – will shed light, it is hoped, on the larger context of EC environmental policy. It is argued, in particular, that economic interests pervade this policy area. Economic integration in a Common (or Internal) Market has been both the main driving force in the development of EC car emission regulation and a major constraint on national efforts in this field. At the same time, the objective to harmonize as much as possible the conditions for market entry of automobiles – important both as a consumer good and as an item of intra-Community trade – has imposed a legalistic and technical style of regulation. Because, on the other hand, the technical questions have been closely associated with economic and political interests in the Member States, technical regulation has been highly politicized. The technical constraints, and the economic and political pressures associated with a policy issue, influence not only the outcome of the policy-making process but also the form of the process itself.

Community legislation on car emissions is an example of a continually expanding field of regulation.[1] Since the first EC directive covering carbon monoxide (CO) and hydrocarbon (HC) emissions from petrol cars in 1970 (EC, 1970a), the scope of regulation has been extended to diesel cars, vans and heavy-duty vehicles. Soot emissions from diesel engines were first included in 1972 (EC, 1972), nitrogen oxides (NO_x) in 1976 (EC, 1977), and hydrocarbon evaporative emissions in 1991 (EC, 1991). Work has started to add carbon dioxide (CO_2) emissions to the list, in response to the greenhouse effect. While throughout the 1970s, regulation proceeded at a leisurely pace and without much political attention, this situation changed in the 1980s with strong environmental pressures stirring up the established actors. Initially, it was German concerns about air pollution which forced the issue onto the Community agenda. The 'Luxembourg Compromise' of 1985 on passenger cars represented a first uneasy agreement between Germany's demands and the resistance of the car industries mainly in France, Britain and Italy. Afterwards, only the introduction of qualified majority voting in the Council of Ministers by the Single European Act in 1987 (see Chapter 2) unblocked a two-year stalemate caused by a Danish veto. The Small Car Directive of 1989 (EC, 1989) marked a breakthrough in bringing EC emission standards in line with stringent US standards. It reflected the adaptation of car manufacturers to new environmental constraints, the more 'environmental' outlook of the EC Commission and the strengthened position of a 'green' European Parliament. The provisional keystone to this body of regulation was put in place with the 1991 Consolidated Directive (EC, 1991) which confirmed the requirement to apply state-of-the-art technology.

The following analysis restricts itself to events since the early 1980s, and renounces a strict chronological order in favour of a clearer analytic structure. First, the emergence of EC car emission regulation as a free trade-related policy is outlined. A second section briefly reviews the technical and economic implications of stringent exhaust emission standards for the car industry. Following this, the politicization of technical regulation at the Community level is illustrated in relation to the roles of the EC Commission and the European Parliament, and to the conflicts between Member States in the Council of Ministers. This section also emphasizes the important role of the Member States at all stages of the EC policy process.

Free Trade Versus Environmental Protection

Community regulation on car emissions is a good example of the economic policy roots of EC environmental legislation (see Chapter 2), being a child of free trade and early concerns about urban air pollution. The first directive on exhaust emissions was passed in 1970 after France and West Germany had adopted national exhaust gas regulations liable to hinder intra-Community trade in cars. This directive was later amended, and today's body of car emission regulation consists of these amendments, all based on Article 100/100a. Actually, standards on exhaust emissions are only one part of a larger legislative programme for a common approval system for motor vehicles (see EC, 1970b).

Slowly, though, car emission regulation has been emancipated from its economic past. Thus particulates and nitrogen oxides (NO_x) were added to the two pollutants covered initially. While in the 1970s emission standards were worked out largely in the framework of the United Nations Economic Commission for Europe (ECE) in Geneva and then adopted by the EC, at the beginning of the 1980s the Community took the lead. Within the EC Commission, the Directorate-General for the Internal Market, originally in charge of car emission legislation, had to share its responsibility in this field with the environment division. And what had been optional harmonization until then, simply forbidding Member States from excluding vehicles complying with EC standards from their markets, became mandatory in 1989. Since then, directives require emission standards to be met by all new cars manufactured under what can now be seen as true environmental regulation.

However, the co-existence between the free-trade objective as one of the traditional cornerstones of the EC and the environmental policy dimension which gradually emerged has never been an easy one. Indeed, from a purely free-market angle, the only tenable position is to have a uniform set of standards which allow the Common Market to function. The importance of keeping open the car market in the Community ensues from the contribution which motor vehicles make to infra-Community trade and, concomitantly, the dependence of car manufacturers on exports. Moreover, although high standards may be desirable in environmental terms they often entail higher costs which have to be borne by producers and consumers. From an environmental policy point of view, in contrast, the stringency of standards is the crucial point. Obviously, these economic and environmental concerns are valued differently by different actors.

Before the 1980s, environmental concerns were insufficiently articulated to challenge seriously the priority given to free trade. The latent tension between the free-trade and the pollution-abatement objectives could only materialize when the pollution issue was given higher prominence by one powerful actor: the West German government (see Chapter 12). The Federal Republic was followed in this by The Netherlands, Denmark and Greece. Together, they questioned the free-trade priority on environmental grounds. Had it not been for the interest shared by industry and governments to keep a Common Market for automobiles. Community regulation on exhaust emissions might not have survived.

The politicization of the car exhaust issue was reflected in the EC Commission abandoning the adaptation committee procedure. Community law provides for a mechanism by which an existing directive can be adapted, in response to technical advances, by the Commission in a simplified procedure with reduced involvement of Member States. The condition for the use of this procedure is that the new legislation does not extend the scope of the original directive. Its objective is to prevent the creation of new trade barriers due to technological development. Such a mechanism had been set up for technical regulation on cars, and the car emission directives of 1976 and 1978 had been passed under this adaptation clause.[2] Although in principle car emission directives could still be passed under the same procedure, the Commission has since chosen to route them through the Council.

The Threat of 'Going-it-Alone'

The environmental challenge to free trade arose in two forms. For a range of domestic reasons (see Boehmer-Christiansen and Skea, 1991), car pollution became a top political issue in Germany around 1982 and Bonn started to press for tight car emission standards within the EC. This move met with little enthusiasm from some and open resistance from other EC partners who were less preoccupied with forest damage attributed, in the Federal Republic at least, to car emissions. Some foreign observers even detected industrial interests behind the German call for higher standards.[3] Frustrated with the blocking of the initiative at the EC level, German public opinion supported the possibility of 'going-it-alone', ie of setting standards nationally if no Community solution could be agreed. This, however, would have meant the deathblow to a common market in cars. Manufacturers would have had to tailor their cars for different requirements in different countries.

What interests were at stake in the early 1980s for the European car industry and indeed for all car manufacturers operating in the European market? First, at a general level, producing a variable product to different requirements engenders costs, costs that each industry wants to avoid. The 'economies of scale' argument is one of the core reasons for creating a Common Market in the first place.

Second, and more specifically, at the beginning of the 1980s differences in engineering know-how related to pollution control existed between European manufacturers. Some manufacturers would have had less problems than others to make their car models meet higher emission requirements within a short time. These manufacturers would have been advantaged on the new 'tough standard' German market, at least initially.

The reason for this situation was twofold. In the first place, the presence of manufacturers in the US market played an important role. The USA had imposed stringent emission standards already since the 1970s (see Mills and White, 1978; Crandall et al, 1986) which required the use of catalytic converters as the best available emission control technology. It was these standards that served as a point of reference for the German call for new European norms. While catalytic conversion was a basic technology which was in the hands of all European car companies, the adaptation of this technology to individual car models required costly and time-consuming development work. This favoured those producers who had exported many of their models to the US market and had thereby gained a lead in development work – mainly the manufacturers of large expensive automobiles (Mercedes, BMW, Volvo, etc).

A second reason for car companies having differing capabilities to adapt quickly to new high standards was that they had pursued different technological options for treating car exhaust gases. Besides catalytic conversion, the so-called lean-burn engine was being developed mainly by the British motor industry and the French Peugeot group, particularly for small and medium-sized cars. In fact, the lean-burn engine was originally an engineering answer to the energy efficiency concerns after the oil crises of the 1970s. At the same time, the German car industry in particular – not least because of its interest in the US market – had oriented its research and development (R&D) towards catalytic conversion. While the lean-burn technology seemed attractive as it combined lower fuel consumption with lower emissions, it appeared unlikely to meet standards equivalent to US norms as envisaged by the German government. The potential availability of a technological alternative to catalytic converters, however, was a crucial factor influencing the position of some car manufacturers in the regulatory debate.

Generally speaking, then, important parts of the German car industry (Mercedes, BMW, Volkswagen) would have adapted relatively easily to a tightening-up of car emission norms in the EC as a whole, or to Germany 'going-it-alone'. Their competitors, on the contrary, would have found themselves at a comparative disadvantage for some time and feared losing their market shares. Their concern was to prevent a rapid and unilateral German move towards higher standards which would have partly closed the German market to their products. A Community-wide solution was clearly needed from their point of view, with extended lead times and generous emission limits.

It might be thought that German manufacturers would have benefited from Germany 'going-it-alone' as this would have reduced foreign competition on their home market. However, it would have risked a trade war within the EC, a horrifying possibility for a sector as export-dependent as the German car industry. Thus the German car companies joined their foreign counterparts in calling for EC-wide emission standards. At least on the issue of national versus EC standards, the European car industry stood united.

Faced with this united front, the spectre of national German standards quickly disappeared. Political pressure from the other EC Member States was probably not even needed to make Bonn restore the priority given to free trade. The most convincing arguments presumably came from the German car companies. Besides, the new Liberal-Conservative government which came to power in 1982 was deeply committed to deregulation, free trade and European integration. 'Going-it-alone' would have meant transgressing its own convictions. Thus, the initial German push for a tightening of car emission legislation was translated into action at the EC level where it had to compromise with the interests of other countries.

Denmark was less hesitant in taking a separate route. Not being exposed to pressures from a national car industry, the Danish Folketing, in 1984, had decided to implement stringent US standards which would finally come into force in 1990.[4] This step prompted immediate protests from the European car industry to the EC Commission. A legal case against Denmark was averted soon afterwards, however, when Denmark declared that future standards under the Consolidated Directive were equivalent to US norms, and would therefore be accepted.

Fiscal Incentives

In their efforts to accelerate the introduction of the 'clean' car, both the German and the Dutch governments in 1985 and 1986 respectively, resorted to a tax rebate scheme for less-polluting vehicles. Granted to buyers of cars complying with certain emission standards, they supported the sales of these cars. On the other hand, those manufacturers who could not offer such car models were at a disadvantage. Fiscal incentives might thus distort competition and constitute barriers to trade.

The question of fiscal incentives has been one of the major issues in EC car emission regulation since 1985. The various national incentive schemes caused particular criticism with car-producing countries (mainly Britain and France) which feared the damage that could be done by these schemes to their manufacturers' sales. In 1988/89, a newly introduced Dutch scheme linking the tax rebate to compliance with US standards seriously disturbed the ongoing negotiations on the Small Car Directive, and led the Commission to start legal proceedings against The Netherlands (Corcelle, 1989, p521; Wessels, 1989). Contemporaneous Danish plans for a similar scheme further provoked the European car lobby's protests.

The Small Car Directive of 1989 permitted Member States to grant tax rebates subject to certain conditions. These provisions were defensive in character in that they prevented EC standards from being undermined – and the uniformity of the Common Market from being disrupted – by fiscal incentives. Later, the EC discovered the fiscal instrument as a means of generating an effective environmental policy. The preface to the 1991 Consolidated Directive states that 'the environmental impact of the more stringent standards would be greatly increased and speeded up if the Member States were to grant ... tax incentives' (EC, 1991). In the run-up to this directive, the Commission had proposed a new 'two-step approach' to car emission regulation. Besides the standards imposed by the directive itself (first step), target values would be specified which, subject to review, could become mandatory at a later stage (second step). Fiscal incentives could then embrace these target values, and speed up their voluntary implementation. This proposal, however, failed in the European Parliament which, in the vote on the Consolidated Directive, could not muster the majority necessary to amend the Council's agreed position.

Both the aborted debate in West Germany on the possibility of 'going-it-alone' and the question of fiscal incentives highlight the central part played by the pursuit of a common (or internal) market in the interconnected development of the environmental policies of individual Member States and EC environmental policy. The car emission case supports two more general points in this context. First, the free-trade rule promotes a separate EC environmental policy in that it necessitates the transfer of many environmental problems to the European level where common policy is established. Indeed, proposals by individual Member States to legislate on environmental matters often force the Community to regulate environmental matters to prevent distortions of competition or barriers to trade.[5] Second, the need to compromise within the Community tends to create adulterated policies from an environmental point of view. On individual issues and for individual countries, EC environmental policy may act more as a brake than as a stimulus for the solution of environmental problems.

The Technical and Economic Side of EC Car Emission Regulation

As the objective to create a common economic area between EC Member States has been one of the reasons why Community environmental policy developed in the first place, so EC environmental policy is often closely linked to economic concerns. Economic considerations, in turn, often have to do with the technical implications of potential legislation. In fact, it is not the protection of the environment which is to the fore in many actors' minds but competitive advantage, R&D strategies or product image. Politicians have to take industry's views into account, and at the same time watch out for their voters' feelings. If interest splits run along national lines, these non-environmental interests become strongly politicized in the negotiations at the EC level. In order to understand the EC environmental policy process, it is necessary to understand the technical and economic factors underlying the decisions to be taken.

The technical debate around car emission abatement in the early 1980s started out from three basic technological options, each with different emission reduction potentials and different cost implications. First, the three-way catalytic converter was and still is the best available technology for controlling the 'traditional' emissions, ie CO, HC and NO_x. Unfortunately, the three-way catalyst is a relatively sophisticated and expensive technology. The oxidation catalyst, the second technological option, is cheaper than the three-way catalytic converter but also considerably less effective: particularly, it leaves NO_x emissions uncontrolled. Finally, the lean-bum engine was an attractive, yet undeveloped technology. It aimed to control emissions by changes in engine design. Thereby, the emission of both CO and NO_x would be reduced while the emission of HC increased slightly, which could be controlled by a simple oxidation catalyst. An additional advantage of the lean-burn engine would be decreased fuel consumption. However, the major problem with the lean-bum concept was that at the beginning of the 1980s it was still in the process of development, and unable to match the emission abatement potential of the three-way catalyst. In fact, a fully developed lean-burn engine never saw the light of day. Furthermore, it should be noted that catalytic converters and the lean-burn engine were only the basic technological options. Various other technical devices were also available to engineers and different combinations of technical means were considered to meet particular limit values.

The crucial question in relation to the different technological options was whether the stringency of individual emission standards would require the use of the three-way catalytic converter or allow the use of a less effective but also less costly technical device. The exact thresholds at which some more sophisticated emission control device becomes necessary to meet the standards vary between individual car models, although some generalization according to classes of cars is possible.

Importantly, it is not the absolute but the relative cost increase that matters. As, roughly speaking, the price of a car rises with car size, the sensitivity to cost increases diminishes with size. The effect is compounded by the fact that three-way catalytic converters require electronic fuel injection to work, a gadget which is more expensive than the catalyst itself and which is a standard fitting in large cars. They would thus be hit least by the regulation-induced cost increase, not only in relative but even in absolute terms. The car industry calculated that the price increase to make existing models meet stringent US 1983 emission standards was around 5 per cent for cars with engines of 1.8 to 2.0 litres, and about 17 per cent for cars with engines between 0.75 and 1.0 litre capacity. At a macro-level, these factors were reflected in the costs imposed on entire national car fleets by emission regulation. For instance, as the market share of cars under 1.4 litres is 84 per cent in Italy as compared with 37 per cent in Germany, disproportionally high costs would have been imposed on Italian customers by uniformly strict emission standards (Henssler and Gospage, 1987, p75).

Increases in production costs are passed on to the consumer in the form of a higher price, and may lead to a decrease in the competitiveness of the product. At least in the short term, price increases may lower the demand for cars as owners postpone the replacement of their old vehicles. These are the economic impacts feared by manufacturers. A lot obviously depends on the willingness of consumers to bear the costs associated with cleaner car exhaust fumes. If customers are willing to pay a higher price for less-polluting cars without changing their buying behaviour, car companies can easily proceed to apply more sophisticated emission control technology and should not object to more stringent standards. As the home markets are still the setting for car companies' market assessments, consumer attitudes in the UK, France, Germany and Italy were a decisive factor in the various companies' response to the setting of new emission standards.

Consumer attitudes differed markedly between these four countries. Air pollution was the environmental problem which Germans cared about most at the beginning of the 1980s. In addition, the 'greening' of the German market was furthered by tax rebates for less-polluting cars. Later, the 'cleanness' of a car became an important component of its resale value. Thus, the demand for new cars with emission control rose steadily on the German market from 1985 onwards. In France, Britain and Italy, in contrast, the national markets did not give similarly 'green' signals to car companies.[6] The fact that market demand does make a difference for car producers was made clear by Fiat's announcement in late 1984 that it would offer some models equipped with catalysts in Germany from 1985. Otherwise, Fiat objected strongly to higher standards.

Due to the factors outlined above, the situation of the German car manufacturers was essentially different from the situation of the car industry in the other EC countries. The German automobile producers, BMW, Mercedes-Benz and Volkswagen, had adapted at least some of their models to stringent US requirements already. Opel could probably draw on experience from its US parent company General Motors. In addition, the German firms' home market was ready to follow stricter car emission requirements, and the sales of the large expensive German cars showed little price sensitivity in any case. Moreover, for large cars, the lean-burn engine was never considered a viable option. All this also applied to part of the model range of companies that produce both smaller and larger cars (ie practically all other major European car companies) and for the other European luxury car manufacturers (Rolls-Royce, Jaguar, etc).

Resistance of car manufacturers was directed not against stringent standards for big cars but mostly against the tightening of standards for small and medium-sized cars, and came mainly from the French (Renault, Peugeot), British (British Leyland, Ford) and Italian (Fiat) car companies which have a big stake in these market segments.[7] In addition, the French, British and Italian markets were not so favourable to 'clean' cars. Another reason for producers of small and medium-sized cars to oppose stricter emission requirements was the potential seen in the lean-bum engine. Thus, standards were demanded that were not set so high as to exclude from the outset the use of that technology. Ford (Britain) pushed this point especially for medium-sized cars.

Although it is not possible in this chapter to analyse the interactions between the car industry and the national governments in Bonn, London, Paris and Rome, there is little doubt that the respective car companies' interests were crucial in determining the national negotiating positions at the EC level. While the German government was faced with strong environmentalist pressures and relatively little resistance against stringent standards from the German car industry, the British, French and Italian governments defended their industries' interest in avoiding a tightening of regulations. The so-called 'Luxembourg Compromise' of 1985 (see below) clearly reflected the issues at stake in that it differentiated requirements by car size, with smaller cars being subject to more lenient standards than large cars.

The link between technical and economic factors and the EC policy-making process is surely not a strictly causal one. Economic interests may not be sufficiently organized to influence a government's negotiating position in Brussels or may be overridden by wider political concerns and accords; strategic objectives of policy-makers may curb sectoral industrial interests; and the dynamic of the EC political process can create its own, sometimes unintended results. A deterministic approach to EC politics would hence be inappropriate. Notwithstanding this, the influence of technical and economic constraints in EC policy-making cannot be overlooked. Transferred into the intergovernmental bargaining arena, technical and economic arguments become the matter for dispute and compromise.

Between Technical Regulation and Politics

As has been shown above, complex technical questions and related industrial and political interests loom in the background of much EC environmental policy. On the one hand, the technical problems call for an appropriate regulatory solution. On the other hand, at least when industrial interests align themselves nationally, the fact that EC policy-making is still very much an intergovernmental enterprise translates technical and economic factors into political matter. The EC environmental policy-making process is thus not only affected and contemporaneously fuelled by the constraints arising from the free-trade rule, but is also characterized by an interweaving of technical regulation and politics.

In the following, evidence from EC car emission regulation is taken to illustrate the close links between economic and political factors in Community decision-making, as well as the importance which the EC's institutional set-up has for the policy-making process. First, more generally, the need for technically specific regulations will be explained by reference to the purpose of EC legislation and to the separation between rule-making and implementation in the Community policy process. After that, the politicization of technical problems in the interplay within and between the EC Commission, the Council of Ministers and the European Parliament will be highlighted.

The Emphasis on Detailed Technical Specifications

It has been jokingly remarked that, EC legislation is more concerned with, for example, roll-over protection structures for tractor seats (EC, 1987) than with the unification of Europe. Indeed, EC regulation often consists of exhaustively detailed stipulations which blur the overall objective. Community stagnation in the 1970s and early 1980s had to do with, among other things, the impossibility of harmonizing the detail of national standards for a growing range of products. One way out of this impasse is now seen in the 'new approach' to harmonization which delegates standard-setting tasks to private standardization bodies (Nicolas, 1988). Today this strategy is crucial to the Internal Market programme. Regulation on cars, however, is one of the areas in which the need for detailed technical specifications in Community law itself persists.

In comparative politics, the concept of 'regulatory styles' denotes the specific character of national and/or sectoral regulation (Freeman, 1985). Formal/informal, conflictual/consensual, and active/reactive are some of the dichotomies used to describe regulation in a specific country or sector. In particular, the implementation of regulation has to be seen as an inherent part of the regulatory process. Imprecise rules administered closely by government and industry can be as effective as detailed legal provisions.

The nature of different regulatory styles can partly be attributed to the institutional and general political context in which they develop (Vogel, 1986). Informal regulatory mechanisms imply that rules are implemented on the ground by public authorities invested with discretionary powers. The authorities then are directly responsible for the correct application of statutes that specify objectives rather than means. An executive civil service is the precondition for such an informal regulatory style. As EC law is implemented by the Member States, informal regulatory mechanisms are not possible – regulation has to be legally prescribed simply because the 'informal' alternative is not available. The institutional mechanics of the EC are thus conducive to a regulatory style which emphasizes legalistic precision.

In addition, the purpose of EC regulation to create uniform conditions for economic activity has to be remembered. In order to achieve it, clear standards have to be set out against which implementation of the rules can be judged. Loopholes must be avoided which might allow Member States to apply the law inadequately, be it in response to political or economic pressures or due to differing national regulatory systems. The detailed nature of Community law is thus necessary to ensure the intended uniformity of effect, often under very different national conditions. In a common market, product standards in particular have to specify clearly what conditions the product must satisfy. As the products concerned are inherently complicated, specifications tend to be complicated as well. In addition, any vagueness could be used to inhibit its market entry and trade barriers might ensue. Even if EC directives only lay down performance requirements and do not stipulate specific technical solutions, the result can still be highly technical legislation. Indeed, the emission directives need a car engineer to understand their annexes.

The Commission in the Preparatory Stage of Legislation

The EC Commission is sometimes portrayed as a monolithic technocratic apparatus, subject to no democratic control. Indeed, due to the limited powers of the European Parliament, parliamentary control of the Commission is weak as compared with parliamentary control over national governments. On the other hand, the Member States exercise considerable influence on the Commission. Moreover, within the Commission different interests are represented and oppose each other. Thus, even at the preparatory stage of legislation, the politicization of the EC decision-making process is high.

As between ministries within a government, differences of perceptions and interests also exist between the various Directorates-General (DGs) within the Commission. Thus, the Environment DG (XI) aims at effective environmental regulations, while the DG for the Internal Market and Industrial Affairs (DG III) is widely seen as an advocate of industrial interests. Both DGs co-operate in car emission policy. Generally speaking, DG XI has slowly emerged as a more equal partner to DG III in this field, while DG III itself has become more open to environmental considerations. In any case, the struggle over the technical details of environmental legislation begins within the Commission, with different divisions (and, at the highest level, different Commissioners) taking different sides. In the autumn of 1989, for example, the two DGs were pitched against each other on the limit values for gaseous pollutants to be set by the Consolidated Directive. While the arguments were couched in technical terms, they reflected differences on the question of how stringent the new standards should be.

The main forum for the gathering of the technical expertise necessary to draft a new car emission directive is the Motor Vehicle Emission Group (MVEG). This advisory committee is composed of national experts (mostly civil servants) delegated by Member States' governments, as well as industry, and consumer and environmental organizations. MVEG provides the Commission with the technical data it needs and from them proposes technical specifications. Its work is based on material furnished mainly by the car industry and national government experts. These data are discussed within the group, and the positions taken by the national experts in general anticipate the positions which their governments will take in the Council later. Within MVEG, the technological and economic problems of EC car emission regulation are translated into the language of engineers and discussed as technical questions. Expertise is what counts. However, all participants are aware of the stakes involved.

With the participation of national and industrial experts, MVEG is both a forum for technical discussion, and a quasi-intergovernmental exercise. For much of its evidence it is reliant on car industry sources. Some questions – such as what is feasible or not in terms of emission abatement, and at what cost – can only be answered by the car companies themselves. But an information monopoly of the car industry in a crude sense does not exist. At least on the sensitive questions, evidence is checked by counter-evidence from other sources, and a strict review of arguments is thus possible. National governments and the Commission are able to muster independent expertise to challenge the manufacturers' information. They may also be able to exploit differences between car companies, or draw on examples from other countries. It is only difficult for the relatively weak EC-level consumer and environmental groups to participate in the process because of their lack of technical expertise.

Even in its preparatory work, the Commission is thus highly sensitive to political considerations (see Chapter 9). Not only does the Commission act as mediator between Member States in the Council but it also takes into account their potential positions in drafting its legislative proposals. By pointing to problems, providing information and announcing their intention to legislate nationally on newly recognized problems, the Member States have a strong influence on the Commission's proposals even before they reach the Council. In practice, the Commission shares its role of initiating action with the Member States. In addition, the demands expressed by the European Parliament are now more seriously considered by the Commission, especially when the House is involved in legislation under the co-operation procedure.

Conflicting National Interests in the Council of Ministers

The link between economic and technical considerations and politics is clearest in the negotiations in the Council of Ministers. While the EC is a supranational political system which deeply encroaches on Member States' sovereignty, its decision-making procedures are still prescribed by the final say of the Member States in the Council. Intergovernmental negotiations and compromises, be it under unanimity or qualified majority voting rules, are at the core of Community politics. Finding a consensus or building a qualified majority in the Council of Ministers is an onerous and time-consuming task, especially when important national interests are at stake.

The case of car emission regulation illustrates nicely the politicization of technical and economic factors and the weakness of central EC government. Since the early 1980s, a group of countries pressing for more stringent standards – the Federal Republic of Germany, The Netherlands, Denmark and Greece – has stood against the other Member States' reluctance to set tough norms. Especially the UK, France and Italy, as the other Member States with their own national car industries – besides Germany – opposed stringent legislation. The positions of the different governments were determined by the balance of internal political and economic pressures weighing on them and by different perceptions of the problem.

The greatest conflict over EC car emission regulation occurred during the run-up to the so-called 'Luxembourg Compromise' of 1985. Under the impression of a German threat to 'go-it-alone', the Commission, in 1984, had presented proposals for a reduction of emission limit values in two stages up to 1995, when US 1983 standards would apply to all new cars. Resisted by the governments in London, Paris and Rome, these proposals were significantly changed in the negotiations in the Council. The outcome reflected the opposed interests involved and bound them together in an overall package. First, the reference of the new European standards to US standards was loosened. The Luxembourg Compromise took as a baseline 'the ultimate effect on the environment' achieved by new standards and it was this effect which had to be 'equivalent' to US conditions. Equivalence of standards with US norms on a car-by-car basis was thus no longer aimed at. Second, the Luxembourg Compromise differentiated standards between three different categories of cars, ie small cars (below 1.4 litres engine capacity), medium-sized cars (between 1.4 and 2.0 litres) and large cars (above 2.0 litres). Standards for large cars were more stringent than those for smaller cars. The rationale given for the variation of standards was that 'compliance with Community requirements' had to be allowed 'at a reasonable cost and using different technical means' (EC, 1988). Only the limit values fixed for large cars clearly required the application of three-way catalytic converters as the best available technology. Third, the legal start dates by which the limit values had to be implemented differed between new models and other new cars. Thus, sufficient lead time was granted to manufacturers to apply emission control technology to their whole range of car models. Lastly, as a concession to environmental demands, another stage of limit value reductions was envisaged for small cars in 1987.

The Luxembourg Compromise, finalized in June 1985, was a package deal characteristic of Community policy-making. On the one hand, the Community, under pressure from some of its Member States, embarked on a more ambitious car pollution control policy than had previously been considered. Although not formally in the directive itself, Germany was nonetheless allowed to further the introduction of less-polluting cars by fiscal incentives (Corcelle, 1986, p129). Lenient requirements were imposed on the particularly cost-sensitive category of small cars. The technological implications for medium-sized vehicles were not clear. In addition, extended deadlines for the application of the new requirements were granted. Overall, the Luxembourg Compromise, in its basic structure of differentiation between car categories, reflected the interests of the car industry. Putting this package together was a matter of hard negotiation in the Council, against a background of mutual suspicion in the Member States. In Germany, public opinion held that the Federal Republic's EC partners would let its forests die from acid rain. The EC was seen as blocking effective German action. In the UK and France, Germany was accused of trying to give its car industry a competitive advantage under the cover of environmental concerns. Probably, only the overall objective of maintaining a common market for motor vehicles prevented the failure of negotiations.

Although a compromise had thus been laboriously established by the main protagonists, the legislative process provisionally came to nothing. Under the unanimity requirement of Article 100, Denmark vetoed the car emission agreement as it considered the compromise reached to be unsatisfactory from an environmental point of view. This fate of the Luxembourg Compromise shows the lack of decision-making power affecting the EC under the unanimity rule. Notwithstanding the objective merits that the minority view may have and the necessary safeguard clause as regards essential national interests, it is clear that the vetoing power of individual Member States inhibits progress at the EC level. With the understanding that European integration is inherently a 'give-and-take' exercise which requires compromises, a unanimity requirement allowing for national vetoes is counterproductive.

Had it not been for the Single Act coming into force in July 1987, the impasse created by the Danish veto and the ensuing legal uncertainty for the EC car industry would have persisted. The change in the rules of the game as regards Internal Market legislation, from a unanimity to a qualified majority principle, broke the stalemate (see Chapter 2). In December 1987, the Luxembourg Compromise, presented again by the Commission under the new Article 100a, passed through Council against the votes of Denmark and Greece and became Directive 88/76 (EC, 1988). It was the first time that the Council acted under a qualified majority on the basis of Article 100a.

Clearly, conflicts of interest and of political objectives as well as the opposition of powerful interest groups to government policies also exist at the national level and are not peculiar to EC politics. It is also true that the need for federal/state co-ordination and agreement, coalition politics and legislation requiring a more-than-simple majority may constrain central authority within the nation-state. However, in general, these constraints do not affect national governments to the extent to which the unanimity or qualified majority rules determine EC affairs. The events around the Luxembourg Compromise and its de-blocking by the possibility of deciding by qualified majority are indicative of the importance of voting requirements in the EC. Indeed, since the Single Act, most EC exhaust emission legislation has passed through Council despite votes against it from some Member States; these acts would not have passed under the unanimity rule.

Since the Luxembourg Compromise, political conflicts around EC car emission regulation have somewhat subsided. The Small Car Directive of 1989 abandoned the principle established under the Luxembourg Compromise that less stringent standards be applied to smaller cars. Indeed, as the resistance of car manufacturers to strict standards had weakened and under the pressure of the European Parliament (see below), the Council imposed new limit values for small cars which were lower than past limit values on large cars. A balancing act, however, was required to forge a qualified majority in the Council for this directive. In 1988, the Commission's proposal was initially opposed by France, on the one hand, because it considered the requirements too stringent; and The Netherlands, Denmark and Greece, on the other side, calling for still tougher norms. This strange coalition of opponents and proponents of high environmental standards could have thwarted the Commission's proposal in the Council. Finally, France and The Netherlands changed their positions and the directive was enacted (Corcelle, 1989, pp520–23). This episode shows the difficulties of Community decision-making even under qualified-majority rule.

For the time being, the keystone to EC car emission regulation is the Consolidated Directive of 1991 (EC, 1991). This directive aligns the limit values for all categories of cars with the values of the Small Car Directive and transposes them onto a new European car testing cycle. A second stage of particulate emissions for diesel cars is enacted. In addition, for the first time, a limit value for evaporative emissions is set and provisions for a durability test for anti-pollution devices are made. In sum, the Consolidated Directive integrates and completes earlier directives. While negotiations on this latest piece of car emission regulation produced differences between Member States on individual points, they were a far cry from the political struggles surrounding the Luxembourg Compromise. In the end, the Consolidated Directive was passed in the Council by unanimity vote even though a qualified majority would have sufficed.

The Role of the European Parliament

The political aspect of EC regulatory processes is heightened by the role played by the European Parliament. It is true that its position in the Community's institutional system is not comparable to that of a parliament in a true parliamentary democracy, but nonetheless, the Parliament's influence should not be underrated (see Chapter 8). Parliamentary questions to the Commission or the Council may highlight problems of EC policy-making and thus exercise some control over Community affairs. Generally speaking, the Commission now takes the House more seriously than was the case previously. This change has been furthered since 1979, with Parliament being directly elected, and by its revaluation through the Single Act of 1987.

The Single Act, under the new co-operation procedure (new Article 149), increased Parliament's powers in the legislative process. While environmental legislation does not generally come under the co-operation procedure, acts of legislation at the interface between Internal Market and environmental policy do. Accordingly, Parliament is often credited with the breakthrough towards tougher 'clean car' regulation achieved with the Small Car Directive of 1989. This shows how political the regulatory process can be with the participation of the House.

The Council's common position on the Small Car Directive, which went before the Parliament in April 1989, had not taken up earlier proposals made by the House in the first reading, aimed at strengthening the legislation. The common position had been adopted by the Council with a qualified majority against the votes of The Netherlands, Denmark and Greece. Parliament, in the run-up to its re-election in June 1989, was eager to present itself as the advocate of a tough environmental policy. The Commission, for its part, had signalled its support for some parliamentary amendments to be made to the Council's common position. Under the co-operation procedure parliamentary amendments, if supported by the Commission, can be rejected by the Council only by a unanimity vote. However, they can be adopted by the Council by a qualified majority. This was precisely what happened. Having entered into a tacit alliance with the Commission on the amendments that the latter would be willing to support. Parliament amended the common position with an overwhelming majority. As these amendments were not so radical as to arouse new resistance within the Council, which would have undermined the existing qualified majority, these amendments were indeed adopted by the Council, and thus found their way into the new directive.

This episode certainly does not show the Parliament 'forcing its will' on the Council. The House benefited from a propitious situation, and restrained itself to those amendments which could be supported by the Commission and a qualified majority in the Council. Indeed, looking at the amendments from a technical point of view, they really did not make a big difference. The most important development in the months before the parliamentary vote had been that the resistance by some car manufacturers to standards requiring three-way catalytic converters had dwindled. Since the mid-1980s the industry had had time to prepare for more stringent legislation, and had adapted itself to new environmental requirements. This had released especially the Italian and the French governments from pressure to resist higher standards (Corcelle, 1989, p522ff). What the example does show, however, is political games being played in the Community's regulatory process. Public attention focused on the matter and Parliament's amendments were motivated at least as much by its political quest for a better standing as by its wish to improve legislation. The European Parliament thus contributes, within its limited means, to the politicization of technical EC regulation.

Conclusion

The intention of this chapter was not to give a historical account of the evolution of EC regulation on car exhaust emissions or to describe the existing body of legislation in this field. Rather, the objective was to contribute to an analysis of the EC political system generally by taking exhaust emission regulation as an illustration of what is thought to be more general features of EC environmental policy-making.

In particular, the fact that EC environmental policy is often less about the protection of the environment, and more about economic objectives and interests has been stressed. Indeed, much of Community environmental regulation is motivated by the need to prevent trade barriers and distortion of competition in the first place (see Chapters 2 and 12). The car exhaust case is an example of legislation which grew out of this concern and only lately was turned to the achievement of environmental objectives. It should be remembered that even now, car exhaust directives are based on the Internal Market Article 100a of the EEC Treaty.

A look at Community car emission regulation also suggests the importance of technical and economic factors in the EC policy-making process which are politicized in intergovernmental negotiations. When economic and political interests differ along national lines and when they have a strong enough leverage on the respective national governments, technical constraints and possibilities inevitably become central stakes in Community politics. Technical regulation, already complicated enough, is then intertwined with politics. As the position of the Member States in the EC political process is strong, this politicization may lead to the blocking of legislation (see Chapter 12). Conversely, the fact that multiple actors with different interests participate in the regulatory process from the outset ensures checks and balances concerning the technical expertise on which rule-making is based. Although happening behind closed doors, EC standard-setting is thus in some sense an open process, as evidence is provided, and reviewed, from different sides. As the politicization of technical regulation is a characteristic of EC policy-making in general, understanding the technical and economic ramifications of regulation is, in turn, crucial to understanding the policy process. As far as the outcome of this process is concerned, the provisions of the Luxembourg Compromise directive, for example, can only be understood against the background of the practical ramifications of regulation for the car industry.

The major role played by the Member States in EC environmental policy is another crucial point highlighted by a study of car emission regulation, whether in blocking progress at the EC level, or in acting as catalysts (see Chapter 10). France, the UK, Italy, Denmark, The Netherlands and Greece, at different times and for different reasons, opposed new legislation, and partly hindered it from being enacted. On the other hand, had it not been for German and Dutch insistence, no serious headway on car emission control would have been made in the 1980s.

Indeed, despite the institutional development of the EC and its importance, the national arena is arguably still the main playing field for most interest groups. This is particularly so for public interest groups, including environmentalists. While different environmental organizations are now represented with their own offices in Brussels, their political leverage at the Community level is weak (see Chapter 10). This is mainly due to the fact that environmental groups gain their political clout mainly through public attention and support. As long as the nation state continues to be the most important framework for public opinion and as long as only the national and sub-national governments but not the Commission and the Council of Ministers have to be concerned about re-election, environmental pressures come to bear more effectively within the Member States than at Community level. Because of the final say that Member States still have in Community politics, exercising pressure on one's own national government remains the most important way of influencing EC regulation.

Notes

1. For a good overview, see Corcelle (1985, 1986, 1989).
2. Interestingly, the 1976 directive actually extended the scope of EC legislation by, for the first time, setting a limit value for NO_x (EC, 1977). The fact that it was nevertheless passed under the simplified adaptation procedure is indicative of the low degree of politicization of car emission regulation in the 1970s.
3. For a brilliant analysis of French perceptions around the acid rain issue raised by Germany, see Roqueplo (1988).
4. Indeed, the Single Act of 1987 introduced a clause (Article 100a(4) EEC) under which higher standards than those contained in EC law can be justified under certain conditions even at the expense of the free movement of goods.

5. Another example for EC environmental legislation prompted by a national initiative is the large Combustion Plant Directive (Crijseels et al, forthcoming).
6. See, for example, an opinion poll done by the EC Commission in 1986,
quoted in *Parlement Européen* (1987, pp11–13).
7. In 1987, only 0.6 per cent of West German car production was in the category below 1.0 litres cylinder capacity, in comparison to 9.7 per cent in
France, 14.3 per cent in the UK and 43.6 per cent in Italy. The small to
medium-size category (1.0 to 1.5 litres) comprises about 60 per cent of car
production in Britain, 40.1 per cent in France, 33.1 per cent in Italy but
only 19.5 per cent in Germany (SMMT 1988, p11, p39ff).

References

Boehmer-Christiansen, S. and Skea, J. (1991) *Acid Politics: Environmental and Energy Policies in Britain and Germany*, Belhaven Press, London/New York.

Corcelle, G. (1985) 'L'introduction de la 'voiture propre' en Europe', *Revue du Marche Commun*, No.287, pp258–63.

Corcelle, G. (1986) 'L'introduction de la 'voiture propre' en Europe: suite et fin?', *Revue du Marche Commun*, No.295, pp125–31.

Corcelle, G. (1989) 'La 'voiture propre' en Europe: le bout du tunnel est en vue!', *Revue du Marché Commun*, No.331, pp513–26.

Crandall, R. W., Gruenspecht, H. K., Keeler, T. E. and Lave, L. B. (1986) *Regulating the Automobile*, Brookings Institute, Washington D.C.

European Communities (1970a) Council Directive of 20 March 1970 on the approximation of the laws of the Member States relating to measures to be taken against air pollution by gases from positive-ignition engines of motor vehicles (70/220/EEC), *Official Journal*, L76, 6 April.

European Communities (1970b) Council Directive of 6 February 1970 on the approximation of the laws of the Member States relating to the type-approval of motor vehicles and their trailers (70/156/EEC), *Official Journal*, L42, 23 February.

European Communities (1972) Council Directive of 2 August 1972 on the ap-
proximation of the laws of the Member States relating to the measures to be taken against the emission of pollutants from diesel engines for use in vehicles (72/306/EEC), *Official Journal*, L190, 20 August.

European Communities (1977) Commission Directive of 30 November 1976 adapting to technical progress Council Directive 70/220/EEC of 20 March 1970 on the approximation of the laws of the Member States relating to measures to be taken against air pollution by gases from positive-ignition engines of motor vehicles (77/102/EEC), *Official Journal*, L32, 3 February.

European Communities (1987) Council Directive of 25 June 1987 on roll-over protection structures mounted in front of the driver's seat on narrow-track wheeled agricultural and forestry tractors (87/402/EEC), *Official Journal*, L220, 8 August.

European Communities (1988) Council Directive of 3 December 1987 amending Directive 70/220/EEC on the approximation of the laws of the Member

States relating to measures to be taken against air pollution by gases from the engines of motor vehicles (88/76/EEC), *Official Journal,* L36, 9 February.

European Communities (1989) Council Directive of 18 July 1989 amending with regard to European emission standards for cars below 1.4 litres, Directive 70/220/EEC on the approximation of the laws of the Member States relating to measures to be taken against air pollution by emissions from motor vehicles (89/458/EEC), *Official Journal,* L226, 3 August.

European Communities (1991) Council Directive of 26 June 1991 amending Directive 70/220/EEC on the approximation of the laws of the Member States relating to measures to be taken against air pollution by emissions from motor vehicles (91/441/EEC), *Official Journal,* L242, 30 August.

Freeman, G. P. (1985) 'National Styles and Policy Sectors: Explaining Sstructured Variation', *Journal of Public Policy,* Vol.5, No.4, pp467–96.

Grijseels, H. C. D., Liefferink, J. D. and van der Velde, M. (forthcoming) *Environmental Policy in the European Community: Negotiating the Directive on Air Pollution from Large Combustion Plants.*

Henssler, H. and Gospage, S. (1987) 'The Exhaust Emission Standards of the European Community', SAE, *Technical Paper Series,* No.871080.

Mills, E. S. and White, L. J. (1978) 'Government Policies Toward Automotive Emissions Control' in Friedlaender, A. F. (ed), *Approaches to Controlling Air Pollution,* MIT Press: Cambridge/London.

Nicolas, F. (with the cooperation of J. Repussard and published as a document of the EC Commission) (1988) *Common Standards for Enterprises,* Office for Official Publications of the European Communities: Luxembourg.

Offermann-Clas, C. (1983) 'Die Kompetenzen der Europäischen Cemeinschaften im Umweltschutz', *Zeitschrift für Umweltpolitik,* Vol.6, No.1, pp47–64.

Parlement Européen (1987), (1987–1988) *Année européenne de l'environnement,* Serie environnement, santé publique et protection des consommateurs, No.10.

Roquepio, P. (1988) *Pluies Acides: Menaces pour l'Europe,* Economica, Paris.

Schumann, W. (1991) 'EG-Forschung und Policy-Analyse: Zur Notwendigkeit, den ganzen Elefanten zu erfassen', *Politische Vierteljahresschrift,* Vol.32, No.2, pp232–57.

SMMT (Society of Motor Manufacturers and Traders) (1988) *Motor Industry of Great Britain 1988 – World Automotive Statistics,* London.

Vogel, D. (1986) *National Styles of Regulation: Environmental Policy in Great Britain and the United States,* Cornell University Press: Ithaca and London.

Wallace, W. (ed) (1990) *The Dynamics of European Integration,* Pinter Publishers: London/New York.

Wessels, P. (1989) *EC Law, Politics and the Environment: The Case of Stricter Emission Standards for Small Cylinder Cars,* (mimeo).

Institution-building from Below and Above: The European Community in Global Environmental Politics

Alberta Sbragia

The European Community was created in a post-war world of proliferating regional and global institutions. Its unique characteristics did not insulate it from the international environment. How the Community was to relate to that environment was contested both within the Community and within its counterpart international institutions. What role should the Community play on the international stage?

The Member States which formed the Community retained their sovereign right to negotiate unilaterally in the myriad international organizations created after World War II. Their participation in the Community did not automatically pre-empt their right to negotiate and represent themselves at international bargaining tables. The one exception was clearly the GATT as the Treaty of Rome gave the Community exclusive competence for commercial policy (although the Community itself did not become a signatory to the GATT). (See, for example, Woolcock and Hodges, 1996.) Given the retention of national sovereign rights in the international field outside of the GATT, the Community's role in external relations was problematic. Many of the Member States assumed that the international powers of the Community would be 'enumerated' powers and that they, the Member States, would control that process of institutionalization.

In 1997, as we examine the international role of the Community, we find it playing a major role in many international fora concerned with 'civilian' issues. While its negotiating cohesiveness is not as stellar as the proponents of a federal Europe would wish, its international presence is far more significant than the Treaty of Rome would predict. This is particularly true in the global environmental arena. How did the Community gain the power to be represented when the Treaty of Rome did not even mention the notion of environmental protection?

How did this international presence emerge? What were the dynamics? For its part, how did the global system react to the Community's representation once it was legitimated within the Community itself?

The emergence of the European Community as a player on the stage of global environmental politics raises two questions: (1) how did the Community qua Community gain the powers to act and (2) how did the international system respond to the Community's demands for participation? The first question leads us to consider the process of institutionalization at the Community level while the second leads us to the process of institutionalization at the global level.

The European Union and External Relations

The power to negotiate and make treaties quickly emerged as one which the Commission wanted to institutionalize as a competence of the Community rather than resting primarily with the Member States. In the words of Eric Stein:

> *[I]n its earliest years the Community was understandably absorbed in the demanding internal task of building the common market; but because it was born into an interdependent world economy it was from the outset compelled to deal with third countries and the proliferating international organizations. By the nature of things, the treaty power was the principal instrument for the Community to replace bilateral relationships between its members and third countries and to create new relationships* (Stein, 1991, p141).

The Treaty of Rome specifically granted the Community the power to conduct external relations in the area of foreign commercial policy. The external role of the EEC in the trade arena was exercised without contestation. The EEC was not a signatory to the GATT, but given that it was the sole negotiator for the Community, its status was not challenged by the USA (see, for example, Meunier, 1996). The EC did, however, become a member of the World Trade Organization in its own right. (The EU's Member States also became contracting parties.) In fact, the EC's newly found status in the international trade arena 'gives formal international recognition to the role of the EC as laid down in the Treaty of Rome' (Scheuermans and Dodd, 1995, p35).

More recently, the European Court of Justice has given the Member States a much greater role in negotiations having to do with trade in services than they were given in trade in manufactured goods. Nonetheless, the capacity of the Community and the Commission in trade can be viewed as the most 'federal' of all external relations. The Community, represented by the Commission, is generally able to act as a unitary actor in trade negotiations.[1] It is important to note here that the European Parliament plays a minor role in the formulation of external trade policy. That is not surprising. National governments, when operating in the international arena, are executive-driven: foreign affairs are relatively insulated from legislative control in all democratic systems. The process of democratization (as well as judicial review) was held at bay when it came to foreign affairs.

In contrast to the Community's role in trade relations, its position in other global arenas has been viewed as weak. The external (as well as EU) dimension of internal security policy (pillar 3) is widely viewed as ineffective, and studies of common foreign and security policy (CFSP) often argue that it is embryonic. The Community's international environmental relations, however, have received very little scholarly attention in spite of the explosion of activity in that area and the high level of scholarly interest in global environmental politics generally.

The Community's international environmental relations are at first glance interesting because they reside in pillar 1 (typically viewed as the most effective pillar) but their subject matter is not economic in the strict sense of the word. The legal status of environmental policy as a Community policy was unusual until the Single European Act (SEA), in that the Community approved environmental directives and entered multilateral environmental agreements without having the environment mentioned in the Treaty of Rome. It is a policy area in which the Community and the Member States share competencies, rather than being in the same category as trade, agriculture or fisheries. In environmental policy, the Community's powers are of a 'concurrent nature' and are characterized by 'the (only) partial delegation of power' (Hession and Macrory, 1994, p157). Therefore, international environmental agreements are known as 'mixed agreements' (O'Keeffe and Schermers, 1983; Groux and Manin, 1985, pp61–9; Lang 1986).

Looking at the question from the perspective of the Community's internal arrangements, how did the Community organize itself to deal at the international level? How were the relative competencies of the Commission and Member States sorted out? How did the balance between the Commission and the Member States manifest itself in this area of external relations?

Finally, the global (and often regional) dimension of environmental policy is addressed within the UN framework. The United Nations and its specialized agencies are perhaps the most prototypical of international organizations. The Community is merely an observer rather than a member.

The politics of global environmental politics highlight the barriers the international system qua system poses for the EU as an external actor outside the trade arena. Institution-building at the EU level does not merely involve sorting out the various competencies of the Commission, the Member States acting within the Community context, and the Member States acting unilaterally. It also involves the circumvention by the Member States of the structural barriers within the system to the EU's emergence as an international 'actor'. It is important to note here that the system is not only hostile to the juridical representation of an organization such as the Community but that it is not set up to even acknowledge the institutionalized 'pooling of sovereignty' at the global level. Thus, how did the Community come to have international status as a party to some treaties? Given that it is not a sovereign state, and that contracting parties to treaties are in fact typically sovereign states, how has the Community acquired that status?

The EU and the International Arena

The role of the EU in the international arena, the environmental arena included, has been nurtured by the implications of creating a common market on the one hand and by the European Court of Justice on the other. The institutionalization of the Community's international role occurred gradually, driven by the substantive aims of the Community, the ambitions of the Commission, and the decisions of the ECJ.

The Common Market

The attempt to create a common market led the Commission in 1968 to propose a program to harmonize national regulations which threatened to create non-tariff barriers and distort competition. The national regulations which concerned the Commission included those in the field of environmental protection. The first environmental directives therefore were based on Article 100 of the EEC Treaty, for they involved ensuring the free movement of goods. In general, the Commission used the objective of ensuring free movement to enhance its own reach; environmental protection was one avenue to such enhancement (Dietrich, 1996; Pollack, 1996).

Although the Commission became more concerned with environmental protection as such, the implications of environmental regulations for the functioning of the Common Market were always a major concern. As Frank Boons has pointed out, 'environmental programmes that are adopted in one country can have substantial consequences for economic actors in other countries' (Boons, 1992, p85). Furthermore, environmental regulations often raise questions of economic competitiveness (Golub, 1998). The economic implications of environmental protection led the Community to focus on international environmental agreements.

As the Member States became active in negotiating and signing multilateral environmental agreements, the Commission began to fear that 'differences in national implementation measures would lead to disparities which, in turn, would hamper the proper functioning of the Common Market'. The Commission therefore included 'co-operation' with third parties as a component of the very first environment action program (Leenen, 1984, p94). It subsequently became a party to a large number of multilateral conventions.

At a substantive level therefore the concern with the construction of the common market focused attention on international environmental agreements as these began to proliferate. National governments, acting unilaterally in negotiation and implementation, could well create non-tariff barriers under the rubric of environmental protection, barriers detrimental to the functioning of the market. Furthermore, the Commission saw environmental protection as giving it a policy reach which had not been included in the Treaty.

But while the substantive reasons might well have been compelling, the ability to be represented at the international level in the arena of environmental protection was not in the Treaty. In fact, environmental protection itself was not mentioned in the Treaty. The Member States had certainly not expected the

Community to be represented in international environmental fora. How did the Community manage to become represented? Why was the international dimension able to be included in the very first action program on the environment? Here we turn to a key Community institution – the European Court of Justice.

The ERTA decision by the Court (see Chapter 7) coupled with the decision by the heads of government to include the environment in the Community's policy competence gave the Community the opening to participate in international environmental politics. The SEA and Maastricht reinforced the ability to participate. The Court, through its case law, institutionalized the power of the Community to exercise external powers once the Member States decided that environmental protection was an arena in which EC legislation could be adopted.

The European Court of justice

The fact that the EU has emerged as an identifiable international actor in the field of environmental protection is rooted in the actions of the European Court of Justice. In Nollkaemper's words:

> [T]he field of the external relations of the Community is, together with the problems of the direct application and priority of Community law, the field in which the Court of Justice has played its most innovative part. The extent to which the Community has become able to claim a place on the international plane over the years is mainly a consequence of the substantial body of case-law developed by the Court (Nollkaemper, 1987, 61).

The ERTA (1971) case served as the keystone to the Community's emergence as an international actor because it created the 'link ... between internal and external powers' (see Chapter 7). The Court ruled that if the Community had been given the power to legislate internally to the Community, it implicitly had been given powers to act externally as well. In its judgement it ruled that:

> [E]ach time the Community, with a view to implementing a common policy envisaged by the Treaty, lays down common rules, whatever form these may take, the Member States no longer have the right, acting individually or even collectively, to contract obligations towards non-Member States affecting these rule. (Mastellone, 1981, p104)

The ERTA case has emerged as the most significant benchmark for delineating the Community's role in international environmental politics. Typically, the Community first legislates and then exercises external jurisdiction. The Court's case law did not, however, clarify whether the Commission or the Council Presidency would represent the Community in international fora. There is no automatic assumption that in external relations the Commission is the Community; the Council Presidency can fulfill that role. Furthermore, the Court's decision did not change the international status of the Community's Member States. In Eric Stein's words:

[R]egardless of the scope of the horizontal and vertical transfer that distinguishes the Community from any other international organization, the Member States remain undisputed subjects of international law and retain their international personality. We thus have no less than 13 international persons, that is 12 sovereign states with a partially circumscribed sovereignty, as well as a new international person ... endowed with a substantial international capacity and external relations powers (Stein, 1991, p129).

Community and Member States Entangled

International treaties highlight the entangled situation described by Stein. They cover areas not covered by the Community's directives – areas which therefore remain in the competence of the Member States. Because the implementation of international environmental treaties will involve the competencies of both the Community and the Member States, such agreements are signed by both the Community and the Member States. They are known as 'mixed agreements' and reflect the 'mixed competence' intrinsic to environmental policy.[2] Mixed agreements are legally very complex,[3] but for our purposes, it is enough to say that they involve ratification by both the Community and the individual Member States. They symbolize the complex intertwining of Member State governments and supranationality which characterizes the Community (see Chapter 7).

The importance of the link drawn between internal and external powers lies in the fact that:

the EC's external powers expand without the express approval of the Member States simply in the course of developing the EC's internal policies. An extra constraint has therefore been added to EC internal policy-making, since the Member States should now always consider whether the adoption of some desirable item of EC legislation might not result in the undesirable (to them) loss of external competence. (Haigh, 1992, p239)

For example, Member States refused to approve a directive on the dumping of wastes at sea which the Commission 'had put forward at least partly to be able to accede to international dumping conventions (the Oslo and London Conventions)' (Haigh, 1992, p240).

The Member States have never recognized international environmental relations as belonging to the exclusive competence of the Community and have gone to some length to ensure that their role is safeguarded. In the case of the Basel Convention on the transport of hazardous waste, for example, the Member States used 'two marginal provisions ... on technical assistance and research to argue that the convention did not come into the sphere of exclusive competence of the Community, but that it was a mixed agreement, ie that it contained provisions for which the Community was responsible and others which were of the competence of Member States' (Kramer, 1995, pp85–6).

While the Member States have worked to ensure that they will not be excluded from the international arena, they have also ensured that the Community would be a presence in that same arena. The SEA and subsequently the Maastricht Treaty gave 'express competence to the Community to conclude international environmental agreements, which then are binding on the institutions of the Community and on the Member States' (Kramer, 1995, p84). Before the coming into force of the SEA, however, the Community became a party to a number of important conventions. In Ziegler's words, the Community's 'own competence to do so and the autonomous possibilities for its Member States were clarified only later by the jurisprudence of the Court of Justice' (Ziegler, n.d., p2). For example, in 1975 it became a party to the Paris Convention of 4 June, 1974 for the prevention of marine pollution from land-based sources, in 1977 to the Barcelona Convention of 16 February, 1976 for the protection of the Mediterranean Sea against pollution, and to the Bonn Convention of 3 December, 1976 for the protection of the Rhine against chemical pollution, in 1981 to the Bonn Convention of 23 June, 1979 on the conservation of migratory species of wild animals, in 1982 to the Bern Convention of 19 September, 1979 on the conservation of European wild life and natural habitats, and in 1981 to the Geneva Convention of 13 November, 1979 on long-range transboundary air pollution (ibid, pp2–3).

The link between the Community and other international bodies was explicitly recognized by the European Council held in Stuttgart in June 1983. The Council stated it saw 'the necessity to take co-ordinated and effective initiatives both within the Community and internationally, particularly within the ECE' in combating pollution (Johnson and Corcelle, 1995, p22). The SEA, for its part, in Article 130r(5) stated that 'within their respective spheres of competence, the Community and the Member States shall co-operate with third countries and with the relevant international organizations'. It gave the Community a legal basis for the negotiation of international environmental accords. In 1987, the heads of state and government at the Dublin Summit decided that the Community should play a key role in the area of international environmental activity.

The Maastricht Treaty reflected that commitment. Article 130r included a new objective for Community action: Community policy on the environment should contribute to 'promoting measures at international level to deal with regional or worldwide environmental problems'.[4] That new provision indicated how far-reaching the internationalization of environmental problems had become. It also strengthened the Community's prerogative in the international field. In Hession's and Macrory's words, the new language in the Treaty:

> *confirms the independent nature of the Community's external power. This latter point is important as the Community previously had to rely on the existence of internal measures to justify external competence in application of the ERTA principle. [It] strengthens the argument that the Community's interest is general and is unrelated to any functional relationship with internal problems or measures* (Hession and Macrory, 1994, p158).

The Commission and International Organizations

The framers of the Treaty of Rome were well aware of the international organizations whose universe they were joining. The role of the EEC multilateral fora was explicitly dealt with in the Treaty of Rome. The Treaty in fact gave short shrift to external relations (other than foreign commercial policy) except in regard to international organizations. In particular, the UN, GATT, OEEC (later OECD), and the Council of Europe were given special mention. Article 229, for instance, specifically empowered the Commission to handle relations with international organizations, with specific reference to the UN, its specialized agencies, and GATT. In 1971, the EEC was only just about to upgrade the head of its Washington office to Director-General and yet it maintained 'permanent liaison, falling only just short of diplomatic missions with GATT in Geneva and OECD in Paris. When OEEC become OECD a special protocol gave to the EEC Commission the task and right to be involved in its work' (Henig, 1971, p10).[5]

Although the Community was only given observer status in those organizations, it is important that the Commission was explicitly given the role of representing the Community with regards to the international organizations mentioned. In what is known as pillar 1 in the post-Maastricht era, therefore, the Commission was given an international role although it was constrained by the very important fact that the Community was not a member of the organizations named. Furthermore, Article 229 does not authorize the Commission to engage in binding commitments (Macrory and Hession, 1996, p135). As the Community de facto became more important in the international arena and its competencies expanded, its official role within the international arena became more complicated.

In a report examining the relationships between the Community and global and regional intergovernmental organizations, the Commission wrote:

> *Not only does the Community have wide ranging relations with these intergovernmental organizations, but these have also undergone a certain evolution. New policies such as that relating to the environment, have involved it in new fields. Similarly, a larger place has increasingly been made for the Community by the international organizations such as the UN system, since in the exercise of its competence it has come to play a larger role* (CEC, 1989, p21).

The Community's participation in intergovernmental organizations, however, is often problematic. Given that the Community is now far more than an international organization but is not a state and that its unique structure is not recognized in international law, its role in international organizations is an awkward one. In the Commission's words:

> *The Community often shares observer status with intergovernmental organizations of the traditional type and is therefore in practice placed on the same footing as those organizations, at least for the present. The Community should be given a status higher than that of observer when the international organization in question is discussing matters falling within the jurisdiction of the Community, but in practice an approach along those lines often runs into difficulties. The basic problem is that traditional international law can accommodate only nation states, or groupings of nation states. Therefore, there has been some resistance to the implied change which is necessary in order for the traditional doctrine to accommodate the new legal entity constituted by the Community* (CEC, 1989, p19).

The key issue for the Commission has been to gain for the Community a separate 'right of access to, and participation in, the work of the deliberative organs of international organizations and conferences'. It was not sufficient for the Member States to agree to a common position among themselves and then have one of them state it within an international organization. The Community wanted to be recognized as a distinct entity with an international personality, and the acquisition of a separate status within international organizations symbolized that recognition. The recognition of such status was of 'great importance' (Groux and Manin, 1985, p43).

In fact, the right of the Community to 'have a seat' in the sense of taking part in meetings (but still officially as an observer and therefore without a vote) at international conferences or within international organizations did not come easily. In the case of the UN General Assembly, the Community did not receive the right to participate until 1974.[6] (While the Commission can speak at meetings of commissions of the UN General Assembly, it is not allowed to address the Plenary Assembly.) By the mid-1980s, 'this battle (could be] considered as almost over since the great majority of permanent international organizations have officially allowed ... the EEC to take part in their proceedings' (Groux and Manin, 1985, pp43, 49). Nonetheless, the Community has no status with the Security Council, the Trusteeship Council, and the International Court of Justice (Brinkhorst, 1994, p610).

In the case of UN international conferences for specific negotiations, the Community must receive the right to participate in each case. The Community is represented at the UN by the Head of the Delegation of the Commission who, however, does not hold ambassadorial status and by the Permanent Representative of the country holding the Presidency of the Council (Brinkhorst, 1994, p610). Brinkhorst, the former Director-General of DG XI, the DG responsible for international environmental negotiations, argues that 'there is a growing disparity between this patchy legal situation of the Community and its political projection at the UN' (ibid, p611). The Community as such has less legal standing than its political profile would suggest.

In the case of the environment, the Commission has had contacts with the United Nations Environment Programme (UNEP) since the latter was founded in December 1972. The relationship was formalized in an exchange of letters between Dr Mostafa K. Tolba, Executive Director of UNEP, and Gaston E. Thorn, President of the Commission in June 1983. Those letters call for regular contacts between the two institutions, exchange of documentation, participation of the Community in UNEP meetings, and consultations on the Regional Seas program, activities pertaining to the assessment of the environment, and environment and development (CEC 1989, pp85–6).

Up until the mid-1980s, however, the Community generally did not try to be recognized as an official member of an international conference organized under the auspices of the UN. The refusal of the Soviet Union and the East European countries to recognize the Community in any fashion was thought to bode ill for any such initiative (Groux and Manin, 1985, pp45–6). As we shall see, the Commission did make a strenuous effort at the negotiations leading to the Vienna Convention to become a contracting party to that Convention –

that effort as well as its eventual success signaled a new era for the Community in the international arena.

In many cases, the Commission is a non-voting participant but the Member States are members of the international organization and field national delegations. Furthermore, the organization often deals with matters which fall under both Member State and Community jurisdiction. Those areas are known under the rubric of 'mixed competence'. Thus, Community representation is often that of 'dual representation.' In such cases, the Community is represented by both the Commission and the Member State holding the Presidency of the Council. The Commission typically speaks on those issues which fall under the Community's exclusive competence although it may also be asked to speak in areas of mixed competence. Such 'dual representation,' for example, is in place at the UN General Assembly, the Economic and Social Council, and UNCTAD (CEC 1989, p21).

It is important to note that 'dual representation' – which includes the Commission and the Presidency as representatives of the Community – incorporates both the 'supranational' and the 'intergovernmental' in the Community's external face. That type of representation in bodies such as the UN does not date from the going into force of the Maastricht Treaty with its provisions for CFSP. Rather, it has its institutional roots in the original mandate in the Treaty of Rome which gave the Commission the right to be involved with the UN and the ECJ's ERTA decision which coupled internal and external powers.[7] Institutionalization has been influenced by a wide variety of factors – not the least of which has been the new prominence of environmental regulations as challenges to cross-border trade – but clearly the Court has played a pivotal role in setting out the essential framework within which the Community's external representation would evolve. Over time, the Community has become a unitary actor more frequently, has worked out a working relationship between the Commission and the Council Presidency, and has secured international recognition. Each step in this process was hard-fought, but the Community is clearly more unitary, more 'balanced', and more recognized than it was in 1973 when environmental policy was added to its competencies.

Global Environmental Politics

The dynamics found in the field of global environmental politics reflect the tensions found in the international arena more generally. Although environmental protection is a relatively new field within global politics, the Community did not find it easy to be accepted by the global system. Although unique, the Community was not a state, and the system (the USA in particular) had difficulty in accepting it as a negotiating counterpart. The legal complexities of 'mixed agreements', the shifting patterns of competencies over time, the evolution of power from the Member States acting unilaterally to their collective action on the international stage in partnership with the Commission, the general lack of precedents and benchmarks in understanding the Community's international role, and the problems for monitoring compliance of these ambiguities were instrumental in making it difficult for the diplomats to accept negotiating with the Community. From the point of view of third parties, it was difficult to know which authority – Brussels or the national governments – would be responsible for implementation and enforcement. That ambiguity made acceptance of the Community particularly problematic.

Internationalization of Environmental Issues

The Community has had to face the question of its international standing in the field of environmental protection because of the explosion of multilateral activities in this area. In Edith Brown Weiss's words:

> *In 1972 international environmental law was a fledgling field with less than three dozen multilateral agreements. Today international environmental law is arguably setting the pace for co-operation in the international community in the development of international law. There are nearly 900 international legal instruments that are either primarily directed to international environmental issues or contain important provisions on them. This proliferation of legal instruments is likely to continue* (Weiss, 1994, p30).

The density of environmental negotiations at the international level is striking. According to Weiss, 'between 1990 and 1992, there have been about a dozen highly important multilateral negotiations occurring more or less in parallel' (Weiss, 1994, p30). Not surprisingly, the implications of this much activity for traditional notions of sovereignty have not gone unnoticed.[8]

Scholars have increasingly paid attention to the creation of global institutions (regimes) in the environmental arena (Young, 1989, 1991, 1993; Hurrell and Kingsbury, 1992; Alker and Haas, 1993; Haas et al, 1993). The UN plays an important role in such an effort. In particular, the establishment of the UNEP at the 1972 UN Conference on the Human Environment in Stockholm 'was probably the most important institutional consequence of increased concern with global environmental change in the Cold War era' (Alker and Haas, 1993, p15). UNEP's impact has been felt at the regional as well as at the global level. The Mediterranean Action Plan was an offshoot of UNEP, for example (Haas, 1990).

The most recent example of such global institution-building is the Framework Convention on Climate Change, signed at the UN Conference on Environment and Development (UNCED) in Rio de Janeiro in June 1992, the Conference on Environment and Development with its resulting Rio Declaration, Agenda 21, and Commission on Sustainable Development, and the Convention on Biodiversity also signed at Rio.

International Negotiation

EU participation in international negotiations is complex. Its participation in binding commitments is rooted in Article 220. Typically, in areas characterized by mixed competence, the Commission will be the negotiator acting under a mandate unanimously agreed to by the Council. The Commission, while it is negotiating, 'continuously consults with a special committee composed of Member States' representatives. In practice, Member States also participate in the negotiation of the environmental agreements' (Kramer, 1995, p84). In areas where the Member States retain jurisdiction, they will negotiate on their own. Given the institutional evolution of the Community, each treaty negotiation has had a different dynamic. The actual representation of the Community is more flexible than the legal scholars might predict. At times the Commission may be asked by the Council to speak for the Community in areas which do not fall within the exclusive competence of the Community while at other times the Presidency may speak even in such areas. When the Presidency speaks for the Community, it will do so using the formula 'on behalf of the Community and its Member States' (Macrory and Hession, 1996, p136).

The following cases give a brief sketch of the key elements of the institution-building process – and its interaction with what can be seen as 'the' key third party, the USA – which has characterized the Community's involvement in international environmental negotiations.

Global Treaties and Institution-Building

CITES

In the case of the 1973 Convention on International Trade in Endangered Species, (CITES) the major global treaty on nature protection, the Community was not a signatory but did enact a regulation implementing the Treaty (EEC/3626/82) which protected more than 250 species of fauna and flora more stringently than did the CITES Convention itself (Johnson and Corcelle, 1995, p306). The fact that the Community was not a signatory was at least partly a question of timing – it did not have competence for environmental protection at the time the Treaty was negotiated. The Member States in 1977 agreed that it should become a signatory, but the Treaty did not allow for the accession of regional economic integration organizations (Johnson and Corcelle, 1995, p417; Weiss, 1996). In 1983, an amendment to the Treaty (the so-called Gaborone Amendment) was negotiated with the USA acting as the principal negotiator. The Gaborone Amendment would have allowed the Community to accede to the Treaty, but the USA, concerned that the institutional structure of the EC would not be able to effectively implement CITES restrictions, decided not to follow through and accept the amendment. The Community is therefore not yet a signatory, primarily because of US opposition.

The knotty question of whether the EC can actually ensure compliance with global treaties as effectively as can national governments operating at the national level has remained largely unresolved from the US point of view. It is the concern with whether the EC can comply on the ground that has undergirded a sustained US skepticism or opposition to the EC's being recognized as an actor in international environmental negotiations.

Although the Community was not a signatory, the Member States' participation in the Conference of the Parties held in 1985 in Buenos Aires was co-ordinated on a daily basis by the Italian Presidency. It must be remembered that in 1985 no treaty basis for environmental protection existed and the Community had not been allowed to sign – yet a regulation implementing CITES had been approved at the Community level and the Member States were acting in the EC framework because of that regulation. In those areas where a common position had been formulated, those positions 'were presented to the Conference on behalf of the Community by the presidency, the Commission, or by the delegation of the Member States having a special interest or specific knowledge on the matter' (CEC, 1985a, p729, final, 2).

Nonetheless, in the Commission's words, 'the Conference witnessed a number of Community incidents' (CEC 1985a, p729, final, 2). The Member States disagreed with the Commission on a variety of issues as well as disagreed with each other. In some contentious areas, no common position was arrived at.

Thus, both the Commission and the Presidency played an important role in the negotiations. While the Community did act in a unitary fashion on some issues, disagreements in both discussions and voting indicated that it was not yet ready to act in a unitary fashion. Clearly, the Community would have been more influential if it had been able to act more cohesively. Yet it is unprecedented for a non-signatory to have the kind of influence which it did have on some issues.[9]

Ozone

American (as well as Soviet) opposition to the Community's emergence as a signatory to global treaties persisted throughout the 1980s. The USA originally opposed the EC signing both the Vienna Convention on the ozone layer and the Montreal Protocol, at least partially because treating the Community as one political unit had implications for how individual Member States might or might not comply with the treaty (Haigh, 1992, p242; Hampson with Hart, 1995, p265). In those treaties, however, the Member States backed the Commission's insistence on the Community becoming a contracting party.

The politics of ozone, however, have one clear feature. The Commission's 'insistence on special statutory treatment' became a key negotiating point, one which, from the point of third parties, was typically shrouded in confusion over what the power of the Community in the area actually was. The question of whether and when the Community exercised exclusive competence was particularly difficult to answer from a legal standpoint. The political ramifications of an answer to that question were often too problematic. As the Community's legal adviser John Temple Lange put it, 'precisely because the limits of exclusive competence are politically important, they are particularly difficult and controversial to define' (cited in Benedick, 1991, p95). The confusion over the entanglement between Community and Member States fuels concern over compliance. Who is responsible for ensuring compliance with the final treaty – Brussels or national capitals? Given the importance for economic actors of the Montreal Protocol, it was particularly important for many countries, the USA included, that the accountability for compliance be relatively straightforward.[10]

In spite of the irritations caused to third parties (and at times to the Member States themselves) by the Commission's relentless pursuit of ensuring its international status, the Community was so important it could not be ignored or dismissed. The cohesion of the Community in the area of ozone generally has been such that it has emerged as a key actor (Szell, 1993, p36; Litfin, 1995a/b). During the Vienna Convention negotiations, the European position was so cohesive in its opposition to binding commitments that a framework convention laying out general principles only was seen as the only feasible option. The Community was in fact a unitary actor, with the Member States and the Commission acting in unison (Jachtenfuchs, 1990, p264).

Leaving aside the content of the environmental restrictions adopted, the Commission strenuously negotiated to be allowed to become a contracting party without restrictions (Benedick, 1991, p95). Given the lack of explicit competence for environmental protection before the adoption of the SEA, the Commission viewed the negotiations as a way to 'obtain greater competence in environmental affairs within the Community. Had it succeeded, it could claim the right to propose Community legislation to implement the ozone convention and future protocols' (Jachtenfuchs, 1990, p263). The Council had agreed in January 1982 that the Community should become a contracting party, and in October 1984 had agreed that the Community should be allowed to become a contracting party without any conditions being attached. However, both the USA and the USSR had proposed restrictions. The USA wanted 'a prior participation by one Member State' and the USSR wanted prior participation by a majority of the Member States (CEC, 1985b, p8, explanatory memorandum). A compromise was finally reached which was acceptable to the Commission.

Negotiations over the Montreal Protocol to the Vienna Convention had some of the same features. The status of the Community – which had both symbolic and substantive implications – was the subject of heated debate and only a last-minute compromise put forth by New Zealand's Environment Minister allowed the negotiations to conclude (Hampson with Hart, 1995, p265). Richard Benedick, the American negotiator, gives a sense of how important the dispute became:

> *After a nerve-racking midnight standoff over this issue, during which the fate of the protocol hung in the balance, a compromise was reached at the last possible moment ... this concession would obtain only if all member countries plus the EC Commission became parties to the protocol and formally notified the secretariat of their manner of implementation* (Benedick, 1991, pp96–7).

However, the issue of competence was highlighted when the issue under discussion was a fund to help developing countries obtain advanced technology. The Community could not be involved, and 'on this point the Member States acted on their own' (Haigh, 1992, p241).

During the Protocol negotiations, the Community again kept the agreement from being as stringent as the USA and the Scandinavians wanted. After a political change at the Community level which transformed the politics of ozone, the Community emerged as a policy leader during the negotiations for the London and Copenhagen amendments. Regardless of whether the Community was a 'leader' or a 'laggard', however, the Community was cohesive enough to emerge as a key negotiating partner.

Climate Change

By the time the climate change negotiations began officially in February 1991, the EC had become a recognized power in the area of international environmental politics. The UN General Assembly had created the Intergovernmental Negotiating Committee (INC) for a Framework Climate Convention under whose auspices the negotiations were conducted. Within that framework, 'the EC assumed a lead role in the negotiations by virtue of its commitment to returning its joint carbon dioxide emissions to 1990 levels by the year 2000' (Porter and Brown, 1996, p95).

While the Community's commitment did indeed provide a benchmark, the Commission's role in the actual negotiation of the Framework Convention was rather limited. The Member States, however, were involved.

Given the role of the USA in international politics, environmental politics especially, it was essential for the success of the Rio Conference (at which the UN Framework Convention on Climate Change was to be signed) that President Bush personally attend. The US position, however, was opposed to binding commitments to reduce carbon dioxide emissions to a specific level by a specific date. The European Community was viewed by the USA as a key adversary, and President Bush demanded the Europeans change their position. Bush 'personally called German Prime Minister Helmut Kohl to ask him to drop his government's demands for the stabilization commitment in return for Bush's participation in the Earth Summit' (Porter and Brown, 1996: 96). Whether that call was to Kohl as a German or whether it was to Kohl as a key player in the ECs politics of climate change is impossible to say, but it may be irrelevant. By that point, the European Community and its Member States were so entangled in a way which does not easily fit the legal language of 'competencies'.

Member-states used their bilateral contacts with Washington to lobby the Bush administration to support the EU's position (unsuccessfully of course). The Member States and the Community were intertwined in such a way that the EC could be seen as a unitary actor using multilateral diplomatic channels to convince the USA to change its position (Porter and Brown 1996, p95). In the context of transatlantic negotiations, the Member States have been in a much stronger position than has the Commission (a situation which began to change under the Clinton administration).[11] The Member States clearly dominated that exchange – but acted in a unitary fashion. From the US point of view, it was the EC/Germans/Dutch/British who were lobbying rather than the Member States acting unilaterally.[12]

The entanglement of the Community and the Member States when dealing in transatlantic negotiations is evident in the negotiation of Article 4 (2) of the Convention. In Nigel Haigh's words:

> [T]he UK Secretary of State for the Environment, Michael Howard, allegedly with the encouragement of some other Environment Ministers from EC Member States, travelled to the USA and agreed a form of words with US officials which forms the basis of Article 4(2) of the Convention. Whether this can be regarded as an EC contribution to the framing of the Convention is a matter of opinion. Formally it was not

since no formal Council decisions were taken on the subject, but without the ma-
chinery provided by the EC for discussion between ministers it may not have hap-
pened (Haigh, 1996, pp181–2).

The USA is such an important actor that it is difficult to analyze the EU's role
without taking into account the impact of US policy. Given that climate
change policy is essentially an issue of international political economy because
of the wide-ranging impacts on industrial activity and structure of carbon dioxide
emission reductions,[13] the economic interdependence within the industrialized
world cannot be ignored by the EU. It is for that reason that in 1992 EU Finance
Ministers insisted that any EU carbon tax be implemented only on condition
that the USA and Japan acted in kind. Japan agreed on condition that the USA
enact some kind of carbon tax. The Clinton administration refused. Although
there are significant Member State differences on the carbon tax issue (the UK
opposes it in principle), there is no doubt that a change in the American position would transform the politics of the carbon tax debate within the EU as well
as the international politics of climate change (Zito, 1995; Porter and Brown,
1996, p149).

The climate change negotiations once again highlighted the concern of third
parties that implementation be transparent. Article 22 (2) specifies that regional
economic integration organizations which accede to the Convention (ie the Community) must 'declare the extent of their competence with respect to matters governed by the Convention' (Macrory and Hession, 1996, p114). The entangled legal
situation in areas of 'mixed competence' and 'mixed agreements', however, makes
this difficult. Thus far the Community's statement is lacking specifics. That perhaps is not surprising, especially given the lack of specifics in the Framework Convention on Climate Change itself. As Macrory and Hession point out:

[i]n the absence of a clearly defined area of exclusive Community competence for climate
change and in the absence of a clear obligation detailing specific action it is extremely
difficult to isolate Community and Member State obligations (ibid, 1996, p114).

UNCED

Once the General Assembly in December 1989 decided to convene a UN Conference on Environment and Development in 1992, the question of the European Community's participation arose. In March 1992, the Council of Ministers approved the full participation of the Community in the UNCED – 'on
equal terms with the Member States' (Jupille and Caporaso, 1996, p20). However, as Jupille and Caporaso point out, when Portugal, in the exercise of the
Community Presidency, asked during the New York PrepCom (IV) meeting
that Commission President Delors be treated during the concluding ceremonies
at Rio as if he were a head of state, a fierce dispute erupted with the USA and
the Member States themselves were unwilling to go that far (ibid, 1996, p21).[14]

A compromise position was put together which acknowledged the special
position of the Community in the world of international affairs. The compromise
allowed the Community to participate fully in the UNCED deliberations – the

only international organization to be given that privilege. This privileged position was however not to be viewed as a precedent, and the Community would still not be allowed to vote. The following excerpt summarizing the compromise gives a sense of how the Community's actual participation was to take place:

> *The EEC will represent exclusively the Community's position to the Conference on issues falling within the EEC's exclusive competence. In cases of mixed competence, the EEC and its Member States will determine which, as between them will represent the positions of the Community and its Member States. The EEC shall inform the UNCED secretariat prior to consideration of an agenda item by the Conference if the EEC will be representing a position of the Community and its Member States with respect to specific matters within the scope of that agenda item.* (Jupille and Caporaso, 1996, p21)

On April 13, 1992, the General Assembly approved a special decision to grant the Community's request to be granted 'full participant status'. Brinkhorst, then the Director-General of DG XI, describes the content and significance of that decision in the following terms:

> *This status conferred on the EEC rights enjoyed by participating states, including representation in committees and working groups of the conference, the right to speak and to reply, and to submit proposals and substantive amendments. On two counts the position would be different from that of Member States: the EEC would not have the right to vote (including the right to block a consensus) nor to submit procedural motions. Although EC representatives made it clear from the beginning that the EC would not request a 13th vote, no new ground could be broken on this point in view of the clear language to the contrary of the UN Charter ... the decision was considered as an important breakthrough of the general procedural rules prevailing at meetings of UN conferences* (Brinkhorst, 1994, p612).

The Community had played what Brinkhorst characterizes as a 'certain mediating role' between developing countries on the one hand and the USA and Japan on the other. The G-77 therefore actively supported the granting of 'full participant status' to the Community (Brinkhorst, 1994, p613).

The Council Presidency played an active role during the negotiations. According to one negotiator from a non-Member State, at certain points the Presidency on behalf of the Community was negotiating with the G-77 with the USA and Russia sitting on the sidelines. In his words, 'the Community was a powerhouse'. Although the Commission's presence was weakened by the refusal of the Commissioner for the Environment to attend, the Community played an important role. The Commission's civil servants were involved and the Council Presidency was very visible. Third parties certainly interpreted the Presidency's actions as those of the Community. Given the codes of international negotiations, the fact that Ken Collins, the Chair of the important parliamentary committee on the environment, did not attend mattered much less than did the fact that the Council Presidency was active.

The relationship between the Commission and the Presidency seems to have been relatively smooth. The Council of Ministers had decided in March 1992 that the Presidency would typically represent and negotiate for the Community in areas of mixed competence but that the Commission could act in the same fashion if it were so agreed. In areas where important EC directives had been approved – toxic chemicals, waste, and fisheries – 'the Commission representatives spoke exclusively on behalf of the Community' (Brinkhorst, 1994, p613).

The Community in fact was able to act in a unitary fashion more easily on environmental issues than on those dealing with development aid policy. No common EC position had been developed, and the Community in that area was unable to exert the kind of influence it did in the environmental arena (Brinkhorst, 1994, p614).

The Community did sign Agenda 21 even though it is not a legally binding document. From a legal perspective, such a signature was unusual. Martin Hession argues that 'the general powers of the Commission to maintain all appropriate relations with organs of the UN (Article 229) cannot be considered sufficient for such general political declarations' (Hession, 1995, p156).

In fact, the Community has been active in its relations with the Committee for Sustainable Development (CSD) which was established by Chapter 38 of Agenda 21 as a Commission of the UN's Economic and Social Council. The General Assembly, in establishing the CSD in January 1993, explicitly called for the full participation of the Community. The Council of Ministers had on 23 November 1992 accepted a Commission recommendation that the Community should participate fully in CSD activities. The Member States which were elected to membership on the Commission (the Community itself would not seek election) would, on issues within the Community's exclusive competence:

exercise their votes on the basis of a Community position decided on in Community co-ordination. On issues of mixed competence, co-ordination would take place with a view to securing a common position on the basis of which the Community members of the CSD should vote (Brinkhorst, 1994, p615).

The Council of Ministers in its meeting of 4 March 1996 laid out the guidelines to be used by the Union during the 4th Session of the Commission which met in New York from 18 April to 3 May 1996. These guidelines were also to be used in the preparation for the EU's participation in the 1997 special session of the UN General Assembly which is to review the progress made in the implementation of the commitments made at Rio (Council of Ministers 1996, p5309/Presse 45, pp5–7).

Conclusion

The EC has over time developed the international standing and the capacity to become an important international actor in the area of international environmental relations. Third parties as well as the UN system have gradually acknowledged the Community's unique status vis-à-vis its Member States and are in the process of adapting international institutions to accommodate its unusual demands.

What is striking about the Community's role is that an institutionalized balance between the Commission and the Member States acting collectively within the framework of the Union is being constructed at the same time that the Community is emerging as an important actor in the global environmental context. The Presidency is a key Community institution in the foreign environmental affairs of the Community. The Commission, for its part, is playing a role much more important than might have been expected given the importance of states in the international system. The Member States, although in constant conflict with the Commission over the internal allocation of responsibilities, are nonetheless consistently agreeing to have the Community play an important international role in the environmental arena.

The institutionalization of 'dual representation' represents an innovative way for the Community to be represented while maintaining a central role for the Member States. The Community has found a way to incorporate both intergovernmentalism (in the form of the Council Presidency) and the 'federal' (in the form of the Commission) in its external personality.

Significantly, the external role of the Commission was legitimized by the European Court of Justice. The Court, as it has so often, gave a powerful 'federal' impetus to the Community by recognizing the external dimension of what we now know as pillar 1. It, however, did not exclude the Member States. The entanglement between the Community and the Member States is packaged under the rubric of 'mixed competence' and 'mixed agreements'. The arcane and convoluted legal spiderwebs which make up the area of 'mixed competence' and 'concurrent powers' are in fact the foundation stones for the balance between Brussels and national capitals which makes the Community both so complex and so successful as an instrument of integration (see Chapter 12).

The environmental arena has proven to be a fruitful arena for institution-building. The Community has been able to increase its stature, its international reach, and its effectiveness within international organizations. Each global treaty has proven to be a step in a process of institution-building which is still ongoing. Its future role in the Commission for Sustainable Development and General Assembly activities in the post-Rio period is likely to continue on a similar trajectory – incremental steps which increase its status as well as its access to the decision-making centres within international fora (such as informal meetings), and therefore the likelihood that it will be able to act in a unitary fashion.

The Council Presidency, flanked by the Commission, and the Commission, flanked by the Council Presidency, are likely to force the international system to acknowledge an entity which does not require the constituent units to subordinate themselves to a 'federal' government or to a 'centre' as conventionally understood. The ever-more institutionalized coupling of the 'supranational' and the 'intergovernmental' in the conduct of international environmental politics represents a case of institution-building at both the Community – and the global – level.

Notes

1. Woolcock and Hodges (1996, p323), for example, conclude that in the Uruguay Round, 'in fourteen of the fifteen negotiating groups, the EC performed on a par with, for example, the USA, if not better, in terms of presenting coherent consistent positions'.
2. Pillar 1 includes areas of exclusive competence – trade in manufactured goods – and areas of so-called 'mixed competence'. The latter is seen by many Commission officials as far from ideal. In the words of one, 'pillar one is being polluted by 'mixicity' – the notion of mixed competencies'.
3. John Temple Lang defines a mixed agreement in the following fashion: 'International agreements are described as 'mixed' when both the European Community and some or all of its Member States become, or are intended to become, parties. In practice this is usually where the Community has exclusive competence over part of the subject matter of the agreement and non-exclusive or concurrent competence over the rest of the subject matter. However, the phrase 'mixed agreements' is also used to describe the much rarer situations in which either part of the subject matter of the agreement is outside the competence, even the concurrent competence, of the Community, or the Community becomes a party even though it has no exclusive competence over any part of the subject matter' (Lang, 1986, pp157–8).
4. The other three objectives are preserving, protecting, and improving the quality of the environment, protecting human health, and the prudent and rational utilization of natural resources.
5. With regards to the OECD, the Commission points out that 'although the Community is not a member of that Organization, its status there is higher than that of an observer. Supplementary Protocol No. 1 to the Convention on the OECD stipulates that the Commission shall take part as of right in the work of the Organization and that representation of the Communities shall be determined with the institutional provisions of the Treaties' (CEC 1989, p19).
6. Much to its dismay, however, the Community has the same formal status vis-à-vis the UN General Assembly as the Commonwealth Secretariat, the International Committee of the Red Cross, the League of African Unity, and the Organization of the Islamic Conference. It is certainly true that such organizations have little similarity with the Community, representing 'both in law and in their factual position a totally different political reality' (Brinkhorst, 1994, p610).
7. The trade arena stands as a contrast. In the case of the Uruguay Round, Member States did not field national delegations. The Commission was the sole representative and the Presidency was not a partner nor was it included in the negotiating team. The Member States gave the Commission the right to negotiate for the Community even in those areas (such as services and intellectual property rights) characterized by 'mixed competence' (Woolcock and Hodges, 1996, p302).
8. See eg Hurrell and Kingsbury (1992); Conca (1994); Litfin (1995a/b).
9. For a more in-depth discussion of the EU's role in CITES, see Sbragia with Hildebrand (1998).

10. The politics of ozone depletion have been very much concerned with economics. As Jeffrey Berejikian argues, 'the central concern of the EC was the economic impact of ozone layer protection' (Berejikian, 1997, p790).
11. For a discussion of how the Clinton administration began to view the Community as a more important transatlantic partner, see Gardner, A. (1997); Sbragia (1996).
12. The Member States, however, maintained control of the negotiations over the Global Environmental Facility. The Community is not a member of the GEF but is trying to become one. At least some of the Member States, however, are opposed to the Community's membership.
13. Michael Grubb has argued that the impact of reducing greenhouse gases will be significant. In his words 'No previous environmental problem has been at once so closely related to major sectors of economic activity'. Cited in Sell (1996, pp106–7).
14. I have drawn heavily from Jupille and Caporaso's excellent paper. Preparatory committees were very important in the UNCED process. In Stanley Johnson's words, 'Few international conferences can have been so thoroughly prepared as the UN Conference on Environment and Development. UNCED's Preparatory Committee (which became known as PrepCom) held four meetings, each of them four or five weeks in length, which were attended by most of the Member States of the United Nations, by the intergovernmental bodies both inside and outside the UN system, by a host of non-governmental organizations including the business, scientific and academic communities, as well as the representatives of 'green' groups and charitable and other bodies interested in the environment and development. The task of these successive meetings of UNCED's PrepCom was to define the issues, to help shape the programmes and other proposals, to assess financial implications where this was possible and, finally, to narrow down the areas of disagreement so that the Rio Conference might ultimately be confronted with a manageable agenda' (Johnson, 1993, p19).

References

Alker, H. R., and Haaz, P. (1993) 'The Rise of Global Ecopolitics', in Choucri, N. (cd), *Global Accord: Environmental Challenges and International Responses*, Cambridge, Mass: MIT Press.

Benedick, R. E. (1991) *Ozone Diplomacy: New Directions in Safeguarding the Planet*, Cambridge, Mass: Harvard University Press.

Berejikian, J. (1997) 'The Gains Debate: Framing State Choice', *American Political Science Review*, Vol.91, pp789–806.

Boons, F. (1992) 'Product-oriented Environmental Policy and Networks: Ecological Aspects of Economic Internationalization', *Environmental Politics*, Vol.4, pp84–105.

Brinkhorst, L. J. (1994) 'The European Community at UNCED: Lessons to be Drawn for the Future', in Curtin, D. and Heukels, T. (eds), *Institutional Dynamics of European Integration*, Dordrecht: Martinus Nijhoff.

Commission of the European Communities (CEC) (Serial) *Directory of the Commission of the European Community*, Luxembourg: Office for Official Publications of the European Communities (1985a) *On the Main Results of the Fifth Meeting of the Conference on the Parties to the Convention on International Trade in Endangered Species of Wild Fauna and Flora*, COM (85) 729.

Commission of the European Communities (CEC) (Serial) *Directory of the Commission of the European Community*, Luxembourg: Office for Official Publications of the European Communities (1985b) *Concerning the Negotiation for a Global Framework Convention on the Protection of the Ozone Layer*, COM (85) 8.

Commission of the European Communities (CEC) (Serial) *Directory of the Commission of the European Community*, Luxembourg: Office for Official Publications of the European Communities (1989) *Relations between the European Community and International Organisations*, Luxembourg: Office for Official Publications of the European Communities.

Conca, K. (1994) 'Rethinking the Ecology–Sovereignty Debate', *Millennium*, Vol.23, pp701–11.

Corbett, R. (1989) 'Testing the New Procedures: The European Parliament's First Experience with its New 'Single Act' Powers', *Journal of Common Market Studies*, Vol.27, pp359–72.

Dietrich, W. F. (1996) 'Harmonization of Automobile Emission Standards under International Trade Agreements: Lessons from the European Union Applied to the WTO and NAFTA', *William and Mary Environmental Law and Policy Review*, Vol.20, pp175–221.

Gardner, A. L. (1997) *A New Era in US–EU Relations? The Clinton Administration and the New Transatlantic Agenda*, Brookfield, Vermont: Ashgate.

Golub, J. (1998) 'Global Competition and EU Environmental Policy: Introduction and Overview', in Golub, J. (ed), *Global Competition and EU Environmental Policy*, London: Routledge.

Groux, J. and Manin, P. (1985) *The European Communities in the International Order*, Luxembourg: Office for Official Publications of the European Communities.

Haas, P. M. (1990) *Saving the Mediterranean: The Politics of International Environmental Co-operation*, New York: Columbia University Press.

Haigh, N. (1992) 'The European Community and International Environmental Policy', in Hurrell, A. and Kingsbury, B. (eds) *The International politics of the Environment: Actors, Interests, and Institutions*, Oxford: Clarendon Press.

Haigh, N. (1996) 'Climate Change Policies and Politics in the European Community', in O'Riordan, T. and Jager, J. (eds), *Politics of Climate Change: A European Perspective*, London: Routledge.

Hampson, F. O., with Hart, M. (1995) *Multilateral Negotiations: Lessons from Arms Control, Trade, and the Environment*, Baltimore: Johns Hopkins University Press.

Henig, S. (1971) *External Relations of the European Community: Associations and Trade Agreements*, London: Chatham House.

Hession, M. (1995) 'External Competence and the European Community', *Global Environmental Change: Human and Policy Dimensions*, Vol.5, pp155–6.

Hession, M. and Macrory, R. (1994) 'Maastricht and the Environmental Policy of the Community: Legal Issues of a New Environment Policy', in O'Keeffe, D. and Twomey, P. M. (eds), *Legal Issues of the Maastricht Treaty*, London: Chancery Law Ltd.

Hurrell, A. and Kingsbury, B. (1992) 'The International Politics of the Environment: An Introduction', in Hurrell, A. and Kingsbury, B. (eds), *The International Politics of the Environment*, Oxford: Clarendon Press.

Jachtenfuchs, M. (1990) 'The European Community and the Protection of the Ozone Layer', *Journal of Common Market Studies*, Vol.28, pp261–77.

Johnson, S. P. (1993) *The Earth Summit: The United Nations Conference on Environment and Development (UNCED)*, London: Graham & Trotman/Martinus Nijhoff.

Johnson, S. P. and Corcelle, G. (1995) *The Environmental Policy of the European Communities*, 2nd edn, London: Kluwer Law International.

Jupille, J. H. and Caporaso, J. A. (1996) 'The European Community in Global Environmental Politics', ECSA Workshop, The Role of the European Union in the World Community, Jackson Hole, Wyoming, 16–19 May.

Kramer, L. (1995) *EC Treaty and Environmental Law*, 2nd edn, London: Sweet & Maxwell.

Lang, J. T. (1986) 'The Ozone Layer Convention: A New Solution to the Question of Community Participation in 'Mixed' International Agreements', *Common Market Law Review*, Vol.23, pp157–76.

Leenen, A. T. S. (1984) 'Participation of the EEC in International Environmental Agreements', *Legal Issues of European Integration*, 1984/1, pp93–111.

Litfin, K. T. (1995a) 'Rethinking Sovereignty and Environment: Beyond Either/Or', presented at SSRC Workshop, Rethinking Sovereignty and Environment, University of Washington, 13–15 October.

Litfin, K. T. (1995b) 'Framing Science: Precautionary Discourse and the Ozone Treaties', *Millennium: Journal of International Studies*, Vol.24, pp251–77.

Macrory, R. and Hession, M. (1996) 'The European Community and Climate Change: The Role of Law and Legal Competence', in O'Riordan, T. and Jager, J. (eds), *Politics of Climate Change: A European Perspective*, London: Routledge.

Mastellone, C. (1981) 'The External Relations of the E.E.C. in the Field of Environmental', *International and Comparative Law Quarterly*, Vol.30, pp104–17.

Meunier, S. (1996) 'Divided but United: European Trade Policy Integration and EC–US Agricultural Negotiations in the Uruguay Round', presented at the ECSA Workshop, The Role of the European Union in the World Community, Jackson Hole, Wyoming, 16–19 May.

Nollkaemper, A. (1987) 'The European Community and International Environmental Co-operation – Legal Aspects of External Community Powers', *Legal Issues of European Integration*, 1987/2, pp55–91.

O'Keeffe, D. and Schermers, H. G. (eds) (1983) *Mixed Agreements*, Boston: Kluwer Law and Taxation Publishers.

Pollack, M. A. (1996) 'Ignoring the Commons: International Trade, the International Environment, and EC Environment Policy', paper presented at the

Council for European Studies Conference of Europeanists, Chicago, 14–16 March.

Porter, G. and Brown, J. W. (1996) *Global Environmental Politics,* 2nd edn, Boulder, Colorado: Westview.

Sbragia, A. (1996) 'Transatlantic Relations: An Evolving Mosaic', International Conference, Policy-Making and Decision-Making in Transatlantic Relations, Universite Libre de Bruxelles, 3–4 May.

Sbragia, A. with Hildebrand, P. (1998) 'The European Union and Compliance: A Story in the Making', in Weiss, E. B. and Jacobson, H. (eds), *Engaging Countries: Strengthening Compliance with International Environmental Accords,* Cambridge, Mass: MIT.

Scheuermans, F. and Dodd, T. (1995) 'The World Trade Organization and the European Community', Working Paper, External Economic Relations Series, E-1, Brussels: European Parliament, Directorate-General for Research, External Economic Relations Division.

Sell, S. (1996) 'North–South Environmental Bargaining: Ozone, Climate Change, and Biodiversity', *Global Governance,* Vol.2, pp97–118.

Stein, E. (1991) 'External Relations of the European Community: Structure and Process', *Collected Courses of the Academy of European Law,* 1, Book 1, Deventer: Kluwer Law International.

Szell, P. (1993) 'Negotiations on the Ozone Layer', in Sjostedt, G. (ed), *International Environmental Negotiation,* Newbury Park, California: Sage.

Weiss, E. B. (1996) 'The Natural Resource Agreements: The Living Histories', unpublished MS.

Weiss, E. B. (1994) 'International Environmental Law: Contemporary Issues and the Emergence of a New World Order', *Business and the Contemporary World,* Vol.6, pp30–44.

Woolcock, S. and Hodges, M. (1996) 'EU Policy and the Uruguay Round', in Wallace, H. and Wallace, W. (eds), *Policy-Making in the European Union,* Oxford: Oxford University Press.

Young, O. R. (1989) *International Co-operation: Building Regimes for Natural Resources and the Environment,* Ithaca, NY: Cornell University Press.

Young, O. R. (1991) 'Political Leadership and Regime Formation: On the Development of Institutions in International Society', *International Organization,* Vol.45, pp281–308.

Young, O. R. (1993) 'Negotiating an International Climate Regime: The Institutional Bargaining for Environmental Governance', in Choucri, N. (ed), *Global Accord: Environmental Challenges and International Responses,* Cambridge, Mass: MIT Press.

Ziegler, A. R. (n.d.) 'International Co-operation for the Protection of the Environment in the European Community: Shared Tasks and Responsibilities of the Community and the Member States', unpublished MS.

Zito, A. (1995) 'Integrating the Environment into the European Union: The History of the Controversial Carbon Tax', in Rhodes, C. and Mazey, S. (eds), *The States of the European Community, III: Building a European Polity,* Boulder, Colorado: Lynne Rienner.

Part 5
FUTURE CHALLENGES

17

The Implementation of EU Environmental Policy: A Policy Problem without a Political Solution?

Andrew Jordan

The Community is at a crucial point in its environmental policy. The first stage of its policy, that of legislating ... has developed substantially as a result of the Community's work in the past two decades ... We are now moving into a second stage of strengthening and consolidating the acquis communautaire *through bringing about changes in current trends, practices and attitudes ... Achieving the goal of a high level of environmental protection is only possible if our legal framework is being properly implemented. If the strong* acquis communautaire *on the environment is not properly complied with and equally enforced in all Member States, the Community's future environmental policies cannot be effective ... The environment will either remain unprotected or the level of protection in different Member States and regions of the Community will be uneven and might, inter alia, lead to distortions of competition* (CEC, 1996, p1).

To govern is not to write resolutions and distribute directives; to govern is to control the implementation of the directives (Joseph Stalin).

Implementation is very much at the 'sharp end' of the European Union (EU) environmental policy process. The success of EU policies – and with them the whole integration project – must ultimately be judged by the impacts they have on the ground. If, as the Commission warns above, the *acquis* is not fully implemented, EU environmental policy risks becoming a paper exercise with little tangible effect on environmental quality.

Krislov et al (1986, p68), authors of one of the first systematic studies of EU environmental policy, noted a 'growing problem of compliance' across all sectors of EU law. A special investigation by the EU's Court of Auditors *(OJ* 1992b) revealed that environmental directives were 'being implemented slowly' and pointed to a 'significant, gap between the set of rules in force and their actual application'. A damning report by the highly regarded House of Lords Select Committee on the European Communities (HOLSCEC, 1992a, p35) in the UK concluded that:

> *Implementation and enforcement of environmental legislation go to the heart of Community policy. But Community environmental legislation is being widely disregarded, and the Community has paid insufficient attention to how its policies can be given effect, enforced or evaluated. The time has come to redress the balance (p35).*

In this chapter I investigate why implementation was neglected throughout most of the first decade of EU environmental policy, outline the responsibilities and interests of the main actors involved, and discuss possible solutions to the 'gap' between the stated aims of policies and their practical impact on the ground in Member States. Recent years have, however, witnessed a new willingness on behalf of Member States to remedy past failings and give higher priority to making new policies fully implementable. The chapter concludes with a comparison of the Commission's recent communication on implementation with other popular recommendations for closing the implementation 'gap' afflicting EU environmental policy.

Implementation: The 'Missing Link' in Policy Analysis?

Why should a seemingly well-conceived policy that has the political blessing of every state go adrift during the process of being implemented? In one of the first systematic studies of policy implementation. Pressman and Wildavsky (1973) showed why a politically popular federal employment programme in the US failed to live up to prior expectations. The subtitle of their book paraphrases its central message: 'How great expectations in Washington are dashed in Oakland; or, why it's amazing that federal programmes work at all ...'. They showed how successful implementation requires linkages to be built between the bewilderingly large number of actors whose co-operation is needed to turn a policy statement into action (what they termed the 'complexity of joint action'). Using relatively simple arithmetical calculations they concluded that, even where there is a high chance of obtaining clearance from a single participant at a given 'decision point' in the implementation chain, when all the probabilities are multiplied together the overall chances of success are extremely slender. In a revised edition, they warned politicians not to promise what they could not deliver; to do so leads only to 'disillusionment and frustration' with the policy process (Pressman and Wildavsky, 1984, p6).

However, if there is one thing the EU is unequivocally good at, it is producing large quantities of highly ambitious regulation.[1] The Commission in particular is a precocious entrepreneur, constantly on the lookout for opportunities to expand its competence in areas regarded as peripheral by the Member States. But when it comes to putting the *acquis communautaire* into effect at the national level, the Commission is on a steep upward slope, possessing neither the political resources nor the legal competence to delve substantially into national affairs. This begs the question of why the architects of the EU constructed an international organization with an inbuilt 'pathology of non-compliance' (Mendrinou, 1996) – in other words, a political entity with insufficient capacity to achieve its objectives. More puzzling still, far from creating political disillusionment in the policy process, EU environmental policy continues to be one of the few elements of the European project that enjoys genuine public appeal, despite being poorly implemented. And instead of reducing the output of new legislation and concentrating on strengthening policy delivery structures, with the exception of a few recent blips, the tide of new environmental regulation emanating from Brussels remains as strong as ever (Haigh, 1997, Section 2.2; Zito, 1999).

What explains these paradoxical features? A major contributory factor is the EU's institutional structure, which shares out power unevenly between the main actors. This structural imbalance ensures that the EU's constituent bodies, namely the Commission, the European Court of Justice (ECJ), and so on, are geographically and politically dissociated from what goes on at the ground level in Member States. In Pressman and Wildavsky's terms, the 'complexity of joint action' required to give effect to European rules framed at the supranational level is many orders of magnitude more elaborate than that required to give effect to a national statute. Majone (1996) argues persuasively that, partly by accident and partly by conscious design, the states of Western Europe have created a *regulatory* state at the pan-European level. Possessing only very limited 'tax-and-spend' powers of its own (and virtually none in the environmental field), maximalist actors such as the Commission and the European Parliament have a powerful incentive to disregard Pressman and Wildavsky's admonition and propose ambitious pieces of legislation which impose their primary costs on the actors, namely Member States and private organizations, charged with implementing them. The need, moreover, to secure agreement among the many actors in the EU policy process leaves the Commission with little incentive to point out the full implications of its proposals.

Given these incentive structures it is hardly surprising that so many 'great' environmental expectations in Brussels and Strasbourg are dashed by weak and inconsistent enforcement at the national level. In fact, conflicts surrounding the speed and scope of implementation are an integral part of the political game playing between state and non-state actors, described by Zito (1999) in this issue. Supranational actors propose legislation which is deliberately ambitious in an attempt to upgrade the common interest and further integration; states resist when policies fail to fit their national interests.

The accumulation of such a sizeable implementation 'deficit' during the past 25 years raises grave doubts about the overall effectiveness of EU environmental policy at resolving, as distinct from simply addressing, environmental problems. In this chapter it is argued that the gap between the declared objectives of EU environmental policies and their political effect raises interesting theoretical questions about the process of task expansion (Jordan, 1997a, 1997b, 1999b). Systematic non-compliance poses a particularly awkward problem for those who claim that European integration has developed its own expansive logic, which states struggle to control even when they act in concert (see Zito, 1999). On the contrary, by controlling the speed of implementation states seem able to fine-tune European regulations to domestic political and economic exigencies, thereby checking the speed and scope of the integration process. For 'new' realists the implementation deficit plaguing EU environmental policy is no accident – it is the *inevitable* corollary of developing an elaborate multilevel environmental governance system. However, it is not immediately clear why there should be compliance problems at all if the EU is, as realists claim, dominated by states'.[2] Specifically, why do states not 'erode' (Hogwood, 1987, p180) policies they regard as unfavourable at the decision-making phase rather than undergo all the uncertainties and political embarrassment associated with protracted infringement proceedings?

What is an Implementation Deficit?

The EU was by no means unique in neglecting the implementation of policy. Implementation has often been the poor relation of policy analysis, only emerging as a separate focus of sustained academic study in the late 1960s (Jordan, 1996). Those that rushed to respond to Pressman and Wildavsky's *cri de coeur* discovered that the enunciation of a policy was not a predictable, bureaucratic operation, but was often just the beginning of a decisive process of determining what actually happens on the ground (Sabatier, 1986). More often than not, implementation involves intense political interaction between those who framed the policy in the first place and those charged with implementing it. Accordingly, it is misleading to think of there being a sharp distinction between policy-making and implementation – the two are interconnected. What is especially curious about implementation in the EU, however, is that, in sharp contrast to national policies, Member States are simultaneously the policy-makers – the power to adopt policies rests with the Council of Ministers – and the primary implementing agents (although many functions are performed by subcentral actors and in some policy areas the Commission enjoys substantial management powers of its own).

The terms implementation 'deficit' and 'gap' are normally used in 'top-down' accounts of implementation (see Ham and Hill, 1993, pp97–113) to describe the shortfall between the goals embodied in particular directives and their practical effect in Member States. But there are other, equally valid, perspectives on implementation. Weale (1992, p45) has developed a simple 2×2 matrix which differentiates between four different types of deficit (table 17.1). Following Easton (1965) he distinguishes between policy outputs 'the laws, regulations and institutions that governments employ in dealing with policy problems' (Weale, 1992, p45) and policy outcomes ('the effects of those measures upon the state of the world'). Most implementation analyses are designed to investigate the extent to which policy outputs conform to the objectives set out in legislation (cell 1). In other words, was the necessary implementing legislation enacted or were new government agencies put in place? In the EU, this involves transposing European policies into national law and nominating national competent authorities. Many of the 'black-letter' accounts of implementation by lawyers fall into this category.

Table 17.1   *Types of implementation failure*

Orientation to problem	Focus of analysis	
	policy output	policy outcome
Orientation to policy goals	1	2
Orientation to policy problem	3	4

What such studies conspicuously fail to address, however, is the 'real' implementation problem: delivering political outcomes. Accordingly, implementation studies can also investigate whether policy outcomes match the goals set out in a policy (cell 2). Important research questions here include establishing whether polluting emissions were reduced by the required amount and calculating the corresponding impact on environmental quality. Intuitively, these seem more pertinent given that the ultimate purpose of EU policy is to safeguard the environment. Sabatier (1986) argues that such an approach usefully reveals whether the causal theory embodied in a policy is sound. Studies undertaken from the 'bottom up' have shown that some policies are ineffective not because they are poorly implemented but because they are poorly conceived (Hill, 1997).

This chapter is mainly concerned with cells 1 and 2, but it is important to be aware of at least two other types of deficit which receive less recognition in the continuing debate about implementation in the EU. These relate to situations in which policy outputs (cell 3) and outcomes (cell 4) are insufficient to address the underlying policy problem. In other words, do the chosen policy outputs represent a *sufficient* response to the problem, given other possible alternatives? Is it, for instance, possible to conceive of a better package of outputs which, for whatever reason, was not adopted? For Weale (1992, p46) this somewhat wider perspective is justified because 'sins of omission may be as important as sins of commission' in explaining why things are not achieved by the policy process (p46).³ The questions suggested by cells 3 and 4 are not only normative but also somewhat hypothetical. The likelihood of reaching clear answers is not going to be that great. Take type 4 implementation deficits, for example. First, the analyst would need to specify a desirable mix of policy instruments to tackle a particular problem, then he or she would have to investigate the likelihood of their being implemented: not easy!

Many analysts would instinctively shy away from such questions on the grounds that they are speculative or too normative. This wider, more political, perspective does, however, raise profound questions about the ability of the policy process to solve problems, about where 'policy' should be determined (that is, whether in the Environment Council or during the process of implementation), and about how goal shortfall should be interpreted. For instance, does the Habitats Directive provide a sufficient response to biodiversity loss in Europe? Is the EU's climate-change strategy sufficiently stringent in the light of the best scientific predictions of future damage? Lenschow's account (1999) of the barriers to environmental policy integration is a good example of a type 3 implementation failure.

Scharpf (1988) argues that the multilevel arrangement of the EU renders it vulnerable to 'joint decision-making traps' which drag policies down to the lowest common denominator of state preferences. Although history shows that joint decision-making has not retarded the development of the environmental *acquis,* it is important to remember that possibly the most fundamental, but elusive, implementation 'problem' of all is the loss of the most progressive policy proposals during the process of policy framing. And, of course, gaps between the 'ideal' mix of policy outputs and what eventually emerges from the policy process stand a good chance of being widened still further by Member States if they choose to sabotage the policy during the implementation process proper.

The 'Unpolitics' of Implementation

In political science it is just as important to explain why certain issues fail to make the political agenda for debate and decision-making (the 'unpolitics' of policy-making) as it is to account for what actually emerges from the policy process in the form of laws and policies (Crenson, 1971). Until relatively recently, the implementation of the environmental acquis was a taboo subject, rarely discussed in policy circles. None of the major players had any reason to raise its political profile, so a conspiracy of silence prevailed. For obvious reasons states prefer not to advertise their own failings and there is a well-established 'gentleman's agreement' not to draw attention to one another's failings. I explained in my introductory paper (Jordan, 1999b) that the Commission had good reason to concentrate on building a framework of environmental law given the absence of a firm treaty base for the environment. Writing in the mid-1980s, Rehbinder and Steward (1985, p238) observed that the Commission had 'never tried to probe into the actual implementation and enforcement activities of Member States'. The Third Environmental Action Programme (OJ 1983) dealt with implementation in just three lines, and the first ever book written on EU environmental policy by a well-known 'insider' devoted only two pages to formal compliance and said nothing at all about practical compliance (Johnson, 1979).[4] According to one British Minister, David Trippier, it was not until an Environment Council meeting in 1991 that the states 'actually studied what had gone on in the past; what was already on the European statute book; how it was being monitored and enforced' (HOLSCEC, 1992b, p185).

There are at least four interlinked reasons why implementation languished in the political doldrums throughout the 1970s and early 1980s: political symbolism, the depth of European integration, bureaucratic politics and institutional power relations.

Political Symbolism

In the past, EU environmental policy was commonly appraised on the basis of the amount of legislation adopted rather than its effectiveness at solving environmental problems. During his long tenure in the UK Department of the Environment (DoE), William Waldegrave (HOLSCEC, 1987, p12) observed that the sharing of the Presidency of the EU among the Member States on a rotating six-monthly basis created an unhealthy competition to agree as much legislation as possible. In the 1970s and early 1980s the political profile of the environment remained low, and public pressure on the Commission to track the implementation of directives was not that great.

Extent of European Integration

According to Macrory (1992a, p350) many of the first laws were adopted when directives were commonly viewed as a 'commitment of policy intention' rather than a 'genuine legal obligation'. In advance of a firm indication from the ECJ that directives were binding in their entirety, a distinctly *de minimis* view of European law prevailed. The British in particular regarded environmental directives as 'flexible instruments, the implementation of which could take considerations of finance, time and vested interests into account' (Haigh and Lanigan, 1995, p23). However, if Pierson (1996) is to be believed, the tendency for national politicians to claim the political credit for EU policies without inquiring too closely into the possible long-term implications is not unique to environmental policy.

Bureaucratic Politics

During the first decade of EU environmental policy, the Commission concentrated upon establishing Community competence and enhancing its own bureaucratic position, leaving the economic and technical aspects of implementation to Member States. Community-wide compliance-cost assessments were rarely, if ever, undertaken (Pearce, 1998). Other Directorates-General of the Commission regarded DG XI as a weak and peripheral player and did not scrutinize its proposals as carefully as they do now. Significantly, the policy process at the European level was institutionally 'thinner' and much more technocratic than it is today, so many of the first directives sailed through the adoption phase relatively unopposed (see Jordan, 1999b).

Institutional Power Relations

Responsibility for implementing EU law is apportioned by the founding Treaties. Article 155 identifies the Commission as the legal 'guardian of the treaties' with responsibility for ensuring their provisions are applied. The Commission may take action under Article 169 against non-compliant states. But the treaties leave open the matter of how cases of non-compliance are to be processed. Consequently, the Commission has developed its own informal enforcement procedure. However, Article 130r(4) makes it abundantly clear that, subject to strictly limited and carefully delineated exceptions, Member States are primarily responsible for undertaking the implementation of measures adopted by the Council. As far as environmental protection is concerned, the EU therefore breaches Stalin's First law of 'sound' governance; its primary task is to propose and to adopt policy, not to implement it. This unequal sharing of competences leaves the Commission, which is not directly elected, in a weak and 'invidious position' (Williams, 1994). It prefers not to stir up trouble with non-compliant states in case it endangers the wider integrationist project or offends the publics which elected them.

The common exceptions are when a particular state's behaviour is plainly egregious or when national groups strongly support enforcement action (Puchala, 1975, p513). It is only when the Commission senses an opportunity to 'cultivate' political spillover by responding to national political demands for fuller implementation that it directly and openly confronts states (Jordan, 1999a).

The Politicization of Implementation

Since the mid-1980s, a number of factors have pushed the issue of implementation up the political agenda in Europe. These include the following ten factors.

*   *The internal market programme:* in the 1980s awareness grew, particularly within industry circles, of the need for comparable regulatory effort in order to promote free and fair competition (Anderson, 1988; Weiler, 1988). It was immediately obvious to Lord Cockfield, the chief architect of the programme, though not, it seems, to state officials, that the internal market would remain a paper exercise unless and until the 300 proposals mentioned in the Commission's 1985 White Paper were put fully into effect. But in supporting the programme, sceptical states were forced to acknowledge, perhaps unwittingly, the need for the EU to be vested with greater regulatory powers than had hitherto been the case.[6] The programme also underlined the need for evenhanded enforcement by supranational agents, especially the Commission.
*   *The growth of the environmental acquis:* a body of binding legislation is a vital prerequisite for an implementation 'problem'. By the mid-1980s, the EU had adopted over 200 environmental statutes.
*   *Greater unity of purpose:* the 1980s witnessed an increasingly common environmental agenda among Member States, covering cross-border issues such as acid rain, ozone depletion and marine pollution. Only when this was established could actors supporting the inclusion of high environmental standards in legislation turn their attention to the achievement of policy outcomes.
*   *Rulings by the European Court:* from the 1960s the Court sought to emphasize the supremacy and 'direct effect' of EU legislation (Macrory, 1992a, p351).[7] According to neofunctionalist (see Chapter 10) legal scholars, its rulings followed a much more 'maximalist' interpretation of EU law and were made against the wishes of states (Alter, 1998).
*   *Institutional crises:* the disappearance of several drums of chemical waste from a chemical factory in Seveso, Italy, in 1982, prompted the European Parliament to establish its first ever committee of inquiry (ENDS, 1984). The committee pushed the Commission to take a much tougher line and to publish and disseminate information.
*   *Pressure from EU institutions:* members of the European Parliament were instrumental in forcing the Commission to develop improved surveillance apparatus and to publish annual reports on implementation, starting in 1983.

- *Growing public concern:* the number of official complaints submitted by individuals and pressure groups to DG XI about poor compliance mushroomed from just 9 in 1984 to over 460 in 1989 (Wägenbaur, 1990, p462). The Commission designated 1987 'European environment year' in recognition of the growing public interest in environmental matters.
- *Environmental campaigning:* as well as submitting complaints, national environmental pressure groups began to publicize suspected breaches and to call governments to account.
- *Passing of deadlines for full compliance:* many of the water directives adopted in the 1970s were to have been fully implemented by the mid-1980s.
- *Greater academic interest in the impact of the acquis:* Haigh's handbook (1984) established a new research agenda which others soon followed (Siedentopf and Ziller, 1988).

Above all, the fundamental transformation of EU environmental policy in the 1980s (Jordan, 1999b) profoundly altered the *nature* of the commitments that states had willingly entered into when environmental concern and support for integration were much less pronounced. Weiler (1988) ascribes the subsequent tightening of the legal and political context of directive framing and implementation to 'judicial activism' ('law without political consensus') on behalf of the Court. The 'supremacy' and 'direct effect' doctrines, which were not included in the Treaty of Rome but derive from Court judgements in the 1960s and 1970s, have, Macrory believes (1991, p227), helped to blur the traditional distinction between regulations and directives:

> *Member states can no longer consider the commitments contained within Directives as representing best intentions similar to those contained within conventional international treaties. Instead, they must be considered as real legal obligations, giving rise to potential legal action both before national courts and the European Court.*

Heightened public expectations, more strenuous pressure-group campaigning, and greater public support for EU environmental policy also played a big part in making non-compliance a live political issue in Europe. The internal market programme in particular galvanized political support for fuller implementation. The Commission's influential 1985 White Paper on the completion of the internal market drew attention to the 'large volume of complaints' received about poor implementation and argued that efforts to ensure the free movements of goods and services would 'be in vain if the correct application of rules is not ensured' (CEC, 1985, p12).

Individual personalities were also important. The environment commissioner in the period 1985–89, Stanley Clinton-Davis (4 July, 1996, interview with author), a lawyer inculcated with a strong respect for the 'sanctity' of the law, began to raise at Environment Council meetings the issue of poor implementation, encouraged the Commission's Legal Service to push the most serious breaches, and tried to rationalize enforcement procedures by dealing with groups of cases rather than dealing with cases individually. He favoured a more *proactive* and interventionist approach, and targeted *practical* compliance problems rather than simply 'paper' failures of transposition and notification (Table 17.2).

Table 17.2 *European Union environmental policy: Infringement proceedings, 1982–1990*

Year	Incomplete transposition	Non-notification[a]	Poor application[b]	Total
1982	1	15	0	16
1983	10	23	2	35
1984	15	48	2	65
1985	10	58	1	69
1986	32	84	9	125
1987	30	68	58	156
1988	24	36	30	90
1989	17	46	37	100
1990	24	131	62	217
Total	163	509	201	873

[a] A failure to inform the European Commission of national implementation measures
[b] A failure to achieve the necessary practical policy outcomes
Source: Jordan, 1997a

His successor, the flamboyant and outspoken Italian socialist Carlo Ripa di Meana, was equally unwilling to engage in bargaining games with errant states (Haigh and Lanigan, 1995, pp24–5). Rather than following the convention of keeping correspondence between the Commission and national governments confidential, both he and Clinton-Davis publicized cases – even holding press conferences in some cases.

A standard form was produced to streamline the official complaints procedure. The arrival of Ludwig Kramer, a German environmental lawyer, in DG XI's enforcement section was an equally important factor in the politicization of implementation. Well known for his green attitudes, he disliked secrecy, believed strongly in public participation, and refused to compromise on issues of legal principle (Krämer, 1989). Kramer set about the task of enforcing environmental directives with much greater vigour than any of his predecessors, embroiling the Commission in a series of politically controversial standoffs with Member States, over polluted water and environmental impact assessment.

These mounting levels of concern provoked a range of institutional responses. The June 1990 European Summit of state leaders in Dublin declared that 'Community environmental legislation will only be effective if it is fully implemented and enforced by Member States'. A political declaration attached to the Maastricht Treaty emphasized that 'each Member State should fully and accurately transpose into national law the Community Directives addressed to it within the deadlines laid down', to ensure that EU law is 'applied with the same effectiveness and rigour [as] ... national law' (see Chapter 3).

Since 1984 the Commission has presented an annual report to the European Parliament on the application of EU law, though they say more about transposition than practical implementation. Implementation was a cornerstone of the

Fourth (1987–1992) Action programme (OJ 1987), and the Fifth (1993–2000) (OJ 1992a) devotes a full chapter to implementation and enforcement issues.

The Causes of the Implementation 'Deficit'

In many respects, the tension – or what Weiler (1981) terms the 'dualism' – between the intergovernmental and supranational aspects of the EU is more starkly revealed in the implementation phase than in any other. Somehow, a *supranational* legal order spun by actors with maximalist beliefs has to be reconciled with a state-dominated system of policy implementation. Scharpf (1994, pp221–2) argues that the' EU's capacity for autonomous action is severely curtailed. In stark contrast to fully federated states such as Germany or the US, it lacks a common political culture and public opinion, political parties operating at both levels of governance, and a high degree of economic and cultural homogeneity. It also has a relatively small and largely non-executant bureaucracy. In contrast to other policy fields such as competition, merger control, or fisheries protection,[8] DG XI does not have direct powers of enforcement; in the very places that EU environmental policy is supposed to 'bite' – in factories and on river banks and beaches – it has little or no physical presence.

The Commission is also disadvantaged by the preferred tool of EU environmental policy – the *directive*. Directives are so called because they direct Member States to legislate or take other effective action. They are binding in terms of the overall objective to be achieved but leave states to determine the detailed arrangements for putting them into practice. Not surprisingly, Member States almost always prefer directives to other forms of regulation because they offer sufficient flexibility to address local peculiarities. EU law is thus deliberately *flexible* to allow for adjustment to national circumstances. Crucially, directives are primarily addressed to Member States. In legal parlance, they have a direct effect on states or their 'emanations' (vertical direct effect) as distinct from the private bodies or persons (horizontal direct effect) upon whom compliance often depends. Even the Commission's ultimate sanction, a reference to the ECJ, is a relatively blunt weapon. Although the ECJ can rule that Member States are in breach of EU environmental law, it has virtually no power to enforce its decisions, being, for instance, unable to send erring ministers to prison. There are Member States who have still not complied with environmental rulings issued by the Court in the early 1990s (see Macrory and Purdy, 1997, Appendix 1).

That said, states remain under a legal obligation to implement EU legislation. Crucially, the power to determine the extent of that obligation rests with supranational bodies – ultimately the ECJ – not states. Given that complete disavowal of EU obligations is illegal and often politically unfeasible, most enforcement disputes between the Commission and Member States therefore centre on the precise timing and extent of implementation rather than on whether it should proceed at all. Enforcement therefore is not top-down but is informal, involving bargaining and negotiation. The Commission cannot command national or subnational actors, public or private, and it normally only resorts to court proceedings when it has exhausted every diplomatic avenue (Snyder, 1993).

Several other features of EU environmental policy exacerbate implementation problems, as follows:

- *Policies tend to have vague and/or contradictory objectives:* this is in many respects inevitable given the need to reach consensus in the Council of Ministers, and the Commission's tendency to concentrate on getting laws adopted without worrying too much about problems buried away in the fine print (Collins and Earnshaw, 1992, p225; Wyatt, 1998).
- *Issues pertinent to implementation are disregarded during the process of negotiation:* the Commission allegedly proposes, and some states accept the principle of, legislation without paying sufficient attention to the practicalities of implementation (HOLSCEC, 1992a, 1997). Their Lordships believe that the EU should think in terms of a 'regulatory chain' through which implementation and enforcement issues are considered when policies are designed and adopted.
- *Legislation is poorly drafted and prepared:* specialist legal draftspeople are not always involved as early or as intensively as they might be (Bennett, 1993, p27; Macrory and Purdy, 1997, p46).
- *The body responsible for proposing legislation, the Commission, is not substantially responsible for its application and implementation:* this may explain why some proposals are not as well drafted as they might be (Weiler, 1988, p352) and the absence of comprehensive compliance-cost assessments.
- *There is an absence of powerful and committed 'vested interests':* it is a common characteristic of environmental politics that the interests fighting for public goods such as environmental quality are politically weak and geographically dispersed (HOLSCEC, 1992b, p5).
- *There is too little consultation with affected parties:* the Commission does not always use advisory committees as well as it might (HOLSCEC, 1992a, p9), and much of the scientific and technical advice used to prepare proposals is not made public (HOLSCEC, 1997, pp15–18). The activities of the hundreds of COREPER and comitology committees which implement and amend policies are shrouded in secrecy (for a more detailed analysis, see Docksey and Williams, 1994; Dogan, 1997).
- *Enforcement proceedings are slow, secretive, inflexible, complex and dominated by states and the Commission:* following the tradition in international diplomacy, the legal correspondence between the Commission and Member States remains strictly confidential.[9] Complainants are not always notified and the Commission is under no obligation to explain the reasons for its decisions.[10] Individuals and pressure groups have limited means of redress, being unable to take public interest cases against non-compliant states before the ECJ, unless they are directly and individually concerned (that is, when they can establish *locus standi*).[11]

How Big is the Implementation Deficit?

The 15 Member States of the EU are large, mature democracies with relatively well-developed bureaucracies. Therefore one would imagine that estimating what has or has not been achieved is a relatively straightforward task; after all, a directive is either implemented or it is not implemented. Nearly three decades of implementation research has, however, revealed that the size of the deficit is hugely dependent upon the normative standpoint of the observer and the criteria used (Hill, 1997). Indeed, the very word 'deficit' implies that policy distortion is somehow undesirable when it may be an unavoidable corollary of, inter alia, unforeseen events and changing political priorities.

In his *Manual of EU Environmental Policy*, Haigh (1992, Section 1.4) distinguishes between *formal* compliance (the legal process of transposing EU law into national legislation) and *practical* compliance (determining whether the ends specified in the directive are actually achieved). These two correspond with cells 1 and 2 in Table 17.1. Consequently, there are two main implementation gaps: the first relating to *legal transposition,* the second to the *practical implementation* and enforcement of laws. Macrory (1992a, p354) argues that the first are difficult but by no means impossible for the Commission to detect,[12] requiring scrutiny of the relevant national legislation, whereas the latter can be extremely difficult to identify. This is because the Commission is almost entirely dependent upon Member States reporting back on what they are actually doing, on costly and time-consuming consultancy reports, or on whatever national environmental groups and private actors choose to submit via the formal complaints procedure (Wilkinson, 1994). A recent House of Lords report concluded that the problems of collecting and assessing information 'make any comprehensive assessment of Member States' compliance with EU obligations virtually impossible at this stage' (HOLSCEC, 1992a, p26).[13] DG XI's powers of inquiry are limited to seeking comments from Member States. On-site visits and other 'spot checks' by Commission officials are of limited value: they are usually extremely time-consuming, politically fraught, and can easily be blocked by Member States who are under no legal obligation to co-operate. Consequently, they tend to be undertaken infrequently.[14] The Commission's reliance on other actors to flag lapses in compliance is amply reflected in the figures presented in Table 17.3.

Even if the Commission had access to all the information it needed, it is debatable whether it has the resources to chase up every errant Member State.[15] There is one 'desk officer' in DG XI's enforcement unit [about 0.002% of the total work force (490 in 1996–1997)] assigned to deal with all suspected cases of

Table 17.3 *Suspected infringements, 1988–1994: Origins*

Origin	Year						
	1988	1989	1990	1991	1992	1993	1994
Complaints	929	1199	1274	1052	1185	1040	1145
Parliamentary questions	82	46	32	126	45	30	5
Petitions	8	105	18	18	33	23	6
Cases detected by Commission	752	962	268	237	282	247	277
Total	1771	2312	1592	1433	1545	1340	1433

Sources: OJ, 1991, 1995

non-compliance in each Member State. It is no wonder that there is an average delay of six years between the Commission first receiving a complaint and a judgement by the Court (Krämer, 1995, p136). Nor is it surprising that the Commission concentrates on areas where it can achieve some success, namely enforcing formal rather than practical compliance, and combating what it considers to be the most egregious breaches of the law.

The situation changed markedly in the late 1980s, although restrictions on private enforcement action still leave the Commission to shoulder most of the responsibility.[16] Proceedings relating to practical compliance grew significantly, reflecting both Clinton-Davis's desire for stronger enforcement and vocal demands from national pressure groups for the law to be fully and, perhaps more importantly, consistently enforced. It is notable, however, that the majority of environmental cases that reach the ECJ have tended to be brought by the Commission under the Article 169 procedure, rather than by individuals (Article 173) and Member States (Article 170), or via references from national courts (Article 177) (Sands, 1990, p694).

It is unwise to rely too heavily on the Commission's data when searching for trends and patterns (Macrory and Purdy, 1997, p39; Williams, 1994, p374). First and foremost, the recent rise in complaints and infringement proceedings may simply reflect the Commission's determination to tighten up on enforcement rather than increasing lawlessness among Member States. The Commission routinely acknowledges that failures are more often the product of inefficiency and incompetence on behalf of states than deliberate disobedience. It is also significant that the majority of cases still relate to failures of formal rather than practical implementation. Second, just as in national and local contexts, legal enforcement is an exceedingly complicated activity, involving bargaining and the application of discretion. Consequently, many potential or 'real' implementation problems fail to appear in the Commission's figures. Snyder (1993, p29) shows that the Commission relies heavily on the tried and tested techniques of quiet negotiation and bargaining to accelerate compliance in spite of the rhetorical commitment to tougher enforcement. For instance, an Article 169 letter sent to Britain in 1991 regarding compliance with the drinking water directive was apparently preceded by no less than ten written exchanges and three meetings (Collins and Earnshaw, 1992, p228). In fact, a guide from the UK Department of Environment, Transport and the Regions (DETR) to negotiating in the EU openly extols the benefits of quiet persuasion to lobby Commission officials:

> *Infraction cases are more like civil than criminal proceedings. Discussion, compromise and the application of reason are all permitted. Therefore informal channels of communication are kept open ... .This is one of the more occult areas of the infraction system and should not be discussed openly, particularly with colleagues from other Member States (who seem to make much less use of such channels). [DETR] officials can have an important role to play in convincing the Commission that the UK Government's case is a good one* (Humphreys, 1996, pp131–2).

Even when formal proceedings are initiated, something like 80 per cent are settled before they go to court (CEC, 1997, p8). Court cases tend to be long-winded, extremely complicated, stretch the Commission's meagre resources, and endanger the goodwill of states. Decisions to take cases to the Court are not taken lightly; they must be sanctioned by the Commission's Legal Services and receive the support of the College of Commissioners. Being so political, recourse to court proceedings is normally considered as a very last resort.

For obvious reasons, the Commission adopts a tougher stance in relation to high-profile cases which have been the subject of complaints from the public (Krämer, 1989, p246). Pressure groups provide DG XI with the 'eyes and ears' it needs to detect infringements and the political legitimacy to confront recalcitrant states. But as Krämer (1995, p142) himself admits, a public demand-led approach, although in some respects inevitable, is biased towards the most politically contentious issues which are 'not necessarily the most serious or the most urgent cases'.

Attempts to draw cross-national comparisons should also be interpreted with caution as they often say more about a particular state's internal administrative culture and political relations with the Commission than about the actual quality of the environment (see Tables 17.4 and 17.5). Other important factors include the energy of national pressure groups and the appetite of different national media for environmental stories. Krämer's (1995, p143) comment about infringement proceedings making a bigger splash in Britain with its 'outstanding, highly sensitive journalism' reveals a lot about the Commission's political strategies. Longitudinal analyses are also made difficult by the Commission's reluctance to adopt a consistent approach to reporting its findings (see Macrory and Purdy, 1997).

Table 17.4 *Progress in notifying environmental directives, 1996*

Country	Directives applicable on 31 December 1996	Directives for which measures were notified	
		number	percentage
Denmark	136	133	98
The Netherlands	136	133	98
Luxembourg	136	131	96
Germany	138	132	96
Ireland	136	130	96
Sweden	134	127	95
UK	136	128	94
Austria	132	124	94
Portugal	140	131	94
Spain	140	131	94
France	136	126	93
Greece	141	128	91
Belgium	136	117	86
Finland	134	115	86
Italy	136	116	85

Source: CEC, 1997, page 107

Table 17.5 *Progress in notifying environmental measures, 1994–1996*

Country	Directives for which applicable on measures were 31 December notified (%)			Average
	1994	1995	1996	
Denmark	100	98	98	98.7
The Netherlands	98	98	98	98.0
Ireland	97	95	96	95.0
Sweden	na	94	95	94.5
France	94	95	93	94.0
Germany	91	94	96	93.4
Luxembourg	93	92	96	93.4
Austria	na	92	94	93.0
Spain	86	90	94	90.0
UK	82	93	94	90.0
Greece	85	88	91	88.0
Portugal	82	87	94	87.7
Finland	na	87	86	86.5
Belgium	85	83	86	84.7
Italy	76	85	85	82.0

na not applicable
Sources: CEC, 1997, p107; OJ 1995, 1996b

Bearing in mind these complicating factors, can we say whether implementation is comparatively worse in the environmental Field than in other policy areas? The Commission's own figures suggest that they are (OJ 1996b), although there is a long tradition of poor compliance in the areas of competition and the internal market. Between 1988 and 1992, the ECJ made more rulings on environmental matters than in any other field except the internal market (DG III), and customs and indirect taxation (DG XXI) (OJ 1993b, p108). This is relatively high bearing in mind that the Commission normally prioritizes breaches relating to internal market legislation. Again, official figures should be treated with caution. Obvious distortions include the conflictual style of national environmental politics in some countries and the limited means of legal redress at the national level.

Closing the Implementation Gap

A number of measures have been proposed to ease the EU's implementation problem. These include, inter alia:

- creating a centralized environment inspectorate with powers to investigate alleged breaches and levy fines;

- allowing the Commission to take proceedings against local implementing officials and subnational actors;
- devolving justice to the national level by allowing citizens to take action in national courts;
- creating an enforceable right to environmental quality on a par with the right to free movement of goods enshrined in Article 30;
- making greater use of regulations rather than directives;[17]
- improving the poor record of reporting both by Member States and by the Commission;
- improving the legal and technical drafting of directives;
- making greater use of non-regulatory instruments such as taxes, tradable permits and voluntary agreements;
- reducing the national veto by extending the application of qualified majority voting (QMV);
- providing greater financial assistance to the 'cohesion' states in the south of the EU;
- making the Article 169 procedure more transparent and open to independent scrutiny.

Many of these are deeply at odds with the realpolitik of the EU which, despite all the evidence of greater supranationality, is still dominated by 15 Member States, each with its own political culture, set of legal traditions, administrative practices, economic structures and environmental circumstances. Given this heterogeneity, slow or at least *differential* implementation is probably inevitable. The question, then, is one of determining precisely how far national practices should be allowed to deviate from European norms. From DG XI's perspective, striking the right balance is extremely difficult:

> *The legal culture is different from one Member State to the other and inevitably where you have a uniform product, an EEC made Directive, and it meets this different legal culture it is differently absorbed, differently integrated and also differently perceived which makes it rather difficult sometimes to get the right balance between ... national considerations and the purposes and spirit of what was decided at Community level* (Krämer, in HOLSCEC, 1992b, p12).

These dilemmas will be instantly familiar to those who subscribe to a more bottom-up view of implementation. For them, implementation involves bargaining and negotiation, not rigid, top-down control. 'Bottom-uppers' would tend therefore to take a more sanguine view of the implementation 'crisis' in the EU, viewing it as the inevitable outcome of trying to squeeze a diverse group of states into a common framework.

Of course, the Commission understands full well the political constraints it is under and has learnt to think tactically and to act cautiously. One only has to look at the chapter on implementation in the Fifth Action Programme to see this. This Programme contains a number of proposals to: strengthen consultation (via the creation of a number of 'strategic groups' linking national inspectorates and interest groups); increase national reporting; enhance auditing; and promote the use of non-regulatory instruments. Reflecting the post-Maastricht demands for greater subsidiarity (see Chapter 3), the overarching theme is one of fostering 'joint responsibility' among actors, complementing the traditional top-down approach to enforcement (OJ, 1993a). Directives on standardized national reporting [Directive 91–692 (Haigh, 1992, Section 11.6)] and public access to environmental information, a British-inspired commitment to discuss implementation issues more regularly in the Council of Ministers, and an informal network of national inspectorates (IMPEL) were some of the main institutional initiatives designed to improve the flow of information. The Commission has also attempted to make the Article 169 process more transparent, by issuing press releases at each stage.

Some progress has been made in developing alternative instruments – the ecomanagement and audit scheme (EMAS) and ecolabelling schemes being prominent examples – but legislation remains the principal form of action. For the time being, the continuing need for unanimity in the Environment Council on all fiscal matters remains a formidable impediment to ecological tax reform. The continuing auto-oil programme aside, voluntary agreements are still conspicuous by their absence. IMPEL has concentrated on exchanging information on large industrial plant and is still a long way short of becoming what the UK once described as an 'inspectorate of national inspectorates'. A European Environment Agency (EEA) was established in 1994 after Jacques Delors campaigned for an environmental inspectorate. The prospect of Brussels bureaucrats taking water samples and scrutinising environmental records was greeted with great suspicion and even outright hostility by Member States. The establishment of the EEA was delayed for two years by a bitter dispute between states about where it would be sited. The information collected by the EEA will help clarify the precise situation in every Member State, but its remit is restricted to gathering and disseminating data. Despite strong pressure from MEPs, states were very careful to prevent it becoming involved in frontline enforcement and implementation activities. For the time being, it is almost entirely reliant on what Member States submit, being unable to undertake its own fact-finding missions.

Wilkinson (1992, p226) observes that better consultation and the use of soft (that is, non-legislative) instruments allows the Commission to achieve its environmental objectives without being seen to interfere directly in the affairs of Member States. There has, however, been no let up in its determination to enforce the acquis across all policy areas, despite a sharp decline in the number of public complaints (down 29 per cent in the period 1994–1996) (CEC, 1997, pp6–7).[18] In 1996, the Commission issued 435 reasoned opinions (a 224 per cent increase on 1995), made a record number of referrals to the ECJ (93 cases), and dispatched 1142 Article 169 letters (a 7 per cent increase on 1995).

Three macro-level initiatives were introduced by the Maastricht Treaty in 1993 (see Jordan, 1999b) which may help remedy the situation in the medium to long term, as follows.

• *Financial penalties for non-compliance:* Article 171 was amended to allow the ECJ to fine states that persistently disregard its rulings. The delay in ratifying the Treaty delayed their use and it was a further two and a half years before DG XI issued a communication explaining how it would calculate the level of daily fines (OJ 1996a, p6). The first applications were made by the Commission in 1997, but none has been the subject of a ruling by the Court. However, the fact that the majority of cases for which requests were made have been quickly settled does suggest that the new article is already having some practical impact.

- *Financial assistance for poorer states:* a cohesion fund was established to help the 'cohesion' Member States meet the cost of environmental improvements. Implementation of the urban wastewater treatment directive has been a major priority for the fund but, as Andrea Lenschow (1999) explains, investments are not subject to environmental safeguards and there is persistent criticism that individual projects are not always designed with sufficient environmental sensitivity.

- *Extension of QMV:* majority voting could prove to be a double-edged sword as far as implementation is concerned. On the one hand it may substantially upgrade the adoption of environmental legislation by ameliorating the 'joint decision trap'; on the other hand any improvement in the level of protection may be undone if states are forced to implement legislation they consider to be unacceptable. Implementation problems could in other words worsen not improve if states are robbed of the first part of their 'double veto' over European affairs (see Jordan, 1999b) (see Chapter 3).

It is notable that none of these initiatives significantly disturbs the institutional balance of power as far as implementation is concerned; vital questions will continue to be resolved by states and supranational actors, with little direct input from private actors. Despite the best efforts of the ECJ to establish a 'new legal order', conferring judicially enforceable rights and obligations on all legal persons, public, and private,[19] the opportunities for public interest litigation to protect the environment remain extremely limited. The Treaty does not provide for individuals to bring public interest litigation in environmental matters before the Court, many impediments prevent environmental laws having direct effect at the national level (Holder, 1996), and, despite much speculation, individuals have found it very difficult to obtain compensation under the Frankovich[20] ruling for damages suffered where a Member State has failed in its environmental duties.

In 1996 the Commission issued a communication (CEC, 1996) setting out its thoughts on how to improve implementation after the Commission and Parliament had co-organized public hearings in 1996. The tenor of the document is cautious and discursive; rather than announcing new policy interventions, many items are simply flagged for further discussion. As one might expect, the document is peppered with references to subsidiarity, shared responsibility and deregulation. Three new policy ideas are discussed in some detail, as follows.

1   *Development of EU-wide minimum criteria for inspection tasks in the Member States:* these would address matters such as site visits, inspection plans and public access to information.

2   *The setting of minimum criteria for handling complaints and carrying out investigations in Member States:* overloaded by complaints from the public and MEPs, the Commission is keen to devolve some of the burden of enforcement to the national level. It will therefore 'consider' the need for new ad hoc bodies, including national-level 'ombudsmen'.

3   *The issuing of guidelines on access to national courts:* the Commission has been actively exploring opportunities to widen public access to environmental justice at the national level for some time. On this occasion, legislation is rejected in favour of 'soft' interventions such as granting *locus standi* to non-governmental organizations 'recognized' by states, improving the clarity of EU rules, and raising awareness among national judges.

So far, there has been little administrative follow-up. The Environment Council duly adopted a resolution on implementation in 1997 reaffirming previous pledges to consider implementation matters more regularly, and the Belgian government appended a declaration on improving access to national courts [which gained the support of only three other states (Europe Environment, 1997)]. At the time of writing, the only legislative proposal to emerge relates to minimum criteria for site inspections. Although this will greatly enhance IMPEL's institutional position, it seems likely to be opposed by some Member States on the grounds that it interferes with subsidiarity (ENDS, 1998).

Future Challenges

The EU has travelled a long way from the essentially intergovernmental structure established by the Treaty of Rome, but states remain deeply reluctant to address the underlying cause of the implementation deficit, namely the structural imbalance in the institutional makeup of the EU. Clinton-Davis (1992, p201) is of the view that the only viable, long-term answer is to vest the Commission with the same powers it enjoys in the field of competition, fisheries and agriculture. However, persistently poor performance will only feed demands, which are currently muted, for greater EU competences. It is not, of course, inconceivable that the EEA will eventually develop into a centralized inspectorate with the same powers as those in the fisheries and competition fields, but for the moment the main levers of power remain firmly in the hands of states.

This decidedly informal and low-key political response to implementation will face its stiffest challenge as and when the EU enlarges eastwards to encompass parts of the former Eastern Bloc. A recent Communication from the Commission warned that 'none of the candidate countries of Central and Eastern Europe will be able to achieve full compliance with the environmental *acquis* in the short to medium term' (CEC, 1998). Early indications suggest that the environment will be the single most expensive policy area in the context of enlargement.[21]

To force the new entrants to achieve existing standards at a stroke would result in massive levels of non-compliance that could fatally undermine political confidence in the acquis communautaire. The Commission outlines two possible options:

1. negotiate strategies to align current national practices gradually with the acquis;
2. mobilize public and private resources to help the new entrants leapfrog polluting and resources-intensive technologies.

At the time of writing, entry negotiations are still at a very early and delicate stage. Decisions will eventually have to be made about which countries to invite first and which areas of legislation to give primacy to.

There is, of course, another line of argument which suggests that now implementation is so deeply politicized the gap will endure regardless of what is done to close it. On this view, which has obvious affinities with the neofunctionalist literature (see Chapter 10), the implementation deficit is regarded as a symbol not of policy failure, but of success measured in terms of heightened public expectations of higher environmental quality. Armed with handbooks explaining how to exploit EU law (EEB, 1994; Macrory, 1992b), domestic pressure groups in the existing Member States have come to expect higher levels of performance and will harass states that try to disavow their commitments. If this experience is replicated in the candidate countries of Eastern Europe over the next 25 years, we may have to accept large implementation deficits as a fact of life in the wider and more devolved Europe of the future.

In many important respects, the troublesome implementation of EU environmental policies is a microcosm of the wider story of integration and the conflicting forces and contradictions which have characterized the EU throughout its journey from an intergovernmental agreement to a multilevel polity. These contradictions include the maintenance of unity in diversity, the competition between national priorities and supranational imperatives, and the distribution of powers between actors at different spatial levels of government. If anything, they are more starkly revealed in the implementation phase when the EU's policies are put to the test than at earlier stages in the policy process, where symbolic gestures and rhetorical commitments are more likely to secure consensus. Implementation is at the sharp end of the EU policy process, where a burgeoning supranational legal order meets a decentralized policy delivery system dominated by states.

In this chapter I have argued that implementation deficits are built into the structure of the EU; they help to maintain the delicate 'balance' between governmental and supranational elements (Sbragia, 1993). It is significant that 'maximalist' agencies such as the Commission and the Parliament have been at the forefront of attempts to publicize and resolve failures of non-compliance, whereas Member States have sought to maintain a tight grip over policy delivery and ensure that it remains 'the last strong-hold of national control' (From and Stava, 1993). By setting the question of implementation in a wider political context, I hope to offer in this chapter a corrective to the common perception that EU policies are necessarily 'good and that poor implementation is necessarily pernicious. Rather, 'postdecisional' (Puchala, 1975) politics are an integral part of the continuing struggle between actors at different administrative levels to control the integration process.

Acknowledgements

I am extremely grateful to Tim O'Riordan and to two referees for their comments on earlier drafts of this chapter.

Notes

1. In 1960 the Community adopted just ten legal instruments; in 1993 it adopted 546 (Rometsch and Wessels, 1996, p33).
2. Krislov et al (1986, p61) refer to this as the 'paradox of non-compliance'.
3. Jordan and Richardson (1987, p238) make the telling point that there are 'probably more policies which are never introduced because of the anticipation of resistance, than policies which have failed because of resistance'.
4. At the time Johnson, who was formerly an official of the Environment and Consumer Protection Service, was Vice-Chairman of the European Parliament's Environment Committee. He later became a special adviser to the Director-General of DG XI.
5. This now has four stages, the first three being administrative, the final one legal: (1) writing informally to the state in question seeking clarification (a 'pre-Article 169 letter'); (2) issuing an 'Article 169 letter' to which the state in question is obliged to reply; (3) issuing a formal 'reasoned opinion', setting out the legal justification for commencing legal proceedings against the state; (4) bringing a case before the ECJ.
6. Even previously sceptical states became firm supporters of better implementation. Lord Cockfield (1994, p88) recalls that Margaret Thatcher, a redoubtable opponent of European political union, dispatched a note to each and every Member State government during the UK's 1986 Presidency encouraging them to speed up implementation of internal market measures.
7. Put simply, a directive may be enforced against the state or its 'emanations' (for example, local authorities and pollution-control agencies) in national courts if it is sufficiently precise to the rights granted and the ends to be achieved and if the date for implementation has passed (Krämer, 1996b). The direct effect doctrine is supposed to prevent states frustrating the objectives of policy by failing to enact implementing legislation. In a word, it gives EU law *autonomy:* unlike international law, EU law does not rely on the legal constitutions of the Member States.
8. The Commission can act on its own initiative to investigate anticompetitive situations, prevent governments subsidizing their industries if it prevents free and fair competition, and impose fines where it finds the law has been broken.
9. Williams (1994, pp384–394) provides a fascinating 'insider' perspective on the Commission's politically charged confrontation with the UK over the application of the environmental assessment directive.

10. Williams (1994, pp399–400) explains that the Commission's dual role as both the political 'motor' of European integration and the impartial enforcement authority put it in an 'invidious' position with regard to noncompliant states. He makes the case for 'radical' changes to restore public faith in the system, centring on an independent, open and accountable body with sufficient clout to conduct on-site investigations and confront states.

11. In a typically bullish article on the restrictions upon public interest litigation, Krämer (1996a) argues that the Commission is required by the Treaties to open proceedings when it detects an infringement. It *only* has the discretion to decide whether or not to seek a ruling from the ECJ. Correspondence between states and the Commission is not normally disclosed to third parties. Neither individuals nor the European Parliament can compel the Commission to open proceedings against a state. Their role is restricted to bringing suspected breaches to its attention. Without a more formal and better resourced system of enforcement, coupled to greater opportunities for public interest action by individuals, Krämer believes that the Commission will be 'over exposed' to political pressures in trying to fulfil its role as 'guardian of the environment' (1996a, p9).

12. This is not always the case. Some directives are transposed into national law by up to 50 or 60 separate pieces of legislation (HOLSCEC, 1992a, p2).

13. Of the 15 states, only three, Denmark, Finland and Sweden, regularly submit 'concordance tables' to the Commission, specifying the measures taken to transpose EU legislation into national law (CEC, 1997, p94).

14. In the period to 1987, only three had been undertaken (HOLSCEC, 1987, p12). Krämer (1995, p143) argues that they amount to little more than 'fact-finding missions' because their purpose is to clarify points rather than investigate instances of suspected noncompliance.

15. The EU has a total budget of less than 1.2 per cent of Community gross domestic product (GDP), 70 per cent of which is swallowed up by the Common Agricultural Policy and the structural funds.

16. Holder (1996, pp324–325) outlines the limits on the applicability of the direct effect and Francovich rulings in the environmental sphere.

17. The Sutherland Report recommended that all directives be transformed into regulations after a period of harmonization (CEC, 1993).

18. The number of environmental complaints received by the Commission fell by 27 per cent in the same period.

19. See especially the Court's ruling in *Van Gend en Loos* (C-26/62, ECR [1963], p1). For good accounts of the 'constitutionalization' of EU law see Wincott (1995) and Burley and Mattli (1993).

20. The Court's ruling in Frankovich permits individuals who have suffered losses as a result of a Member States' failure to implement directives to sue them in national courts for financial compensation for any damages thereby incurred. For Frankovich to apply, the directive in question must grant 'rights' to individuals, the content of those rights must be identifiable, and there must be a clear causal link between the failure to implement the directive and the damage for which compensation is being sought (see Somsen, 1996).

21. Provisional estimates put the cost of harmonization with existing environmental standards at ecu 120 billion – around a third of the total cost (ecu 300–400 billion) of implementing the acquis communautaire in new entrant states (Bjerregaard, 1998, p5).

References

Alter, K. (1998) 'Who are the "Masters of the Treaty"? European Governments and the ECJ', *International Organisation*, Vol.52, No.1, pp121–144.

Anderson, D. (1988) 'Inadequate Implementation of EEC Directives: A Roadblock on the Way to 1992', *Boston College International Comparative Law Review*, Vol.11, pp91–102.

Bennett, G. (1993) 'The Implementation of EC Environmental Directives' *The Science of the Total Environment*, Vol.129, pp19–28.

Bjerregaard, R. (1998) 'EU Enlargement – An Environmental Challenge', *UKCEED Bulletin*, pp525–6.

Burley, A. and Mattli, W. (1993) 'Europe before the Court', *International Organization*, Vol.47, No.1, pp41–76.

CEC (1985) COM(85) 310 final, 14 June, Commission of the European Communities, Brussels.

CEC (1993) *The Internal Market after 1992: Meeting the Challenge*, report to the EEC Commission by the High Level Group on the Operation of the Internal Market Commission of the European Communities, Brussels.

CEC (1996) COM(96) 500 final, 22 October, Commission of the European Communities, Brussels.

CEC (1997) COM(97) 229 final, 29 May, Commission of the European Communities, Brussels.

CEC (1998) *Agenda 2000: The Future for European Agriculture*, Directorate-General of Agriculture, Commission of the European Communities, Brussels.

Clinton-Davis, S. (1992) 'Memorandum by the Lord Clinton-Davis', in *Implementation and Enforcement of Environmental Legislation. Volume II – Evidence*, House of Lords Select Committee on the European Communities, House of Lords paper 53–11, The Stationery Office: London, pp200–201.

Cockfield, A. (1994) *The European Union*, Wiley Chancery Law: London.

Collins, K. and Earnshaw, D. (1992) 'The Implementation and Enforcement of EC Environmental Policy', *Environmental Politics*, Vol.1, No.4, pp213–249.

Crenson, M. A. (1971) *The Un-politics of Air Pollution*, John Hopkins University Press: Baltimore, Maryland.

Docksey, C. and Williams, K. (1994) 'The Commission and the Execution of Community Policy', in *The European Commission*, Edwards, G. and Spence, D. (eds), Cartermill: London, pp117–145.

Dogan, R. (1997) 'Comitology: Little Procedures with Big Implications', *West European Politics*, Vol.20, No.3, pp31–60.

Easton, D. (1965) *A Framework for Political Analysis*, Prentice-Hall: Englewood Cliffs, NJ.

EEB (1994) *Your Rights Under EU Environmental Legislation*, European Environmental Bureau: Brussels.

ENDS (1984) 'After Seveso: A New Focus on the Implementation of EEC Legislation', *ENDS Report 111*, April, pp9–10, Environmental Data Services Ltd, Unit 24, 40 Bowling Green Lane, London EC1R 0NE.

ENDS (1998) 'DG XI Plans Directive on Environmental Inspections', *ENDS Report 277*, February, pp43–44, Environmental Data Services Ltd, Unit 24, 40 Bowling Green Lane, London EC1R 0NE.

Europe Environment (1997) 'Ministers Debate EU Law, Voluntary Accords and Climate Change', 502, 24 June, pp5–6.

From, J. and Stava, P. (1993) 'Implementation of Community Law', in *Making Policy in Europe*, Andersen, S. and Eliassen, K. (eds), Sage: London, pp55–67.

Haigh, N. (1984) *EEC Environmental Policy and Britain*, Environmental Data Services Ltd, Unit 24, 40 Bowling Green Lane, London EC1R 0NE.

Haigh, N. (1992) *Manual of Environmental Policy*, Longman: Harlow, Essex.

Haigh, N. (1997) *Manual of Environmental Policy*, Cartermill: London.

Haigh, N. and Lanigan, C. (1995) 'Impact of the EU on UK Policy-making', in *UK Environmental Policy in the 1990s*, Gray, T. (ed), Macmillan, Basingstoke, Hants, pp18–37.

Ham, C. and Hill, M. (1993) *The Policy Process in the Modern Capitalist State*, Harvester Wheatsheaf: London.

Hill, M. (1997) 'Implementation Theory', *Policy and Politics*, Vol.25, pp375–385.

Hogwood, B. (1987) *From Crisis to Complacency*, Oxford University Press: Oxford.

Holder, J. (1996) 'A Dead End for Direct Effect?', *Journal of Environmental Law*, Vol.8, pp313–335.

HOLSCEC (1987) *Fourth Environmental Action Programme*, House of Lords, papers 25, House of Lords Select Committee on the European Communities, The Stationery Office: London.

HOLSCEC (1992a) *Implementation and Enforcement of Environmental Legislation: Volume 1 – Report*, House of Lords, Papers 53–1, House of Lords Select Committee on the European Communities, The Stationery Office: London.

HOLSCEC (1992b) *Implementation and Enforcement of Environmental Legislation: Volume II – Evidence*, House of Lords, Papers 53–11, House of Lords Select Committee on the European Communities, The Stationery Office: London.

HOLSCEC (1997) *Community Environmental Law: Making it Work*, House of Lords, Papers 12, House of Lords Select Committee on the European Communities, The Stationery Office: London.

Humphreys, J. (1996) 'A Way Through the Woods: Negotiating in the EU', Environmental Protection: Strategy Europe Division, Department of the Environment, London; published in a revised form as Humphreys J. (1996) *Negotiating in the European Union: How to Make the Brussels Machine Work for You*, Random House: London.

Johnson, S. (1979) *The Pollution Control Policy of the European Communities*, Graham and Trotman: London.

Jordan, A. (1996) 'Implementation Deficit or Policy-making? How do we Theorise the Implementation of EC Environmental Policy?', WP GEC 95–18, Centre for Social and Economic Research on the Global Environment, University of East Anglia, Norwich.

Jordan, A. (1997a) 'Overcoming the Divide between Comparative Politics and International Relations Approaches to the EC: What Role for "Post-decisional Polities"'?, *West European Politics*, Vol.20, No.4, pp43–70.

Jordan, A. (1997b) *Post-decisional Politics in the EC: The Implementation of EC Environmental Policy in the UK*, unpublished PhD thesis, School of Economic and Social Studies, University of East Anglia: Norwich.

Jordan, A. (1999a) 'EC Water Standards: Locked in or Watered Down?', *Journal of Common Market Studies*, Vol.13, No.1, pp13–37.

Jordan, A. (1999b) 'The Construction of a Multilevel Environmental Governance System', *Environment and Planning C: Government and Policy*, Vol.17, pp1–17.

Jordan, G. and Richardson, J. (1987) *British Politics and the Policy Process*, Allen and Unwin: London.

Krämer, L. (1989) 'Enforcement of Community Legislation on the Environment', *Journal of the Regional Science Association*, Vol.137 (March), pp243–248.

Krämer, L. (1995) *EC Treaty and Environmental Law 2nd edition*, Sweet and Maxwell: London.

Krämer, L. (1996a) 'Public Interest Litigation in Environmental Matters Before European Courts', *Journal of Environmental Law*, Vol.8, No.1, pp1–18.

Krämer, L. (1996b) 'Direct Effect of EC Environmental Law', in *Protecting the European Environment*, Somsen, H. (ed), Blackstone Press: London, pp99–134.

Krislov, S., Ehlermann, C. and Weiler, J. (1986) 'The Political Organs and the Decision-making Process in the US and the EC', in *Integration Through Law: Volume I, Book 2*, de Gruyter: The Hague.

Lenschow, A. (1999) 'The Greening of the EU: The Common Agricultural Policy and the Structural Funds', *Environment and Planning C: Government and Policy*, Vol.17, pp91–108.

Macrory, R. (1991) 'The Implementation and Enforcement of EC Eenvironmental Laws: A New Form of Federalism?', in *The Constitution and The Environment*, Clark, J., Cromelin, P. and Saunders, A. (eds), Centre for Comparative Constitutional Studies, University of Melbourne: Melbourne, pp223–241.

Macrory, R. (1992a) 'The Enforcement of Community Environmental Laws: Critical Issues', *Common Market Law Review*, Vol.29, pp347–369.

Macrory, R. (1992b) *Campaigners' Guide to Using EC Environmental Law*, Council for the Protection of Rural England, Warwick House, 25 Buckingham Palace Road, London SW1W 0PP.

Macrory, R. (1996) 'Environmental Citizenship and the Law', *Journal of Environmental Law*, Vol.8, No.2, pp219–235.

Macrory, R. and Purdy, R. (1997) 'The Enforcement of EC Environmental Law Against Member States', in *The Impact of EC Environmental Law in the UK*, Holder, J. (ed), John Wiley: Chichester, pp27–50 and 335–368 (addendum).

Majone, G. (1996) *Regulating Europe*, Routledge: London.

Mendrinou, M. (1996) 'Non-compliance and the European Commission's Role in Integration', *Journal of European Public Policy*, Vol.3, No.1, pp1–22.

OJ – Official Journal of the European Communities:

1983 26 C46, 17 February.

1987 30 C328, 7 December.

1991 34 C338, 31 December.

1992a 35 C138, 17 May.

1992b 35 C245M, 23 September.

1993a 36 C138, 17 July.

1993b 36 C233, 30 August.

1995 38 C254, 29 September.

1996a 39 C242, 21 August.

1996b 39 C303, 14 October.

Pearce, D. (1998) 'Environmental Appraisal and Environmental Policy in the European Union', *Environmental and Resource Economics*, Vol.11, pp489–501.

Pierson, P. (1996) 'The Path to European Integration', *Comparative Political Studies*, Vol.29, pp123–163.

Pressman, J. and Wildavsky, A. (1973) *Implementation*, University of California Press: Berkeley, CA.

Pressman, J. and Wildavsky, A. (1984) *Implementation*, 2nd edn, University of California Press: Berkeley, CA.

Puchala, D. (1975) 'Domestic Politics and Regional Harmonization in the European Communities', *World Politics*, Vol.27, pp496–520.

Rehbinder, E. and Steward, R. (1985) 'Environmental Protection Policy', in *Integration through Law, Volume II*, Capelletti, M., Seccombe, M. and Weiler, J. (eds), de Gruyter: Berlin, pp137–175.

Rometsch, D. and Wessels, W. (eds) (1996) *The EU and Member States*, Manchester University Press: Manchester.

Sabatier, P. (1986) 'Top-down and Bottom-up Approaches to Implementation Research', *Journal of Public Policy*, Vol.6, No.1, pp21–48.

Sands, P. (1990) 'European Community Environmental Law', *Modern Law Review*, Vol.53, pp685–698.

Sbragia, A. (1993) 'The EC: A Balancing Act?', *Publius: Journal of Federalism*, Vol.23, pp23–38.

Scharpf, F. (1988) 'The Joint Decision Trap', *Public Administration*, Vol.66, pp239–278.

Scharpf, F. (1994) 'Community and Autonomy: Multi-level Policy-making in the EU', *Journal of European Public Policy*, Vol.1, pp219–242.

Siedentopf, H. and Ziller, J. (1988) *Making European Policies Work*, Sage: London.

Snyder, F. (1993) 'The Effectiveness of European Community Law', *Modern Law Review*, Vol.56, No.1, pp19–54.

Somsen, H. (1996) 'Frankovich and its Application to EC Environmental Law', in *Protecting the European Environment*, Somsen, H. (ed), Blackstone Press: London, pp135–150.

Wägenbaur, R. (1990) 'European Communities Policies on Implementation of Environmental Directives', *Fordham International Law Journal*, Vol.14, pp455–477.

Weale, A. (1992) 'Implementation: A Suitable Case for Review', in *Achieving Environmental Goals*, Lykke, E. (ed), Belhaven Press: London, pp43–63.

Weiler, J. (1981) 'The Community System: The Dual Character of Supranationalism', *Yearbook of European Law*, Vol.1, pp257–306.

Weiler, J. (1988) 'The White Paper and the Application of Community Law', in *1992: One European Market?*, Bieber, R., Dehousse, R., Finder, J. and Weiler, J. (eds), Nomos: Baden-Baden, pp337–358.

Wilkinson, D. (1992) 'Maastricht and the Environment', *Journal of Environmental Law*, Vol.4, pp221–239.

Wilkinson, D. (1994) *The State of Reporting by the Commission in Fulfilment of Obligations Contained in EC Environmental Legislation*, Institute of European Environmental Policy, 52 Horseferry Road, London SW1P 2AG.

Williams, R. (1994) 'The European Commission and the Enforcement of Environmental Law: An Invidious Position', *Yearbook of European Law*, Vol.14, pp351–400.

Wincott, D. (1995) 'The Role of the Law or the Rule of the Court of Justice?', *Journal of European Public Policy*, Vol.2, pp583–602.

Wyatt, D. (1998) 'Litigating Community Environmental Law', *Journal of Environmental Law*, Vol.10, pp9–19.

Zito, A. R. (1999) 'Task Expansion: A Theoretical Overview', *Environment and Planning C: Government and Policy*, Vol.17, pp19–35.

18

European Environmental Policy by Stealth: The Dysfunctionality of Functionalism?

Albert Weale

Consider the following (paradoxical) features of European Union (EU) environmental policy:

1. The EU is an international organization founded on liberal principles, including the free movement of goods, services, capital and people. Yet in its approach to environmental policy it has made little use of economic instruments; less use indeed than have some countries more closely identified with social democracy than with economic liberalism.
2. The European Commission is formally and legally independent with respect to Member States. Yet in practice it is heavily dependent on those Member States both for the development of particular policy measures and for the enunciation of general policy principles.
3. The European Parliament is a latecomer to the EU institutional scene. Yet it has had more influence on environmental measures than is typically true for more well-established national parliaments.
4. Rational principles of institutional design would suggest that the EU should concentrate on the protection of environmental public goods at an international level. Yet the EU has often been active in policies for the protection of subnational local public goods such as urban air quality, bathing water and drinking water. How are we to understand these paradoxes?

In answer to this question my thesis in this chapter can be easily stated. All four features are related to one another as the effects of a common cause: European political unification 'by stealth' (Hayward, 1996), as implied by the Monnet method of institution-building. If this thesis is true, then it carries implications for the way in which we study European environmental policy. It is often said (indeed, I have said it myself) that, if it is to be successful, environmental policy needs to be integrated with other sectors of public policy, as environmental problems are typically the by-product or runoff of otherwise legitimate activities (industry, transport and agriculture). We also need to consider reverse influences, however. What effect does spillover from other policy sectors have on the shape and character of environmental policies? A central feature of the Monnet method of European integration is the establishement of conditions producing spillover of concerns from one policy sector to another. As a result, environmental policy in Europe needs to be studied as much as effect as cause.

The remainder of this chapter has three sections. In the first, I set out a characterization of the Monnet method, examining its effect on the development of EU environmental policy. The second looks at how the four paradoxes can be understood in the light of the Monnet method, and a brief concluding section considers the implications for institutional redesign suggested by the first two.

European Unification by the Monnet Method

The present EU system of environmental governance emerged from the Monnet method of European integration. This method is one of integration by stealth. Instead of confronting the major questions of constitutional principle involved in the integration of European societies, the Monnet method requires policy-makers to focus upon apparently technical matters of a 'low polities' variety in order to advance greater political co-operation among Member States. From this beginning it then posits: issue linkage and spillover from one policy sector to another; the indeterminate extension of such spillovers; the creation of a shared system of authority in which Member States are locked into a broad process of integration; and an emphasis upon continual momentum rather than the enjoyment of achievements (compare Schmitter, 1996). Although logically distinct from one another, these elements all share in common an emphasis upon process rather than end state.

At the European level the Monnet method has been remarkably successful. In retrospect it is easy to lose sight of the fact that, at the time when the European Coal and Steel Community (ECSC, the forerunner of the EU) was founded, there were a great many movements and projects offering models for European integration, including the European Union of Federalists, the International Committee for a Socialist United States of Europe, the United Europe Movement, the European League for Economic Co-operation, the European Parliamentary Union, and the proposals for the European Political Community and the European Defence Community (see Griffiths, 1995, pp14–28; Mazey, 1996, pp24–39). That the Monnet method emerged as the most successful approach in this highly competitive environment presumably says something about the way that its presuppositions and implications suited the political realities of the time.

As is well known, Monnet's own view was that European integration required a piecemeal pragmatic approach, rather than the implementation of a previously conceived grand design, and it was this belief that lay behind the stress on putting technical issues first. In his own memoirs, he stressed that the starting point for European integration had to be limited achievements, leading to de facto 'solidarity' from which a federation would grow. The notion of 'solidarity' appeared, for Monnet, to be defined in terms of the existence of common interests, created for example in the 'pooling' of coal and steel resources. He wrote that the ECSC provided for a breach in national sovereignty that was 'narrow enough to secure consent, but deep enough to open the way towards the unity that is essential to peace' (Monnet, 1978, p296). In this view, European integration had to be achieved by small incremental steps in policy sectors where issues of national sovereignty were not likely to be raised, rather than in the high politics of defence and foreign policy (compare Mazey, 1996, p29). Indeed, this was the main feature of Monnet's method that marked it out from contemporaneous attempts at European federalism.

As Hayward (1996, p252) has pointed out, this method has its origin in a French political system in which politicians had only a short expectation of high office in any government and in which bureaucrats were mere used to inertia than to innovation. In Hayward's view, such origins led to the founding of the EU by a few self-conscious agents of change. In these circumstances, elite, non-elected leadership, focusing upon apparently technical questions of economic harmonization, could accomplish much, establishing what Wallace (1996) has called 'government by committee', subsequently solidified in the EU's system of 'comitology'. European integration is thus a process of dealing with the 'low-polities' issues of the harmonization — more recently the mutual recognition — of standards to create the conditions for market integration. Conversely, and by implication, it is an important feature of this approach that large constitutional questions should be avoided or sidestepped.

Unification by stealth led to government by appointed officials chosen for their technical competence rather than for their political representativeness. Both Monnet and Hallstein stressed the importance of making the high authority of the ECSC independent of elected representatives in contrast to those who, like Dirk Spierenburg, wished for greater political control (Laursen, 1996). Hayes-Renshaw (1996) points out that the technocratic bias of the EU is reinforced by much Council business being settled through negotiations in COREPER.

The Monnet approach also depends on the idea of issue linkage. In other words, integration is not only focused on technical matters, it also involves an issue dynamic (which we can define as the set of further questions and issues which a solution to a particular policy problem involves) drawing broader considerations into the decision-making process, perhaps without anyone ever seeing that they are involved. Thus, just as the creation of a single market had a logic leading to a single currency (Cameron, 1992, pp25–7), so it also had a logic leading to the strengthening of environmental policy (Weale and Williams, 1992). Just as Monnet himself stressed the potential for industry and agriculture to provide the basis for the common interests which the pooling of sovereignty in certain spheres would enable, so, even in specific areas of policy, Monnet saw the solution to specific problems as raising general concerns, most notably the need for better communications if prosperity was to be achieved. As I note below, the development of environmental policy is entirely consistent, at least in its origins, with this logic of spillover, based on the issue dynamic that is created by the original pooling of resources.

The Monnet method was not implemented in a pure form, however. In the negotiations in which the ECSC was set up, it was the smaller nations who insisted on the injection of political control though a council of ministers. As the pattern adopted for the ECSC was to form the basis of the institutional arrangements of the EU, the division of decision-making authority between the Commission and the Council of Ministers which derived from this original institutional bargain meant that the structure of European governance was superimposed on the political institutions of the Member States. To be sure it may well be the case, as Milward (1992) has argued, that this superimposition is itself built upon a logic through which national politicians seek to strengthen their own position domestically by displacing the costs of policies onto the European level. Yet, whatever the original motivation, the development of European institutions means that the pattern of policy-making authority is vertically complex, necessarily involving complex interactions between institutions at the European level and the Member States.

It is also horizontally complex. That is to say, it is characterized by a complicated pattern of interinstitutional processes at the EU level itself. It has always been an issue in the academic analysis of the EU to determine the exact extent to which it rests on an intergovernmental bargain or derives its legitimacy from the extent to which it is able to meet the felt needs of European citizens (for a good recent review, see Cram, 1996). Clearly, both elements are important. Yet, in the striving for greater popular legitimacy, the creation of the directly elected European Parliament in 1979 and the successive growth in its powers through the 1987 Single European Act, the 1992 Maastricht Treaty, and the 1997 Amsterdam Treaty have had important effects on decision-making processes. In particular, the growth of parliamentary power now means that the EU incorporates a principle of the separation of powers in its policy-making – a separation that is compounded by the role of the European Court of Justice over matters of compliance and implementation. Such a separation leads to horizontal complexity in the making of policy (see Chapter 12).

In addition, European integration following the Monnet method should be seen as an open-ended process, not as the implementation of a constitutional blueprint. The bicycle metaphor is the one that is frequently used in this connection: European unification is like riding a bicycle – you need to keep going forward in order not to fall off. The Monnet method thus rests upon the steady accumulation of powers at the supranational level, and not on a once-and-for-all constitutional bargain among contracting parties.

What are the consequences of the Monnet method for the decision-making structure of the EU? In many ways, environmental policy can be regarded as a textbook illustration of the method at work. As Jordan points out in his editorial introduction (Chapter 1), the Treaty of Rome did not find a place for environmental policy. Yet, even in the 1960s the harmonization of technical standards called for attention to environmental rulemaking. By the early 1970s, with the rise in popular concern about the environment, heads of government decided to take the matter more seriously and the first action programme was developed. With the intense German interest in environmental policy in the early 1980s, the politics of the environment became important in EU relations and formal competence was incorporated into the Single European Act (Chapter 2). Thus, environmental concerns were taken up into an institutionalized domain of policy in its own right. Completely unanticipated in 1957, environmental policy had moved from silence to salience within 30 years. This is not to say that functional spillover was the sole, or even prime, mover in the development of European environmental policy. Patterns of environmental policy are not be explained by the pure logic of spillover (Chapter 12). Other pressures and trends associated more generally with the rise of international environmental politics as well as developments wholly within the realm of domestic politics have played their part. Yet, without the impetus of functional spillover, the domestic and European politics of environmental policy would have been different.

The Monnet Method and Environmental Policy

To say that the logic of the Monnet method underlies the development of EU environmental policy is not to say that the legacies of that logic are unexceptionable or without problems. Indeed, I suggest in this section that the original four paradoxes with which I began can be seen as consequences of the Monnet method and the subsequent processes of political integration to which it has given rise. I consider each of the four paradoxes in turn.

Illiberal Instruments and Liberal Foundations

The basis upon which European political unification developed was economically liberal: the creation of a Common Market without barriers to trade in goods and services and allowing the free movement of capital and people. No doubt in the development of this orientation Monnet's own career background in international business was important, as well as his hostility to the traditional French policy of protectionism. Of course, economic liberalism is not the whole story, as the existence of the interventionist Common Agricultural Policy testifies. Nevertheless, the liberal elements were of crucial importance. Such a view of European integration must represent more than a personal vision on the part of Monnet himself. That Jacques Delors was able to revive the pace of European integration in the 1980s by stressing the importance of the completion of the Single Market, and the added impetus that the 1992 programme gave to integration, are likely to reflect important features of the underlying dynamic of the process. Enough Member States could see enough advantages over a suitably defined range of issues to give the completion of the Single Market priority. It is not evidence against this conclusion to note that the implementation of the programme has not been perfect and the protectionist sentiments have not been eliminated.

The pace of the development of environmental policy increased at the same time as the Single-Market programme was developed for reasons that were in part related to that programme, although there was no attempt to consider environmental effects arising from the Single Market at the time (Weale and Williams, 1992). There is, over a number of issues, a potential conflict arising from the completion of the internal market and the achievement of EU environmental goals, most obviously related to increased transport flows and the way in which waste is handled as a commercial product. Within this context Majone has identified the case for saying that there is a liberal argument for the EU developing a strong environmental policy, in order to correct for market failure (1996, pp28–31).

The essence of Majone's argument rests upon the claim that there is often a strong liberal argument for regulation by the political authorities in order to promote economic efficiency. In the case of environmental policy this argument arises because pollution can be seen as an economic externality. Such externalities exist when the full costs of production and exchange are not borne solely by the beneficiaries of the exchange, but fall in part upon third parties. For example, water pollution from agricultural runoff will adversely affect downstream fishing or water abstraction for human consumption, imposing costs on those who are not parties to the contract between farmers and those who buy from them. (The example is mine, not Majone's.) In these circumstances, a case for public intervention exists on grounds of economic efficiency alone. Correcting for the externality by forcing producers to internalize the costs will lead to a better use of resources. On such liberal grounds, the case is especially strong for the regulation of international environmental pollution by the EU, as its boundaries are extensive enough to ensure that externalities are internalized across the full extent of its authority, whatever national boundaries are involved.

It is common, though by no means universal, in neoclassical treatments of the externality problem to underline the extent to which regulation by means of economic instruments is superior, by the test of economic efficiency, to regulation by means of administrative rules (for a range of views see, inter alia. Brown and Johnson, 1984; Burrows, 1974; Dolan, 1990, Hanley et al, 1990). Such economic instruments include: taxes on emissions, usually by volume emitted; refund schemes for returnable items, ranging from cars to bottles; taxes on polluting substances, for example, fuel oil or pesticides, and so on. The arguments favouring such measures are many and varied, depending on the case at hand. Such measures allow greater freedom for producers to find least-cost solutions to their pollution problems than do uniform emission limits. Economic instruments, such as taxes on pesticides, are likely to be more effective at dealing with dispersed, nonpoint sources of pollution. And where pollution arises from consumption rather than from production externalities, economic instruments are often only the effective instruments.

The merits of these arguments applied to any particular case are less relevant than is their appeal to those holding to liberal principles. If international conflict is to be constrained by the liberal policy of free trade within the boundaries defined by the treaty parties, then it would seem that a liberal approach to pollution control would be the logical corollary. In fact, the EU Commission and Council have long accepted the logic of the argument that an effective approach to pollution control requires the need to internalize the external costs arising from pollution. Acceptance of the polluter-pays principle, for example, is to be found in the First Action Programme on the Environment of 22 November 1973, and a 1983 Memorandum by Directorate-General XI to the House of Lords inquiry into the polluter-pays principle makes it clear that in the Commission's thinking, acceptance of the principle rests upon economic grounds associated with the optimal allocation of resources (SCEC, 1983, p102). The 1987 Fourth Environmental Action Programme took as one of its priority areas the 'development of efficient instruments such as taxes, levies, State aid, authorization of negotiable rebates' with the aim of implementing the polluter-pays principle (cited by SCEC, 1987, p28), and the 1992 Fifth Action Programme asserted the importance of getting market prices right and the need to create market-based incentives for environmentally friendly economic behaviour (CEC, 1992, p67).

Despite these commitments of principle, it is striking that little opportunity has been taken for making use of economic instruments in the attainment of environmental objectives. For example, in policies aimed at the reduction of sulphur dioxide emissions the sort of permit trading that has been developed in the USA in order to achieve least-cost reductions has not been used. This is so despite the structural similarity of the problems on both sides of the Atlantic, as sulphur deposition both in Europe and in the USA arises in large measure from spatially concentrated electricity-generating sources, often operating with old plant, and the regions which suffer the pollution are asymmetrically situated with respect to those causing it. Similarly, the Commission has not attempted to extend and make mandatory in all Member States the successful use of emissions charges relating to water pollution that exist in some. Most striking, perhaps, is the failure at the European level to develop economic instruments for the control of greenhouse gases, of which the failed carbon-energy tax is the clearest example (Chapter 14).

Indeed, the failure to develop instruments is even more striking than these examples suggest, as the resistance to economic instruments can go as far as the Commission wishing to prevent Member States from using such instruments to meet their own pollution-control objectives. The clearest example here is probably provided by the Commission's opposition to the Dutch attempt, in the 1980s, to encourage cleaner cars (Chapter 15). In the wake of the Council decision of 1985, which established the framework within which subsequent measures on emissions controls for cars were negotiated, the Dutch government introduced a subsidy to encourage the purchase of cleaner vehicles (Schrama and Klok, 1995). This stimulated opposition from other Member States, most notably France, which protested to the Commission about the measure. In 1989 there was even the threat of a European Court of Justice reference by the Commission, though it was not acted on in the end. Thus, we not only find little use of economic instruments, but we even find instances where there is opposition to their use at Member State level.

In large measures these restrictions stem from the legal constraints imposed by EU treaties. The effect of these treaty agreements is to give Member States veto powers over the development of taxed-based instruments for environmental protection at the European level. Under the Maastricht Treaty, the use of fiscal instruments for environmental-policy objectives is subject to unanimous voting in the Council of Ministers, rather than qualified majority voting, thus giving veto power to any one Member State (see Chapters 3 and 4). A clear example of the use of such veto powers was seen in the opposition of the UK to the proposed carbon-energy tax. To be sure, there were doubts about the wisdom of the tax in the UK environmental-policy community (SCEC, 1992) but the UK government opposed the measure on the grounds of principle that the EU should not acquire more tax-raising capacity (see Chapter 14).

We have in this case therefore an indication of the inherent limits of functional integration. In order to avoid raising the large constitutional questions about sovereignty, the Monnet method adopts the approach of focusing on the low-politics issues of technical standards and market integration. However, if there is a need to use fiscal instruments in order to raise standards, it is impossible to avoid intruding on one of the responsibilities, tax policy, which by any definition is at the heart of the modern state. If we than embed the Monnet method in a system of decision-making which gives the Member States a privileged, if not all-powerful, place in the making of policy, the limits of functional integration are reinforced by the desire of Member States to preserve their own resources.

However, in addition to these inherent limits of the Monnet method (or rather the combination of the Monnet method and the institutional concessions granted to Member States in the original treaty bargains), there are other factors at work limiting the extent to which we might expect to see the development of economic instruments at the European level. One of these is the dependence of the Commission upon the Member States for the form and character of environmental measures. The general consequences of this dependence are touched on below. Here it is simply worth noting that emissions trading to control sulphur dioxide was unlikely to emerge at the European level, given that the original impetus for the measure came from Germany, a state which itself has shown little desire to experiment with the development of economic instruments in the field of air-pollution control. Indeed, to the extent to which Germany has been a leader in European environmental policy (for contrasting evaluations, see Jänicke and Weidner, 1997; Pehle, 1997), we might expect its own preference for administrative regulation to be reflected in EU measures.

Political integration through market integration also has distinctive effects on patterns of environmental policy. It is striking that the Nordic states, strongly influenced by social democratic party ideology and principles, have nonetheless been among those countries who have most extensively developed the use of economic instruments (see European Environment Agency, 1996). With the exception of Denmark, these countries were outside the EU until 1995 (Norway and Iceland still are, of course) and so were not constrained in their choice of policy instruments by the Single-Market programme, with is inherent suspicion of environmental taxes and subsidies as a form of ecoprotectionism (see Weale and Williams, 1992). All this suggests that liberalism, as a set of principles for economic management, has an ambiguous significance for the development of environmental policy. On the other hand its endorsement of market integration, and the implication this has in turn for the development of environmental policy, suggest that functional spillover operated to link the Single-Market and environmental issues. On the other hand liberal economic policy, in the form of the creation of an integrated market, and in the absence of a political capacity to develop a full range of measures to correct for market failure, imposes limits on the development of environmental policy.

Yet, there is also a large question begged in the above analysis: to what extent is European integration truly a liberal project? To be sure, the creation of the European Single Market and the emergent consequences of economic and monetary-union are the effective instruments of political integration. This does not mean, however, that the liberal credentials of the Single-Market programme are uncontested or have a uniform interpretation. It is clear that the support which Delors received from EU leaders for the pursuit of the Single-Market programme stemmed from a variety of motives, not all of which were compatible with one another (Garrett, 1992). On the other side were those who, like the UK government, favoured the project because they saw it as creating a free-trade area in Europe. On the other side were those who saw the Single Market as the necessary condition under which Europe could collectively take on the economic contest with the USA and Japan. This second group were more productivist and corporatist in ideology than liberal, and there is no reason to expect them to be especially sympathetic to an economic instrument such as ecotaxation as distinct from subsidies that might support infant eco-industries. In other words, the Single Market encapsulated the struggle of what Albert (1993) calls 'capitalism against capitalism'. In this context, it is not surprising that key economic instruments remain undeveloped at the European level.

The Dependent Supranational Commission

Independent supranational authority is intrinsic to the Monnet method, and its role is reinforced by various features of the formal, legal and institutional arrangements of the EU. The Commissioners themselves, though nominated by the Member States, undertake to be independent of national affiliation and loyalty. Their appointment and term of office is protected by their being, in effect, immune to parliamentary censure and removal. And the Commission is given the sole formal right to initiate measures, though in practice this has been qualified by the growth of various conventions which allow the Council and the Parliament to bring to the attention of the Commission items which they want on the agenda. Moreover, the Commission operates according to the ethos of the continental public functionary, from which Weber's (1947) picture of the bureaucrat was drawn: technically competent, careful of the rules, and deferential to the norms of legal-rational authority This is not to say, of course, that these formal norms are always upheld in practice. It has been rumoured among the Commission staff, for example, that a French Commissioner took a strong and partisan interest in protecting the interests of the French car industry during negotiations on exhaust-emissions directives in the 1980s. But, if true, these would be venial human failings, not institutional characteristics.

Against this background it is striking that, in the development of proposals for environmental measures, the Commission is highly dependent upon the Member States. The clearest example to occur during the 1980s concerned the development of large-combustion-plant directive. However, Héritier and her colleagues have shown that this is not an instance of a more general 'pioneer' role played by Germany but, rather, part of a pattern in which individual countries try, and sometimes succeed, to transpose their own domestic policy concerns and approaches onto the European stage (Héritier et al, 1994). Thus, the development of procedural measures, for instance directives on eco-audit or integrated pollution control, was heavily dependent upon the UK government's attempt to secure its approach within the EU. How does it come about, then, that the formal independence coexists with this de facto dependence?

Once again, the answer is the Monnet method: such de facto dependence is built into the policy process by the form which integration has taken. Monnet's own predilections, both when developing French economic planning and in the original staffing of the ECSC, was for a small-scale bureaucracy. In his view this both encouraged esprit de corps and, in the development of French planning, prevented other ministries from being envious of resources. This approach was transferred to the EU. As he rather nicely put it in his memoirs, Monnet's principle was that a few hundred European civil servants would be enough to set thousands of national experts to work (Monnet, 1978, p373). In addition, as Peters (1997, p28) has noted, the Commission is highly fragmented for a bureaucracy of its size, so that the staff of any one directorate general is likely to be small in relation to the tasks at hand. To be sure, Directorate General XI has grown significantly in size from the mid-1980s, but a large part of this expansion is accounted for by temporary staff.

Moreover, as Scharpf (1994, p222) has noted (cited also by Hurrell and Menon, 1996, p391), the EU lacks those attributes which confer a high degree of policy-making autonomy on federal states: a relatively homogeneous political culture, a party system operative at the federal level, and a high degree of economic and cultural homogeneity. The lack of these characteristics would make for a weak centre in any system of governance, so it is hardly surprising that their effect is most keenly felt by the Commission as the body responsible for initiating European legislation. In the case of environmental policy, there is some offsetting pressure contrary to these centrifugal trends from the strong commitment which a number of observers have noted among staff in Directorate General XI to the cause of the environment (Peterson, 1995, p482). However, common conviction in the importance of the issue you are dealing with does not of itself make for an autonomous policy-making capacity.

To some extent this problem highlights a flaw in the Monnet method itself. Monnet's own predilection for a small and committed staff made a great deal of sense in the immediate postwar context of French economic planning, where there was a need for a strategic core staff to promote economic reconstruction. It also made sense in the context of the ECSC, where there was a clearly delimited sphere of competence and it was important to live within the expectations of Member States. But in a system of multilevel governance like that of the EU, with an intrinsically heterogeneous issue like that of the environment, a small Commission staff becomes vulnerable to whatever parallelogram of forces is most active at the time (Chapter 9), and it is made more vulnerable by the absence of the common 'formation' to which all civil servants would be subject if they were staffing national bureaucracies.

Moreover, the national pressures to which Héritier and her colleagues point are likely to become stronger, not weaker, with the development of EU environmental policy. In part, the motive for Member States to push their own priorities and approaches stems from the fact that implementation is made easier if EU legislation borrows from the pattern of one's own national system. Fewer changes in standard operating procedures need to be made and measures are likely to be less costly to implement if they are incremental changes from a national status quo. So, a relatively small Commission faces states with strong incentives to advance their own conceptions of environmental policy (Chapter 12).

The European Parliament: The Power of the Parvenu

Regarded from the point of view of parliamentary systems in Europe, the powers of the European Parliament appear few. It is not the formal source of legislation. It does not appoint or overthrow governments. Its party alignments are not well established. It is less attractive than national parliaments to those for whom politics is a career rather than a form of early retirement. It does not have the last say on legislative matters. In short, it still has to make the transition fully from a consultative body to a legislative body holding the executive to account. Moreover, by comparison with the Council of Ministers, its formal powers are few. The EU system of governance is thus unbalanced, with what Lodge (1996, pp197–8) refers to as 'horizontal rivalry', involving imperfect bicameralism, imperfect parliamentary supervision of ministers, imperfect co-operation among the institutions, different interpretations of the decision rules, and inadequate information sharing among the institutions.

There is much truth in this view. However, the more we accept it, the more we are presented with a paradox. The environmental rule-making and standard-setting process in national political systems is not one in which parliaments play a strong role once the legislative powers under which governments can set standards are in place. It is possible to find examples where there is a strong parliamentary influence in matters of environmental policy, for example, the collapse of the Christian Democrat – Liberal coalition in The Netherlands in 1989 or the rejection by the UK Parliament of the proposals for VAT on domestic fuel at the standard rate, and in Germany the *Länder* are able to have their say on proposed measures in the *Bundesrat*. However, by and large, the initiative for the changing of standards comes from the government, and typically involves bureaucratic, rather than parliamentary, activity.

The European Parliament, by contrast, has assumed significant environmental-standard-setting capacity, particularly since it acquired more powers through the adoption of the co-operation procedure under the Single European Act in cases where environmental measures were implicated in single-market legislation (see Chapter 8). The clearest example was that of car-exhaust legislation in 1989, in which the Parliament forced on the Council the acceptance of so-called 'US83' standards of emissions for all cars manufactured after 1992 (Chapter 15). However, the Parliament was also important in placing the issue of poor implementation on the European political agenda, extending the powers of the European Environmental Agency (Chapter 17) and most recently sending back to the Council draft directives on landfill and the control of auto oils (see ENDS, 1998a; 1998b, p41). In each case, the Parliament has taken a tougher proenvironment position than the common, or agreed, position of the Council. In the case of the last two, though the crucial decisions have still to be made at the time of writing, it seems as though the Parliament will succeed in strengthening the directives in terms of environmental protection.

How does it come about that a 'weak' parliament can exercise such strong powers? In part the answer to this question depends, as Tsebelis (1994) has explained, on the logic of the decision rules. According to the co-operation procedure, the European Parliament can amend a proposal coming from the Council, and if the Council wishes to reaffirm its original decision then it must do so by unanimity, even when the original decision was taken by a qualified majority (as most single-market legislation was). If there is a majority in the Council in favour of a move from a status quo point, then the Parliament can pull the whole Council further in the direction of stronger environmental measures than the Council would go on its own by presenting amendments to the Council's agreed position. It does this, in effect, by presenting the majority in the Council with a stark alternative: either some movement is accepted in the direction the Parliament wishes, or the status quo prevails. Faced with such a choice, the majority of the Council will sometimes concede to the Parliament, as it did on exhaust emissions.

Of course, in practice, the choice is never as simple or as stark as this explanation suggests. For example, with the car-exhaust-emissions directive there was a great deal of negotiation with the Commission before a text emerged which the Council could agree to (Chapter 8). Tsebelis's account, nonetheless, makes a great deal of sense of what would otherwise be obscure. In effect, he offers the theoretical explanation of what seasoned observers like Haigh have inferred from experience: since the Single European Act, 'the Commission and the Parliament acting together can put considerable pressure on the Council, since it can only change a revised proposal by unanimity' (Haigh, 1992, Sections 6.8–7).

In noting that the European Parliament does not control a government in the way that national parliaments do, we are simply committing a category mistake if we then infer that the Parliament's influence on environmental policy is weak. The correct comparison is not with the powers of national parliaments in Europe, but with a system like that in the USA, in which there is a separation of powers between the executive and the legislature. To be sure, the European Parliament does not have the powers of the US Congress, but it would be surprising if it did after so short a period in its history. Even so, the co-operation procedure has, under some circumstances, given the Parliament important powers, which were further strengthened by the Amsterdam Treaty.

The agenda-setting powers given by the existing rules are not the whole of the story with respect to the European Parliament, however. The Parliament had begun to flex its muscles in the early 1980s, before the Single European Act, in respect of the right of initiative, and had devised an informal procedure by which the Commission would follow up on its suggestions. Moreover, the Environment Committee is among the most important of the European Parliament's committees, and there is strong political interest in the selection of its chair, probably because, with party groupings relatively weak, it is possible for parliamentarians to form ad hoc coalitions on issues that are not captured along the single left–right spectrum of economic issues.

It would be a mistake to see the strength of the European Parliament as a direct consequence of the Monnet method. The attempt to secure political legitimacy for European integration through a directly elected parliament came late in the development of European institutions. However, the power of the Parliament can be seen as an indirect consequence of Monnet's approach, as once the process of European integration had reached a certain level it was difficult not to attach the legitimacy of direct elections – the principal form of legitimacy in the modern world (Manin, 1997) – to the institutions of Europe.

Supranational Authority and Subnational Public Goods

The EU is clearly more than an international regime, even though it may be constrained in its development and freedom of manoeuvre by its constituent national states. The legal doctrine of the direct effect of Community law, its powers of implementation, and the extensive scope of the issues with which it deals all mark it out as a supranational authority of a distinct kind. However, this fact alone highlights our fourth paradox: how does it come about that a supranational body, which might be thought best tailored to the protection of international public goods, has spent a great deal of time and effort on matters concerned with local public goods, including urban air quality, bathing water and drinking water? In other words, how has it come about that task assignment in EU environmental policy has taken the form that it has?

Task assignment involves the specification of functions and competences to different levels within a multilevel system of governance. If we were looking for a coherent rationalization of task assignment, then one obvious source would be within welfare economics and the utilitarian tradition more generally. According to this approach, policy competence and political authority should be placed at the level at which it will be most effective and efficient. In particular, jurisdictional competence for the protection of public goods should be set at the level at which the publish authorities are large enough to internalise the relevant externalities (for example, see Peltzman and Tideman, 1972, p962; Rothenberg, 1970, p34, though most of the arguments were anticipated by Sidgwick, 1891, pp496–500). A contrast with this approach would be the principle of subsidiarity, according to which (in its most natural interpretation, at least), there should be a bias towards the local in the assignment of functions, and a distrust of centralization. Logically speaking, a proponent of the principle of subsidiarity ought to be prepared to countenance forgoing some of the benefits of centralization in order to preserve the advantages of local control. Whichever of these two views we take, however, neither would suggest that an international organization like the EU should be regulating the supply of subnational public goods. Kay (1994, p14) put the point bluntly, but from the point of view of these two standard principles correctly, when he argued that regulation should be at the lowest feasible level and that 'If we [the UK population] choose to drink and bathe in dirty water, that is really our own business, and for Brussels to fine us when we admit to doing so is only to add public insult to private injury' (p14). The question, therefore, is whether it is simply an accident that 'interference' from Brussels should exist in matters of subnational environmental quality.

Once again, in answering this question, we need to look at the specific features of the Monnet method. Integration through functional interaction is bound to the logic of spillover. The solution to one set of problems leads on to the other problems. Just as the customs union led to the Single Market, which in turn led to economic and monetary union, so we cannot say in advance where the resolution of policy problems will lead. The efficiency secret of this approach, to use Bagehot's (1867) useful term, is the *acquis communautaire*. Roughly speaking, this means that having acquired a competence, the EU will not give it up. There is therefore no role in the constitutional politics of the EU for an equivalent to the tenth amendment of the US constitution, which states that powers not expressly granted by the states to the federal government remain reserved to the governments of the states. The *acquis* is central to the Monnet method of European integration, as it imparts a bias against the ability of Member States to reclaim their historic rights against the supranational authority of the EU (for water policy, see Jordan, 1999c).

Moreover, this distinctive feature of the constitution of the EU is reinforced by the form in which functions are assigned. In this respect, to the extent to which the EU is federal in form, it follows the logic of German federalism rather than US federalism. Scharpf (1988, p242) has argued that the EU is one of a class of political systems in which decision-making authority is not allocated in a zero-sum fashion between different levels of government, but is, instead, shared. Thus, the German federal government shares authority with the *Länder* through the need to secure a majority in the Bundesrat, and in many matters the division is not one of responsibility for policy sector but for stages of the policy process, with *Länder* governments having the responsibility for the implementation of policies agreed at the federal level. This pattern applies in environmental policy within the EU, as the typical mode of carrying out environmental measures is for the Member States to implement, according to their own procedures and laws, the measures that are contained in environmental directives (see Jordan, 1996b) (see Chapter 17). So, rather than a neat division of sectors of policy between Europe and the Member States, we have the less clear-cut distinction of responsibility for different phases of the policy process.

Following the first Danish referendum on the Maastricht Treaty in June 1992, the British government secured an EU review of environmental legislation in an attempt to see whether some responsibilities could be repatriated (Jordan, 1999c). The argument was that the principle of subsidiarity, according to which functions should be carried out at the lowest feasible level, implied that the regulation of bathing-water quality, for example, should be a matter for the Member States and not for the EU. However, the review did not recommend a change of responsibility. As Flynn (1997) has shown in his review of the Commission's response to the Edinburgh decision, the application of the principle of subsidiarity was not used to reassign competences for particular issues of policy. Rather it was interpreted as an opportunity to assert the importance of 'soft law' approaches to environmental regulation. In place of the formal directives and regulations that had characterized environmental policy during the 1980s, there would be a greater stress placed on voluntary agreements, negotiated rulemaking, and other non-legal forms of environmental policy control. Significantly, not a single piece of legislation has been repealed and reform of the drinking-water and bathing-water directives is taking a great deal of time.

Conclusion: Dysfunctional Functionalism?

There is a growing body of opinion that the Monnet method has run its course, and that in place of integration by stealth we should have an explicit constitutional contract that would refine and redefine the powers and principles under which European institutions should operate. We could imagine, for example, a constitutional convention, on the model of 1787 in the USA, in which political representatives bargain and debate the shape and future of Europe. In any such constitutional process, environmental policy would obviously be a central topic of concern. It is politically important to European mass publics and there is a growing body of expert opinion to the effect that the protection of the environment involves large-scale and serious social and economic changes. Creating an institutional system in which the relevant issues could be properly debated and discussed is therefore an important priority. How much reform is required is, of course, an open-ended matter and would require discussion.

If we look at the history and character of environmental policy in the EU, it is easy to conclude that the functional method of European integration has been dysfunctional from the point of view of environmental policy. EU environmental policy may be thought too uniform in scope and form for the environmental diversity of Europe, with too much attention being paid to the post-materialist concerns of northern Europe and insufficient attention to the sustainable-development concerns of southern Europe. It can be charged with pursuing expensive solutions to marginal improvements to water quality, while ignoring the damage caused by water abstraction in the more arid regions of Europe. Some might think it intervenes too much at the subnational level, while being insufficiently vigorous on issues such as global climate change. Its decision-making procedures can be indicted for being slow and cumbersome, paying too much attention to special interests and not enough attention to the diffuse, but nonetheless real, interests of European citizens at large. Environmental policy is made by a bureaucracy in which the environmental right hand is ignorant of, or cannot control, the left hand of economic growth. In short, the Monnet method can be said to have yielded a system of environmental governance that is pervaded by pathologies.

All this may be true. It is equally true, however, that EU environmental policy has brought a degree of international accountability to the way in which national governments in Europe tend and manage their environmental resources that is unparalleled in any other part of the world among sovereign nation states. Moreover, the Monnet method has been one of the devices by which the countries of Western Europe have enjoyed more peace and stability in the last 40 years than they enjoyed in the previous hundred. This is no small achievement. How far a constitutional convention would wish, after reflection and deliberation, to undo and refashion the achievements of the Monnet method in environmental policy is an intriguing, but perhaps unanswerable, question.

Acknowledgements

This chapter is drawn from the research project 'Environmental standards and the politics of expertise' funded by the Single European Market Programme (award no. W113 251 025) of the Economic and Social Research Council of UK. I should like to thank my co-researchers in the project (Michelle Cini, Brendan Flynn, Dimitrios Konstadakopoulos, Geoffrey Pridham, Martin Porter, and Andrea Williams) for discussions and material relevant to this chapter. I am also grateful to Andrew Jordan and an anonymous referee for comments and suggestions. Remaining errors are my responsibility.

References

Albert, M. (1993) *Capitalism against Capitalism*, Whurr Publishers: London.

Arp, H. (1993) 'Technical Regulation and Politics: The Interplay between Economic Interests and Environmental Policy Goals in EC Car Emission Legislation', in *European Integration and Environmental Policy*, Liefferink, J. D., Lowe, P. D. and Mol, A. P. J. (eds), Belhaven Press: London, pp150–171.

Bagehot, W. (1867) *The English Constitution*, edited, with an introduction by Crossman, R. H. S. (1963) Fontana/Collins: London.

Brown, G. M. Jr. and Johnson, R. W. (1984), 'Pollution Control by Effluent Charges: It Works in the Federal Republic of Germany, Why Not in the United States?', *Natural Resources Journal*, Vol.24, pp929–966.

Burrows, P. (1974) 'Pricing Versus Regulation for Environmental Protection', in *Economic Policies and Social Goals*, Culyer, A. J. (ed), Martin Robertson: Oxford, pp273–283.

Cameron, D. R. (1992) 'The 1992 Initiative: Causes and Consequences', in *Euro-Politics: Institutions and Policymaking in the 'New' European Community*, Sbragia, A. M. (ed), The Brookings Institute: Washington, D.C., pp23–74.

CEC (1992) *Fifth Environmental Action Programme*, COM (92) 23 final, Commission of the European Communities: Luxembourg.

Cram, L. (1996) 'Integration Theory and the Study of the European Policy Process', in *European Union: Power and Policy-making*, Richardson, J. J. (ed), Routledge: London, pp40–58.

Dolan, E.G. (1990) 'Controlling Acid Rain', in *Economics and the Environment: A Reconciliation*, Block, W. (ed), The Fraser Institute: Vancouver, B.C., pp215–232.

ENDS (1998a) 'Parliament Declares War on Auto/Oil Standards', *Ends Report*, 277, February, p44, Environmental Data Services Ltd, Unit 24, 40 Bowling Green Lane, London EC1R 0NE.

ENDS (1998b) 'EC Climate Policy Takes Shape, Progress on Landfills, Air Pollution', *Ends Report* 288, March, pp39–41, Environmental Data Services Ltd, Unit 24, 40 Bowling Green Lane, London EC1R 0NE.

European Environment Agency (1996) *Environmental Taxes: Implementation and Effectiveness*, European Environment Agency: Copenhagen.

Flynn, B. (1997) 'Subsidiarity and the Rise of Soft Law', OP-40 Human Capital and Mobility Network, University of Essex: Colchester, Essex.

Garrett, G. (1992) 'International Cooperation and Institutional Choice: The European Community's Internal Market', *International Organisation*, Vol.46, pp533–560.

Griffiths, R. T. (1995) 'The European Integration Experience', in *Orchestrating Europe: The Informal Politics of the European Union 1973–95*, Middlemas, K. (ed), Fontana Press: London, pp1–70.

Haigh, N. (1992) *Manual of Environmental Policy: The EC and Britain,* Catermill: London, release 12 November 1997.

Hanley, N., Hallett, S. and Moffatt, I. (1990) 'Research Policy and Review 33: Why is More Notice not Taken of Economists' Prescriptions for the Control of Pollution?', *Environment and Planning, A*, Vol.22, pp1421–1439.

Hayes-Renshaw, F. (1996) 'The Role of the Council', in *The European Union: How Democratic Is It?*, Andersen, S. S. and Eliassen, K. A. (eds), Sage: London, pp.143–163.

Hayward, J. (1996) 'Has European Unification by Stealth a Future?', in *Elitism, Populism, and European Politics*, Hayward, J. (ed), Clarendon Press: Oxford, pp252–257.

Héretier, A., Mingens, S., Knill, C. and Becka, M. (1994) *Die Veränderung van Staatlichkeit in Europa*, Leske und Budrich: Opiaden.

Hurrell, A. and Menone, A. (1996) 'Politics Like Any Other? Comparative Politics, International Relations and the Study of the EU', *West European Politics*, Vol.19, pp386–402.

Jänicke, M. and Weidner, H. (eds) (1997) *Germany in National Environmental Policies: A Comparative Study of Capacity-building*, Springer: Berlin, pp133–155.

Jordan, A. (1999a) 'Editorial Introduction: The Construction of a Multilevel Environmental Governance System', *Environment and Planning C: Government and Policy*, Vol.17, pp1–17.

Jordan, A. (1999b) 'The Implementation of EU Environmental Policy: A Policy Problem Without a Political Solution?', *Environment and Planning C: Government and Policy*, Vol.17, pp69–90.

Jordan, A. (1999c) 'European Union Water Standards: Locked in or Watered Down?', *Journal of Common Market Studies*, Vol.37, No.1. pp13–37.

Judge, D. (1992) '"Predestined to Save the Earth": The Environment Committee of the European Parliament', *Environmental Politics*, Vol.1, No.4, pp186–212.

Kay, J. (1994) 'Clever Trick but the Cracks Remain', *Financial Times*, 16 August, p14.

Laursen, F. (1996) 'The Role of the Commission', in *The European Union: How Democratic Is It?*, Andersen, S. S. and Eliassen, K. A. (eds), Sage: London, pp119–141.

Lodge, J. (1996) 'The European Parliament', in *The European Union: How Democratic Is It?*, Andersen, S. S. and Eliassen, K. A. (eds), Sage: London, pp187–214.

Majone, G. (1996) *Regulating Europe*, Routledge: London.

Manin, B. (1997) *The Principles of Representative Government*, Cambridge University Press: Cambridge.

Mazey, S. (1996) 'The Development of the European Idea: From Sectoral Integration to Political Union', in *European Union: Power and Policy-making*, Richardson, J. J. (ed), Routledge: London, pp24–39.

Milward, A. (1992) *The European Rescue of the Nation State*, Routledge: London.

Monnet, J. (1978) *Memoirs*, translated by R Mayne, Collins: London.

Pehle, H. (1997) 'Germany: Domestic Obstacles to an International Forerunner', in *European Environmental Policy: The Pioneers*, Andersen, M. S. and Liefferink, D. (eds), Manchester University Press: Manchester, pp161–209.

Peltzman, S. and Tideman, T. N. (1972) 'Local Versus National Pollution Control: Note', *American Economic Review*, Vol.62, pp959–963.

Peters, B. G. (1997) 'Escaping the Joint-decision Trap: Repetition and Sectoral Politics in the European Union', *West European Politics*, Vol.20, No.2, pp22–36.

Petersen, J. (1995) 'Playing the Transparency Game: Consultation and Policy-making in the European Commission', *Public Administration*, Vol.73, pp473–492.

Rothenberg, J. (1970) 'Local Decentralization and the Theory of Optimal Government', in *The Analysis of Public Output*, Margolis, J. (ed), Columbia University Press: New York, pp29–64.

SCEC (1983) 'Memorandum: The 'Polluter Pays' Principle', in House of Lords, Select Committee on the European Communities, *The Polluter Pays Principle Report 10*, Session 1982–83, The Stationery Office: London, pp102–103.

SCEC (1987) *House of Lords Papers and Bills: Session 1986–87: Fourth Environmental Action Programme*, HL 135, Select Committee on the European Communities, The Stationery Office: London.

SCEC (1992) *House of Lords Papers: Session 1991–92: Carbon/Energy Tax*, HL 52, Select Committee on the European Communities, The Stationery Office: London.

Scharpf, F. W. (1988) 'The Joint-decision Trap: Lessons from German Federalism and European Institutions', *Public Administration*, Vol.66, pp239–278.

Scharpf, F. W. (1994) 'Community and Autonomy: Multi-level Policy-making in the European Union', *Journal of European Public Policy*, pp219–242.

Schmitter, P. C. (1996) 'Examining the Present Euro-polity with the Help of Past Theories', in *Governance in the European Union*, Marks, G., Scharpf, F. W., Schmitter, P. C. and Streeck, W. (eds), Sage: London, pp1–14.

Schrama, G. J. I. and Klok, P.-J. (1995) 'The Swift Introduction of "Clean Cars" in The Netherlands, 1986–1992: The Origin and Effect of Incentive Measures', in *Successful Environmental Policy: A Critical Evaluation of 24 Cases*, Janicke, M. and Weidner, H. (eds), Edition Sigma: Berlin, pp203–222.

Sidgwick, H. (1891) *The Elements of Politics*, Macmillan: London.

Tsebelis, G. (1994) 'The Power of the European Parliament as a Conditional Agenda Setter', *American Political Science Review*, Vol.88, pp128–142.

Wallace, W. (1996) 'Has Government by Committee Lost the Public's Confidence?', in *Elitism, Populism and European Politics*, Hayward, J. (ed), Clarendon Press: Oxford, pp238–251.

Weale, A. (1996) 'Environmental Rules and Rule-making in the European Union', *Journal of European Public Policy*, Vol.3, pp594–611.

Weale, A. and Williams, A. (1992) 'Between Economy and Ecology? The Single Market and the Integration of Environmental Policy', *Environmental Politics*, Vol.1, No.4, pp45–64.

Weber, M. (1947) *The Theory of Social and Economic Organization*, translated by Henderson, A. M. and Parsons, T., Oxford University Press: Oxford.

Further Reading

The European Union

Until relatively recently there were very few good textbooks on the EU, but now this is no longer the case. Currently, the best summaries are:

Cram, L., Dinan, D. and Nugent, N. (eds) (1999) *Developments in the European Union,* Macmillan: Basingstoke.*

Dinan, D. (1999) *Ever Closer Union* (2nd edn), Macmillan: Basingstoke.

Nugent, N. (1999) *The Government and Politics of the European Union* (4th edn), Macmillan: Basingstoke.

Hix, S. (1999) *The Political System of the European Union,* Macmillan: Basingstoke.

George, S. (1996) *Politics and Policy in the European Union* (3rd edn), Oxford University Press: Oxford.

Wallace, H. and Wallace, W. (2000) *Policy Making in the European Union,* Oxford University Press: Oxford.*

Currently, the best review of the most popular theories of EU politics and European integration is:

Rosamund, B. (1999) *Theories of European Integration,* Macmillan: Basingstoke.

EU Environmental Policy

Nigel Haigh's annually updated *Manual of Environmental Policy* describes each and every item of EU environmental policy and its impact on Britain:

Haigh, N. (2001) *Manual of Environmental Policy: The EU and Britain,* Elsevier: Oxford (in looseleaf, annually updated).

Sadly, there are precious few textbooks on EU environmental policy. In the meantime, the following are well worth consulting:

Bomberg, E. (1998) *Green Parties and Politics in the European Union,* Routledge: London.

Liefferink, D., Lowe, P. and Mol, A. (eds) (1993) *European Integration and Environmental Policy,* John Wiley: Chichester.

Lowe, P. and Ward, S. (eds) (1998) *British Environmental Policy and Europe,* Routledge: London.

---

* Contain a separate chapter on environmental policy.

Weale, A. (1992) *The New Politics of Pollution*, Manchester University Press: Manchester.

Zito, A. (1999) *Creating Environmental Policy in the European Union*, Macmillan: Basingstoke.

Academic journals such as *Environmental Politics*, the *Journal of European Environmental Policy* and *European Environment* regularly carry articles on recent developments in EU environmental policy. For up to date reviews of developments in policy and legislation, consult one of the many media publications such as *Environmental Data Services (ENDS) Report*, *European Voice*, *Europe Environment*, *Agence Europe* and *Environment Watch: Western Europe*.

Index